Green Culture

GREEN CULTURE

Environmental Rhetoric in Contemporary America

Edited by

Carl G. Herndl

and

Stuart C. Brown

The University of Wisconsin Press

The University of Wisconsin Press
2537 Daniels Street
Madison, Wisconsin 53718

3 Henrietta Street
London WC2E 8LU, England

5 4 3 2

Printed in the United States of America

Library of Congress Cataloging-in-Publication Data
Green culture: environmental rhetoric in contemporary America
   edited by Carl G. Herndl and Stuart C. Brown.
         p.   cm.
   Includes bibliographical references and index.
   ISBN 0-299-14990-0 (cloth: alk. paper).
   ISBN0-299-14994-3 (pbk.: alk. paper)
   1. Green movement—United States.   2. Environmentalism—United States.
   I. Herndl, Carl George.   II. Brown, Stuart C. (Stuart Cameron), 1955–
GE195.G72   1996
363.7—dc20   95-43809

Contents

Preface

This book provides an opportunity for us, the editors, and for the contributors to combine two abiding interests: our professional work in rhetorical criticism and our concern for the environment. Most of us are hikers, campers, canoeists, climbers, or bird-watchers. We worry about what is happening to our communities, to the people in them, and to the natural resources around them. And like many other people, the contributors to this volume have followed and participated in the public debate over the environment. The chapters that follow offer a way to understand that public discussion about the environment and why it takes the shape it does.

Rhetoricians study the ways people use language to construct knowledge and to do things in the world. The chapters gathered here provide rhetorical analyses of the environmental debates that occur in a wide variety of institutional and cultural locations, from public hearings on nuclear waste sites to nineteenth-century landscape painting. These studies describe some of the historical and cultural sources of the rhetoric used to talk about the environment, and they offer careful analyses of how that language shapes our contemporary debates. Each chapter explains with scholarly care the way language functions in a particular case or in a powerful written genre. These chapters also make available to readers some of the tools of rhetorical criticism that will allow them to better understand and participate in the public debates about the environment.

This book represents the work of a great number of talented people, particularly the colleagues who have contributed chapters to this collection. We are very much indebted to them. These colleagues have been generous with their time, their ideas, and their energy. And they have been patient throughout the long process of designing and producing this book. We doubt that many collaborative efforts are as enjoyable as this has been. We would also like to thank Jack Selzer, Gretchen Schoff, and Curt Meine for their careful reading. They provided abundant criticism and very useful advice on the working manuscript. And we would like to thank Allen

Fitchen and the staff at the University of Wisconsin Press; they were both expert and easy to work with.

Finally, we thank our spouses and colleagues, Diane Price Herndl and Leslie Coutant, for their many suggestions and for their support and encouragement.

CARL G. HERNDL AND STUART C. BROWN

Contributors

CHARLES BERGMAN teaches writing and literature at Pacific Lutheran University in Tacoma, Washington. He has written extensively on environmental issues for magazines such as *Audubon* and *Orion,* as well as *Wild Echoes: Encounters with the Most Endangered Animals in North America* (McGraw Hill, 1990). His new book is *Orion's Legacy: A Cultural History of the Male as Hunter* (E.P. Dutton, 1996).

ROBERT L. BROWN directs the Freshman Composition Program at the University of Minnesota, studying and teaching rhetoric, linguistics, and cultural theory.

STUART C. BROWN teaches rhetorical history and criticism at New Mexico State University. He is the coeditor with Theresa Enos of *Defining the New Rhetorics* (Sage, 1993) and *Professing the New Rhetorics* (Blair, 1994), as well as author and coauthor of several composition textbooks (Allyn & Bacon, forthcoming) and a number of book chapters and journal articles.

JAMES G. CANTRILL is Associate Professor of Communication and Performance Studies at Northern Michigan University. He has coordinated national conferences on environmental advocacy and has published in journals such as *Journal of Environmental Education, Communication Research Reports,* and *Journal of Applied Communication Research.* His current research focuses on the cognitive processes of environmental communications.

GREGORY CLARK is Professor of English at Brigham Young University. He wrote *Dialogue, Dialectic, and Conversation: A Social Perspective on the Function of Writing* (Southern Illinois University Press, 1990) and coedited with S. Michael Halloran *Oratorical Culture in Nineteenth-Century America: Transformations in the Theory and Practice of Rhetoric* (Southern

Illinois University Press, 1993). His current project is a study of travel as a metaphor for national collectivity in early American literature and culture.

MARILYN M. COOPER is Associate Professor of Humanities at Michigan Technological University. She publishes on social and political issues in writing pedagogy and writing theory, including environmental and technological issues. She is a contributing member of both The Nature Conservancy and Earth First! as well as a number of other environmental groups.

S. MICHAEL HALLORAN is Professor of Rhetoric at Rensselaer Polytechnic Institute, where his research and teaching focus on the theory and history of rhetoric, with special emphasis on rhetoric as an art of civic discourse and on the rhetoric of scientific discourse. Among his recent publications is *Oratorical Culture in Nineteenth-Century America: Transformations in the Theory and Practice of Rhetoric,* coedited with Gregory Clark (Southern Illinois University Press, 1993).

CARL G. HERNDL is Associate Professor of English at New Mexico State University, where he teaches and writes about discourse theory and cultural studies. He has published in *College English, College Composition and Communication, Rhetoric Review,* and numerous edited collections.

ZITA INGHAM is Assistant Professor of English at Arkansas State University in Jonesboro. She is presently on leave and teaching at Southwestern Oregon Community College in Coos Bay. She has contributed essays and articles to the *Journal of Business Communication, Rhetoric Review,* and *Puerto Del Sol,* and is currently the coordinating editor of the bibliography project of the Association for the Study of Literature and Environment.

STEVEN B. KATZ is Associate Professor of English at North Carolina State University. He has articles on writing, technology, ethics, and culture in several journals and has just published *The Epistemic Music of Rhetoric: Toward the Temporal Dimension of Reader Response and Writing,* (Southern Illinois University Press, 1995). His article "The Ethic of Expediency: Classical Rhetoric, Technology, and the Holocaust" (*College English,* 1992) won the 1993 NCTE Award for Best Theoretical Article on Scientific and Technical Communication.

M. JIMMIE KILLINGSWORTH is Professor of English at Texas A&M University. He is the author of books and articles on rhetoric, American literature, and technical communication, including most recently *Ecospeak: Rhetoric and Environmental Politics in America,* coauthored with Jacqueline Palmer (Southern Illinois University Press, 1992), *Signs, Genres, and Communities in Technical Communication,* coauthored with Michael Gilbertson (Baywood, 1992),and *The Growth of Leaves of Grass: The Organic Tradition in Whitman Studies* (Camden House, 1993).

CAROLYN R. MILLER is Professor of English at North Carolina State University, where she teaches rhetorical theory and criticism, as well as various writing courses. Her primary research interest is in the rhetoric of science and technology. She has published essays in *Argumentation, College English, Quarterly Journal of Speech, Rhetorica,* and the *Rhetoric Society Quarterly,* as well as in numerous essay collections. She is 1996–98 President of the Rhetoric Society of America.

JACQUELINE S. PALMER is a researcher and trainer with the Southwest Educational Development Laboratory in Austin, Texas. She is the author of several articles on science and environmental education and communication and the coauthor (with Jimmie Killingsworth) of *Ecospeak: Rhetoric and Environmental Politics in America* (Southern Illinois University Press, 1992).

SCOTT SLOVIC is the author of *Seeking Awareness in American Nature Writing: Henry David Thoreau, Annie Dillard, Edward Abbey, Wendell Berry, Barry Lopez* (1992) and coeditor of *Being in the World: An Environmental Reader for Writers* (1993). Slovic is Director of the Center for Environmental Arts and Humanities at the University of Nevada, Reno. He served as the founding president of the Association for the Study of Literature and the Environment (ASLE).

H. LEWIS ULMAN is Associate Professor of English at Ohio State University, where he teaches courses in composition, literature, and rhetorical and critical theory. His recent publications include books and articles on eighteenth-century British philosophy and rhetoric. His current research focuses on computers and literacy and on self-representation in American nature writing.

CRAIG WADDELL is Associate Professor of Rhetoric and Technical Communication in the Humanities Department at Michigan Technological University. His principal research area is the rhetoric of science policy. He is particularly interested in the rhetoric of environmental policy, in public participation in policy formation, and in the role that pathos plays in this process. He has published in *Philosophy and Rhetoric, Sci-*

ence, Technology, and Human Values, the *Quarterly Journal of Speech,* and *Social Epistemology.*

ALLISON WOODFORD received her B.S. in Communication and is completing requirements for the M.S. in Technical Communication at Rensselaer Polytechnic Institute.

Green Culture

Introduction

CARL G. HERNDL and STUART C. BROWN

Rhetorical Criticism and the Environment

> Words are used as signs, arbitrary and temporary, even as language reflects (and informs) the shifting values of the peoples whose minds it inhabits and glides through. We have faith in "meaning" the way we might believe in wolverines—putting trust in the occasional reports of others or on the authority of once seeing a pelt. But it is sometimes worth tracking these tricksters back.
>
> —Gary Snyder

This book is about an idea, the environment, and about the language we use to talk about it. For most rhetoricians who write essays such as those collected in this book, the environment is not a thing you could go out and find in the world. Rather, it is a concept and an associated set of cultural values that we have constructed through the way we use language. In a very real sense, there is no objective environment in the phenomenal world, no environment separate from the words we use to represent it. We can define the environment and how it is affected by our actions only through the language we have developed to talk about these issues. As rhetorical theorists have long argued, what we know, how we know it, and who can speak about it authoritatively are largely determined by our language.

We are not claiming that there is no such thing as nature or that pollution has no effect outside the arena of environmental discourse. What we are suggesting is that the environment about which we all argue and make policy is the product of the discourse about nature established in powerful scientific disciplines such as biology and ecology, in government agencies such as the Environmental Protection Agency and its regulations, and in nonfiction essays and books such as Rachel Carson's *Silent Spring* or Paul Ehrlich's *The Population Bomb*. Beyond this, the values and beliefs we hold about the environment are established through the discourses of a be-

3

wildering variety of genres, institutions, and media. For example, the value
the environment holds in our culture is shaped not only by documents such
as environmental impact statements, but also by books like Thoreau's *Walden: Or Life in the Woods* or television shows such as Mutual of Omaha's
Wild Kingdom that we watched as children. The language of these various
discourses determines what exists, what is good, and what is possible. Furthermore, as our brief list suggests, the field of environmental rhetoric is
immense and remarkably varied, so varied in fact that we think it connects
almost every part of our social and intellectual life, crossing the boundaries
between various academic disciplines and social institutions.

The environment is certainly a political issue; in 1988, George Bush ran
as "the environmental president," and the Rio Earth Summit reminded us
all that the environment is an important foreign policy problem. The continuing and bitter arguments between advocates of economic growth and
advocates of environmental preservation divide communities. Work in biology and ecology has made environmental study the center of powerful
scientific disciplines. Debates over what Garrett Hardin calls the "commons" add complex moral issues and have led to the development of an
entire subdiscipline called "environmental ethics." The concentration of
pollution and waste sites in minority and ethnic communities has come to
be seen as environmental racism. The tradition of American landscape
painting and the many books, stories, and poems written about our relation to nature and the power of natural beauty have made attention to the
environment part of our culture's aesthetic.

The ubiquity with which the environment pervades our lives makes it
an important issue for everyone. But for rhetoricians who study the way
we use language to construct our world and to conduct our lives, this
wide range of environmental discourse is both interesting and problematic. The variety of very different contexts in which we talk about the
environment suggests that there is not one environmental discourse but
many, a polyphony that makes it difficult to understand and resolve environmental disputes.

At different points in its history, the study of rhetoric has been understood as a way to help citizens participate in their government. Rhetoric
has been understood not only as Aristotle defined it as "the discovery of the
possible means of persuasion" but also as a tool that allowed people to
explore significant social and moral issues and make wise or prudent decisions. For example, as Greg Clark and Michael Halloran have demonstrated, the purpose of formal rhetorical education in nineteenth-century
America was to help citizens participate in the public discussions necessary
for democratic government. Certainly our society has changed, but famili-
arity with rhetoric and its analytic methods can help us understand the

nature of our environmental debates and their outcomes. As Barry Brummett argues, rhetoric is "the social function that influences and manages meanings," and it does so in both professional forums and popular culture (xiv). Brummett concludes that "If we could see how we are influenced [by rhetoric], if our repertoires for making reality were broadened, we might make the world into something different" (xxii).

In order to demonstrate the way rhetorical analysis might elucidate our discourse about the environment and the way that discourse shapes our relations to the world, we begin with two brief examples. The first example is drawn from Diane Ackerman's essay "Albatrosses," which appeared in the *New Yorker* magazine. The essay describes an expedition to survey short-tailed albatrosses, an almost extinct species that lives on Torishima, a remote island off the coast of Japan. Like most essays in the *New Yorker* genre, the narrative of the expedition is punctuated by the sobering facts of environmental degradation and with fascinating biography, in this case the life story of Peter Harrison, a remarkable naturalist and noted illustrator. What interests us about this text is the way it frames the albatross and the environmental issues of preservation and loss within a powerfully romantic discourse about the spiritual vision of private individuals and the kinds of social action it encourages or discourages.

The essay is quite long, covering twenty-seven pages with relatively few advertisements, but we need not reproduce the whole essay; a few salient examples will illustrate our argument. It focuses on the expedition to Torishima by the writer along with Peter Harrison and Hiroshi Hasegawa, the Japanese scientist who has fought to preserve the island and the short-tailed albatross. Throughout, this is a story of solitary individuals fighting to save the last remnants of a once abundant species. The three adventurers struggle against government intransigence and cross typhoon-ravaged seas to reach the barren rock where the last colony of short-tailed albatross cling. They make a "pilgrimage," an "arduous religious journey to discover what is sacred, . . . beset by many unavoidable steps and hardships on [their] quest" (66). The narrative invokes a private, religious, and romantic context. The environmentalist becomes the knight-errant or the wandering visionary. And this sense of the protagonist as an individual set apart is compounded when we are introduced to the essay's hero, Peter Harrison.

We learn that Harrison grew up in a seamen's orphanage on the northern coast of England where he spent his childhood sailing whaleboats into the North Sea and scaling the sea cliffs looking for birds' nests. At one point, Harrison recalls an earlier expedition during which he climbed barren rock towers off Cape Horn in stormy seas to make the first survey of the gray-headed albatross. He tells of falling 125 feet into the freezing surf, and then, after a couple of restorative shots of whiskey, climbing back up the tower. His comment: "this was certainly the closest I've ever come to death, and not just once or twice a day but many times" (70–71). His feats seem superhuman as he literally defies death to overcome the "hardships on [his] quest."

The romantic vision of this essay is perhaps clearest in the passage where Harrison describes his feelings for the sea:

> There is a rhythm to the sea, and the sea obliges you to adopt it. . . . You haven't any choice. So I sometimes think of the ocean as the heartbeat of the world. If you stand anywhere on any shoreline, even if it is just at a lake, and just listen, letting the stillness descend around you, it doesn't matter where you are—there's always a rhythm, a beat. I love being part of that bigger self. (68)

In the vision Harrison articulates, nature is the province of the solitary figure: an exceptional person acts out of a separate, intimate, and personal connection with a mysterious and wild nature. We could easily find these lines about being "part of that bigger self" in a poem by a leading figure among the nineteenth-century British romantic poets, William Wordsworth. In fact, the description of Harrison's childhood exploits echoes Wordworth's poems about his childhood on this same northern English coast, complete with the gathering of birds' eggs along the sea cliffs. Harrison's sense of the unity of nature, of belonging to a "bigger self," recalls Wordworth's description of a benevolent and unified nature, the spirit that "rolls through all things," in poems such as "Tintern Abbey," or a poem like "The Eolian Harp" in which Samuel Taylor Coleridge, Wordsworth's contemporary, speaks of "the one Life within us and abroad" that he feels in nature.

This mythologizing is one version of our engagement with nature, but with its own particular ideological origins and political consequences. The individualism that lies at the center of this romantic vision considers knowledge and action as private affairs and sees nature as an aesthetic, even religious, object. The kinds of discourse and social engagement provided by this construction of nature and our relations to it, however, simply do not fit our urban, postindustrial age. Indeed, as scholars have argued, this myth didn't even fit the historical conditions of the early nineteenth century, but was itself a nostalgic desire for an agrarian culture that was already lost or may never have existed. In many ways this vision of nature emerged as a reaction against the urbanization brought on by the industrial revolution.

As interesting as the historical sources of the romanticism in the *New Yorker* essay are, the consequences of this vision for our relations to the environment are at least as important. The model of knowledge and of the contemplation made possible by a romantic vision makes it nearly impossible to think of the environment as a social responsibility, to think of nature as a scientific, an economic, or an institutional construction or problem. This form of romanticism celebrates the inner life of the exceptional individual who is engaged in a private relationship with nature. The kinds of actions necessary in our contemporary political context are those in which individuals act within social communities and the ethical values at play are often those of social responsibility rather than private pleasure and spiritual reverie.

Our argument here is similar to the one Jimmie Killingsworth and Jacqueline Palmer recently made in an article, "How to Save the Earth," in which they analyze the rhetoric of the new and widely read genre of environmental "how-to" books. Among their conclusions Killingsworth and Palmer point out that even if these books reach audiences who would not read Barry Commoner,

The green consumer movement is all too open to be appropriated by forces whose long term interests are anything but environmentalist. . . . Emphasis on small scale actions or personal agendas that ignore public causes may function ideologically, blinding the general public to the need for massive shifts in government policy and curtailments of large scale industrial activity. (399)

In the *New Yorker* essay, seemingly a direct descendant of nineteenth-century romanticism, the poetics of individual vision perform precisely this function. The literary critic Marjorie Levinson, for example, has pointed out that the pastoral landscape Wordsworth idealized in his famous poem "Tintern Abbey" was actively being cut and burned even as Wordsworth gazed upon it (29–30). But this social, industrial problem, and any appropriate shift in government policy, are invisible, absent from the romantic lyric Wordsworth produced. He literally looked the other way, ignoring the impact of industrialism as he described a vision of nature that became, like Harrison's sense of the sea, "the nurse, / The guide, the guardian of my heart, and soul / Of all my moral being" ("Tintern Abbey"). Levinson has argued convincingly that the great power of Wordsworth's lyric comes precisely from his ability to present the social and political problem as a spiritual and aesthetic issue. By idealizing nature, Wordsworth, inadvertently or not, contains or even dismisses the threat of industrial change and makes the idealized landscape part of his internal poetic vision rather than part of a public dilemma.

The ideology that concentrates on the private at the expense of the public and social is striking in the *New Yorker* article. Introducing the depredation of the once abundant albatross, Ackerman notes that "In barely a hundred years, plume hunters slaughtered almost every one of these birds"

(61). A page later, the writer describes watching two pieces of film footage of the island, one old, one new. She describes the first film and then moves to the second.

Just offshore, the waves appeared permanently whitecapped, so large and dense were the rafts of magnificent birds. Next, in sharp contrast, a color film shows us the few birds that are left, and we shake our heads in disbelief. How could such a thing have happened? (62)

The naiveté of this disbelief is remarkable enough, but Killingsworth and Palmer's prediction that the individualism of much environmental rhetoric may actually be used to promote anti-environmental agendas is fulfilled when we consider the advertisements that are interleaved throughout this *New Yorker* essay. Among the advertisements that share the page with this text is one for a $24,000 jewel-encrusted broach; one promoting the nuclear power industry and warning us of the "dangers" of "unpredictable" "foreign oil"; and, the most apropos, an advertisement for the "overwhelming furs" of Copenhagen's Birger Christensen furriers. Because the romantic ideology of Ackerman's essay celebrates the individual's private vision and excludes the social and material from her discourse, it leaves no room to contest this commercial appropriation of her narrative. A story about the depredation of the albatross by plume hunters becomes a vehicle to sell exotic furs.

To avoid the implication that the romantic ideology of private, individual consciousness is the only problem in environmental rhetoric, we offer one other very brief analysis of environmental discourse. The genre of environmental writing that probably reaches the most people in American and that may come to define the environmental rhetoric for millions of people is direct mail solicitations. Greenpeace alone sends out forty-seven million pieces of direct mail annually. Greenpeace activists Peter Bahouth and Andre Carothers describe the mailbox as "a sanctuary and a lifeline: a sanctuary for delivering those political views that cannot survive the media's censorship, and a lifeline for the growth and preservation of the issues" (55). Bahouth and Carothers stress that direct mail helps establish a community that cannot be built in any other way.

As important as direct mail is to the efforts of groups like Greenpeace, the Nature Conservancy, or the Wilderness Society, the consequences of their rhetorical construction are not all beneficial. For example, a recent mailing from the Nature Conservancy has a sandhill crane on the envelope and the crane seems to be glowering at you. The enclosed letter describes the crane's sanctuary as "prime real estate," and its postscript suggests that your $15 donation will buy the crane's "first motel stop." The rhetoric of real estate values, motel prices, and neighborhood preservation makes the crane just another consumer competing in the marketplace, thus reinforcing the very commercial ideology that has destroyed much of the crane's habitat. Direct mail campaigns are a technology designed to make a sale, and environmental groups who use them often position themselves as just another group in a consumer economy.

Our second point about direct mail is that such letters offer only two options: ignoring the letter, or sending money to the group. Thus the possibilities for participation and rational engagement are radically limited. Such letters do not ask readers to explore the complexities of the environmental situation. They do not offer readers a chance to participate in the making of environmental policy decisions. This limitation, perhaps one largely imposed by the medium, reduces the process of ethical decision making so severely that it essentially guts any viable sense of collective, community-based ethical action. As a number of rhetorical scholars suggest, such letters compromise the ethics of the environmental discourse (see, for example, Johannesen; Porter; Wallace).

Unfortunately, environmental discourse is not as straightforward as the simple dichotomies our examples suggest. If the romantic ideology we have described in the *New Yorker* essay tends to discourage social analysis and collective action, it can also provide an emotional and spiritual language that maintains a value and love for nature. Peter Harrison may be a daring adventurer set radically apart from the lives of his readers, but he is also a figure with whom many readers can identify, at least emotionally. Through Ackerman's romantic narrative about Harrison and the albatross, readers may very well come to share some of Harrison's love and reverence for nature. And if the language of the Nature Conservancy's direct mail campaign reinforces the dominant view of nature as just another commodity, this same language has built unusual political and social coalitions and raised funds that have protected large areas of sensitive habitat.

Our examples and the complications that arise in them demonstrate the need for rhetorical and cultural analyses of environmental rhetoric. Whether we think our language practices privilege some kinds of thinking and some forms of knowledge at the expense of others, or whether we think of the genres of environmental writing—e.g., EPA reports, *New Yorker* essays, books such as *Silent Spring*—as recurrent forms of social action (Miller), it is clear that environmental discourse is a historically developed cultural form maintained by rhetorical activity. As Roderick Nash, Max Oelschlaeger, Carolyn Merchant, and others demonstrate, our "ideas" about nature have long been a defining characteristic in human culture.

Our brief examples demonstrate some of the ways rhetorical criticism examines the details of a text and considers its relation to the context in which it circulates. Rhetorical critics determine how some texts succeed in particular situations and why. Unfortunately, rhetorical criticism cannot always dictate rhetorical practice. Rhetorical acts are embedded in their immediate context, and this context changes. Thus, the analysis of past rhetorical activity does not always tell us what to say or how to say it in future situations. But rhetorical criticism does provide a method for analyzing our public rhetoric, and principles which can guide our rhetorical practice in the future.

In order to organize analysis of environmental rhetoric we offer the following model. This model is designed to identify the dominant tendencies or orientation of a piece of environmental discourse. Loosely adapted from Ogden and Richards' rhetorical triangle (11) and from Killingsworth and Palmer's "Continuum of Perspectives on Nature" (*Ecospeak* 14), the model ask us to determine the attitude, or in Kenneth Burke's term, the "motive," of a particular text regarding an environmental topic. Burke's influential theory of rhetoric says that the motives and purpose of a document can be found in the "scene" from which the document emerges, and that we can understand a text only if we understand the relations between the scene and the other elements of any rhetorical action. Burke calls this "dramatism," a "technique of analysis of language and thought as basically modes of action rather than as means of conveying information" (*Language as Symbolic Action* 54). As a description of action, dramatism is an epistemological system that can be used as a heuristic to generate new knowledge. What we learn in analyzing a text gives us a broader understanding of the world; it provides "*equipments for living*" (*Philosophy of Literary Form* 304).

Of particular interest here is Burke's argument that our understanding of the world comes through the symbols provided in our language. The way we use these symbols to represent the world is determined by motives that emerge from the rhetorical scene. Our model is designed to help clarify the connections between a text, a writer, and the setting from which a piece of writing comes in an effort to elicit the underlying motives around a text or topic. As we will see later, this model can also help us apply the results of rhetorical criticism to practice.

The regulatory discourse at the top of the model represents the discourse of the powerful institutions that make decisions and set environmental policy. This discourse usually regards nature as a resource, one among many others, to be managed for the greater social welfare. In many ways this discourse is the legacy of Gifford Pinchot's vision of a utilitarian management of natural resources which eventually won out in the contest with John Muir's wilderness philosophy. As a result, we call this an ethnocentric discourse, one devoted to negotiating the benefits of environmental policy

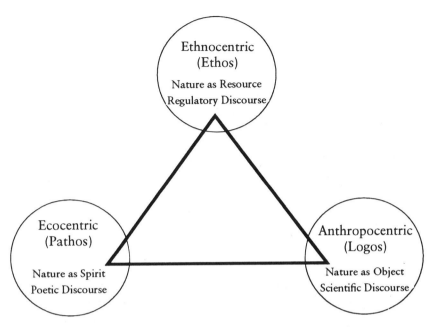

A rhetorical model for environmental discourse

measured against a broad range of social interests. The U.S. Department of the Interior's policy of multiple use in national forests and the broad appeal of the Nature Conservancy direct mail campaign are representative examples of this position. The breadth of the interests represented, of course, is precisely one of the contested issues in many environmental disputes. The political power of this discourse comes from its institutional context, but its rhetorical power emerges from the rhetorical notion of ethos, the culturally constructed authority of the speaker or writer who represents these institutions. As we will see in the essays that follow, the failures of many policy-making processes emerge, in large part, from the failure to construct an acceptable authority from which to promulgate decisions.

The scientific discourse in the model represents the specialized discourse of the environmental sciences. Within this discourse, nature is usually regarded as an object of knowledge constructed through careful scientific methodology. Because this discourse locates the human researcher as outside and epistemologically above nature, we call this anthropocentric discourse, one grounded in its faith in the human ability to come to know nature's secrets. The immense cultural power of this discourse comes from our rationalist faith in science and in the productivity of the scientific method. The rhetorical power of this discourse emerges from the rhetorical notion of logos, the appeal to objective fact and reason. This is the discourse to which the policy makers often turn to ground their arguments; technical data and expert testimony usually represent the basis of policy decisions, often at the expense of other participants or other forms of rhetorical appeal.

The poetic discourse in the model refers to the language we use to discuss the beauty, the value, the emotional power of nature. In this discourse, nature is usually regarded as a spiritual or transcendent unity. Because this discourse largely considers humanity as part of nature and seeks to locate human value in a harmonious relation to the natural world, we call this an ecocentric discourse. The power of this discourse comes largely from aesthetic or spiritual responses to the rhetorical notion of pathos, or appeals to the emotions of the audience. Thoreau's *Walden: Or Life in the Woods,* Henry Beston's *The Outermost House,* and Diane Ackerman's essay "Albatrosses" are good representatives of this kind of emotional appeal.

Our model identifies the main characteristics of three powerful environmental discourses, but these discourses are not pure. As the following chapters demonstrate, successful writing often combines the styles, forms, and rhetorical appeals of more than one of these discourses. Like any model, ours identifies only the dominant tendencies and is perhaps most useful as a heuristic that helps us navigate the sometimes bewildering variety of discourses on the environment, their cultural importance, and the array of rhetorical techniques available to the critic or the writer.

The Essays

> Statements are made but partially— Things are said with reference to certain conventions or existing institutions.— not absolutely.
>
> —Henry David Thoreau

The first three chapters examine the writing of a number of influential nature writers such as Rachel Carson, Aldo Leopold, Barry Commoner, and Loren Eiseley. These essays describe in detail the way these writers adapt well-known textual strategies to suit their specific context and purposes. We would locate the genre of nature writing along the bottom of our model. Nature writing often combines a scientific knowledge of nature with a desire to reenchant science, to connect scientific knowledge to a spiritual sense of nature and its beauty. Thus, nature writing often uses conventions and forms more characteristic of poetic discourse and appeals to pathos as well as to reason. These important texts do not set policy, but they do construct the cultural understanding of nature and our relation to it whereby policy decisions will be judged.

In the first chapter, Killingsworth and Palmer trace the recent history of the apocalyptic form in environmental writing. Starting with Rachel Carson's famous opening to *Silent Spring*, Killingsworth and Palmer discuss the changing shape and context of the apocalyptic form in writers such as Paul Ehrlich, Barry Commoner, and even James Watt. They argue that in the three decades since the publication of *Silent Spring,* this important form of environmental writing has changed as political and cultural contexts have changed. Thus, Carson's strident warning suits the Cold War context in which she can associate the danger of pesticide contamination with the threat of nuclear destruction. Paul Ehrlich's *The Population Bomb,* published in 1968, uses a less polemical style while maintaining a powerful attack on the ideology of industrial progress. But Barry Commoner, writing in the environmentally active 1970s, eschews the radical apocalyptic rhetoric and adopts a moderate voice more suited to what was then a part of mainstream culture. Ironically, it is the radical anti-environmentalist James Watt who adopts the explicitly Christian apocalyptic rhetoric during the Reagan era's fight against environmentalism. Identifying the connection between rhetorical form and cultural context allows Killingsworth and Palmer to see the apocalyptic narrative as a rhetorical strategy rather than a literal argument. They demonstrate that writers have used the apocalyptic form as a way to attract new members to the environmental movement, and that these narratives should be read not as predictions, but as emotional and political appeals to a wide readership.

Taking his title, "Thinking like a Mountain," from one of the most famous essays in *A Sand County Almanac,* Louis Ulman examines the writings of Aldo Leopold as examples of the way nature writing can help us resolve environmental dilemmas. Ulman defines nature writing as a genre that exists on the border between scientific writing about natural history and autobiographical writing about the way individuals relate to the natural world. Nature writing combines the objective description of natural history with the personal insight of autobiography to give its readers a model of how, individually and collectively, we should relate to the nonhuman world. Thus, Ulman argues that Leopold's most enduring contribution to conservation is the essays in which Leopold presents "an ethical vision of humanity's place in nature." Using the rhetorical concepts of *ethos, persona,* and judgment to explain the way Leopold changes his essays to suit different contexts and purposes, Ulman demonstrates how Leopold came to construct the powerful persona that inhabits *A Sand County Almanac.* He argues that the ecological essays in the middle of *A Sand County Almanac* weld the personal experience of the first section to the philosophical essays of the last section in a fashion that has become a dominant rhetorical model in American nature writing.

In his chapter, "Epistemology and Politics in American Nature Writing," Scott Slovic traces the rhetorical strategies at work in the writing of Henry Beston, Loren Eiseley, Aldo Leopold, and Rachel Carson back to the early American sermons of Cotton Mather and Jonathan Edwards. He describes the way these two New England preachers used a rhapsodic celebration of nature to inspire wonder and love of God in their listeners and how, at other moments, they used the shrill warning of the jeremiad to instill obedience. After demonstrating the pervasiveness of these two styles in contemporary nature writing, Slovic evaluates the different effects these strategies have on readers. By doing so, he provides environmentalists with a way to decide how best to persuade specific audiences to respect the environment and to alter their actions.

The next four chapters examine the shape environmental discourse takes in the powerful institutions that make decisions and set policy. These essays examine various aspects of the regulatory discourse located at the top of our model. They examine procedures such as risk analysis as methods for making policy and consider the degree to which citizens can effectively participate in this institutional discourse. Each chapter develops its analysis through an extended case study of a specific environmental issue, and as a group, they explore the ways we succeed or fail in constructing the kind of social and rhetorical authority necessary to make and promulgate environmental policy.

Katz and Miller trace the process through which the North Carolina Waste Management Authority, charged with selecting a site for a low-level waste repository, conducted its investigation and came to a decision. They take the five-year process involved in this case as typical of the way state and federal agencies make decisions about locating facilities that are opposed by the communities in which they are to be located. They demonstrate that the procedures and assumptions built into the techniques of "risk communication" that guide the institutional decision-making process on this and other environmental issues "can help account for the communication and decision-making failures." After years of work, over 350 hearings, and more than $3,500,000 spent on public information campaigns, debate and public opposition to the Authority's siting decision remain widespread. By examining the documents and testimony involved in this case, Katz and Miller explain how the "engineering model" of communication embedded in risk communication reduces public participation to a passive reception of information, turning what should be dialogue into a public relations campaign. They conclude that the model of communication used in risk analysis depends on an erroneous faith in the social and political neutrality of information and scientific fact, and that, as a result, the model excludes the attitudes, values, and emotions of the affected community from the decision-making process.

Craig Waddell's discussion of the International Joint Commission on Great Lakes Water Quality offers a sharp contrast to the analysis Katz and Miller offer. Established by the Boundary Waters Treaty between the United States and Canada, the International Joint Commission investigates disputes about water quality and quantity, and, most recently, monitors both governments' compliance with the Great Lakes Water Quality Agreement. Unlike the North Carolina Waste Management Authority, however, the International Joint Commission is notably successful in resolving disputes and encouraging public participation. Through his analysis of documents, public testimony, and personal interviews, Waddell demonstrates that, in this case, public participation took the form of what he calls the "social constructionist model"; to a greater or lesser extent both information and values passed from the public to the commission. Waddell demonstrates that despite the common conflict between "rational" experts and "emotional" members of the public, emotional appeals were common in the testimony of both groups, and that they were effective in persuading the commission and moving them to take action. His analysis suggests that environmentalists combine emotional appeals that describe the effect of policies on human life and health with the power of ecocentric appeals, those based on the intrinsic value of the environment separate from human interests.

The complex of rhetorical positions involved in resolving environmental disputes with which Waddell closes is the central focus of James Cantrill's ethnographic study of the Beartooth Alliance in Cooke City, Montana. Here, Cantrill explores the uneven success with which a small town constructs a sense of community and wages its environmental fight. Cooke City faces the threat of the New World Project, a hugh gold-mining operation that would drastically alter the physical and social environment that Cooke City residents treasure. By analyzing the themes that recur in the way members of the Beartooth Alliance talk about themselves, the Alliance, and the mine, Cantrill explores the way the rhetoric of grassroots organizations both creates a rhetorical community and limits the effectiveness of groups' attempts to shape public policy. He argues that the tensions and divisions revealed within the Beartooth Alliance are symptomatic of the fissures and differences that run through most environmental organizations in this country. Thus, the uncertain future and uneven success of the Cooke City group provide a useful cautionary tale for environmental groups everywhere.

In the last chapter in this section, Zita Ingham examines the value of rhetorical education in changing community values. In the small town of Red Lodge, Montana, as elsewhere across the country, environmental preservation is tied to disputes over land use, economic growth, and private property rights. The problem here is exacerbated by the fact that the area around Yellowstone National Park that includes Red Lodge is one of the fastest-growing areas in the United States. In her study of the way the people of Red Lodge respond to change, Ingham describes how one town constructs its sense of community through rhetorical activity that combines reason and emotion, outside experts and local citizens. Central to the success of this process is the idea that "rhetorical dialogue about the environment ties the health of the environment to the rhetorical health of the community." In the case of Red Lodge, the rhetorical principle of "identification" between speaker and audience helps consolidate a sense of community, and the rhetorical notion of dissensus, the willingness to explore the reasons for differences rather than enforce an artificial consensus, lead townspeople to an ongoing process of dialogue and collective action. In many ways, the rhetorical education going on in Red Lodge is an example of the more democratic models of risk communication advocated in the previous chapters by Waddell and by Katz and Miller.

The last four chapters describe the cultural and historical background in which the writers discussed in the first section and the institutional debates described in the second section take place. These essays examine some of the history of environmental rhetoric, and how ideological positions are established and negotiated through the language of environmental discourse. In various ways, these four chapters describe environmental discourse as the scene of cultural conflict and struggle. These essays explore the power of the poetic discourse at the bottom of our model, its historical development, and the cultural context within which these values and emotions are formed and combined with regulatory or scientific discourse. These four chapters make more explicit what the earlier chapters left implicit: the politics and details of environmental discourse must be understood within a broad cultural context. The connections between Thoreau, or Edwards and Mather, and current environmental debates, for example, emerge only as part of the historical development of American culture. Or as we suggest about the *New Yorker* essay "Albatrosses," romantic ideology can transcend narrowly defined political or institutional conflicts and reside, finally, in our shared cultural sense of the world and our place in it.

In the first of these essays, Robert Brown and Carl Herndl examine the environmental writing of the John Birch Society. They read one of the society's publications devoted to a discussion of the 1992 Rio Earth Summit as an example of the way the unequal relations of power between social groups affects environmental discourse. Using the cultural theory of

French critic Pierre Bourdieu, they argue that the society's seemingly irrational rhetoric is not evidence that its writers are uninformed or illogical. Rather, the radical discourse of society publications serves to establish the social identity of society members and to consolidate power within their group. Brown and Herndl argue that for members of politically marginal groups such as the John Birch Society this oppositional rhetoric and its spokespersons offer a powerful, idealized persona with which sympathetic readers identify. Thus, the society's rhetoric, like that of other environmental discourses, must be understood as part of a complicated social negotiation of power and identity.

In her essay "Environmental Rhetoric in the Age of Hegemonic Politics," Marilyn Cooper points out that the fundamental dilemma facing environmental organizations is the degree to which we must change our lifestyle to preserve the environment. Must we make the radical changes advocated by the deep ecology movement and groups like Earth First! or simply manage our environment better as groups like the Nature Conservancy suggest? Cooper focuses on an essential rhetorical construct: the nature of persuasion. Specifically, she is concerned with how we can best persuade people to change their lifestyles and how we can gauge the success or failure of the rhetorical strategies of different environmental groups. Cooper compares the policies of the Nature Conservancy and Earth First! and examines the rhetorical structure of representative pieces of their writings. She analyzes these two groups through the perspective of radical democratic politics, a theory that examines the way groups struggle to create a position or point of view that people in a society will accept as a commonsense basis for their actions. Social change is successful when groups can link new values to accepted political positions in a society. Using this theoretical approach, Cooper concludes that the environmental movement needs to forge connections between the very different rhetorical strategies of Earth First! and the Nature Conservancy.

The books, essays, and community discussions analyzed in earlier chapters all represent the environment in language; after all, we negotiate our cultural and political consensus, or our lack of one, through language. But as Clark, Halloran, and Woodford demonstrate, the language we use to discuss and debate environmental policy is partly determined by the way we have historically depicted nature and our relations to it in art, here the paintings of the Hudson River School. This distinctly American tradition of landscape art provides us with images that carry with them political and cultural assumptions about the relationship between humans and nature. As Clark, Halloran, and Woodford argue, the paintings of Thomas Cole establish a rhetoric in which humans are alienated from the natural world, which then becomes the potential object of human domination. They set this artistic tradition in the context of the nineteenth-century development of the land and connect this rhetorical representation to contemporary debates over the environment. The images of the Hudson River School are an important source for the contemporary sense of nature as a resource to be used and the opposing position that humans are a destructive intrusion into nature.

In the last chapter, Charles Bergman explores the ways in which our artistic images speak to us about the alienation of men and women both from the natural world and from themselves, from their own bodies. Moving from prehistoric paintings etched on the walls of Spanish caves to the pastoral tradition in Western literature, Bergman traces the connection between nature and the human body. He interprets these images as signs that help us understand the cultural myths that have constructed our relationship to nature as one of power and desire. Bergman finds the clearest expression of this relationship in the prehistoric cave paintings; he argues that we have always invested the body of nature with the desires that control our relation to our own bodies. Noting the absence of desire and sexualized imagery from American nature writing, he calls for a transformation of our relationship to nature and the the relations of power and control that mark our alienation from the natural world.

The environment has become a central topic in a wide range of institutions and forums. Discussions of environmental matters now not only occupy entire fields of study, but cross disciplinary boundaries and include the distinctly American genre of nature writing, several sciences, politics, economics, ethics, law, and spirituality. Despite this widespread concern, however, scholars have produced very few concentrated analyses of the rhetoric of these debates. This collection begins to address that lack and provides a scheme for defining the emerging field of rhetorical analyses of environmental discourse. Although the chapters in this collection examine a range of methods, sites, and issues, there is a great variety of environmental discourse that remains to be examined. Environmental discourse in the mass media, writing in sciences such as biology and ecology, and the growing body of work in environmental racism and ecofeminism provide rich sites for future analysis.

As the essays in this collection demonstrate, rhetorical criticism offers a means to investigate and evaluate, as Sonja Foss notes, "rhetorical acts and artifacts for the purpose of understanding the rhetorical process" of language at work in the world (5). Rhetorical criticism can provide "a form of interrogation, of performed response, of appreciation, interpretation, explanation, and judgment," according to Thomas Benson (xxii). The essays collected here analyze environmental discourse produced in a wide variety of sites and genres and offer explanations of how these very different discourses are constructed rhetorically.

Questions of environmental action and policy are notoriously difficult to resolve—the pervasive nature of the problems, their breadth and variety, as well as the encompassing range of professional and social interests involved all create a seemingly intractable complexity. Often competing arguments seem incommensurate, not only because they represent opposing interests, but because of differences in institutional, disciplinary, and social discourses. The various essays presented here examine these differences and provide analytic tools to investigate the language through which environmental issues are constructed and contested. Further, they suggest how rhetoric as a discipline can help resolve environmental disputes. Many of the studies in this book suggest that writing intended for a large public audience is most successful when it combines the rhetorical resources of more than one kind of discourse. For example, the power of nature writing to alter our cultural values and influence action comes from the writer's ability to combine scientific information with some of the forms and appeals characteristic of poetic discourse. As our relations to nature are not purely rational, not solely a matter of scientific knowledge, so our discourse must acknowledge the emotional and spiritual elements of our relation to nature. But perhaps most importantly, if we live in an "age of missing information," as Bill McKibben argues, rhetorical analyses of how we talk about the environment provide a means to recover some of what is missing.

WORKS CITED

Ackerman, Diane. "Albatrosses." *New Yorker,* 24 September 1990, 61–88.

Bahouth, Peter, and Andre Carothers. "In Defense of Junk Mail: Mailbox as Public Square." *Utne Reader* (Nov./Dec. 1990):55–58.

Benson, Thomas W. Introduction. *Rhetorical Criticism.* The Landmark Essays Series. Davis, CA: Hermagoras P, 1993. xi–xxi.

Brummett, Barry. *Rhetorical Dimensions of Popular Culture.* Tuscaloosa: U of Alabama P, 1991.

Burke, Kenneth. *Language as Symbolic Action: Essays on Life, Literature, and Method.* 1966; Berkeley: U of California P, 1968.

Burke, Kenneth. *The Philosophy of Literary Form: Studies in Symbolic Action.* 3d ed. Berkeley: U of California P, 1973.

Clark, Greg, and S. Michael Halloran, eds. *Oratorical Culture in Nineteenth-*

Century America: Transformations in Theory and Practice of Rhetoric. Carbondale: Southern Illinois UP, 1993.

Foss, Sonja K. *Rhetorical Criticism: Exploration and Practice.* Prospect Heights, IL: Waveland P, 1989.

Foucault, Michel. *The Archaeology of Knowledge.* Trans. A. M. Sheridan Smith. New York: Pantheon, 1972.

Halloran, Michael. "Rhetoric in the American College Curriculum: The Decline of Public Discourse." *Pre/Text* 3.3 (1982):245–69.

Hardin, Garrett. "The Tragedy of the Commons." In *The Environmental Handbook,* ed. Garrett De Bell. New York: Ballantine, 1980. 31–50.

Johannesen, Richard L. *Ethics in Human Communication.* 3d ed. Prospect Heights, IL: Waveland P, 1990.

Killingsworth, M. Jimmie, and Jacqueline S. Palmer. *Ecospeak: Rhetoric and Environmental Politics in America.* Carbondale: Southern Illinois UP, 1992.

Killingsworth, M. Jimmie, and Jacqueline S. Palmer. "How to Save the Earth: The Greening of Institutional Discourse." *Written Communication* 9.3 (1992):385–403.

Levinson, Marjorie. *Wordsworth's Great Period Poems: Four Essays.* New York: Cambridge UP, 1986.

McKibben, Bill. *The Age of Missing Information.* New York: Plume, 1992.

Merchant, Carolyn. *The Death of Nature: Women, Ecology, and the Scientific Revolution.* San Francisco, 1980.

Miller, Carolyn R. "Genre as Social Action." *Quarterly Journal of Speech* 70 (1984): 151–67.

Nash, Roderick. *The Rights of Nature: A History of Environmental Ethics.* Madison: U of Wisconsin P, 1989.

Nash, Roderick. *Wilderness and the American Mind.* Rev. ed. New Haven: Yale UP, 1973.

Ogden, C. K., and I. A. Richards. *The Meaning of Meaning: A Study of Influence of Language upon Thought and of the Science of Symbolism.* New York: Harcourt, 1923.

Oelschlaeger, Max. *The Idea of Wilderness: From Prehistory to the Age of Ecology.* New Haven: Yale UP, 1991.

Porter, James E. "Developing a Postmodern Ethics of Rhetoric and Composition." In *Defining the New Rhetorics,* ed. Theresa Enos and Stuart C. Brown. Newbury Park, CA: Sage, 1993: 207–26.

Snyder, Gary. "The Etiquette of Freedom." *The Practice of the Wild: Essays by Gary Snyder.* San Francisco: North Point, 1990. 3–24.

Thoreau, Henry David. *A Year in Thoreau's Journal: 1851.* Ed. H. Daniel Peck. New York: Penguin, 1993.

Wallace, Karl. "An Ethical Basis of Communication." *Speech Teacher* 4 (1955):1–9.

CHAPTER 1

Millennial Ecology

The Apocalyptic Narrative from
Silent Spring to *Global Warming*

M. JIMMIE KILLINGSWORTH and JACQUELINE S. PALMER

> More and more it seems to me that the philosopher, being *of necessity* a man of tomorrow and the day after tomorrow, has always found himself, and *had* to find himself, in contradiction to his today: his enemy was ever the ideal of today. So far all these extraordinary furtherers of man whom one calls philosophers, though they themselves have rarely felt like friends of wisdom but rather like disagreeable fools and dangerous question marks, have found their task, their hard, unwanted, inescapable task, but eventually also the greatness of their task, in being the bad conscience of their time.
>
> —Nietzsche

> I'll walk to the depths of the deepest forest,
> Where the people are many and their hands are all empty,
> Where the pellets of poison are flooding their waters,
> Where the home in the valley meets the damp dirty prison,
> Where the executioner's face is always well hidden,
> . . . It's a hard rain's a-gonna fall.
>
> —Bob Dylan

Apocalyptic narratives, long recognized as a major thematic and structural component in science fiction (Slusser, Greenland, and Rabkin), as well as in both canonical and postmodern American literature (Bercovitch; Dewey; Jameson; Newman; Robinson; Tichi), have for the last three decades also served as a standard feature of environmentalist polemic (DeGregori; Emsley). In depicting the end of the world as a result of the overweening desire to control nature, activists have discovered a rhetorical means of contesting their opponents' claims for the idea of progress with its ascendent narratives of human victory over nature (Killingsworth and Palmer). How are we to receive the words of these latter-day prophets?

21

Beyond proclaiming the literal possibility that the world may end, what do they hope to signify or bring about by invoking the onset of the last days?

At least partly, the new millennialism represents a radical attempt to re-place the ideology of progress and to dislodge from power its primary per-petuators and beneficiaries in big business, big government, and big science—to overturn the technocapitalist enterprise that fuels the econ-omy of the developed world. In this essay, however, we argue that, contrary to initial impressions, literal readings, and the assumptions of anti-environmentalists, the most influential apocalyptic narratives do not un-dertake a wholesale attack on the ideology of progress or its attendant faith in science, technology, and liberal democracy. These texts appear not as the rhetorical equivalent of total war but as shock tactics to win the hearts and minds of the general public at crucial historical periods in which the need is perceived to extend and broaden commitments to the environmental move-ment. One such historical watershed formed in the 1960s, when the envi-ronmental movement enjoyed its first surge of public support under the inspiration of Rachel Carson's visionary polemic *Silent Spring*. By charting the responses and reactions to Carson's influential use of apocalyptic narra-tive in the literature of environmental advocacy, we argue that millennial rhetoric bears a dialectical relation to public support for the environmental movement. It alternately reflects and builds a growing public awareness. It aims to transform the consciousness that a problem exists into acceptance of action toward a solution by prefacing the solution with a future scenario of what could happen if action is not taken, if the problem goes untreated.

We begin our analysis by establishing two extreme positions as critical poles. At one pole, we find the radical position of millennial ecology, which offers a thoroughgoing critique of progressive ideology and fosters a to-talizing vision of political transformation in the tradition of Christian millennialism—an outsider's gambit to reverse the trends of a degenerate orthodoxy (see Cohn; Tuveson).[1] At the other pole, we have the anti-environmentalist position, which defends orthodox progressivism against the attack of the millennialists. After sketching the broad outlines of these two positions, we go back to trace the historical development of the con-flict, beginning with what we see as the key source of millennial ecology—Carson's *Silent Spring*. We then follow the stream of Carson's influence to the recent turbulence over the issue of global warming. We conclude with a brief look at the implications of historical study both for environmental rhetoric and for rhetorical theory.

Critics of Progress—and Its Apologists

A true millennial ecologist, the eco-anarchist Murray Bookchin claims that our society is haunted by "nightmares of an ecological apocalypse."[2] In

Remaking Society: Pathways to a Green Future, he writes, "We live under the constant threat that the world of life will be irrevocably undermined by a society gone mad in its need to grow—replacing the organic by the inorganic, soil by concrete, forest by barren earth, and the diversity of life-forms by simplified ecosystems; in short a turning back of the evolutionary clock to an earlier, more inorganic, mineralized world that was incapable of supporting complex life-forms of any kind, including the human species" (20). The subtle connection of mechanistic characteristics in this passage with the idea of the regression to an inorganic state—the mention of "concrete" and "clock"—suggests a dialectical move typical of radical environmentalist rhetoric. The ideology of progress connected with the mechanistic and instrumental rationality of modernism is aligned with environmental degradation so that progressivism itself comes under question. The material progress associated with technological development is shown ultimately to turn back upon itself. Such development may have been dressed by it advocates in organic language—with terms like "growth" and "evolution"—but it ultimately represents the negation of organic life. It spreads but it does not grow. It destroys rather than creates.

In Bookchin's hands, apolcalyptic rhetoric signifies a radical undertaking, the aim of which is to root out the conceptual underpinnings of a polluting culture—in particular the ideal of progress—and establish new foundations for communal action. In mounting a critique of progress, the radical ecologist attacks the master narrative of liberal democracy in use since the Enlightenment. As Ernest Tuveson noted in 1949, to criticize the concept of progress is to risk heresy in Western cultures: "no higher commendation could be accorded than to say an idea or plan or person is 'progressive'—an adjective that has come to have all the force of 'righteous' and 'good,' " so that "to challenge the certainty and inevitability of progress" may well seem "as outrageous as to challenge the doctrine of the Atonement a few centuries ago" (x). Progress has thus become a "*total* ideology" as defined by Daniel Bell—"an all-inclusive system of comprehensive reality, . . . a set of beliefs infused with passion" that "seeks to transform the whole of a way of life," to convert ideas into a "social lever" (399–400). As Robert Nisbet has suggested, the ideology of progress "has been able to survive a great deal of adversity in its twenty-five hundred years: mass poverty, plagues and famines, devastating wars, economic depressions, eruptions of political and religious tyranny" (317). Its durability depends upon the bonding strength of its central premises—"belief in the value of the past; conviction of the nobility, even superiority, of Western civilization; acceptance of the worth of economic and technological growth; faith in reason and . . . scientific and scholarly knowledge . . . ; and, finally, belief in the intrinsic *worth* of life on this earth" (317). But now, millennial ecology suggests that this constellation of values has come undone, that both scientific reason and the moral commitment to sustaining life no longer support either the superiority of Western culture or large-scale economic and technological growth. It attempts to transform environmentalism into a total ideology that competes with the dominant ideology of progressivism. Like Nietzsche's philosopher, then, the millennial ecologists live "in contradiction to [their] today"; they are "dangerous question marks" representing "the bad conscience of their time" (Nietzsche 137).

Murray Bookchin is hardly alone in attempting to radicalize environmentalism. Though he has disagreed ideologically with the so-called "deep ecologists" (*Remaking Society* 12–15; Manes 154–55), he shares with them the vision of ecological apocalypse and total societal transformation. Christopher Manes, for example, the most eloquent and fervently political advocate for deep ecology, argues that Western society has opted to perpetuate a "culture of extinction," which pursues "short-term affluence at the cost of impoverishing nature and raising the specter of ecological collapse" (24). In the destruction of diversity among plant and animal species, Manes reads the fate of humanity and indeed all the earth. He sees "apocalyptic angst" as a leading motivator in the "rise of radical environmentalism" (24).

What is most remarkable about millennial ecology is not that it should arise as a form of criticism; apocalyptic prophecies have appeared throughout modernity as a kind of rhetorical and ideological counterweight to the scientific worldview, technological development, and liberal democracy that characterize the dominant culture. What is remarkable is rather that millennial ecology should have gained a hearing at all. Despite the strong popular sentiment supporting environmentalist values in the American culture of the 1990s (Killingsworth and Palmer 264–65; Norton 63–64), sentiment in favor of progressivism remains so strong that most people cannot even imagine a view of history that eliminates the concepts of growth and progress. Because of the hold that progressivism enjoys over the popular imagination, the public is usually slow to sympathize with apocalyptic prophecy. Millennialists from William Miller, the nineteenth-century founder of the Millerite sect, to David Karesh, the martyr of the Branch Davidians in our own time, have most frequently been regarded as either harmless cranks or dangerous fanatics.

By associating environmentalists with other, more fanatical millennialisms, anti-environmentalists have begun systematically to exploit the popular appeal of the progressive ideology.[3] The politician and scientist Dixy Lee Ray, for example, enumerates the discomforts of a childhood lived "close to nature" on a small farm during the Depression, summoning the old argument that environmentalists want to turn back the clock of progress until we are all living in caves. She thus presents us with a kind of reverse apocalyptic narrative, the message of which is more or less that, if we don't keep going, we'll fall back into the degradation of a past age.

The journalist Ronald Bailey, another defender of the progressive ideal, condemns "the false prophets of ecological apocalypse" for "their faulty analyses, their wildly inaccurate predictions, and their heedless politicization of science" (xi). Blaming sensationalistic mass media for the undeserved attention awarded to the millennialists, Bailey attempts to undermine their authority by reclaiming science for the party of hope and aligning radical environmentalism with the Millerites and other fanatic sects of the nineteenth century and with the Marxist belief that capitalist society will collapse of its own rottenness. For Bailey, apocalyptic rhetoric becomes a sign of unreliability; anyone who stoops to millennialism should not be trusted as a voice in the public forum, he warns. Such admonitions are certainly not new; the charges of inaccurate prediction and "wolf-crying" have haunted environmentalists' use of apocalyptic rhetoric, at times even alienating sympathizers to the cause (Bramwell 225–27; Killingsworth and Palmer 292 n. 2). But Bailey is perhaps the first to treat apocalyptic rhetoric as the grounds for a wholesale dismissal of the environmentalist movement.

More philosophical, but equally dismissive of millennialist claims, is the critique presented in the widely read book *The End of History and the Last Man* by Francis Fukuyama. Writing after the fall of Marxism in Eastern Europe, Fukuyama feels free to reintroduce a Hegelian defense of Western liberal democracy and scientific progress. While admitting the reality of environmental degradation (which Ray and Bailey seem hardly able to accept because of their deep distrust of millennial rhetoric and their commitment to the progressive ideal), Fukuyama identifies radical environmentalism with the old enemy Rousseau and the ill-informed belief in the recoverability of a state of nature. All so-called nature, he suggests, ended long ago, so that now every part of the natural world bears the mark of advanced society. Even Rousseau's lament over lost nature was belated, says Fukuyama; so that two centuries later, a book like Bill McKibben's *The End of Nature* can be seen only as doubly belated—and doubly sentimental, since it resurrects a Romantic point of view that was already nostalgic when it was formulated in the late eighteenth century. By that time, the frontier was restricted to only the most remote climes, and most parts of the "natural" world (certainly those known by Rousseau or Wordsworth, for example) had been thoroughly terraformed by centuries of human intervention.

Fukuyama argues that though it is certainly possible to limit technological development, it is virtually impossible to forget the principles that have enabled it. Once instituted, science cannot be undone. With science ever in the collective intelligence of the human race, Fukuyama reasons, the pressure to develop will remain as well, an irresistible temptation that matches the high expectations of those who have lived in the developed world, not to mention the third-world industrialists who desire a developed world of their own. Moreover, Fukuyama argues, we should not limit the development of technology, even if we could, for science and technology are the most likely sources for solving our environmental problems. Thus, Fukuyama concludes, "a truly cyclical history"—the view of history implicit in Bookchin's prophecy and in millennial ecology in general—"is conceivable only if we posit the possibility that a given civilization can vanish entirely without leaving any imprint on those that follow." Though history has certainly known such vanishings, it is not our fate, says Fukuyama: "Modern natural science . . . is so powerful, both for good and for evil, that it is very doubtful it can ever be forgotten or 'un-invented' under conditions other than the physical annihilation of the human race." The "grip of a progressive modern natural science" is thus "irreversible," a fact that supports the Hegelian notion of a "directional history" whose end is not a death but a *telos,* a full realization of the purpose of history—the victory of modern science and "all of the other variegated economic, social, and political consequences that flow from it" (88).

But Fukuyama's critique, for all its appeal, ultimately attacks a straw man. Far from abandoning science to go and live in caves, most environmentalists, even the radicals, are scientifically educated and support their claims with scientifically generated information. This is certainly true of Bookchin, especially in his early work. Likewise, Manes argues that the need to slow down and question, if not stop, technological progress is a feeling not only shared by environmental activists but also "corroborated by the findings of some of the world's most distinguished biologists" (24).

Manes's simultaneous appeal to the authority of science and to the "environmental angst" of the public borrows the key political strategy of *Silent Spring,* the book that arguably inaugurated the modern environmental movement with the millennialist claim that not only are we using up our resources at a dangerous rate (the worry of earlier conservationists), but we may well be killing ourselves more directly and literally with the widespread use of chemical pesticides.[4] But the significance of this apocalyptic rhetoric—particularly its political meaning—underwent a radical shift in the thirty years between Carson's book and Manes's *Green Rage.* To grasp this significance—another instance of the historical maxim that "nothing comes back the same" (Scholes 11)—we must try to reconstruct the recent history of millennial ecology, beginning with *Silent Spring.*

Getting to the Source: Carson's *Silent Spring*

Drawing upon native strains of popular culture and sensing the apocalyptic mood of the nuclear age, Rachel Carson echoed the dark prophecies of street preachers, folksingers, and beat poets with a social critique that connected recent scientific findings with anxieties over the earth's capacity to support the growth of a technologically advanced civilization. She struck a resonant note. Her book quickly became a best-seller when it appeared in 1962 and was regarded by President Kennedy as having significant implications for national policy (Brooks 285; Graham 51). Folksinger Bob Dylan, then a rising star, picked up the theme of *Silent Spring*—"the pellets of poison . . . flooding [the] waters"—in his 1963 "protest song," "A Hard Rain's A-Gonna Fall."

Though not the first book to argue for the pervasiveness of environmental danger—a distinction shared with Bookchin's *Our Synthetic Environment,* also published in 1962 under the pseudonym Lewis Herber—*Silent Spring* possessed a rhetorical power unmatched in its day. The book's accessibility and the popularity of its author made it a much more visible and influential book than any to have preceded it in the environmental movement. Key authors who antedated Carson—such as John Muir and Aldo Leopold—did not really gain a wide readership until after the publication of *Silent Spring.* Before the 1960s, Muir and Leopold were thought of as naturalists who wrote mainly for a limited or specialized audience. Arguably, they were carried into popularity on the wave of environmental awareness that followed the publication of *Silent Spring.*

Carson's rhetoric appealed to the temper of the times in a special way. Her eloquence depended upon the success of carefully embedded emotional "charges," as Kenneth Burke would call them (165–66). "Symbolic intensity," Burke says, "arises when the artist uses subject-matter 'charged' by the reader's experience outside the work of art" (163). The particular experience that Carson tapped into was the public's growing uneasiness over science and the military in the Cold War era, when the threat of Armageddon seemed ever more real. In the postwar years, science had enjoyed much of the credit for societal progress in the West. Moreover, it was hailed for having ended the war by providing America with the ultimate weapon. But public enthusiasm for science, which was supported as never before by big government and big business, moderated toward ambivalence as the Cold War produced crisis after crisis. Carson contributed a new dimension to the more sinister image of science that lurked in the popular imagination. Just as physics had joined with the military to produce the bomb that ended the big war but also left the world on the brink of nuclear disaster, so had agricultural science, as Carson depicted it, joined with agribusiness to produce chemicals that increased agricultural production in the short run but in the long run threatened the environmental safety of the very citizens who prospered from the advances in farming technology.

In a number of places, Carson explicitly aligned nuclear and agricultural science within the same conceptual framework, as in the following passage:

The rapidity of change and the speed with which new situations are created follow the impetuous and heedless pace of man rather than the deliberate pace of nature. Radiation is no longer merely the background radiation of rocks, the bombardment of cosmic rays, the ultraviolet [rays] of the sun that have existed before there was any life on earth; radiation is now the unnatural creation of man's tampering with the atom. The chemicals to which life is asked to make its adjustment are no longer merely the calcium and silica and copper and all the rest of the minerals washed out of the rocks and carried in rivers to the sea; they are the synthetic creations of man's inventive mind, brewed in his laboratories, and having no counterparts in nature (17).

In a related passage, she says, "Next to the possibility of the extinction of mankind by nuclear war, the central problem of our age has therefore become the contamination of man's total environment with substances of incredible potential for harm" (18). Thus, Carson concludes, "genetic deterioration through man-made agents is the menace of our time, 'the last and greater danger to our civilization' " (186).

Recasting the story of technological development in the language of black magic and Faustian mythology, Carson undercuts the classical claims of the Enlightenment—that science frees the world of the dark arts of medieval magic and brings the light of human progress (Killingsworth and Palmer 64–78). The book's epigraph from Keat's "La Belle Dame Sans Merci"—"The sedge is wither'd from the lake / And no birds sing"—sets the stage for a rendering of the human tragedy connected traditionally with the desire to control nature through witchcraft and sorcery. In Carson's own metaphors, agricultural chemicals are "brewed" like the witch's broth and sprayed over the earth as a "chemical death rain" in a "crusade to create a chemically sterile . . . world," a crusade undertaken with "fanatic zeal" (17, 21, 22).

Despite her own eloquence, her own zeal, her angry words against the chemical industry, her mythically and topically charged language, however, Carson never denied the problem of insect infestation or the need for a scientific solution: "All of this is not to say that there is no insect problem and no need for control," she insisted; "I am saying, rather, that control must be geared to realities, not to mythical situations, and that the methods employed must be such that they do not destroy us along with the insects"

(19). Somewhat ironically, her critique was, in many ways, an insider's work. Scientifically trained and a skilled popularizer of scientific knowledge, Carson ultimately argued that it is not science per se that is to blame for the wrongdoings of the pesticide industry, but a particular approach to science, a *paradigm*, to use Thomas Kuhn's well-known term. Carson was arguing not for a return to a prescientific era, but for a "paradigm shift," a *revolution* in science, as Kuhn would call it. She believed that the "Neanderthal age of biology and philosophy" motivated by the "arrogant" drive to "control nature" had run its course and should be abandoned in favor of the holistic work-with-nature model emerging in the relatively new science of ecology (261). Chemical "biocides" could ultimately be replaced, she argued, by ecologically sensitive biological means of protecting crops, with no loss of productivity, no retreat from the progress of the "green revolution" in agriculture. The overall scientific validity of her claims has been vindicated again and again, as has the timeliness and cogency of her vision (Bosso; Dunlap; Hynes).

What made Rachel Carson different from other scientific revolutionaries, such as those discussed by Kuhn and his followers, was that Carson, a science popularizer rather than a specialized researcher, took her case to the public instead of presenting her views in the close quarters of specialized research journals. Exposing not only theoretical diversity but also political dissent within the scientific community, she was arguing for a revolution in science that was not exclusively controlled by science itself, but included the participation of the public and its agents in government. No wonder then that when it came, the reaction of the scientific community to *Silent Spring* was strong, both for and against the positions advocated by Carson.

Those who castigated Carson as well as those who borrowed from her all but overlooked some of the strongest language in her book, such as its final words: "The concepts and practices of applied entomology for the most part date from the Stone Age of science. It is our alarming misfortune that so primitive a science has armed itself with the most modern and terrible weapons, and in turning them against the insects it has also turned them against the earth" (261–62). Far more controversial and influential, by contrast, was the brief, relatively low-key, but apocalyptically charged prologue. "A Fable for Tomorrow." The prologue covers barely two pages, but few texts have caused such a stir in environmental politics. The title says that the "fable" is "for tomorrow," but the prologue is written, like a foregone conclusion, in the past tense: "There once was a town in the heart of America where all life seemed to live in harmony with its surroundings" (13). The fabled town is situated in the pastoral landscape of a farming community, strongly suggesting the antebellum ideal of an agrarian America, an ideal undone by devastating conflicts, the Civil War and the World Wars, each of which extended the industrial revolution in mighty ways. The peaceful scene passes quickly in Carson's prologue, as "a strange blight crept over the area and everything began to change. Some evil spell had settled on the community": the cattle and poultry died; the farmers and their families became ill with diseases that puzzled their doctors; the birds disappeared, leaving silence in the fields; the bees did not come to the apple blossoms; the fish disappeared from the streams; the roadsides, "once so attractive, were now lined with browned and withered vegetation as though swept by fire" (13–14). Who was responsible? "No witchcraft, no enemy action had silenced the rebirth of new life in this stricken world. The people had done it themselves" (14).

With this denial of the conventional external villain, the fable reveals its moral even as it shifts its ground to appear not as a fairy tale but as a more realistic composite portrait. At the end of the prologue, Carson explains:

This town does not actually exist, but it might easily have a thousand counterparts in America or elsewhere in the world. I know of no community that has experienced all the misfortunes I describe. Yet every one of these disasters has actually happened somewhere, and many real communities have already suffered a substantial number of them. A grim specter has crept upon us almost unnoticed, and this imagined tragedy may easily become a stark reality we all shall know. (14–15)

"A Fable for Tomorrow" thus experiments with the merging of genres. It requires readers to view the text simultaneously as a fable, a psychologically complex tragedy (with a flawed protagonist—the community), and a report of actual occurrences. The implication is that the old, simple ways of seeing and acting no longer work; that a new reality requires a new kind of narrative. Above all, the language resonates with the fear of the end of the world, which, though mythic in proportion and venerable in intertextual possibilities, takes on a new reality in the shadow of nuclear weaponry. When Carson asserts that agricultural chemicals "should not be called 'insecticides,' but 'biocides' " (18), she again connects applied entomology with nuclear physics and invokes the specter of "evil science" (embodied in popular culture as the mad scientists of comic books and the egghead aliens of science fiction movies) as the foil of "good science," the progenitor of technological progress and the friend of advanced civilization.

The curious success of *Silent Spring* most likely grows from its willingness to criticize science while holding out hope for a scientific solution, much in the manner recommended by Fukuyama. While "Stone Age" scientists lead us down the dinosaurs' path to extinction, the heroes of ecological holism beckon toward a better path. The last chapter of *Silent Spring* thus begins with this wary but encouraging passage, which appeals to conventional wisdom with allusions to both Robert Frost and the Christian Gospel:

The road we have long been traveling is deceptively easy, a smooth superhighway on which we progress with great speed, but at its end lies disaster. The other fork of the road—the "one less traveled by"—offers our last, our only chance to reach a destination that assures the preservation of our earth. . . . A truly extraordinary variety of alternatives to chemical control of insects is available. . . . All have this in common: they are *biological* solutions, based on understanding of the living organisms they seek to control, and of the whole fabric of life to which these organisms belong. Specialists representing various areas of the vast field of biology are contributing—entomologists, pathologists, geneticists, physiologists, biochemists, ecologists—all pouring their knowledge and their creative inspirations into the formation of a new science of biotic controls. (244–45)

The solution Carson offers is therefore relatively moderate, if not from the perspective of the chemical industry, then certainly from the perspective of the public, but the stakes are high: change or die.

The success of Carson's apocalyptic narrative spawned both criticism and imitation. The work of the literary critic Douglas Robinson suggests that we might expect such a response. "American apocalypses," he says, "at once undermine basic American values and definitely express those values" (xi–xii). Certainly, with its critique of scientific practice and its substitution of a new, holistic branch of scientific learning, *Silent Spring* makes its appeals to readers simultaneously threatened and encouraged by scientific advances.

The scientific community certainly divided over its verdict on *Silent Spring*. Several distinguished authors, including Loren Eiseley and Julian Huxley, wrote admiring reviews (Graham 71). However, *Time* magazine—which would take up environmentalist themes in the late 1980s, but which represented a different political agenda in the early 1960s (Killingsworth and Palmer 151–60)—claimed that Carson had offended a number of "responsible scientists": "[They] may sympathize with Miss Carson's love of wildlife, and even with her mystical attachment to the balance of nature. But they fear that her emotional and inaccurate outburst in *Silent Spring* may do harm by alarming the nontechnical public, while doing no good for the things that she loves" (quoted in Graham 69). Shortly after its publication, the *Time* review was denounced by a reviewer in *Scientific American* for depending too heavily on informants from the chemical industry (Graham 66). Whatever may have been *Time*'s actual debt to such sources, informants with a vested interest were not lacking. Unwilling to give up their share in the mythic status of modern science, industry scientists launched a frenetic counterattack on Carson's position. As Christopher Bosso has suggested, agribusiness and the chemical industry moved quickly "to flood the public consciousness with 'experts' who loudly refuted Carson's claims" (116). The experts were joined by a number of academic scientists offended by Carson's charge that their kind had been "trading . . . professional objectivity for obeisance to the needs of industry and of their own research-funding": "Carson's attack, in this sense, was not only on pesticides but on reputed 'scientific neutrality' " (Bosso 116). The response was predictable; the book was criticized for its "mysticism" and "unscientific statements" (Graham 47).

"A Fable for Tomorrow" seemed particularly "unscientific." Roland C. Clement of the National Audubon Society remembered, "It just 'turned off' many scientists. The chapter is an allegory. But an allegory is not a prediction, which is what the literal-minded readers, with no background in literature, confused it with" (quoted in Graham 64). Yet, ironically, industry responded not with a coolly rational, "scientific" refutation, but with a fire-for-fire imitation of "A Fable for Tomorrow," the Monsanto Chemical Company's pamphlet "The Desolate Year." Published first in *Monsanto Magazine,* then distributed to newspapers and book reviewers across the country, this apocalyptic narrative warns that famine awaits a humanity deprived of agricultural chemicals (Graham 65).

Ehrlich's Bomb

Environmentalists did not allow the new ground broken by *Silent Spring* to lie fallow for long. Within five years, they welcomed yet another strong apocalyptic writer—the Stanford biologist Paul Ehrlich, whose book *The Population Bomb* quickly became a best-seller when it first appeared in 1968. A slightly expanded second edition was issued by the Sierra Club early in 1969. Ultimately, it became "the most popular environmental book ever published," with sales reaching three million copies in its first decade (Sale 22).

If Carson's power lay in her expansive, romantic vision, Ehrlich found his voice in a stripped-down plain style, framing a narrative that refused to hedge or understate the dimensions of the problem, but favored instead the presentation of "worst-case scenarios" as foregone conclusions. "In the 1970s," he states in the Prologue, "the world will undergo famines—hundreds of millions of people are going to starve to death in spite of any crash programs embarked upon now." With the sensibility of a prophet living in the last days, Ehrlich continues: "At this late date nothing can prevent a substantial increase in the world death rate, although many lives could be saved through dramatic programs to 'stretch' the carrying capacity of the earth by increasing food production." At best, however, such programs will provide "a stay of execution unless"—and here is revealed the alternative agenda proposed by Ehrlich—"unless they are accompanied by determined and successful efforts at population control." These efforts should be both mandatory and global, Ehrlich insists, breaking with the liberal ideals of individual autonomy and national sovereignty: "We must have population control at home, hopefully through a system of incentives and penalties, but by compulsion if voluntary methods fail. We must use our political power to push other countries into programs which combine agricultural development and population control" (5–6).

Deftly evoking bourgeois terror in a report of personal experience, Ehrlich suggests that the "population bomb" has already fallen, though its full effects—pestilence, disease, and mass starvation, the "logical conclusion" of current trends (13)—have not yet spread to America:

I have understood the population explosion intellectually for a long time. I came to understand it emotionally one stinking hot night in Delhi a couple of years ago. My wife and daughter and I were returning to our hotel in an ancient taxi. The seats were hopping with fleas. The only functional gear was third. As we crawled through the city, we entered a crowded slum area. The temperature was well over 100, and the air was a haze of dust and smoke. The streets seemed alive with people. People eating, people washing, people sleeping. People visiting, arguing, and screaming. People thrusting their hands through the taxi window, begging. People defecating and urinating. People clinging to buses. People herding animals. People, people, people, people. As we moved slowly through the mob, hand horn squawking, the dust, noise, heat, and cooking gave the scene a hellish aspect. Would we never get to our hotel? All three of us were, frankly, frightened. It seemed that anything could happen. . . . (12)

Dysfunctional machines, people imposing upon you with their desperate needs, open and squalid displays of bodily functions, and an indifferent nature compounding the human misery with dust and heat—a hellish vision indeed for the American middle-class audience with whom Ehrlich sought to identify and whom he sought to influence. His apocalyptic vision found horror in the intruding crowd and denied the reassuring push of democratic humanity as envisioned by the poet Walt Whitman and his fellow romantics, who, a century before, could still sing the benefits of procreation and full population. The time for either romanticism or sentimentality about the freedom of individuals, families, and nations has passed, Ehrlich argues.

Though it is tempting to dismiss his vision as merely an aberration of disaffected bourgeois ideology, we must not overlook the traces of radicalism in *The Population Bomb*. Like *Silent Spring*, which struck at the root of scientific/technological claims on progress, Ehrlich's treatment of the population explosion hints at a devastating reconsideration of liberal and libertarian social theory. If we are to maintain our standard of living as well as the largest measure of our freedom, he claims, we must submit to government control of the family.

The Cooling of the Apocalyptic Temper

Predictably, Ehrlich drew fire from the Catholic church and right-wing organizations. More interestingly, he was criticized by other environmentalists and scientists. The most able was Barry Commoner, whose quarrel with Ehrlich over the centrality of the population question in the environmental debate has gone on continuously since 1971, when Commoner argued in *The Closing Circle* that overemphasis on population blinded the public to the more important cause of environmental degradation—advancing technology in late capitalism (see their latest books, *Making Peace with the Planet* by Commoner and *The Population Explosion* by Ehrlich and his co-author, Anne Ehrlich). In addition to arguing directly that Ehrlich had his emphasis wrong, Commoner indirectly implied that Ehrlich's apocalyptic rhetoric was both unscholarly and ineffective. Introducing his own more modest aim to describe "some of the damage we have done to the ecosphere," Commoner all but apologizes for Ehrlich and his other predecessors: "by now such horror stories are familiar, even tiresome" (*Closing Circle* 13). "Much less clear," he says, "is what we need to learn from them, and so I have chosen less to shed tears for our past mistakes than to understand them" (13). He tries to distance himself from the pathos of writers like Carson and Ehrlich and to maintain his ethos as a scientist, a purveyor of reliable knowledge.

He is particularly anxious in making assertions about the future. In a typical passage, he attaches such an astounding number of qualifications and disclaimers that he all but nullifies his own prediction:

These are the kinds of considerations that lead to my judgment that the present course of environmental degradation, if unchecked, threatens the survival of civilized man. Although it might be convenient if the environmentalist, like some occult seer predicting the end of the world, could set a date for this catastrophe, the exercise would be futile and in any case unnecessary. It would be futile because the uncertainties are far too great to support anything more than guesses. One can try to guess at the point of no return—the time at which major ecological degradation might become irreparable. In my own judgment, a reasonable estimate for industrialized areas of the world might be from twenty to fifty years, but it is only a guess. (*Closing Circle* 232)

In another passage, which tells the story of toxic effects that have issued from the production of plastics, he writes: "[The story] is *not* reported here in order to suggest that we are all about to perish from exposure to plastic automobile upholstery" (*Closing Circle* 231). Commoner thus attempts to curb the full effect of his potentially apocalyptic rhetoric. This strategy is in keeping with his commitment to what Karl Popper (1:157–58) would call "piecemeal social engineering," an approach to social change that opposes "Utopian social engineering" and promotes instead the scientist's preference for stepwise progress based on data produced under carefully controlled conditions. Piecemeal engineering must reject apocalyptic rhetoric, which tends to promote a fully radical transformation of society (*radical* in the original sense—from the *roots* upward).

But even with his preference for stepwise change, Commoner cannot altogether deny himself the apocalyptic temper of the radical environmentalist. In *The Closing Circle,* he criticizes "the blind, ecologically mindless progress of technology" that "has massively altered our daily environment." He concludes in the manner of Rachel Carson: "Unwittingly, we have created for ourselves a new and dangerous world. We would be wise to move through it as though our lives were at stake" (231).

Millennialism in Politics: Environmentalist and Otherwise

Commoner's indecision over the apocalyptic tradition of environmentalist rhetoric may have had less to do with personal or professional preferences and more to do with the history of the environmental movement. With the passage of the National Environmental Policy Act in 1969, with some evidence of a declining birthrate in the United States, and with the popularity of Earth Day in 1970, environmentalists may have felt that they could afford to restrain their rhetoric. They could adopt the ethos of the cautious scientist and advance their agenda with the rhetorical tools of peacemaking and consensus, leaving aside for the moment the warlike, oppositional rhetoric of the apocalypse.

Indeed, by the late seventies, it was the anti-environmentalists who were on the defensive. But when the Reagan administration took office in the early eighties, Secretary of the Interior James Watt came forward with an apocalyptic vision of his own (a vision that more recent antienvironmentalists like Ronald Bailey would prefer to forget) in an attempt to turn the tide of environmentalist sympathy. Now it was Watt's side that needed to regain lost territory in the debate, so it should not surprise us that he took to the offensive with millennial zeal.

Watt's apocalyptic rhetoric followed two paths that can only seem contradictory in retrospect. First, he invoked Christian eschatology as a sanction for ignoring environmental restraints. As Al Gore writes, "For some Christians, the prophetic vision of the apocalypse is used—in my view, unforgivably—as an excuse for abdicating their responsibility to be good stewards of God's creation" (263). This trend within the Christian right finds support in the popular millennialism of Hal Lindsay's notorious *The Late Great Planet Earth*, a book published in 1970 which argued that God had foreordained nuclear disaster (see Keller). For Gore, James Watt comes to mind as the one figure in government who seems to have taken this prophecy seriously and even used it as a guide to public policy: "Former Secretary of the Interior James Watt . . . was once quoted as belittling concerns about environmental protection in part because it would all be destroyed by God in the apocalypse. Not only is this idea heretical in terms of Christian teachings, it is also an appallingly self-fulfilling prophecy of doom" (263).

But Watt also employed a second apocalyptic tactic, one ironically in tune with the rhetoric of his enemies in the environmentalist camp. In this mood, Watt talked as if Armageddon were something to be avoided. He told one interviewer, for example:

We do not have an energy crisis; we have a crisis in government management. If we do not allow the private marketplace to go in and develop these energy sources in a systematic, methodical, and environmentally sensitive way, we will create such a political and economic crisis that Washington will nationalize the industries and attack our energy-rich West in such a manner as to destroy the ecology, primarily because it must get to that energy to heat the homes of the Northeast and keep the wheels of industry going in the Midwest. (Marth 40)

Hinting at a possible future of uncontrolled chaos, Watt connects the environmental dilemma with another more troubling and deeply rooted conflict—the struggle of capitalist democracy to maintain its goals against socialist intrusions. Again and again, Watt would portray his opponents as "anti-American" and would go so far as to stigmatize them as communists and enemies of democracy: "Their real thrust is not clean air, or clean water, or parks, or wildlife but the form of government under which America will live. The environment is a good vehicle to achieve their objectives. That is why you see the hard-line left drifting toward that interest" ("Secretary Watt" 86).

In many ways, Watt—like the defenders of progress in the current debate, such as Dixy Lee Ray and Ronald Bailey—was right. Millennial ecology *does* represent a threat to the industrially intensive way of life that many have identified as quintessentially American, and a number of environmentalists, among them the ostensibly cautious Barry Commoner, have indeed considered socialism as an alternative to technocapitalism (see especially *The Poverty of Power*).

The trouble with Watt's approach is that, in the wake of the Vietnam

War and during a period when the economy was shifting from an industrial base to a service base, Americans were in no mood for ideologically fueled apocalyptic rhetoric devoted to the salvation of heavy industry. Support for environmentalist values was appearing in an ever-widening circle of the general public. Despite the setbacks the environmental lobby suffered during the Reagan years, Watt's offensive campaign and the considerable further efforts of the Reagan administration failed to stifle the popular movement (see Hays 491–92, 505; Norton 64). By 1988, when Reagan left office, the time was ripe for the second coming of millennial ecology, as environmentalism enjoyed another period of increasing public support.

Global Warming and the Revival of the Apocalyptic Narrative

The nineties have witnessed a transformed environmentalism, now no longer a resistance movement but a full-fledged ideology. The "ecological age," writes the cultural historian and millennialist Thomas Berry, demands "not simply adaptation to a reduced supply of fuels or to some modification in our system of social or economic controls"; rather, it calls forth "a radical change in our mode of consciousness[,] . . . a new language, even a new sense of what it is to be human[,] . . . a completely new sense of reality and of value" (41–42). In 1988, in the midst of the hottest summer on record, while fires raged in Yellowstone and medical waste littered beaches on the eastern seaboard, the mass media awoke to the theory that by drastically increasing the amount of carbon molecules in the upper atmosphere, advanced technological societies may have begun an irreversible cycle of global warming that, if it continued unabated, would radically alter the conditions of life on earth. This new awareness stimulated a revival of millennial ecology, culminating in what now appears to be a significant extension of sympathy for the environmentalist cause. This time around, however, weaker versions of the apocalypse seem to have prevailed over the strong.

The title of an article in the 4 July 1988 issue of *Time* magazine, for example asks the question "Is the Earth Warming Up?" In a cautious anticlimax, the subtitle answers: "Yes, say scientists, but that may not explain this year's heat wave" (Brand 18). But then the article begins with an apocalyptic prologue, a future scenario whose present-tense narrative invites a strong response from the magazine's broad audience:

The Great Plains has become a dust bowl, and people are moving north into Canada's uplands to seek work. Even in Alaska, changing ocean currents are boosting the fish catch. New York is sweltering in 95° weather that began in June and will continue through Labor Day. In the Southeast the hot spell started six weeks earlier . . . (Brand 18; italics and ellipsis in original)

During the same year, *New Scientist,* the British journal of alternative science, printed stories and editorial essays with such sensationalist headlines as "An Atmosphere in Convulsions" (Gribbon), "Prepare to Meet Thy Doom!" (Tudge), "How the Heat Trap Will Wreak Ecological Havoc" (Pain), and "No Escape from the Global Greenhouse" (Pain). The latter, which deals with the possible decline of biodiversity in the face of global warming, presents an odd mixture of apocalyptic rhetoric and scientific detail. In addition to the apocalyptic title, a gothic icon depicting skeletal figures rising above an earthly plain appears in the "window of emphasis" on the layout (centered in the two-column format, just above the middle of the page), and in the last sentence of the first paragraph—a classic position of emphasis—we read, "Global warming is threatening life on this planet" (Pain, "No Escape" 38).

Like Commoner, however, the scientific journalist seems incapable of a full step into apocalyptic rhetoric. The first sentence of the second paragraph picks up the rhetorical alarm with a confident assertion about the reality of the greenhouse hypothesis, but its subordinate clause begins to soften the claim and to move in the direction of cautious skepticism: "The greenhouse effect is no longer controversial, although estimates of how hot the world will become vary considerably" (Pain, "No Escape" 38). By the time we reach the fourth paragraph, the certainty appears to have withered considerably: "Unfortunately, no one is certain precisely what will happen as the concentrations of carbon dioxide and other greenhouse gases (notably methane) increase" (38). The next paragraph returns, jarringly, to a confident assertion about the reality of climatic changes and offers an apocalyptic narrative that refuses to soften the message with qualifiers and conditionals, projecting events with the full strength of the future tense:

Changes have already begun. Even an increase of 1°C can produce profound ecological change. Perhaps more important from a biological point of view, the increase will vary from place to place. Estimates range from an increase of 1°C at the equator to as much as 12°C at the poles. . . . Other, equally damaging changes will accompany the rise in temperature. Sea level will rise both because water expands as it heats up and because the polar ice will begin to melt. In many parts of the world, storms will be more frequent and more ferocious; heat waves will be longer and hotter and droughts more protracted. Elsewhere, rains will be more severe. Some scientists believe that this year's drought in the US and the recent spate of storms and hurricanes are all signs of the changing climate—and herald worse to come. (38)

But, by the paragraph that follows this one, caution returns: "Ecologists do not wholly understand what controls the distribution of species" (38). And the verb form is altered accordingly: "A species that is successful today *might be ousted* by invaders better suited to the new climate" (38; italics added).

The interplay of apocalyptic intensity and cautious advice also marks the work of the climatologist Stephen Schneider, who, like Barry Commoner, seems to be conflicted about his public role. Should he play the prophet of millennial ecology for the generation of the nineties, or should he accept the traditional role of scientific advisor on matters of policy that his research touches most directly? His *Global Warming: Are We Entering the Greenhouse Century?* begins with an apocalyptic narrative in the tradition of "A Fable for Tomorrow." However, with Carson's experience in the background, and fully aware of the low regard in which the scientific community holds flamboyant displays of rhetoric, Schneider proceeds circumspectly. Whereas *Silent Spring* began with a flourish of romantic sentiment—"There once was a town in the heart of America where all life seemed to live in harmony with its surroundings" (Carson 13)—Schneider begins with a warning about his own rhetorical tactics: "No one can know the future, at least not in detail. But enough is known to allow us to fashion plausible scenarios of events that could well take place if current trends and present understanding are even partly true" (1).

Only after this disclaimer does Schneider offer his story of future life in the "greenhouse century." Whereas Carson's stylized fable drew upon the tradition of ancient wisdom literature, Schneider's text is a parody of a news report, a straightforward narration of sweltering city activities (baseball enduring despite the heat and ozone alerts), browning lawns, health threats to the old and weak, salinity problems in the water supply, threatened shorelines, massive hurricanes, rapid forest dieback, increased risk from toxin, droughts, and regional failures of agriculture. Like Carson, Schneider writes in the past tense both to sustain the parallel to newswriting and to bolster his argument that, though his scenarios probably require a warmer world than we now know, current scientific knowledge suggests that such events are a foregone conclusion if present-day patterns of development continue. We are, he argues, already in the greenhouse century.

In this performance for the general public, Schneider toys with radicalism, calling for "an integrated look at all the consequences associated with our actions," an abandonment of "the piecemeal fashion that has dominated policy making in the past," and a "new dimension of creative, integrated solutions" (*Global Warming* 265). When he addresses his scientific peers, however, in an article in *Science,* he argues for a "tie-in strategy" more receptive to "piecemeal" solutions, which indeed sounds more like Popperian social engineering. In the *Science* article, he advocates policy measures that have been shown scientifically to tie in to solutions for problems smaller than but related to global climate change: "society should pursue those actions that provide widely agreed societal benefits even if the predicted change [in global climate] does not materialize." He thus argues for a fairly limited "energy efficiency strategy" that focuses on emissions reduction ("Greenhouse Effect" 778).

Schneider's caution encourages a literal reading of the apocalyptic narrative, a reading that assumes a commitment to accurate prediction on the part of the narrator. Such readings are only too common among the enemies of millennial ecology. In their view—a view supported (unintentionally, it appears) by Schneider's hedging about "dirty crystal balls" ("Greenhouse Effect" 775)—if the narrative of the future does not come true, the narrator may be dismissed as a doom prophet with no authority as a scientific advisor.

With this reader response in mind, Paul and Anne Ehrlich have recently suggested that it was a "mistake" to depend in *The Population Bomb* on the effect of apocalyptic scenarios—"little stories about the future" presented "as an aid to thinking about it"—because people took the scenarios as predictions and some concluded that because they had not 'come true' the basic message of the book was wrong." "But, of course," they explain, trying to win success out of what they obviously perceive as a rhetorical failure, "the entire purpose of the . . . scenarios was to stimulate the kind of action that would prevent events such as those described in the scenarios from occurring" (*Population Explosion* 269 n. 5). Despite their efforts to preserve the content of the millennial ecology set forth in the earlier book, they have moderated their position considerably in their latest, substituting "cultural evolution" for cultural revolution and countenancing a "whimper" as well as a "bang" theory of ecological Armageddon (*Population Explosion* 48–49, 174–75). Like Commoner and Schneider, the Ehrlichs have stepped back from the radicalism of the 1960s. Their rhetoric shifts to accommodate their move to the political center. Now, they say, "we're avoiding scenarios," but "we would not be surprised . . . if some reviewer dismissed *The Population Explosion* because the scenarios in *Population Bomb* did not actually materialize" (*Population Explosion* 269 n. 5).

The Significance of the Apocalyptic Narrative

Critics of the Ehrlichs—scientific apologists like Dixy Lee Ray, Whig historians like Anna Bramwell, and conservative journalists like Ronald Bailey and Warren Brookes, as well as the authors of halfhearted apocalyptic narratives like Stephen Schneider and Barry Commoner—either miss or resist the central point of environmentalist apocalypses, as explained and defended in *The Population Explosion*. These writings are not to be taken literally. Their aim is not to predict the future but to change it. The scientific credentials of Ehrlich notwithstanding, the value of his work is not scientific, but political. If we can say that he overstated some of the consequences of overpopulation, we may also note—indeed he and Anne Ehrlich have themselves noted—that they *underestimated* and could not have foreseen other effects that may be tied to overpopulation, such as the AIDS epidemic and the extent of global warming. Again, however, to dwell upon the success or failure of the prediction is to ignore the radical import of the apocalyptic narrative and to reduce millennial ecology to a reformist agenda rather than a political transformation.

As Robinson (7) suggests, the distinctive features of apocalyptic narrative are neither thematic nor formal, but rather relational, specifically oppositional and iconoclastic. In the environmental movement, the apocalyptic narrative has appeared in those moments of history when the movement is seeking to expand, to appeal to new segments of the general public, to annex new territories in a kind of rhetorical imperialism. The hyperbole with which the impending doom is presented—the image of total ruin and destruction—implies the need for an ideological shift. If the "predicted" devastation is extreme in the apocalyptic narrative, then the change in consciousness or political agenda recommended by the narrator is correspondingly extreme or radical. As the devastation is moderated, so are the ideological effects intended. Thus the apocalyptic narrative becomes a kind of political barometer in the history of environmental politics in America.

For rhetorical study, the history of millennial ecology has two main implications. First of all, language, genre, medium, or "form" of any kind is never innocent of meaning. Discourse has consequences beyond the linguistic realm (as the public has begun to realize in the recent struggles over "political correctness"). To employ apocalyptic rhetoric is to imply the need for radical change, to mark oneself as an outsider in a progressive culture, to risk alienation, and to urge others out into the open air of political rebellion. The apocalyptic narrative is an expansive and offensive rhetorical strategy.

Second, eloquence—the ability to *move* an audience, to change its political or intellectual orientation by means of effective uses of language—is historically determined. The rhetorical tradition has always realized the importance of situation and rhetorical context. What is not always so clear—what the history of environmental rhetoric amply illustrates—is just how hard it is to predict the effect of a particular discourse on an audience at any given time. Rachel Carson's apocalyptic narrative may have succeeded beyond any design she may have had, but Stephen Schneider's quite similar narrative seems to have fallen flat—not only because of a difference in creative talent or apocalyptic intensity, but because of a difference in the historical period in which each of these texts appeared.

Thus, between rhetorical criticism and practical rhetoric, there lies something of a gap. Our problem in taking what we know about past performance and projecting the success or failure of future performances shares much with the problem policy makers face in struggling with the issues of agricultural technology and global climate change. To think from the known to the unknown requires a leap—the leap of inference, which rests upon interpretation, but which requires faith. And faith can never be a simple matter of calculation and prediction.

NOTES

1. Originally, *apocalypse* meant simply *revelation*. Like the prophets of ecological destruction, who are his rhetorical heirs, the author of the Book of Revelation, the last book of the Christian Bible, known traditionally as the Apocalypse of St. John, foresees the second coming of Christ as a brief period of destruction, the battle of Armageddon, followed by a thousand-year reign of the saints, followed in turn by the final judgment and fulfillment of the Kingdom promise, the establishment of "a new heaven and a new earth." But the word *apocalypse* has come to be associated in modern times almost exclusively with the destructive force of the battle of Armageddon, when worldly kingdoms will be swept away by the King of Kings returning in glory and power: "out of his mouth goeth a sharp sword, . . . with it he [shall] smite the nations, and he shall rule them with a rod of iron; and he treadeth the wine press of the fierceness and wrath of the Almighty God." The defeated kings of the old order and their armies will then be "cast into a lake of fire burning with brimstone" (King James Version, chapters 19–21).

2. If he had been more concerned with etymology and intertextual reference, Bookchin may have preferred the phrase "ecological Armageddon." Following the currently popular usage, he employs the term *apocalypse* to refer generically to a prophecy of destruction followed by a renewal. This use of the term narrows the meaning of *apocalypse* and emphasizes the vision of destruction, the rhetorical force of which is partly responsible, it would seem, for the restriction of meaning. What we are calling "millennial ecology" uses images of future destruction— "apocalyptic narratives"—to predict the fall of the current technocapitalist order. The realization of this fall (in political consciousness if not in actuality) serves as prelude to a "new earth." The true believer thus greets the apocalypse with a mixture of dread and joy. For more on revolutionary millennialism in the Christian tradition, see the two now classic studies by Tuveson and Cohn.

3. This tactic is particularly attractive to those who call themselves "conservatives." Traditionally, of course, conservatives are antiprogressive, but, at least since Ronald Reagan's day, the American right has redefined its mission. Progress has become the ideology of the status quo, while ecological radicalism appears to embrace something very much like traditional conservatism.

4. We follow Kirkpatrick Sale, who, while taking note of writers like John Muir and Aldo Leopold as the advance guard of environmentalism, argues that the environmentalist movement as we have come to know it began with the publication of *Silent Spring*. See Sale's brief but excellent history of the "green revolution." Also see our treatment of the origins of the word *environmentalist* in *Ecospeak*, chapter 1, and the compelling historical work of Samuel Hays.

WORKS CITED

Bailey, Ronald. *Eco-Scam: The False Prophets of Ecological Apocalypse*. New York: St. Martin's, 1993.

Bell, Daniel. *The End of Ideology*. Cambridge: Harvard UP, 1988.

Bercovitch, Sacvan. *The American Jeremiad*. Madison: U of Wisconsin P, 1978.

Berry, Thomas. *The Dream of the Earth*. San Francisco: Sierra Club, 1988.

Bookchin, Murray. *Remaking Society: Pathways to a Green Future*. Boston: South End, 1990.

[Bookchin, Murray.] Herber, Lewis (pseud.). *Our Synthetic Environment*. New York: Knopf, 1962.

Bosso, Christopher J. *Pesticides and Politics: The Life Cycle of a Public Issue*. Pittsburgh: U of Pittsburgh P, 1987.

Bramwell, Anna. *Ecology in the Twentieth Century: A History*. New Haven: Yale UP, 1989.

Brand, David. "Is the Earth Warming Up?" *Time*, 4 July 1988, 18.

Brookes, Warren T. "Stirring Up Environmentalist Hysteria." *Memphis Commercial-Appeal*, 17 Sept. 1989, A4.

Brooks, Paul. *Speaking for Nature: How Literary Naturalists from Henry Thoreau to Rachel Carson Have Shaped America*. San Francisco: Sierra Club, 1980.

Burke, Kenneth. *Counter-Statement*. 2d ed. Los Altos, CA: Hermes, 1953.

Carson, Rachel. *Silent Spring*. New York: Fawcett, 1962.

Cohn, Norman. *The Pursuit of the Millennium*. Revised and expanded edition. New York: Oxford UP, 1970.

Commoner, Barry. *The Closing Circle: Nature, Man and Technology*. New York: Knopf, 1971.

Commoner, Barry. *Making Peace with the Planet*. New York: Pantheon, 1990.

Commoner, Barry. *The Poverty of Power: Energy and the Economic Crisis*. New York: Knopf, 1976.

DeGregori, Thomas R. "Apocalypse Yesterday." In *The Apocalyptic Vision in America: Interdisciplinary Essays on Myth and Culture*, ed. Lois Parkinson Zamora. Bowling Green, OH: Bowling Green U Popular P, 1982. 206–21.

Dewey, Joseph. *In a Dark Time: The Apocalyptic Temper in the American Novel of the Nuclear Age*. West Lafayette, IN: Purdue UP, 1990.

Dunlap, Thomas. *DDT: Scientist, Citizens, and Public Policy*. Princeton: Princeton UP, 1981.

Dylan, Bob. "A Hard Rain's A-Gonna Fall." *Writings and Drawings*. New York: Knopf, 1973. 38–39.

Ehrlich, Paul R. *The Population Bomb.* 1968; 2d ed., San Francisco: Sierra Club, 1969.

Ehrlich, Paul R., and Anne H. Ehrlich. *The Population Explosion.* New York: Simon and Schuster, 1990.

Emsley, Michael. "The Evolution and Imminent Extinction of an Avaricious Species." In *The Apocalyptic Vision in America: Interdisciplinary Essays on Myth and Culture,* ed. Lois Parkinson Zamora. Bowling Green, OH: Bowling Green U Popular P, 1982. 183–205.

Fukuyama, Francis. *The End of History and the Last Man.* New York: Avon, 1992.

Gore, Al. *Earth in the Balance: Ecology and the Human Spirit.* Boston: Houghton, 1992.

Graham, Frank, Jr. *Since Silenct Spring.* Boston: Houghton, 1970.

Gribbon, John. "An Atmosphere in Convulsions." *New Scientist,* 26 Nov. 1987, 30–31.

Hays, Samuel P. *Beauty, Health, and Permanence: Environmental Politics in the United States, 1955–1985.* Cambridge: Cambridge UP, 1987.

Hynes, H. Patricia. *The Recurring Silent Spring.* New York: Pergamon, 1989.

Jameson Fredric. "Postmodernism, or the Cultural Logic of Late Capitalism." *New Left Review* 146(July–Aug. 1984): 53–92.

Killingsworth, M. Jimmie, and Jacqueline S. Palmer. *Ecospeak: Rhetoric and Environmental Politics in America.* Carbondale: Southern Illinois UP, 1992.

Keller, Catherine. "Women against Wasting the World: Notes on Eschatology and Ecology." In *Reweaving the World: The Emergence of Ecofeminism,* ed. Irene Diamond and Gloria Feman Orenstein. San Francisco: Sierra Club, 1990. 249–63.

Kuhn, Thomas. *The Structure of Scientific Revolutions.* 2d ed. Chicago: U of Chicago P, 1970.

Lindsay, Hal. *The Late Great Planet Earth.* Grand Rapids, ID: Zondervan, 1970.

Manes, Christopher. *Green Rage: Radical Environmentalism and the Unmaking of Civilization.* Boston: Little, Brown, 1990.

Marth, Del. " 'I Must Search for Balance': In-Depth Interview with Secretary Watt." *Nation's Business,* Sept. 1981, 36–41.

McKibben, Bill. *The End of Nature.* New York: Anchor, 1989.

Newman, Robert D. *Transgressions of Reading: Narrative Engagement as Exile and Return.* Durham: Duke UP, 1993.

Nietzsche, Friedrich. *Beyond Good and Evil.* Trans. Walter Kaufmann. New York: Vintage, 1966.

Nisbet, Robert. *History of the Idea of Progress.* New York: Basic, 1980.

Norton, Bryan G. *Toward Unity among Environmentalists.* New York: Oxford UP, 1991.

Pain, Stephanie. "How the Heat Trap Will Wreak Ecological Havoc." *New Scientist,* 15 Oct. 1988, 22.

Pain, Stephanie. "No Escape from the Global Greenhouse." *New Scientist,* 12 Nov. 1988, 38–43.

Popper, Karl R. *The Open Society and Its Enemies.* 2 vols. 5th ed. Princeton: Princeton UP, 1966.

Ray, Dixy Lee (with Lou Guzzo). *Trashing the Planet.* Washington, DC: Regnery Gateway, 1990.

Robinson, Douglas. *American Apocalypses: The Image of the End of the World in American Literature.* Baltimore: Johns Hopkins UP, 1985.

Sale, Kirkpatrick. *The Green Revolution: The American Environmental Movement, 1962–1992.* New York: Hill and Wang, 1993.

Schneider, Stephen H. *Global Warming: Are We Entering the Greenhouse Century?* San Francisco: Sierra Club, 1989.

Schneider, Stephen H. "The Greenhouse Effect: Science and Policy." *Science* 243(1989): 771–81.

Scholes, Robert. *Textual Power: Literary Theory and the Teaching of English.* New Haven: Yale UP, 1985.

"Secretary Watt Fires Back at His Critics." *Business Week,* 24 Jan. 1983, 86.

Slusser, George E.; Colin Greenland; and Eric S. Rabkin. *Storm Warnings: Science Fiction Confronts the Future.* Carbondale: Southern Illinois UP, 1987.

Tichi, Cecelia. *New World, New Earth: Environmental Reform in American Literature from the Puritans through Whitman.* New Haven: Yale UP, 1979.

Tudge, Colin. "Prepare to Meet Thy Doom!" *New Scientist,* 7 Jan. 1988, 70–71.

Tuveson, Ernest Lee. *Millennium and Utopia: A Study in the Background of the Idea of Progress.* 1949; Berkeley: U of California P, 1964.

CHAPTER 2

"Thinking Like a Mountain"

Persona, Ethos, and Judgment in American Nature Writing

H. LEWIS ULMAN

> Let us not underrate the value of a fact; it will one day flower in a truth.
>
> —Henry David Thoreau

> That land is a community is the basic concept of ecology, but that land is to be loved and respected is an extension of ethics. That land yields a cultural harvest is a fact long known, but latterly often forgotten.
>
> —Aldo Leopold

Writing at the Border of Science and the Humanities

Communication about environmental issues can get tricky when science, ethics, and rhetoric interact. In many forums, scientists, environmental activists, and policy makers often find themselves at odds with one another, a tension one commentator tellingly evokes in a magazine essay on environmentalist Jeremy Rifkin: "Rifkin and his troops go to the Hill and to court with arguments about how man must be in partnership with his world, must respect the dignity of the planet and what Aristotle called the *telos* (the natural purpose) of each living thing in it. Such rhetoric drives scientists to distraction; politicians' eyes glaze over" (Tivan). Yet such discursive borderlands are rich sites for rhetorical investigation, ethical judgment, literary representation, and political action.

Naturalists have long observed that boundaries between adjacent ecosystems are often lively places. Animals and plants exploit the more diverse habitat of such borderlands, and species characteristic of the different ecosystems reveal their particular strengths and affinities as they confront changing environmental conditions. The definitive characteristics of each ecosystem are more apparent in contrast to those of neighboring systems.

46

This paper concerns a rhetorical analog of such rich and complex borderlands—nature writing. I first consider nature writing as a genre, focusing particularly on the roles of three rhetorical features—persona, ethos, and judgment—in the genre. Next, I turn to a case study of persona, ethos, and judgment in the writing of Aldo Leopold, one of the founders of modern ecology and one of the most influential nature writers of the past fifty years. The essay concludes by examining in more general terms how ecology and ethics have interacted in the borderland of nature writing, exemplified by Leopold's work, to create and sustain a new ecological conscience.

Nature Writing as Genre

That nature writing is for many contemporary readers, writers, and publishers a familiar type of writing seems indisputable, at least judging from the number of anthologies and critical essays devoted to this body of work in the past few years.[1] However, identifying, labeling, and defining textual genres are slippery acts of interpretation requiring at least the argumentative foothold provided by a working description: since Thoreau, much writing about nature has consisted of (typically nonfiction) texts whose rhetorical *focus* or *purpose* is to construct a coherent map of the borderland where, following Aldo Leopold's formulation in the epigraph to this chapter, scientific facts, ethical principles, and cultural values interact. Or, following Thoreau's more teleological formulation, we might say that nature writing models the process by which natural facts "flower in a truth," a process not of objective *dis*engagement from nature but of personal experience and engagement: "We do not learn by inference and deduction and the application of mathematics to philosophy, but by direct intercourse and sympathy" ("Natural History" 29). This working description identifies not a sharply bounded territory but an alignment of rhetorical features useful for taking one's bearings in a discursive borderland—as the presentation of "direct intercourse and sympathy" recedes from view, nature writing moves toward natural history; as natural history recedes from our attention, nature writing moves toward autobiography; when self and scene dynamically blend, we are in the ecotone of nature writing.[2]

To investigate this borderland further, I must expand my working description of nature writing beyond describing what it *is* to asking what it *does*. Consider Carolyn Miller's definition of rhetorical genres (in general) as "typified rhetorical actions based in recurrent situations" (159). This definition treats genre not as a "formal entity" identified by textual features but as "a form of social knowledge—a mutual construing of objects, events, interests, and purposes that not only links them but also makes them what they are" (153). Analysis of nature writing from this perspective holds out the promise of recognizing not only the individual purposes and strategies of nature writers but also the cultural work of the genre, for "as a recurrent, significant action, a genre embodies an aspect of cultural rationality" (165). However, Miller's view of genre as an enactment of cultural rationality raises several questions.

First, we should ask (with apologies to Alasdair Macintyre), "Whose culture? Whose rationality?" The conception of nature writing as a genre in this essay admittedly reflects a Western perspective, perhaps one unique to Euro-American culture. That perspective determines both the cultural construction of environmental problems and ways of addressing those problems. Indeed, recent collections and studies of indigenous cultures' representations of their places in the natural world suggest that the first move we have to make in understanding those representations is to move beyond our own discursive practices—beyond nature writing as it is considered here (see Elder and Wong; McLuhan; Piacentini). In their introduction to *Family of Earth and Sky: Indigenous Tales of Nature from around the World* (1994), John Elder and Hertha Wong note that

"Nature writing" conventionally has been taken to mean personal, reflective essays in a Thoreauvian mode—a species of nonfiction grounded in the appreciation of contemporary science and at the same time remaining open to the physical creation's spiritual and emotional significance. The essays in this genre have been powerful vehicles for integrating observation with revelation, and for bridging the rift between the "two cultures" of science and literature. But they have also projected the voices of solitary—and sometimes alienated—individuals rather more often than they have emphasized how the human *community* might be seen as a part of nature. (3)

In other words, for all the emphasis that nature writing places on integration and bridging, "the very fact that the West has developed a genre called 'nature writing' testifies to a separation between much of human life and the nonhuman world that has developed since the industrial revolution" (3–4). Thus, this study must acknowledge the irony of cultural perspective to which Elder and Wong draw our attention: what serves in this investigation as a principle of integration in a discursive and (intra)cultural borderland appears as a distinguishing principle from a broader, (multi)cultural perspective. From their perspective, Elder and Wong repeatedly present Aldo Leopold's work as emblematic of American nature writing and, therefore, as a particularly useful contrast to the indigenous works they have collected. While this case study focuses on Leopold's contribution to the form of cultural rationality manifest in nature writing, I hope that by knowing one culturally bounded genre better, readers will be better prepared to investigate others.

Miller's view of genre as an enactment of cultural rationality also raises the question of *why* the hybrid, relatively subjective genre of nature writing thrives in a culture that places increasingly high value on specialized, objective knowledge. What role does nature writing play? My presumption is that nature writing does not directly answer our need for expert testimony concerning scientific fact or practical leadership concerning particular matters of public policy, for those judgments are associated more directly with genres such as research reports, environmental impact statements, and legal briefs. Rather, nature writing entails a hybrid mode of interpretation—making available to other persons a symbolic model of cognitive, affective, physical, ethical, and pragmatic relationships to the nonhuman world characteristic of an individual or collective human *subject*. This distinctly ethical interpretation foregrounds the *ethos* or moral character of interpreters—in this case, both writers and readers—as it emerges in relation to the nonhuman world modeled in the interpretation. This mode of interpretation does not entail institutional contexts for judgment like those characteristic of writing in science and government, which are designed to resolve matters of disciplinary knowledge and public policy; rather, nature writing emphasizes the personal knowledge and values that undergird shared knowledge and public decision making.

Of course, I don't mean to suggest that primarily scientific interpretations of nature do not, or should not, present writers' ethos nor that primarily ethical interpretations neglect scientific models of the natural world. Indeed, it is important not to overdetermine the notion of genre; generic distinctions may constitute what Kathleen Hall Jamieson and Karlyn Kohrs Campbell call a *dynamis*, "a potential fusion of elements that may be energized or actualized as a strategic response to a situation" (135), but they do not account for all the significant elements of a given text. Rather, I am arguing simply that texts of whatever stripe *foreground* concerns that are *at issue* and *foreshorten* others that are treated as matters of convention or common knowledge. Thus, traditional scientific writing treats the objectivity of the scientist, the writer's rhetorical stance, as a matter of convention; at issue in such texts are the accuracy of data, the soundness of method, and the validity of knowledge claims. Nature writing, as described above, accommodates natural history but *foregrounds* the construction of writers' personae and ethos in light of ethical judgments about how to be and act at home (i.e, *ecologically*) in the natural world.[3]

Persona, Ethos, and Judgment in Nature Writing

The concepts of persona, ethos, and judgment have been the subject of much recent scholarship aimed at refining their application to contemporary rhetorical studies.[4] *Persona*, as used here, refers to a character *type* bearing some significant relationship to a context in which a rhetor attempts to affect, and an audience attempts to make, judgments—for instance, identifying oneself as, or being recognized as, a scientist when addressing lay persons on matters of environmental policy.[5] In other words, persona refers to a rhetorical construct that focuses an audience's "perceptions of a source of communication" and establishes general expectations of the "value and importance" of an author's message (Yoos 49, 55).[6] *Ethos* (again, as used here) refers to the sum of *particular* intellectual and moral qualities that an audience recognizes in the rhetor's message—for instance, the determination that a speaker or writer is acting as a *competent* and *responsible* scientist.[7] Such evaluations of a speaker or writer's moral character are made in light of expectations appropriate to his or her persona-in-context. That is, while our recognition of genre and character type inevitably establishes expectations based on prior knowledge of such types, those expectations can be altered by a rhetor's discourse in a given situation. Even a habitual liar may tell the truth—or vice versa—and it is a crucial role of rhetorical judgment to discern the difference.[8] Similarly, while we may expect professional scientists to speak with more authority than lay persons regarding scientific knowledge, we may also recognize that such knowledge claims are subject to error and bias. *Judgment* refers to an audience's understanding of their own relationship to the situation or issue at hand.[9] For instance, a lay audience faced with consistent expert testimony concerning the environmental impact of a landfill may conceive of its task not as judging the accuracy of that testimony but as weighing it against the economic and social needs of their community. Faced with conflicting expert testimony, an audience may have to resolve the conflict by judging the character of the expert witnesses. In both cases, the judgment will be made in light of some substantive good—for instance, the healthy, sustainable, and practical conduct of culture in nature.

Analysis of the relationships among persona, ethos, and judgment can help to define from an ethical perspective the substantive goods at stake in a given issue, for we follow the guidance of those who know something about the good. In Aristotle's formulation of rhetoric, for instance, the substantive good, or goal, of human action is happiness, comprising good birth, good friendships, good health, strength, honor, and so on (*On Rhetoric* 1.5). In this model, rhetors can show that they are reliable guides to a substantive good by demonstrating, and appealing to, practical wisdom (*phronesis*), virtue (*arete*), and good will (*eunoia*) in a manner suited to Athenian expectations of various character types, including the young, the old, those in the prime of life, the wellborn, the wealthy, and the powerful (*On Rhetoric* 2.1.5, 2.12–17). Of course, these formulations must be transformed for analyses of environmental rhetoric, for they reflect classical forums for civic judgment (the Athenian senate, courts, and public assembly) and Greek theories of character and substantive goods. Accordingly, this study examines how we construct the alignments of persona, ethos, and judgment that *typify* the rhetorical situation of twentieth-century American nature writing. In order to investigate these aspects of nature writing more concretely, I turn now to a case study of "Thinking Like a Mountain," arguably Aldo Leopold's most famous nature essay and one of the central texts of post–World War II ecology.

The Rhetoric of Aldo Leopold's Land Ethic

A professional forester during a period of great change in our management of natural resources, Aldo Leopold (1887–1948) was also a tireless and eloquent advocate for wilderness. Leopold's career included government and professional service, academic research and teaching, and public advocacy for ecologically informed land management. Trained at Yale (Master of Forestry, 1909), Leopold worked for the U.S. Forest Service from the year of his graduation until 1927, save for the period between January 1918 and August 1919. He served first as a forestry assistant in the territories of Arizona and New Mexico and earned a reputation as a dedicated game preservationist who valued forest lands for their recreational, as well as economic, importance. Leopold's efforts during the 1920s to establish wilderness preserves in the National Forest System rallied the new voices of conservation—chiefly naturalists, ecologists, and sportsmen—to oppose the earlier, generally economic view of natural resources then predominant among professional foresters. In 1924, Leopold rose to the position of Assistant Director of the Forest Products Laboratory in Wisconsin, and in 1933, the same year that he accepted the nation's first chair of Wildlife Management at the University of Wisconsin, he published a now-classic textbook entitled *Game Management*. Leopold's subsequent academic career was marked by distinguished publication and teaching, and he remained in his position at the University of Wisconsin until his death in 1948.

Leopold practiced environmental advocacy in many capacities from his early career in the Southwest, when he developed game protection associations with local hunters, to just before his death, when he accepted a position as consultant for conservation to the United Nations. During the 1940s, the period on which this case study focuses, Leopold helped set the policies of "approximately a hundred different professional societies and committees, conservation organizations, government agencies, research stations, conferences, and journals, culminating with his election in 1947 as president of the Ecological Society of American" (Flader 34). Even more important, in addition to his professional service and writing (*Game Management* is only the most notable example of his extensive academic publications), Leopold wrote about ecology for a broad American public concerned about natural history, game management, and outdoor recreation. His nature essays appeared in such journals as *Audubon Magazine, Condor, Outdoor America, Outdoor Nebraska,* and *The Auk*.[10] Most readers will know this aspect of Leopold's work from his posthumously published collection of essays, *A Sand County Almanac and Sketches Here and There* (1949). Though his empirical research in the nascent field of ecology and his land and game management policies were important, his most enduring contributions to conservation are those nature essays which present to nonspecialists an ethical vision of humanity's place in nature.

Leopold's rhetorical stance toward his public audience was carefully considered and complex. In "Land Use and Democracy," published in *Audubon Magazine* late in 1941, Leopold advocated "trying democracy" rather than relying solely on government specialists to design and implement sound land use policies: "The formula is: learn how to tell good land-use from bad. Use your own land accordingly, and refuse aid and comfort to those who do not. Isn't this more to the point than merely voting, petitioning, and writing checks for bigger and better bureaus, in order that our responsibilities may be laid in bigger and better laps?" (quoted in Meine 431). But as Curt Meine has noted: "One particularly volatile issue—deer management— would embroil Leopold in a bitter debate that would make plain the difficulties involved in 'trying democracy' as a solution to complex conservation problems" (431). The effect of the public debates over deer management on Leopold's optimistic stance in "Land Use and Democracy" can be seen in an undated fragment from the mid-1940s entitled "Conservation Education: A Revolution in Philosophy":

> "If the public were told how much harm ensues from unwise land-use, it would mend its ways." This was once my credo, and I think still is a fairly accurate definition of what is called "conservation education."
> Behind this deceptively simple logic lie three unspoken but important assumptions: (1) that the public is listening, or can be made to listen; (2) that the public responds, or can be made to respond, to fear of harm; (3) that ways can be mended without any important change in the public itself. None of the three assumptions is, in my opinion, valid. (Quoted in Flader 206)

In spite of the exasperation, pessimistic finality, and even the hint of arrogance in these notes, Leopold continued throughout the 1940s to look for ways to make the public listen. In his original foreword to the manuscript that would eventually be published as *A Sand County Almanac,* some of Leopold's pessimism about his ability to reach the public shows through, but he pins his hopes on striking a chord of recognition: "These essays were written for myself and my close friends, but I suspect that we are not alone in our discontent with the ecological *status quo*. If the reader finds here some echo of his own affections and of his own anxieties, they will have accomplished more than was originally intended" ("1947 Foreword" 288). Particularly in his writing about deer management, Leopold found himself in rhetorical situations complex enough to call forth various strategies for conservation education, including one that I believe serves as an exemplar of the rhetorical *dynamis* of contemporary nature writing. Writing about this issue throughout the 1940s as an academic scientist, a popular science writer, a state conservation commissioner, and an essayist or nature writer, Leopold addressed audiences faced with various judgments and struggled in each instance to construct his ethos effectively within the constraints imposed by the occasions, the substantive questions at issue, and his audience's expectations of his personae, which were sometimes fixed by the situation, sometimes more open to his construction. Viewed against this background, "Thinking Like a Mountain" reveals Leopold's own discovery of the rhetorical borderland occupied by nature writing.

The Deer Dilemma: A Case Study in Ecological Judgment

Throughout the 1940s, Leopold wrote about the problem of what he called "deer irruptions"—the tendency of deer herds to grow beyond and, through overbrowsing, eventually reduce the carrying capacity of their range, even after mass starvation drastically reduces the size of the herd. Though game managers had seen indications of this problem in Wisconsin throughout the 1930s, "serious study" of the problem did not begin until 1940 (Meine 438). At about the same time, Leopold was developing a broader sense of the problem. In July and August 1941, Leopold inspected Cooperative Wildlife Research Units in Utah and Oregon for the American Wildlife Institute and witnessed "deterioration of deer range in virtually every corner of the intermountain West" (Meine 417). Leopold argued that the central problem was the size of the deer herds, but officials were managing for a controlled increase in herds reduced by starvation, in part by eliminating predators and relying on hunting seasons to cull the recovering herd as needed. In his report to the Wildlife Institute, Leopold took issue with these practices: "Hunting is a crude, slow, and inaccurate tool, which needs to be supplemented by a precision instrument. The natural aggression of lions and other predators on an overstocked range . . . is the only precision instrument known to deer-management" (quoted in Flader 175). In addition, he proposed an ecological criterion for game management linked not to the numbers of deer but to the carrying capacity of the land: "the true yardstick of progress should be the establishment of *new reproduction of the palatable browse species* to replace the dead stems lost during the irruption" (quoted in Flader 175). In that report were contained the chief matters of fact and policy that Leopold would debate in various capacities for the next seven years: the dynamics of deer irruptions and the effects of various hunting and predator control policies on the process. Addressing these issues, he would also come to articulate an influential land ethic grounded in a transformative sense of self-in-nature.

Leopold addressed the deer problem in numerous essays and public statements, but, for the purposes of this analysis, I focus on six essays written between 1943 and 1947 and on Leopold's major work, *A Sand County Almanac*. The texts consist of one piece of scientific journalism for *Audubon Magazine*, one academic article published in the *Transactions of the Wisconsin Academy of Sciences, Arts, and Letters*, three short articles from the *Wisconsin Conservation Bulletin* written in Leopold's official capacity as Conservation Commissioner of Wisconsin, and "Thinking Like a Mountain," a now-famous essay from *A Sand County Almanac* in which many readers find the most compelling expression of Leopold's environmental ethic (see table 2.1). As a group, these essays demonstrate how Leopold's persona and ethos modulated in keeping with the particular, historically situated, ecologically informed judgments that he was asking his audiences to make. In this context, "Thinking Like a Mountain" aligns persona, ethos, and judgment in a manner that highlights the particular contribution that nature writing, as I have defined it, can make to environmental ethics.

"Deer Irruptions." In September 1942, Leopold was appointed by the Wisconsin Conservation Commission as Chair of the Citizens Deer Committee, which was charged to monitor the Wisconsin deer problem during the winter of 1943 (Meine 439). In November, he was also asked by the Wisconsin Academy of Sciences, Arts, and Letters to chair its newly formed Natural Resources Committee, which was charged to review scientific information on deer irruptions (Meine 439). In a letter written to A. W. Shorger, president of the Academy, shortly after Shorger formed the Natural Resources Committee, Leopold advised setting a strictly scientific task for the academy committee, which he believed "should not try to assess the Wisconsin situation in detail, for its knowledge of the field conditions is second hand. The function of the Academy stops when it deduces from history the important *principles* to be used in arriving at a judgment" (quoted in Meine 439). Further defining the nature of the document that he envisioned the committee would write, Leopold told Shorger that the report should be "drawn with such care as to be unchallengeable as to facts" (quoted in Meine 439). In January 1943, Leopold presented an early version of the Natural Resources Committee's report to the Citizen's Deer

Committee and, in August, published the report in the *Transactions of the Wisconsin Academy of Sciences, Arts, and Letters* under the title "Deer Irruptions."

In this academic article, Leopold writes as a member of the Natural Resources Committee of the Wisconsin Academy of Sciences, Arts, and Letters, a persona made explicit by a headnote, a foreword by the president of the Wisconsin Academy, and the fact that the article appeared in the Academy's *Transactions*.[11] The forum and the foreword construe the audience's judgment as discipline-specific, presenting the paper as one in a series intended to "provide scientific data that can be used as a basis for formulating public policy" (351). The ethos of the article rests on a fairly conventional academic presentation. For instance, Leopold establishes accountability through sixty-two citations to twenty-eight separate sources. Claims are judiciously qualified to reflect the nature of evidence, as when Leopold admits that the committee has not conducted its own field study but cites evidence compiled by another department that "indicates" an advanced irruption in Wisconsin. "If that is correct," he hedges, "then there is imperative need for prompt and decisive herd-reduction" (365). In short, it seems clear that the audience's judgment of Leopold's ethos and argument will reflect criteria appropriate to the scientific persona invoked and sustained in the text.

The inescapable implication of Leopold's study for game management was that if Wisconsin were to avoid the fate of other overpopulated deer ranges, "a substantial reduction in the deer herd was necessary. This inevitably meant instituting a doe season—the first in recent memory, and a move not likely to sit well with any segment of the public" (Meine 442). Leopold would be engaged in this increasingly bitter debate for the remaining five years of his life.

"Excess Deer." In the May–June issue of *Audubon Magazine,* Leopold presented to a broader public audience the results of the Natural Resources Committee's investigation. In general, the essay asks, "Is there a problem with excess deer?" Grounding his argument in an undocumented, informal review of the history and dynamics of deer irruptions, Leopold adopts throughout much of the essay the anonymous, objective persona of the expert defined primarily by what he *knows.* Only in the last two sentences of the essay does he adopt a persona associated more closely with his audience by suggesting that "we" have aggravated the problem of excess deer because "we" have not recognized that predators fill an important ecological niche. This identification may be too subtle to register with many readers (it is reasonable to read "we" as a reference to everyone *except* the speaker, who, after all, *has* recognized "our" shortsightedness). But as Leopold continued to write about deer irruptions in the ensuing years, the

Table 2.1. Selected Rhetorical Features of Aldo Leopold's essays on deer irruptions, 1943–49

	"Deer Irruptions"	"Excess Deer"	"Deer Policy"	"Deer, Wolves . . ."	"Future Deer Herds"	"Mountain"
Issue/Judgment	Disciplinary knowledge: What is/causes a deer-irruption?	Public values: Is there an excess deer problem?	Public Policy: How should we manage deer herds?	Public policy: How should public officials view ecology of deer?	Public policy: Have we chosen the best course?	Private values: Where do our private values lead us?
Persona/Ethos	Member of research committee who demonstrates command of scientific literature and arguments	Member of public who must make informed decisions about conservation	Conservation Commissioner who listens to public opinion	Conservation Commissioner who possesses academic credentials, research and administrative experience, hunting background	Conservation Commissioner who has the courage of his own conviction	At first, a young man "full of trigger itch," then an older, more experienced person who has learned to "think like a mountain"
Audience/Forum	Scientific peers in Wisconsin Academy	Public with general interest in nature	Public interested in game management	Public angry about Leopold's proposals	Public and officials who have made the wrong choices	"We" who strive for safety . . .

Strategies of Inquiry	Critical review of scientific literature (62 citations to 28 sources); quantitative data	Undocumented, informal review of "facts"	Review of quantitative data most relevant to policy decision	Informal, undocumented review of conclusions drawn by scientific studies	Same as "Deer, Wolves . . ."	Personal recollection articulated with professional experience and knowledge
Design	Case histories; graphic presentation of quantitative data; process models	Anecdote	Questions and answers	Statements of opposing views and assumptions paired with his views	Outline of a chain of causes	Narrative; comparison/ analogy; deduction
Claim	A model of process, causes, conditions; a means of intervention	"We" haven't recognized problem because of ignorance	Reduction of deer herd necessary to avoid dire consequences	Leopold takes a broad view of conservation: "forests as well as game."	We must reverse our current policy and take steps now to reduce herd	Too much concern for safety leads to danger in the long run: "Wilderness is the salvation of the world."
Foregrounding	Natural History/Intrinsic Value ⟵		⟶ Audience/Instrumental Value ⟵		⟶	Ethos/Systemic Value

complicity of his public persona in the excess deer problem became an important rhetorical problem.

"Thinking Like a Mountain." In May 1943, Leopold reported to the Conservation Commission the Citizens Deer Committee's recommendation to establish a straight antlerless deer season and lift the bounty on wolves, among other measures to reduce the Wisconsin deer herd (Meine 444). The next month, Leopold's appointment to the Commission was confirmed by the Wisconsin state senate, giving him even greater influence over the state's response to the deer problem (Meine 445). In August, however, under pressure from sportsmen, the Conservation Commission approved a split buck/antlerless deer hunting season—a decision Leopold supported only reluctantly (Meine 449). The heavy deer kill of 128,000 for this split season in 1943 was later branded the "crime of '43" by opponents of Leopold's policies (Meine 452). At this point, Leopold was in the thick of public deliberation on the deer dilemma. As a commissioner, he would no longer be distanced from public policy by the persona of scientific advisor.

Behind the public scene, however, a private correspondence with Hans Albert Hochbaum, one of Leopold's former graduate students (who was then working at a research station in Manitoba), was focusing Leopold's attention on another dimension of his writing.[12] Since the autumn of 1941, Hochbaum and Leopold had been planning in earnest to collaborate on a collection of Leopold's essays—Hochbaum would serve as illustrator. In response to a draft of "Great Possessions," an essay that would later be included in (and lend its title to a draft of) *Sand County Almanac,* Hochbaum wrote to Leopold, "Of all your essays, this is the gem. . . . I like it because of all you have written, this is the first I have read in which you give a picture of yourself. You did so unconsciously; but you, rather than your theme, are the strongest, and for this reason it will be particularly valued by the rest of us" (Hochbaum to AL, 11 Oct. 1943, quoted in Meine 450). During the ensuing months, Hochbaum pushed Leopold to explore further the persona and ethos of his essays. In response to a draft of "Green Lagoons," Hochbaum challenged Leopold to reveal a more dynamic persona, one that had evolved over the course of Leopold's career:

In many of these [essays] you seem to follow one formula: you paint a beautiful picture of something that was—a bear, crane, or a parcel of wilderness—then in a word or an epilogue, you, sitting more or less aside as a *sage,* deplore the fact that brute man has spoiled the things you love. This is never tiresome, and it drives your point deep. Still, you never drop a hint that you yourself have once despoiled, or at least had a strong hand in it. . . . I think your case for the wilderness is all the stronger if, in one of these pieces, you admit that you haven't always smoked the same tobacco. (Hochbaum to AL, 22 Jan. 1944, quoted in Meine 453–54; emphasis added)

Hochbaum was referring to Leopold's earlier efforts as Chief of Operations of the Forest Service's Southwest District to eradicate wolves and mountain lions on game lands. Readers of *A Sand County Almanac* who know little of Leopold's career would no doubt be surprised to learn that in 1920 he wrote the following assessment of predator control in the Southwest: "as the work progresses, the remaining animals become fewer, more sophisticated, and more expensive to catch. It is going to take patience and money to catch the last wolf or lion in New Mexico. But the last one must be caught before the job can be called fully successful" (quoted in Meine 181).[13] Hochbaum clearly felt that Leopold's persona in the essays needed a history, one with which readers whose ecological attitudes were changing would more easily identify.

Curiously, while he seems to have understood Hochbaum's point about the rhetorical effect of his ethos in the essays, Leopold worried about how changes in his ethos might change the "literary effects" of the essays: "I think I can see several opportunities for admitting specifically that we all go through the wringer at one time or another, differing only in the date of emergence. Of course, the question is how to do this without spoiling literary effects" (AL to Hochbaum, 29 Jan. 1944, quoted in Meine 454).[14] Hochbaum pressed his point, urging Leopold not to be distracted from his central purpose by "literary" concerns: "I can't exactly put my finger on your central theme, although I know what it is. What you write about is a state of mind, probably common to all men. For some, like yourself, it is found in the wilderness; but it isn't the wilderness. . . . I find no strong hint in your series that perhaps the greatest unspoiled wilderness is the search for Truth and that he who would seek this wilderness will find the trail just as untraveled behind a white-footed mouse as behind a desert bighorn." Then, worried that his mentor might misunderstand, Hochbaum specifically addresses Leopold's stance toward his audience: "Don't get me wrong; the lesson you wish to put across is the lesson that must be taught—preservation of the natural. Yet it is not easily taught if you put yourself above other men" (Hochbaum to AL, 4 Feb. 1944, quoted in Meine 454).[15] Hochbaum's argument stresses that Leopold's essays are not limited to their concern for the natural places about which he wrote; more important, they construct the ethical world he inhabits. *That* world, Hochbaum reasons, must appear as habitable and dynamic as is the natural world through which Leopold guides his readers.

Just as Leopold would argue in *Sand County Almanac* that every physical landscape has a *numenon*, or "imponderable essence," represented by a particular species ("the grouse is the numenon of the north woods, the blue jay of the hickory groves, the whisky-jack of the muskegs, the piñonero of the juniper foothills," 138), Hochbaum seems to argue that particular ethical landscapes, too, are characterized by such beings:

Perhaps more than anything else, the series is a self-portrait of yourself. Let me say this by way of pointing to the blanks . . . . One of these is your unbounded enthusiasm . . . for the future. . . . The second characteristic is that your way of thinking is not that of an inspired genius, but that of any other ordinary fellow trying to put two and two together. Because you have added up your sums better than most of [us], it is important that you let fall a hint that in the process of reaching the end result of your thinking you have sometimes followed trails like anyone that lead you up the wrong alleys. That is why I suggested the wolf business. . . . Please don't feel uneasy that I should call this a self-portrait. I doubt that you ever thought of it as such. I think it is very important that it should be. If you will put yourself in perspective you might realize that within your realm of influence, which is probably larger than you know, Aldo Leopold is considerably more than a person; in fact, he is probably less a person than he is a *Standard*. (Hochbaum to AL, 11 March 1944, quoted in Meine 456; emphasis added)

Leopold labeled Hochbaum's letter "important" (Meine 456). On 1 April, he wrote "Thinking Like a Mountain," and in June, when he first sent his collection of essays to Macmillan and Knopf, his tentative title was "Thinking Like a Mountain—And Other Essays" (Meine 458,460).

"Thinking Like a Mountain" and *A Sand County Almanac* would reach a broader audience than anything else—perhaps everything else—that Leopold ever wrote. In considering the persona and ethos of that essay, it is important to note the context provided by the rest of the book. Leopold's foreword establishes a very general persona: "There are some who can live without wild things, and some who cannot. These essays are the delights and dilemmas of one who cannot" (vii). In the following pages, Leopold sometimes ironically, sometimes unambiguously adopts more specific personae such as hunter and outdoorsman, prophet, professional naturalist, conservationist, and "great landowner" (an ironic reference to his small sand county farm) among others. But in the first half of "Thinking Like a Mountain," in which Leopold and some companions thoughtlessly kill a wolf with pups, and Leopold's ecological conscience is transformed by watching a "fierce green fire" die in her eyes, we learn that he and the others were "young then, and full of trigger-itch." In the second half we learn that he is much older, much more aware of the disastrous consequences of overzealous predator control, able finally to appreciate that wolves help to prevent the deer from destroying the mountain rangeland— he is able, in short, to think like a mountain. In "Thinking Like a Mountain," Leopold strives to effect a public "shift of values" similar to his changed attitude toward predators (ix), thus linking the substantive good toward which his argument tends—the systemic value of wildness—to the manner in which that value constructs both self and culture. In this essay, that construction is figured as a shift from immaturity to wisdom, both individually and culturally.

The cultural criticism entailed in Leopold's appeal for a shift of values is certainly not unique to "Thinking Like a Mountain." For instance, in the concluding paragraph of *Game Management,* a passage that strikingly echoes the closing paragraphs of "Thinking," Leopold argues that "twenty centuries of 'progress' have brought the average citizen a vote, a national anthem, a Ford, a bank account, and a high opinion of himself, but not the capacity to live in high density without befouling and denuding his environment, nor a conviction that such capacity, rather than such density, is the true test of whether he is civilized" (423). Adopting a similar tone and argument in "Thinking," Leopold writes, "we all strive for safety, prosperity, comfort, long life, and dullness. The deer strives with his supple legs, the cowman with trap and poison, the statesman with pen, the most of us with machines, votes, and dollars, but it all comes to the same thing: peace in our time. A measure of success in this is all well enough, and perhaps is a requisite to objective thinking, but too much safety seems to yield only danger in the long run. Perhaps this is behind Thoreau's dictum: In wildness is the salvation of the world" (133).[16] Leopold's reference to Neville Chamberlain's policy of appeasement toward Nazi Germany and his promise that the Munich Agreement of 1938 had secured "peace for our time" might have been especially effective in the 1940s. But the success of this device surely hinges on the degree to which Leopold has effected a "shift of values," for his opposition was more likely to associate Nazi Germany with wolves than with their own alienation from wildness (see the discussion below of "Deer, Wolves, Foxes, and Pheasants"). Yet Leopold's link between fascism and alienation from wildness rings true insofar as centralization of control in humans and suppression of natural diversity constitute a sort of ecological fascism.

"What Next in Deer Policy?" The articles on deer management that Leopold published in the *Wisconsin Conservation Bulletin* between 1944 and 1947 not only chronicle an intensifying public debate over the proper management of the deer herds (the focus of the audience's judgment in these texts) but also illustrate various strategies Leopold pursued for presenting persona and ethos and influencing ethical judgment. In "What Next in Deer Policy?" (June 1944), Leopold analyzes the 1943 hunting season (the "crime of '43") and argues for further herd reductions. However, in July the Commission voted for a buck season (Leopold dissenting), and in August an opposition newspaper, *Save Wisconsin's Deer (SWD),*

began a series of personal attacks on Leopold. According to Curt Meine, *SWD*'s editor, Roy Jorgensen, edited the paper "with open vindictiveness, ridiculing the 'experts' in Madison and playing on the sentiments of nature lovers. Leopold, because of his high profile in the deer controversy, became and remained until the end of his life the principal target of Jorgensen's verbal abuse" (Meine 463). An example from the August 1944 *SWD* indicates the caustic tone of the attacks: "The infamous and bloody 1943 deer slaughter was sponsored by one of the commission members, Mr. Aldo Leopold, who admitted in writing that the figures he used were PURE GUESS-WORK. . . . Imagine our fine deer herd shot to pieces by a man who rates himself a PROFESSOR and uses a GUESS instead of facts" (quoted in Meine 463). In the offending article, "What Next in Deer Policy?" Leopold dispenses with academic citations but not quantitative specificity. The text fairly bristles with numerical data, tables, and two large figures linking deer populations to various management policies—argumentative apparatus much like those in "Deer Irruptions." By arranging "What Next in Deer Policy?" under a series of questions (How big is the herd? How big a reduction did we make in 1943? What if further reduction is delayed?), Leopold may assume a posture of attentiveness that presumably would reflect well on his ethos as a public official, but the questions are his questions, not the ones his vocal opposition would ask.

"*Deer, Wolves, Foxes, and Pheasants.*" By 1945, Leopold had argued publicly (as a Conservation Commissioner) and privately (in his manuscript of "Thinking Like a Mountain") for the preservation of wolves on deer ranges. His public arguments earned him the enmity of many sportsmen, as evidenced by the following hyperbolic diatribe issued by a Wisconsin sportsmen's club in January 1945: "The wolf is the Nazi of the forest. He takes deer and some small fry. The fox is the sly Jap who takes the choice morsels of game and the song birds. Can Professor Leopold justify their existence because deer meant for human consumption should be fed to the Nazi because we must have that protection for the trees? . . . We must ask [Professor Leopold] a question—'Do you like the wolf better than the man?' " (quoted in Meine 468). In contrast to such vitriolic attacks on Leopold's character, "Deer, Wolves, Foxes and Pheasants" (*WCB*, Apr. 1945) fairly calmly outlines Leopold's vote in January 1945 to *reinstitute* a bounty on wolves, arguing that the bounty was warranted *at that time* "because the increase in coyotes makes it necessary, there is a probability that timber wolves have increased, and it is impracticable to distinguish between the two species in paying bounties" (3–4). Yet the charged atmosphere surrounding the question of predator control shows through. Leopold takes pains to explain that his vote did not violate his underlying ecological principles; indeed, he promises to "fight for again discontinuing the bounty whenever extermination again threatens. We have no right to exterminate any species of wildlife. I stand on this as a fundamental principle" (4). He turns next to his opponents, characterizing them in a manner that only exacerbated his rhetorical problem: "Those who assume that we would be better off without wolves," he writes, "are assuming more knowledge of how nature works than I can claim to possess" (4). Roy Jorgensen quoted the sentence in the June issue of *SWD* and advised his readers to "read [the sentence] again because it has that touch of 'Leopoldian egotism' and insinuates that he, the great Aldo, places his knowledge above that of any Wisconsin citizen" (quoted in Flader 216). In the eyes of his opposition, then, Leopold's persona as a scientific expert and conservation commissioner was transformed into a character type consisting of a single example—"the great Aldo"—whose ethos was judged by degrees of egotism, misplaced affection for predators, and bad judgment. Hochbaum's warnings about the rhetorical dangers of putting oneself "above other men" seems particularly apropos to this episode.

Perhaps because Leopold's position on deer management had become so controversial, the editor's "fill in" his persona as conservation commissioner with a short blurb that surveys his academic title and affiliation, his research and administrative background, and, perhaps to influence sportsmen's ethical judgments, his long and various experiences as a hunter (the blurb goes so far as to tell us that "Prof. Leopold killed his first deer in Wyoming in 1904"!). Leopold then explicitly establishes ethical criteria for his persona as a commissioner and administrative officer: "The public is entitled to direct personal statements from Commissioners and administrative officers, giving their view of current issues. This is an attempt to give my view. It is a personal expression, and does not commit any other Commissioner, nor any officer of the administrative staff" (3). In the course of the article, he states nine positions he believes some in his audience hold (e.g. "Many believe the herd has shrunk too much"), usually followed by his own position, stated in the language of deliberative rhetoric (he "favors" or promises to "fight for" policies and takes a "stand" on fundamental principles). Thus, he displays both attentiveness and decisiveness, though again he retains his privileged persona as expert.

"Mortgaging the Future Deer Herd." In July 1946, when the conservation commission voted 5–1 (Leopold dissenting) for a traditional buck season,[17] Leopold believed that it had bowed to public opinion rather than face the scientifically established need for further herd reductions (see Meine 488). In response to the decision, Leopold published his dissenting opinion as "The Deer Dilemma" (*WCB*, Aug.–Sept. 1946). When the same thing happened a year later, Leopold published "Mortgaging the Future Deer Herd" (*WBC*, Sept. 1947).

In this essay, Leopold addresses an issue of public policy both retrospectively and deliberatively. The question at hand is "Have we chosen the best course?" Leopold goes even further to establish his own particular ethical stance as a Commissioner. At the end of the brief, angry article, he writes, "I am publishing this article because I cannot conscientiously remain a member of the Conservation Commission without giving public notice that I dissent from the policy of postponement [of a doe-hunt] adopted by the majority on July 1" (3). Here he invokes ethical criteria—integrity and having the courage of one's convictions—that might not otherwise be highlighted by his persona as a Conservation Commissioner, but the issue remains polarized as a conflict between expedient and inexpedient policy.

A Sand County Almanac. During the year or so preceding the publication of "Mortgaging the Future Deer Herd," Leopold was hard at work on the collection of essays that would appear posthumously as *A Sand County Almanac.* One of his major challenges in writing and arranging his major work concerned the balance between natural history and ecological argument. Dennis Ribbens's history of Leopold's work on *Sand County Almanac* reveals how central the balance that Leopold struck in "Thinking Like a Mountain" was to his sense of the genre in which he was working and the role of persona and ethos in that genre.

Early correspondence from Knopf about Leopold's plans for the book encouraged him to write "a book for the layman . . . [with] room for the author's opinions on ecology and conservation . . . worked into a framework of actual field experience" (Harold Strauss to AL, 26 Nov. 1941, quoted in Ribbens 92–93). In his response, Leopold pondered "how far into ecology (that is, how far beyond mere natural history) such a book should attempt to go" (3 Dec. 1941, quoted in Ribbens 93). After an intense period of work between September 1943 and June 1944, Leopold submitted to Knopf and MacMillan a collection of thirteen essays, eight of which would eventually appear in part 2 of *Sand County Almanac* along with "Thinking Like a Mountain," the title essay of the collection when he first submitted it for publication (Ribbens 96–97).

Ribbens argues that the emphasis given to "Thinking like a Mountain" at this point in the evolution of *Sand County Almanac* reveals a great deal about Leopold's evolving sense of his rhetorical stance in the collection: in "Marshland Elegy," which had at first lent its name to Leopold's proposed collection, "Leopold stands as aloof critic, the judge of what is right. By contrast 'Thinking Like a Mountain' is personal, experiential, humble, even confessional. . . . It quietly speaks of individual attitude, of Leopold's own change in attitude" (Ribbens 98). At the same time, "Thinking Like a Mountain" balances this personal tone with explicit ecological argument. Knopf, however, was pushing Leopold in the direction of straight natural history, wondering whether he would "consider making a book purely of nature observations, with less emphasis on the ecological ideas which you have incorporated into your present manuscript? It seems to us that these ecological theories are very difficult indeed to present successfully for the layman" (Clinton Simpson to AL, 24 July 1944, quoted in Ribbens 99). Further, Knopf pressed Leopold to find "some sort of unifying theme or principles" for his manuscript (Simpson to AL, 24 July 1944, quoted in Ribbens 99). As Ribbens succinctly observes, "The heart of the Knopf-Leopold debate was the perceived conflict between observation of nature and comment about nature, between aesthetic response and ethical insight, between *nature as other and man's interaction with it*" (Ribbens 100; emphasis added). Of course, the debate appears as well to involve a conflict between Knopf's construction of an audience to whom they could sell books and Leopold's construction of an audience whose values he could engage and transform. The final design of *Sand County Almanac* incorporates these conflicts within a larger rhetorical structure.

The overall structure and rhetorical strategy of *A Sand County Almanac* reveal Leopold's awareness of the relationships among differing stances toward his audience and the natural world. In the foreword, he explains the three-part arrangement of the book in terms of different modes of observation and reflection. Part 1, "A Sand County Almanac," consists of "shack sketches" rooted in his Wisconsin River farm, and arranged seasonally, that record his family's attempts to "rebuild, with shovel and axe, what we are losing elsewhere"—healthy land (viii). The essays that make up part 2, "Sketches Here and There," are set in widely scattered North American locales and examine various issues in ecology and conservation. Part 3, "The Upshot," consists of philosophical essays that present Leopold's attitudes toward the land "in more logical terms." Leopold further identifies three arguments that inform all three parts: (1) "that land is a community"—an ecological concept; (2) "that land is to be loved and respected"—an ethical concept; and (3) "that land yields a cultural harvest"—an aesthetic concept. The essays, he tells us, attempt to "weld" these three arguments together. Finally, he states an explicit rhetorical purpose—to effect a "shift of values" brought about by "reappraising things unnatural, tame, and confined in terms of things natural, wild, and free" (ix).

Leopold also admits that the parts of *Sand County Almanac* have been carefully arranged according to a rhetorical strategy; he saves for his final section those philosophical essays that he feels will daunt all but the "very sympathetic reader" (viii). The successive parts of *Sand County Almanac* gradually foster that sympathy in a manner that mirrors the core concepts of Leopold's land ethic. While all three parts of the book develop aesthetic, ecological, and ethical themes, each part tends to emphasize one stance toward the nonhuman world. For instance, "A Sand County Almanac" emphasizes the rhythms and sensory immediacy of life on the land as a background for the ethical arguments in the rest of the text. "Sketches Here and There" builds on the speaker's capacity for what Thoreau called "direct intercourse and sympathy" with the land but also highlights the ecological object lessons each landscape—and its history—can teach us. "The Upshot" recognizes the value of philosophical formulations and practical designs for telling "the company how it may get back in step" (viii).

In this tripartite structure, "Thinking Like a Mountain" and the other essays of part 2 serve as a rhetorical fulcrum. As Peter Fritzell has observed, in the movement from part 1 to part 2 "The largely psycho-biotic drama of Sand County becomes, in substantial part, the socio-biotic exposition of Wisconsin, Illinois, Iowa, Arizona, New Mexico, Chihuahua, Sonora, Oregon, Utah, and Manitoba. The largely personal and local history of Sand County tends to become generic, regional, American, and even Western" (26). Or in the context of the entire volume, "the stylistic strategy of Part II of *Sand County* is to take the details of a man's relations to land communities . . . to generalize them and lead them toward the major concepts and arguments of Part III; to move gradually away from the personal narrative drama of 'A Sand County Almanac' toward the essentially impersonal explanations and ideas of 'The Upshot' " (28). For Dennis Ribbens, Leopold's design for *Sand County Almanac* highlights "his final conviction that personal descriptive essays on the one end, experience based ecological essays in the converging middle, and philosophical essays on the other end, all have their place in a book about nature" (103). And in that "converging middle," I would argue, lies the rhetorical *dynamis* of American nature writing as it has developed since Leopold.

Along with each discursive mode in the book goes a characteristic persona. For instance, we might characterize Leopold's persona in the three sections of *A Sand County Almanac* as, in turn, the *hermit* in his "refuge from too much modernity" seeking his "meat from God" (vii); the *wandering prophet* of ecology adapting his lessons to various and sundry land communities; and the *teacher* telling "the company how it may get back in step" (viii). Similarly, in light of the correspondence with Albert Hochbaum that prodded Leopold to write "Thinking Like a Mountain," Dennis Ribbens argues that "as his essays evolved, Leopold added Leopold the example to Leopold the preceptor. Only then did be become Leopold the Standard" (105). But as Peter Fritzell points out, interpretation from the perspective of Leopold's land ethic would view persona and ethos not in terms of intrinsic qualities of the human speaker but in terms of the character engaged in a land community: "as the Sand County land community develops [in the text], so the personality of the man in that community develops, and vice versa. . . . When he makes wood in 'February' he becomes a historiographer—saw, wedge, and axe, in turn becoming three distinct, if complementary, approaches to the past" (25). Unfortunately, these nuances in Leopold's textual representation of character have often been overshadowed by stereotypical personae assigned to him as a result more of adulation than of interpretation.

Persona and Ethos as Cultural Values

Given Leopold's struggles to develop an ecocentric, rather than anthropocentric, land ethic and to suggest the transformations of self entailed in such an ethic, it seems incongruous at best to evaluate his ethos in terms of traditional personae. Yet as Curt Meine has noted, "the urge to canonize was difficult to resist; in books and articles, Leopold became the 'priest' and 'prophet' of the environmental movement; *A Sand County Almanac* became the movement's 'bible' or its 'scripture' " (526). Further, environmental historian Roderick Nash notes that Leopold has been called "the father or founding genius of recent environmental ethics," "an American Isaiah," "the Moses of the New Conservation impulse of the 1960s and 1970s," and "an authentic patron saint of the modern environmental movement" ("Aldo Leopold" 68). Nash himself, in *Wilderness and the American Mind*, entitles his chapter on Leopold "Aldo Leopold: Prophet," an emphasis on persona that Nash employs in only two other chapters bearing eponymous titles: "Henry David Thoreau: Philosopher" and "John Muir: Publicizer."[18] Similarly, after noting various personae in *A Sand County Almanac* (the professional field naturalist, erudite man of letters, and "accomplished hunter and outdoorsman") and identifying several more general character traits (earnest, morally responsible to the land, self-confident but humble, "entertaining, engaging, and charismatic"), John Tallmadge offers a rationale for constructing Leopold's persona as prophet: "We might say that Leopold presents himself as a prophet, someone with special knowledge, a history of transformative experiences, and a 'strange power of speech.' . . . He takes his place with Thoreau as an American Jeremiah, judging his culture against the standard of wild nature" (122). Even the U.S. Congress, in a special recognition of Leopold, presents him as another type of cultural leader with a particular resonance in American history—the pioneer (11 Aug. 1988).[19]

Perhaps such traditional characterizations are inevitable. But an ecological view of character challenges us to reevaluate these characterizations, for they can all too easily counter Leopold's efforts to meet his audience on their terms. In a memorial review of Leopold's career, Paul Errington cautions against unwarranted amplification of Leopold's persona and ethos:

"Let no one do him the disservice of fostering Leopoldian legends or Leopoldian dogmas" (350). Rather, Errington argues, the ethical force of Leopold's work requires us to "honor him according to the way we , ourselves,
live and lead" (350). Errington reveals, for instance, that "in order to write
this memorial as reflectively as I could, I waited until my vacation to do it,
to do the writing in a simple log dwelling house near one of the National
Forests," thus reenacting Leopold's own retreats to his Sand County refuge
(348). In this view, rhetorical analyses of persona and ethos in nature writing more properly lead to emulation than adulation, to awareness of the
human self emerging through the practice of culture in nature, reciprocally
shaped by and shaping an environmental ethic. Accordingly, I turn now to
consider Leopold's contributions in the context of ongoing debates over
environmental ethics.

Ecology, Ethics, and Nature Writing

The interface of ecology, ethics, and nature writing is shaped by three overlapping themes: (1) extending our sense of moral community, (2) constructing a theory and practice of self-in-nature, and (3) resolving ethical dilemmas in a manner reminiscent of what Thoreau called "direct intercourse
and sympathy."

Extending the Moral Community

Environmental ethics looks beyond the human sphere, defining human
subjects and informing human behavior not only in the context of human
rights and values but also in relation to nonhuman entities. For instance,
Warwick Fox argues that the deep ecology movement encourages "an
egalitarian attitude on the part of humans not only toward all *members*
of the ecosphere, but even toward all identifiable *entities* or *forms* in the
ecosphere. Thus, this attitude is intended to extend, for example, to such
entities (or forms) as rivers, landscapes, and even species and social systems considered in their own right" (6). Further, ecofeminists highlight
links between the domination of nature and patterns of domination in
human culture. In brief, ecofeminists identify *androcentrism*—male-
centeredness—as the root source of a nature/culture split and the resulting human exploitation of nature.

In response to such arguments, Fox acknowledges the role of
androcentrism in the cultural dynamic of environmental exploitation, but
he sees male-centeredness as but one manifestation of a broader problem—*anthropocentrism,* or human-centeredness: "deep ecologists completely agree with ecofeminists that men have been far more implicated in
the history of ecological destruction than women. However deep ecolo-

gists also agree with similar charges derived from other social perspectives: for example, that capitalists, whites, and Westerners have been far more implicated in the history of ecological destruction than pre-capitalist peoples, blacks, and non-Westerners" (14). In short, Fox argues, "anthropocentrism has served as the most fundamental kind of legitimation employed by *whatever* powerful class of social actors one wishes to focus on" (22).[20] In the context of human culture, such strategies of legitimation are manifested in arguments that members of one group are in some sense more fully human than members of some other group. Because it entails theories of moral character that inform our expectations of rhetorical personae, or types of rhetors, this controversy over the sources of environmental exploitation is particularly important to environmental rhetoric. The controversy is also important to environmental ethics because it concerns principles of exclusion and legitimation in human culture that constitute barriers to extending our sense of moral community to nonhuman nature.

From the perspective of environmental ethics, such principles of exclusion and legitimation ground a hierarchical mode of thinking used to legitimize patterns of domination within and across cultures as well as across a nature/culture split created by that mode of thinking. According to theologian Steven Rockefeller, "just as multiculturalists criticize the positing of the achievements of one group, such as white European and American males, as the norm of fully developed humanity, so some environmentalists criticize an anthropocentric outlook that posits human beings as the final end of the creation process and as inherently superior to all other beings. In both cases there is an attack on hierarchical modes of thought that tend to diminish or deny the value of other beings" (93). As Roderick Nash has noted, the attack on such hierarchical modes of thought in ecology can be traced back to Leopold, whose "most radical ideas, and . . . greatest significance for the 1960s and beyond, concern the *intrinsic* rights of nonhuman life forms and of life communities or ecosystems to exist. . . . Most of the earlier advocates of extended ethics dealt almost exclusively with individual organisms and then, generally, with the higher animals. . . . Leopold's achievement was to follow the road to its termination in ecosystems, environment or, as he preferred, 'land.' He is correctly regarded as the most important source of *environmental* ethics" ("Aldo Leopold" 75–76).

Other ethicists define the moral community in a manner that transcends rather than extends the notion of intrinsic rights. In "Duties to Ecosystems," Holmes Rolston III distinguishes between communities and organisms, noting that organisms are characterized by close coupling of essential parts, whereas ecological communities typically display a relatively loose coupling of individuals that must strive (compete, evolve) with others to create and occupy dynamic niches in the larger system that *emerges* from their interactions. On the one hand, to expect to find in communities the close coupling and cooperation that we expect to find among the parts of organisms "faults *communities* as though they ought to be organismic *individuals*. One should look for a matrix of interconnections between centers, not for a single center, for creative stimulus and open-ended potential, not for a fixed telos and executive program" (255). On the other hand, the principles that shape individuals are themselves coupled through the "matrix of interconnections" to the principles that shape communities: "The *environmental necessity* involves conflict, selection pressure, niche-fittedness, environmental support; the *organic necessity* involves cooperation, functional efficiency, metabolically integrated parts. [Nevertheless,] the skin-in processes could never have evolved, nor can they remain what they are, apart from the skin-out processes" (249; emphasis added). How does all this move environmental ethics beyond the recognition of intrinsic rights possessed by ethical subjects? Distinguishing between *intrinsic value* ("value as an end in itself without necessary contributory reference") and *instrumental value* (the value of "something as a means to an end"), Rolston argues that neither of these traditional categories applies to ecosystems, for these emergent structures have neither ends, purposes, nor "programs," properly speaking, nor do they constitute fixed loci of intrinsic value. Alternatively, he argues that environmental ethics must consider "systemic value": "This cardinal value . . . is not all encapsulated in individuals; it . . . is smeared out into the system. . . . Systemic value is the productive process; its products are intrinsic values woven into instrumental relationships" (270). In Rolston's formulation, recognizing systemic value entails extending our sense of self and of our ethical responsibilities: "When humans awaken to their presence in such a biosphere, finding themselves products of this process too . . . they owe something to this beauty, integrity, and constancy in the biotic community. Ethics is not complete until extended to the land" (270).

In the story of Leopold's engagement in the deer dilemma, we find an exemplar of this ethical extension. As a scientist, Leopold empirically establishes one sort of intrinsic value through his descriptions of the roles of wolves, deer, and landscape in deer irruptions. As a conservation commissioner, he argues axiomatically for the intrinsic right of wolves to survive and pragmatically for the instrumental value of predators and doe seasons in controlling game populations. Finally, as a nature essayist, he recognizes the systemic value of wildness as a defining feature of land and the life forms woven into it—including humans.[21] Leopold also recognized that once we acknowledge the systemic value of land, we transform our sense of self.

Dynamic Theories of Self in Nature

Leopold and others have proposed various explanations for our alienation from the systemic value of nonhuman nature. In *A Sand County Almanac,* Leopold argues that human history should have taught us humility with regard to our *ignorance* of the complex relationships that constitute the natural communities to which we belong: "In human history, we have learned (I hope) that the conqueror role is eventually self-defeating. Why? Because it is implicit in such a role that the conqueror knows *ex cathedra,* just what makes the community clock tick, and just what and who is valuable, and what and who is worthless, in community life. It always turns out that he knows neither, and this is why his conquests eventually defeat themselves" (204). Coming from a professional forester who appeared insufferably arrogant to his opponents in the case of the Wisconsin "deer dilemma," this perspective constitutes a sobering admission of humanity's limited understanding of the complex working of natural ecosystems. For Arne Naess, one of the founders of deep ecology, our alienation from nonhuman nature issues in part from humanity's *repression* of its dependence on the nonhuman world: the "quality [of human life] depends in part upon the deep pleasure and satisfaction we receive from close partnership with other forms of life. The attempt to ignore our dependence [on 'other forms of life'] and to establish a master-slave role has contributed to the alienation of man from himself" (96).[22] Finally, drawing upon her analyses of the relations of science and gender, Evelyn Fox Keller argues that our urge to control nature stems from a deep-seated *fear* of dependency: "constant vigilance and control are the telltale marks of a conception of autonomy that in fact belies its own aims. . . . It betrays particular fears of dependency, loss of self-control, and loss of self" (102). Whether our alienation from nature stems from ignorance of complex relationships, repression of dependency, fear of compromised autonomy—or all of the above and more—working to overcome that alienation has engaged many thinkers in constructing a redefinition of self-in-nature.

As ethicist Jim Cheney puts the case, "an answer to what might be our moral relationship to the nonhuman environment depends upon (1) a complex understanding of what it is to be a human being, what it is to respond to another *as* a human being (whatever that might turn out to be), and (2) an understanding of how those complex webs of relationships that constitute the human moral community might expand to include the nonhuman" (140). However, Cheney and ecofeminists are rightly wary of expansionist or transcendent models of the self that appear to integrate humanity and nature at the expense of recognizing differences, for down that path lies yet another form of domination—the erasure of difference (and that which is different) by those who strive for transcendence.[23] As Ynestra King argues, "an ecological feminism calls for a dynamic, developmental theory of the person—male *and* female—who emerges out of nonhuman nature, where difference is neither reified nor ignored and the dialectical relationship between human and nonhuman nature is understood"(117). In short, such critics argue for theories of the self that recognize difference yet articulate relationships that integrate persons and communities—both human and biological.

One version of ecofeminism focuses on integrating various ways of knowing ourselves and the nonhuman world. King urges us to "fuse a new way of being human on this planet with a sense of the sacred, informed by all ways of knowing—intuitive *and* scientific, mystical *and* rational. . . . This is the potentiality of a *rational reenchantment*. This is the project of ecofeminism" (120–21). Another project examines the various ways in which we organize human communities, reasoning by analogy toward new relationships between human culture and nonhuman nature. For example, Cheney contrasts market economies, in which individuals are defined in terms of what they possess, with gift economies, in which "selves tend to get defined in terms of what I call 'defining relationships'—where our relationships with others are central to our understanding of who we are" (122). This redefinition of self-in-nature also resonates with analyses of self and other undertaken by multiculturalism and feminist psychoanalysis.

In "The Politics of Recognition," Charles Taylor argues that a "crucial feature of human life is its fundamentally *dialogical* character. We become full human agents, capable of understanding ourselves, and hence of defining our identity, through our acquisition of rich human languages of expression. . . . People do not acquire the languages needed for self-definition on their own. Rather, we are introduced to them through interaction with others who matter to us" (32). Similarly, Keller urges us to replace the "static" autonomy of hierarchical, fragmented difference with a "dynamic autonomy that "reflects a sense of self . . . as both differentiated from and related to others, and a sense of others as subjects with whom one shares enough to allow for a recognition of their independent interests and feelings—in short for a recognition of them as other subjects" (99). Of course, relating such work in multiculturalism and psychoanalysis to environmental ethics entails the problem of defining the moral equivalent of subjectivity in what Karla Armbruster has called the "natural other"— animals, plants, ecosystems. Recall that Leopold was accused of liking "the wolf better than the man" because, in the process of reconstructing the subjectivity of mountain rangeland in human terms (i.e., in learning to "think like a mountain"), he appeared to reject the concerns of common men and women in favor of some transcendent consciousness.

Yet Leopold argued that such recognition does not reject the human self but transforms our sense both of the nonhuman world and of ourselves: "a land ethic changes the role of *Homo sapiens* from conqueror of the land-community to plain member and citizen of it. It implies respect for his fellow-members, and also respect for the community as such" (*Sand County Almanac* 204). Such respect for other members of the land community may not preclude ethical dilemmas that arise from conflicting local interests, but it should alter the manner in which humans resolve such problems, for as far as we know, we are uniquely able to awaken to systemic value.

Resolving Ethical Dilemmas in Land Communities

Conflict models of natural relationships, models that highlight predator-prey relationships or competition for limited resources and reproductive opportunities, miss the point of systemic value, according to Rolston: "Although aggrandizing units propel the ecosystem, the system limits such behavior; there is a sufficient but contained place for all the members. . . . The system forces what cooperation there is, embedding every individual deeply in coaction" (248–49). As we have seen, Leopold recognizes this principle when he first reinterprets the predator-prey relationship of wolves and deer in terms of the systemic value of rangeland and then extends that understanding to human attitudes toward safety and wildness. Thus extended to human interactions within ecosystems, this understanding of individuals embedded in coaction constrained by the emergent structures of ecosystems calls for a unique method of ethical argument.

Arguing against a "rights view" of ethics that sees ethical dilemmas as conflicts between autonomous parties, "each with certain interests [or intrinsic values] at stake, interests that can be weighed independently of one another," Jim Cheney admits that "it is much harder to envision decision procedures for cases where the parties to the situation stand in defining relationships to one another"—as do, for instance, wolves, deer, ranchers, game managers, and rangeland. "Rather than simplify," Cheney argues, "we should enrich our description of the situation as much as possible, enrich it, in fact, to the point that appropriate care simply *emerges*" (142). In other words, to resolve ethical dilemmas *solely* on the basis of isolated values—whether intrinsic or instrumental—is to ignore the effects of such resolutions on the web of relationships that define parties to the situation. As Cheney's formulation of this ethical principle of rich description develops, it suggests a *deliberative* role for nature writing. First, he argues that "to contextualize ethical deliberation is, in some sense, to provide a narrative, or story, from which the solution to the ethical dilemma emerges as the fitting conclusion" (144). And further, "the moral point of view wants a storied residence in Montana, Utah, Newfoundland, a life on the tall grass prairie, or on the Cape Cod coastline. . . . Character always takes narrative form; history is required to form character. . . . If a holistic ethic is really to incorporate the whole story, it must systematically embed itself in historical eventfulness" (145). This configuration of history, character, narrative, and ethical deliberation reminds Cheney of Leopold's work and points the way to an understanding of the roles of persona, ethos, and ethical judgment in nature writing.

Referring to Carol Gilligan's account in *In a Different Voice: Psychological Theory and Women's Development* of subjects for whom the solution to moral conflict must emerge from its "compelling representation," Cheney writes, "Perhaps this is the source of the feeling, which one gets from reading Aldo Leopold's *Sand County Almanac,* that the complex understanding that comes from the day-to-day observations of the field naturalist is usually sufficient to generate the sense of care and responsiveness to the biotic community delineated in his land ethic" (143). Leopold lived and worked in the complex ecological borderlands where species and their environments interact. Perhaps that daily exposure led him to a clearer vision of the discursive borderlands in which he drew upon his complex personae and ethos as public official, environmental ethicist, popular author, and academic naturalist. But most of us cannot ground our relationship to nonhuman nature on experiences as professional field naturalists. Rather, Leopold's example helps us, through emulation, conceive of nature writing more generally as constructing the compelling representations of persona, ethos, and judgment necessary if we are to refigure our environmental dilemmas in terms of systemic value, and reconceive ourselves as embedded deeply in coaction with natural others in the borderland between human and nonhuman.

NOTES

Thanks to Karla Armbruster, Stuart Brown, Brenda Bruggemann, Carl Herndl, Rob Stacy, and two anonymous reviewers for the University of Wisconsin Press for reading drafts of this essay and offering very helpful suggestions.

1. Recent anthologies include Lyon; Murray; Lewis; Finch and Elder; and Shore, which includes an introduction by Al Gore. In addition, several literary journals recently devoted special issues at least in part to nature writing: the *Geor-*

gia Review 48 (Spring 1993); *Indiana Review* 16 (Spring 1993); and the *Ohio Review* (no. 49). Recent critical studies of nature writing include Slovic; Sheldon; Cooley; and various essays published in the *American Nature Writing Newsletter* (estab. 1992) and *ISLE*, a journal devoted to interdisciplinary studies on literature and the environment (estab. 1993). Finally, 1993 saw the establishment of *ASLE*, the Association for the Study of Literature and the Environment. See also "The Rise of Nature Writing: America's Next Great Genre? Fifteen Writers Respond to John A. Murray."

Collections of nature and environmental writing intended for use in composition classes have also been appearing regularly over the past three years (1992–95): see Morgan and Okerstrom; Slovic and Dixon; Walker; Ross; and Verburg.

2. John Tallmadge offer the following definition: "The term *nature writing*. . . . usually means descriptive or narrative literature that falls between scientific reportage and imaginative fiction. This genre can include the most diverse subject matter without losing its formal distinctiveness. . . . In general, we might say that whereas scientists use experience and observation to generate 'facts' (that is, theories), nature writers use scientific facts to enrich and deepen their readers' experience" (111). My description agrees with his definition insofar as it places nature writing in a borderland and distinguishes it from natural history in terms of emphasis and purpose.

Similarly, in "Taxonomy of Nature Writing," with which he begins a short history of the genre in *This Incomperable Lande*, Thomas Lyon qualifies his distinctions by noting that "the types I have listed tend to intergrade. . . . nature writing is not in truth a neat and orderly field" (3). Still, he offers his taxonomy in order to highlight the complex dimensions and wide thematic and stylistic range of nature writing. In this essay, I investigate the principle of integration that compels us to view the various kinds of writing that Lyon surveys in relation to one another, as variations on a theme.

3. In classical rhetoric, appeals to *ethos* or moral character were one of three "artistic" or "invented" proofs that might be employed in any rhetorical discourse; the others were *logos* (appeals to reason) and *pathos* (putting the audience in the right frame of mind). Aristotle also identified three species or kinds of rhetoric: *judicial* rhetoric called for judgment about the justice or injustice of past actions; *deliberative* rhetoric called for judgments about the expediency or inexpediency of future courses of action; and *epideictic* rhetoric called for judgments about the nobility or baseness of persons. While all three modes of proof were available in all three species of rhetoric, Aristotle does acknowledge that a given proof will be more or less useful or central depending on the species of rhetoric in which it is employed (*On Rhetoric* 2.1.1–4). It is in this sense that I focus on the centrality of *ethos* in nature writing.

4. Those studies help to clarify the relationship between two elements of Aristotle's doctrine of ethical proof—*exis*, which refers to "a formed and permanent habit of mind," and *ethos*, which refers to a person's "habitual temper or disposition, moral character" (see J. H. Freese's glossary in the Loeb edition of Aristotle's *Rhetoric*). The latter seems to be the more general term associated with "speech

that reveals character" (*On Rhetoric* 1.8.6), as in the following passage: "Next let us go through the kinds of character [*ethe*], considering what they are like in terms of emotions and habits [*exeis*] and age of life and fortune" (*On Rhetoric* 2.12.1). By "emotions," Aristotle tells us, he means "anger, desire, and the like," and by "habits" he means "virtues and vices" (*On Rhetoric* 2.12.2). These first two components of character would seem to apply to people in general. However, Aristotle's analysis of the ages ("youth, prime, and old age") and fortunes ("good birth and wealth and power and their opposites and in general good fortune and misfortune") establishes character *types* about which we might make conventional assumptions (*On Rhetoric* 2.12.2). On the derivation of "ethos" and the distinction between "habits" and "moral character," see Cherry; Corts; Johnson; Grimaldi; and Yoos.

5.   After reviewing traditional uses of *persona* in literary criticism and the derivation of *ethos* (see note 4), Cherry proposes that we distinguish between the two terms on the basis of "authorial distance." My usage agrees with his distinction insofar as a character *type* is more "distant" from the audience than the individual "narrator" or "speaker" whom the audience judges in a given discourse. However, my use of the terms primarily distinguishes between character type (persona) and a situated ethical judgment about an individual who belongs to that type. I do not believe that my argument contradicts Cherry's; authorial distance and moral character are simply two semantic dimensions of *persona* and *ethos*.

6.   Yoos retains the traditional term *ethos* where I use *persona* and employs "ethical appeal" where I use *ethos*. He is making a parallel distinction, however, between the *expectations* an audience has of a given source of communication and the *ethical criteria* by which the audience judges that communication.

7.   These qualities might consist of the traditional rhetorical triad of "practical wisdom [*phronesis*] and virtue [*arete*] and good will [*eunoia*]" (*On Rhetoric* 2.1.5) or of more specific qualities appropriate to a particular persona. See, for instance, Yoos's taxonomy of general ethical appeals.

8.   Thus, Aristotle argues that ethos should be established *in the speech*, not by "a previous opinion that the speaker is a certain kind of person" (*On Rhetoric* 2.1.4). Presumably he recognizes that such opinions do affect our judgment of speakers, but he does not consider them integral parts of the art of rhetoric.

9.   Aristotle writes, "But since Rhetoric is concerned with making a judgment [*kriseos*] . . . it is necessary not only to look to the argument, that it may be demonstrative and persuasive, but also [for the speaker] to construct a view of himself as a certain kind of person and to prepare the judge" (*On Rhetoric* 2.1.2).

10.   For a bibliographies of Leopold's published writings, see Meine (603–20); Leopold (*River* 349–70).

11.   Such devices for establishing persona are, of course, common in academic journals, which often print their contributors' academic rank, institutional affiliation, and major publications.

12.   This important episode in the composition of "Thinking Like a Mountain" is recounted in detail by Meine (450, 453–59).

13.   In a review of Stanley Young and Edward Goldman's *The Wolves of North*

America (1944), Leopold refers explicitly to these earlier beliefs: "I personally believed, at least in 1914 when predator control began, that there could not be too much horned game, and that the extirpation of predators was a reasonable price to pay for better big game hunting. Some of us have learned since the tragic error of such a view, and acknowledged our mistake" (226).

14. Leopold elaborated on the difference between ethical judgment and literary effect in a subsequent letter to Hochbaum: "When you paint a picture, it conveys a single idea, and not all of the ideas pertinent to the particular landscape or action. If you inserted all of your ideas in your picture, it would spoil it.

"In order to arrive at an ethical judgment, however, about any question raised by the picture, you need to consider all pertinent ideas, including those which changed in time. It seems to me therefore, that any artistic effort, whether a picture or an essay, must often contain less than is needed for an ethical judgment. This is approximately what I meant when I said I intended to revise the essays insofar as could be done without spoiling the literary effect" (AL to Hochbaum, 1 March 1944; quoted in Meine 456).

15. Hochbaum's observation echoes Aristotle's comments on *zelos* or emulation; "emulation [*zelos*] is a kind of distress at the apparent presence among *others like him by nature*, of things honored and *possible for a person to acquire*, [with distress arising] not from the fact that another has them but that the emulator does not" (*On Rhetoric* 2.11.1; emphasis added). Here we see how *ethos* and *pathos* might work together, for a rhetor wholly unlike his or her hearers would not be likely to arouse emulation.

16. Leopold had altered this passage; Thoreau actually wrote, "in Wildness is the preservation of the World" ("Walking" 112).

17. The commission had voted against further herd reductions in 1945 by a vote of 5–2, Leopold among the two dissenters (Meine 500).

18. On the history of the characterization of Leopold as an environmental prophet, see Leopold, *River* 30 n. 20.

19. I should also note that the resolution praises Leopold's land ethic, noting that it "changes the role of Homo sapiens from conqueror of the land-community to plain member and citizen" by "simply enlarg[ing] the boundaries of the community to include soils, waters, plants, and animals, or collectively: the land" (U.S. Congress).

20. One might ask, of course, what other perspective is possible for humans. For a brief but trenchant critique of the notion of "biocentrism" championed by some deep ecologists, see Fromm.

21. I do not mean to suggest that Leopold aspires to, or achieves, some transcendent perspective similar to what deep ecologists sometimes call "biocentrism," nor do I believe that recognition of systemic value, as Rolston defines it, necessitates a loss of human perspective. For an insightful analysis of Aldo Leopold's "anthropocentric" biases, including his highly aesthetic sense of nonhuman nature and his apparent streak of disdain for those who did not share that sense, see Fromm.

22. The main lines of Naess's psychological argument have recently received some independent scientific support. Advocates of the "biophilia hypothesis"

claim that "eons of evolution, during which humans constantly and intimately interacted with nature, have imbued Homo sapiens with a deep, genetically based emotional need to affiliate with the rest of the living world" (Stevens B5). Conversely, as David Orr argues, "If we complete the destruction of nature, we will have succeeded in cutting ourselves off from the source of sanity itself" (quoted in Stevens B9).

23.   Cheney argues that "it is the deceptive resemblance of what Freud calls the 'oceanic feeling of fusion' to women's web-like relations, definitive of the self, that (among other things) makes one feel that holistic deep ecology is somehow feminist" (121).

WORKS CITED

Aristotle. *The "Art" of Rhetoric*. Trans. John Henry Freese. Vol. 22 of *Aristotle*. 1926; Cambridge: Harvard UP, 1975.

Aristotle. *On Rhetoric: A Theory of Civic Discourse*. Trans. George A. Kennedy. New York: Oxford UP, 1991.

Armbruster, Karla. Dissertation prospectus. Ohio State University. 28 May 1993.

Callicott, J. Baird, ed. *Companion to A Sand County Almanac: Interpretive and Critical Essays*. Madison: U of Wisconsin P, 1987.

Cheney, Jim. "Eco-Feminism and Deep Ecology." *Environmental Ethics* 9 (1987): 115–45.

Cherry, Roger D. "Ethos versus Persona: Self-Representation in Written Discourse." *Written Communication* 5 (1988): 251–76.

Cooley, John, ed. *Earthly Words: Essays on Contemporary American Nature and Environmental Writers*. Ann Arbor: U of Michigan P, 1994.

Corts, Thomas E. "The Derivation of Ethos." *Speech Monographs* 35 (1968): 201–2.

Errington, Paul L. "In Appreciation of Aldo Leopold." *Journal of Wildlife Management* 12 (1948): 341–50.

Elder, John, and Hertha D. Wong, eds. *Family of Earth and Sky: Indigenous Tales of Nature from around the World*. Boston: Beacon, 1994.

Finch, Robert, and John Elder, eds. *The Norton Book of Nature Writing*. New York: Norton, 1990.

Flader, Susan L. *Thinking like a Mountain: Aldo Leopold and the Evolution of an Ecological Attitude toward Deer, Wolves, and Forests*. Columbia: U of Missouri P, 1974.

Fox, Warwick. "The Deep Ecology—Ecofeminism Debate and Its Parallels." *Environmental Ethics* 11 (1989): 5–25.

Fritzell, Peter A. "Aldo Leopold's *A Sand County Almanac* and the Conflicts of Ecological Conscience." *Wisconsin Academy of Sciences, Arts, and Letters* 64 (1976): 22–46.

Fromm, Harold. "Aldo Leopold: Aesthetic Anthropocentrist." *ISLE: Interdisciplinary Studies in Literature and Environment* 1 (Spring 1993): 43–49.

Grimaldi, William M. A., S.J. "The Auditors' Role in Aristotelian Rhetoric." In *Oral and Written Communication: Historical Approaches,* ed. Richard Leo Enos. *Written Communication Annual 4.* Newbury Park, CA: Sage, 1990.

Gutmann, Amy, ed. *Multiculturalism and "The Politics of Recognition": An Essay by Charles Taylor.* Princeton: Princeton UP, 1992.

Jamieson, Kathleen Hall, and Karlyn Kohrs Campbell. "Rhetorical Hybrids: Fusions of Generic Elements." *Quarterly Journal of Speech* 68 (May 1982): 146–57. Rpt. in Sonja K. Foss, *Rhetorical Criticism: Exploration and Practice.* Prospect Heights, IL: Waveland P, 1989. 135–48.

Johnson, Nan. "Ethos and the Aims of Rhetoric." In *Essays on Classical Rhetoric and Modern Discourse,* ed. Robert J. Connors, Lisa s. Ede, and Andrea A. Lunsford. Carbondale and Edwardsville: Southern Illinois UP, 1984. 98–114.

Keller, Evelyn Fox. *Reflections on Gender and Science.* New Haven: Yale UP, 1985.

King, Ynestra. "Healing the Wounds: Feminism, Ecology, and the Nature/Culture Dualism." In *Reweaving the World: The Emergence of Ecofeminism,* ed. Irene Diamond and Gloria Feman Orenstein. San Francisco: Sierra Club, 1990. 106–121.

Leopold, Aldo. "1947 Foreword." In Callicott 281–88.

Leopold, Aldo. *Aldo Leopold's Wilderness: Selected Early Writings by the Author of "A Sand County Almanac."* Ed. David E. Brown and Neil B. Carmony. Harrisburg, PA: Stackpole, 1990.

Leopold, Aldo. "The Deer Dilemma." *Wisconsin Conservation Bulletin* 11 (Aug.–Sept. 1946): 3–5.

Leopold, Aldo. "Deer Irruptions." *Transactions of the Wisconsin Academy of Sciences, Arts, and Letters* 20 (August 1943): 351–66.

Leopold, Aldo. "Deer, Wolves, Foxes and Pheasants." *Wisconsin Conservation Bulletin* 10 (April 1945): 3–5.

Leopold, Ald. "Excess Deer." *Audubon Magazine* 45 (May–June 1943): 156–57.

Leopold, Aldo. *Game Management.* Illus. Allan Brooks. New York: Charles Scribner's Sons, 1933.

Leopold, Aldo. "Leopold Explains Opposition to Deer Hunting Restrictions." *Milwaukee Journal,* 1 Sept. 1946, 6.

Leopold, Aldo. "Mortgaging the Future Deer Herd." *Wisconsin Conservation Bulletin* 12 (September 1947): 3.

Leopold, Aldo. *The River of the Mother of God and Other Essays.* Ed Susan L. Flader and J. Baird Callicott. Madison: U of Wisconsin P, 1991.

Leopold, Aldo. *A Sand County Almanac and Sketches Here and There.* Illus. Charles W. Schwartz. 1949; New York: Oxford UP, 1979.

Leopold, Aldo. "Thinking Like a Mountain." *A Sand County Almanac and Sketches Here and There.* Illus. Charles W. Schwartz. 1949; New York: Oxford UP, 1979. 129–33.

Leopold, Aldo. "The Varmint Question." *The River of the Mother of God and Other Essays by Aldo Leopold,* ed. Susan L. Flader, and J. Baird Callicott. Madison: U of Wisconsin P, 1991. 47–48.

Leopold, Aldo. "What Next in Deer Policy?" *Wisconsin Conservation Bulletin* 9 (June 1944): 3–4, 18–19.

Leopold, Aldo. Review of *The Wolves of North America,* by Stanley P. Young and Edward H. Goldman. *Journal of Foresty* 43 (January 1945): 928–29. Rpt. in Leopold, *Aldo Leopold's Wilderness* 223–26.

Leopold, Aldo; Lyle K. Sowls; and David L. Spencer. "A Survey of Over-populated Deer Ranges in the United States." *Journal of Wildlife Management* 11 (April 1947): 162–77.

Lewis, Robert W., ed. *Nature Writers/Writing, North Dakota Quarterly.* Grand Forks: U of North Dakota P, 1991.

Lyon, Thomas J., ed. *This Incomperable Lande: A Book of American Nature Writing.* Boston, MA: Houghton Mifflin, 1989.

McLuhan, T. C. *The Way of the Earth: Encounters with Nature in Ancient and Contemporary Thought.* New York: Simon & Schuster, 1994.

Meine, Curt. *Aldo Leopold: His Life and Work.* Madison: U of Wisconsin P, 1988.

Miller, Carolyn. "Genre as Social Action." *Quarterly Journal of Speech* 70 (1984): 151–67.

Morgan, Sarah J., and Dennis Okerstrom, eds. *The Endangered Earth: Readings for Writers.* Boston: Allyn and Bacon, 1992.

Murray, John A., ed. *A Republic of Rivers: Three Centuries of Nature Writing from Alaska and the Yukon.* New York: Oxford UP, 1990.

Naess, Arne. "The Shallow and the Deep, Long-Range Ecology Movement: a Summary." *Inquiry* 16.1 (1973): 95–100.

Nash, Roderick Frazier. "Aldo Leopold and the Limits of American Liberalism." In *Aldo Leopold: The Man and His Legacy,* ed. Thomas Tanner, foreword by Stewart L. Udall. Ankeny, IA: Soil Conservation Society of America, 1987. 53–85.

Nash, Roderick Frazier. *The Rights of Nature: A History of Environmental Ethics.* Madison: U of Wisconsin P, 1989.

Nash, Roderick Frazier. *Wilderness and the American Mind.* Rev. ed. New Haven: Yale UP, 1973.

Piacentini, Pablo, ed. *Story Earth: Native Voices on the Environment.* San Francisco: Mercury House, 1992.

Ribbens, Dennis. "The Making of *A Sand County Almanac.*" In Callicott 91–109.

"The Rise of Nature Writing: America's Next Great Genre? Fifteen Writers Respond to John A. Murray." *Manoa* 4.2 (September 1992): 73–97.

Rockefeller, Steven C. "Comment." In Gutmann 87–98.

Rolston, Holmes, III. "Duties to Ecosystems." In Callicott 246–74.

Ross, Carolyn. *Writing Nature: An Ecological Reader for Writers.* New York: St. Martin's, 1995.

Sheldon, Paul. *For Love of the World: Essays on Nature Writing.* Iowa City: U of Iowa P, 1992.

Shore, William, ed. *The Nature of Nature: New Essays from America's Finest Writers on Nature.* Intro. Al Gore. New York: Harcourt Brace, 1994.

Slovic, Scott. *Seeking Awareness in American Nature Writing.* Salt Lake City: U of Utah P, 1992.

Slovic, Scott, and Terrell F. Dixon, eds. *Being in the World: An Environmental Reader for Writers.* New York: Macmillan, 1993.

Stevens, William K. "Want a Room with a View? Idea May Be in the Genes." *New York Times,* 30 Nov. 1993, B5+ (national edition).

Tallmadge, John. "Anatomy of a Classic." In Callicott 110–27.

Taylor, Charles. "The Politics of Recognition." In Gutmann 25–73.

Thoreau, Henry David. "Natural History of Massachusetts." *The Natural History Essays.* Salt Lake City, UT: Peregrine Smith, 1984. 1–29.

Thoreau, Henry David. "Walking." *The Natural History Essays.* Salt Lake City, UT: Peregrine Smith, 1984. 93–136.

Tivnan, Edward. "Jeremy Rifkin Just Says No." *New York Times Magazine,* 16 October 1988, 38+.

U.S. Senate and House of Representatives. *Special Recognition to the Achievements of Aldo Leopold.* 11 August 1988. S.J. Res. 40.

Verburg, Carol J. *The Environmental Predicament: Four Issues for Critical Analysis.* New York: Bedford-St. Martin's, 1995.

Walker, Melissa, ed. *Reading the Environment.* New York: Norton, 1993.

Yoos, George E. "A Revision of the Concept of Ethical Appeal." *Philosophy and Rhetoric* 12 (1979): 41–58.

CHAPTER 3

Epistemology and Politics in American Nature Writing
Embedded Rhetoric and Discrete Rhetoric

SCOTT SLOVIC

I'm just trying to put out brush fires. . . . I'm standing there with a paint brush in one hand and a bucket of water in the other hand. And if there's no fire around, I'll paint a pretty picture; but if a fire's burning, I've got to dump water on it. So I do separate in my mind, totally, the didactic or political writings from art. It's hard to do, but I try. [To merge the two] is like merging gas and flame. I don't have that possibility and I think it's an incredible danger—it can lure you really close to the edge, and I'm in no way tempted to pursue it further. I already have pushed it about as far as I care to.
—Rick Bass, "A Paint Brush in One Hand and a Bucket of Water in the Other: An Interview with Rick Bass" (1994)

Poetry is least dangerous when the typographical arrangement of words reveals the author's poetic intent. It is most dangerous when the argument is cast in the form of prose, in sentences heavily infected with unacknowledged poetic claims of non-negotiability. In our time the claims of recognized poets are no longer a serious threat to rational thought. The gravest threats to rationality now come from those who employ the rhetorical weapons of poetry from behind an ambush of prose. Popularizers of ecology and advocates of the environment are not the least of the offenders.
—Garrett Hardin, *Filters against Folly: How to Survive Despite Economists, Ecologists, and the Merely Eloquent* (1985)

In their compelling reliance on the rhapsodic (celebratory) and jeremiadic (critical/warning) rhetorical modes, contemporary nature writers such as Richard Nelson, Terry Tempest Williams, and Rick Bass have established an impressive and virtually unexplored phase in the tradition of literary persuasion that stretches, on this continent, back to John Muir and Henry David Thoreau during the latter half of the nineteenth century, and ultimately back to the sermons of Jonathan Edwards and Cotton Mather more than a century before that. Up to now, nature writing scholarship has focused on either the genre's combination of Aristotelian natural history and Augustinian spiritual autobiography or on its ecological messages: see, for example, Peter A. Fritzell's *Nature Writing and America: Essays upon a Cultural Type* (1990) and Frank Stewart's *A Natural History of Nature Writing* (1995). In this essay I aim to place American nature writing in a different Aristotelian context—that of persuasive rhetoric—and thus to suggest that this writing descends from an important, deeply rooted American literary tradition. My particular focus here will be chiefly the tensions between ingenuous exploration of epistemological issues and the explicit voicing of ideology that occur in the early- and mid-twentieth-century works of Henry Beston, Aldo Leopold, Rachel Carson, and Loren Eiseley. In the course of their careers, all four of these writers combined their fascination with natural history and their own places in the natural order with a desire to raise public awareness of contemporary social issues, thus echoing Mather, Edwards, Thoreau, and Muir, and anticipating the rhetorical trends of more recent nature writing in this country.

The prominent human ecologist Garrett Hardin has argued in *Filters against Folly* that nature writers' use of elegant prose that disguises its "patina" of poetic language by not using rhyme and meter impedes the public's ability to think rationally about environmental issues. Furthermore, writes Hardin, "those who use such terms as *non-negotiable, self-evident, must,* and *imperative* try to deny others the right of responding" (33). I would suggest, however, that thinking and discussion—not passive acceptance of environmental ideology—are precisely the goals of the nature writers, even in the process of promoting a particular political agenda. In their discussion of "the rhetoric of scientific activism," M. Jimmie Killingsworth and Jacqueline S. Palmer distinguish between texts that assign "praise and blame" (thus polarizing environmentalists and people who favor development) and other environmental discourse that tries to "create a consensus, a 'we,' among groups formerly at odds with one another or with radically different interests" (*Ecospeak* 76). The deceptive non-negotiability that Hardin warns against may actually, in many cases, be nature writers' efforts to promote concern and attentiveness without necessarily stipulating unanimous agreement or to "build constituencies," as Killingsworth and Palmer put it. Hardin's fears thus seem hyperbolic and inaccurate. In order to understand this, it is necessary to come to terms with the rhetorical shifts and discrepancies within individual literary texts and, in some cases, multiple texts by individual writers.

Like most of the writers I study, I experience a constant and enriching tension between what I call the "epistemological" dimension of nature writing and the "political" dimension of the genre. By "epistemology" I

mean the effort to understand the nature of the universe and the relationship between human beings—or between the human self—and the natural
world. By the term "political," on the other hand, I mean the effort to
persuade an audience to embrace a new set of attitudes toward the environment and, potentially, to implement these enlightened attitudes in the form
of relatively nondestructive behavior. Nature writers have long understood their work as a combination of epsitemological exploration and political persuasion. However, most writers and literary critics have been
reluctant to articulate the precise relationship between epistemology and
politics, possibly because this discussion can degenerate so easily into tru-
isms: any literary text can have both epistemological and political implications; the predominance of either epistemological or political elements in a
given work can depend as much on the social and geographical contexts of
writer and reader as on the actual language; and the balance between epistemology and politics can fluctuate (a work might seem politically neutral
one year, and highly charged at another time). Nonetheless, since nature
writers themselves tend to think of their own work by categorizing it as
political or nonpolitical, scholars must find a way to begin discussing this
aspect of the genre.

In a May 1985 interview, Barry Lopez, one of the leading contemporary
American nature writers, said that the goal of his work is to "create an
environment in which thinking and reaction and wonder and awe and
speculation can take place" (O'Connell 16). This sounds like a quintessentially epistemological enterprise—an exploratory project rather than a persuasive effort. But less than a year later, in his contribution to the "Anno-
tated Booklist" at the back of the fall 1986 special issue of *Antaeus* devoted
to nature writing, Lopez stated: "I suppose this is a conceit, but I believe
this area of writing [nature writing] will not only one day produce a major
and lasting body of American literature, but that it might also provide the
foundation for a reorganization of American political thought" ("Barry
Lopez" 297).

How can creating an environment of "wonder and awe and speculation" somehow contribute to the "reorganization of American political
thought"? These seem like competing goals, and I am trying now to understand this crucial dynamic in American nature writing by categorizing specific nature writing texts as "rhapsody," "jeremiad," or a hybrid form of
the two. I associate the epistemological mode of nature writing with the
rhetorical act of rhapsody (or celebration), for the simple process of expressing deep, ingenuous interest in a subject is, implicitly, a statement of
appreciation—a celebration. Thus E. O. Wilson describes his work in the
biological sciences as the product of "biophilia," or the love of living
things; "to explore and affiliate with life," writes Wilson, "is a deep and

complicated process of mental development. To an extent still undervalued in philosophy and religion, our existence depends on this propensity, our spirit is woven from it, hope rises on its currents" (1). Exploration and affiliation are presented as fundamentally linked states of mind, and when expressed in a literary text, both processes help shape the reader's attitude toward the subject. However, some scholars view the pastoral rhapsody as an inherently limited strategy for social reform; for instance, Lawrence Buell has written that "always at some level there is the chance that the text will tempt the reader to see all sugar and no pill and that even hard thrusts will get deflected into petty excursions. American texts are particularly susceptible to this because of the ease with which dissent can get co-opted as an aspect of consensus" ("American Pastoral Ideology Reappraised" 469). The more overtly political counterpart of rhapsody is the jeremiad (the warning or critique), the primary goal of which is to persuade its audience to adopt a new perspective by pointing out the problems with readers' current way of thinking. We can see the linkage of politics and jeremiadic critique in Lopez's 1991 book *The Rediscovery of North America:*

I'm aware that these words, or words like them, have historically invoked revolution. But I ask myself, where is the man or woman, standing before lifeless porpoises strangled and bloated in a beachcast driftnet, or standing on farmland ankle deep in soil gone to flour dust, or flying over the Cascade mountains and seeing the clearcuts stretching for forty miles, the sunbaked earth, the streams running with mud, who does not want to say, "Forgive me, thou bleeding earth, that I am meek and gentle with these butchers"? (40–41)

This language, posed in the form of a question and mixing contemporary problems with biblical structure and Shakespearean allusion, provides a direct, potent critique of the social order in late-twentieth-century America—it is an example, as Rick Bass says in the epigraph to this essay, of a nature writer trying to put out the world's environmental "brush fires."

In the remainder of this essay, I would like to suggest the historical roots of this rhetorical taxonomy of American nature writing (the opposition between rhapsody/epistemology and jeremiad/politics) and further clarify the taxonomy by examining four important twentieth-century nature writers. From this we can gain an understanding of the essential rhetorical paradigms at work in nonfiction nature writing today. I am particularly interested in the uses of rhapsody and jeremiad in such works as Henry Beston's *The Outermost House* (1928), Aldo Leopold's *A Sand County Almanac* (1949), Rachel Carson's *The Edge of the Sea* (1955) and *Silent Spring* (1962), and Loren Eiseley's *The Immense Journey* (1957) and *The Invisible Pyramid* (1970). Beston and Eiseley are typically remembered as explorers of the relationship between human beings and nonhuman nature, as epistemologists. The other two, Leopold and Carson, are viewed, primarily, as political writers, as environmentalists. But in reality, all four writers demonstrate a combination of epistemological exploration and persuasive social critique. One of the main reasons for their divergent reputations is their use of what I call "embedded persuasive rhetoric," on the one hand, and "discrete persuasive rhetoric," on the other. These rhetorical approaches emerge prominently in American literature as early as the eighteenth-century sermons and narratives of Cotton Mather and Jonathan Edwards. Mather's sermons, such as "The Savior with His Rainbow" (1714) and "A Voice from Heaven" (1719), which tend to merge natural historical information with social/religious exhortation, are examples of the embedded rhetorical form. Edwards, by contrast, tended to work *discretely* in either the rhapsodic mode (see the 1734 sermon "A Divine and Supernatural Light" and his "Personal Narrative," c. 1740) or the jeremiadic mode (the best example of this is the terrifying 1741 sermon "Sinners in the Hands of an Angry God"). Of course, the twentieth-century writers were not addressing physically present congregations, but their work nonetheless exudes a sense of urgency and meaningfulness— whether epistemological or political in emphasis, the rhetoric of nature writing demonstrates a constant awareness of the worldly context of the writer, the reader, and the rhetorical act.

Many nature writing scholars believe that the most important mode of literary nature writing is the rhapsodic, epistemological essay. The branch of the genre that I have described as "political nature writing" tends to evoke the disapproval, even the scorn, of such scholars. For instance, in his 1993 study *Pilgrims to the Wild: Everett Ruess, Henry David Thoreau, John Muir, Clarence King, Mary Austin,* John P. O'Grady complains that "Too often so-called nature writers confine their subjects to limited territories, mere glades of description; in their more adventurous moments, they tend to seize upon a moral. . . . Such writers are eco-moralists, concerned with cultural construction, not clarity of perception; party to ideology, not impact. They issue jeremiads." By contrast, O'Grady expresses his own primary concern with nature writers who "tak[e] the wild as their subject" and demonstrate "the writer's struggle with the impossible: to write that which cannot be written; to write about themselves in relation to that which cannot be written; and to write about themselves in relation to their communities" (19–20). This idea that the most important, the most *literary,* nature writing represents the rhapsodic, epistemological mode seems to mirror the actual history of American writing about the landscape of this continent. Perry Miller has identified a small passage in Samuel Sewall's *Phaenomena quaedam Apocalyptica ad Aspectum Novi Orbis configurata* (1697) as one of the earliest examples of an American writer paying attention to the actuality of the land: "It is not too much to say that this cry of the heart signalizes a point at which the English Puritan had, hardly with conscious knowledge, become an American, rooted in the American soil" (213). This rootedness in the soil takes the form of pure rhapsody as Sewall reflects upon the apparent timelessness of nature in New England:

And as long as Plum Island shall faithfully keep the commanded post, notwithstanding all the hectoring words and hard blows of the proud and boisterous ocean; as long as any salmon or sturgeon shall swim in the streams of Merrimac, or any perch or pickerel in Crane Pond; as long as the sea-fowl shall know the time of their coming, and not neglect seasonably to visit the places of their acquaintance; as long as any cattle shall be fed with the grass growing in the meadows which do humbly bow down themselves before Turkey Hill; as long as any sheep shall walk upon Old Town Hill, and shall from thence pleasantly look down upon the river Parker and the fruitful marshes lying beneath; as long as any free and harmless droves shall find a white oak or other tree within the township to perch or feed or build a careless nest upon, and shall voluntarily present themselves to perform the office of gleaners after barley harvest; as long as nature shall not grow old and dote, but shall constantly remember to give the rows of Indian corn their education by pairs; so long shall Christians be born there, and being first made meet, shall from thence be translated, to be made partakers of the Inheritance of the saints in light. (214–15)

Viewed from the perspective of the late twentieth century, this statement seems either innocently quaint or ominously predictive of the impermanence of such pastoral security, but it seems likely Sewell himself intended no irony with these words. Instead, this pastoral vision is a statement of hopeful celebration—an assertion that the New World's endless bounty will support endless new generations of Puritans. But in the decades following Sewell's *Phaenomena,* it becomes harder and harder to spot such cases of simple rhapsody. We begin to see the clearest precedents for the twentieth-century uses of rhapsody and jeremiad, either embedded together or presented discretely in tandem, in the early eighteenth century.

Many of Cotton Mather's sermons, delivered in Boston between 1710 and 1720, show a keen tension between Lockean empiricism and the desire to extract a socioreligious moral from observed phenomena. The first of my examples, "The Savior with His Rainbow," provides an exegesis of the biblical line "A Rainbow was upon his head" (Rev. 10.1). In fact, although the entire sermon uses the imagery of rainbows and storms, there is no specific mention of an actual storm, only the *idea* of these phenomena as inspired by the scriptural text. The "sight of the natural Rainbow" (225), in fact, simply reminds Mather of the text in question, implying the pri-

macy of Scripture. Yet in this sermon we can see Mather using his characteristic combination of rhapsody and jeremiad, celebration and critique. The
first sections tend to emphasize the cheerful implication of the biblical text:

> It is the Head of your admirable Saviour, which O distressed People of God, now
> appears before you. Oh! behold it, with sweet Encouragements; with just Astonish-
> ments! The Head about which we now see the comfortable Rainbow, is thy Head,
> O thou Church of the Living God; it is he, whom God has placed as thy Head, and
> thou thy self hast chosen him, hast owned him. (219)

But midway through the sermon, Mather complicates his interpretation of
the rainbow, suggesting that this image has a darker side. The rainbow, for
Mather and presumably for his credulous listeners, implies at first the ten-
der attentiveness of God: "O People of God, and you that have Jerusalem
coming into your Minds; look up, look up, see a Rainbow about the Head
of your Saviour; and hear that ravishing Voice come out of his Mouth, I
will take a sufficient Care of my Church in the World. My Covenant for my
Church, there shall be no breaking, no failing of it" (227). This "care"
becomes a more dubious blessing as the tone of Mather's sermon shifts to
jeremiad:

> The Church can't be totally drown'd; the World is: but the Flood of Wickedness,
> which overspreads the whole World, is going off. We have a sad Account of this
> wretched World, I John 5.19. The whole World lies in Wickedness. Alas, the whole
> World is under that Flood, which we find before the Old Flood, and the Cause of it;
> we ought with unutterable Anguish, to make the Complaint, Behold, the Earth is
> corrupt before God, and all Flesh has corrupted his way upon the Earth. A Flood of
> Wickedness, has laid Mankind groaning under the Waters. The Exceptions to the
> Epidemical, the Universal Wickedness of Mankind, are so very few, that we may
> still complain, They are all gone aside; they are together become filthy! But, my
> Brethren, it shall not always be so. The Saviour of Mankind shows himself unto us
> with a Rainbow about his Head. It is to inform us, that the Flood of Wickedness, in
> which the World is at this Day buried, shall one Day be roll'd off. (231)

The rest of this sermon tends to emphasize the persuasive strategy of jeremiad, relying more upon threats than upon enticements to secure the faith
of the congregation. Because of the relatively clean split of the sermon into
rhapsodic and jeremiadic halves, it is possible to argue that this is a case of
"discrete rhetoric," not "embedded rhetoric." However, Mather always
retains at least a sliver of sweetness in his representation of the rainbow,
which should "most movingly invite every Sinner to come in unto [God]"
and at the same time threatens to "pour down terrible Thunderbolts" on
the wicked (236–37).

The rainbow, as George P. Landow explains, "is a prime example of a natural object or event interpreted as part of an allegorical, sacramental universe" (159). Thus, this image lends itself to clear-cut positive-negative readings. Mather's embedding of political critique within epistemological discourse is perhaps more forcefully demonstrated in the 1719 sermon "A Voice from Heaven," which addresses the more ambiguous natural phenomenon of the aurora borealis. The subtitle, "An Account of a Late Uncommon Appearance in the Heavens," strongly implies this mysteriousness. Unlike "The Saviour with His Rainbow," this later sermon begins not with a biblical citation but with a discussion of the actual natural phenomenon, which shifts the initial focus of the sermon from moral exegesis and political exhortation to scientific inquiry—in other words, to epistemology. "We are sensible," begins Mather,

that of Later Times, there has been much Discourse, and some Wonder, about a Meteor, which the Learned agree to call, The Northern Twilight. The Pyramidal Glade of Light, observed by Childrey and Cassim and others in the Northern Haemisphere of the Fixed Stars, has gone by the Name of Aurora Borealis; And an Appearance of Light under various Forms in our Meteorous Regions has had the Name applied unto it. It should seem, that the Appearance of it, grows a little more frequent in the Later Times than it was in the Former; the cause whereof, if the matter of Fact be really so, may be worth Enquiring. (240)

After recounting various European sightings of the atmospheric phenomenon, Mather turns to consider recent occurrences of the northern lights in the skies of New England, including an instance on 11 December 1719, less than a month before the publication of his sermon. Mather devotes a detailed descriptive paragraph to this "Luminous Appearance in the Northern part of the Heavens" (242), but comes up short in his effort to provide a physical explanation for the event: "It is Remarkable to see, how much we are left in the Dark, and how much our Philosophy, is at a loss, about the Lights, that are ever now and then enkindled in the Heavens that are so near unto us" (243). Much like the twentieth-century nature writers, though, Mather is not content merely to *report* experience—he is driven to interpret and explain, to reveal the *meaning* of his own experience of the world.

After admitting that the "philosophy" (natural science) of the day has little to offer as an explanation of the aurora borealis, Mather begins to move, predictably, toward a theological explanation, but he cautiously guards against what might be called an overtly literal or allegorical reading of the natural phenomenon. For several pages, Mather contemplates the difficulty and danger of interpreting nature, for which "the Rules of Prognostication are so Uncertain, Ambiguous & Precarious," while allowing "that Something may be Read sometimes by the Light of those Fires"

(248). Finally, after much delay and equivocation, after what may be viewed as an attempt to embed moral interpretation as thoroughly as possible in an "epistemological inquiry," the author comes to his point:

> But yet, that I may more fully Explain my self, and give you my plain Sentiments on this Point; What Interpretation is to be made of the Aurora Borealis, that Heaven has lately shown unto us? I will say, that tho' I can do very little by way of Prognostic; And I would not say that like the People of Gibeah, when we see a Pillar of Smoke and a Flame ascending in Heaven, we must conclude, That Evil is coming upon us; Nor would I think the Meteor to be a Signal Forerunner of whatever happens to Follow after it, Like the Honest Old Man upon Tenderton Steeple: Nevertheless, No doubt the other Meteors of the Heavens, as well as the Rainbow, are designed for Instructive ones. The Glorious God, who is their and our Creator, (even He, who is also our SAVIOR,) says of us, whom He calls to be the Spectators of them, Surely they will Receive Instruction. (251–52)

What exactly is this "Instruction"? The conservative, careful statement of the meaning of nature contributes to the persuasiveness of Mather's rhetoric. Rather than exaggerating the literal meaning of these "Intimations from Heaven" (252), Mather involves the reader/listener in the subtle philosophical project of determining just how specific a message can be derived from nature. Near the end of his sermon, he notes that in Greenland the northern lights actually provide enough light to enable people to carry on their daily business during the long winter darkness. "We may also render our Northern Light of some use to us, in the Greatest Business of our Lives," Mather continues, "if it awaken in us the Right Thoughts of the Righteous" (253). Just as Henry Beston and other twentieth-century users of embedded persuasive rhetoric seek to muffle the shrillness of their ideological statements, Mather, in sermons such as "A Voice from Heaven," uses this combination of epistemological rhapsody and political jeremiad to convey the author's worldview without repelling the audience.

At first glance, Beston's *The Outermost House* is the least "persuasive" of the paradigmatic twentieth-century texts I have selected—its political dimension is deeply embedded within lengthy passages of eloquent rhapsody. This classic account of the year Beston spent living alone in a small cottage on the Great Beach of Cape Cod is—if we think in purely quantitative terms—almost exclusively about his personal observations of wind and sand and surf and birds and occasional human figures that wander across the landscape. One of the best examples of Beston's dominant epistemological mode is the chapter called "The Headlong Wave," which describes the sight and sound of the ocean, of the water itself, interjecting the author's emotional responses but not promoting any explicit environmentalist messages. A typical paragraph reads as follows:

I can watch a fine surf for hours, taking pleasure in all its wild plays and variations. I like to stand on my beach, watching a long wave start breaking in many places, and see the curling water run north and south from the several beginnings, and collide in furious white pyramids built of the opposing energies. Splendid fountains often delight the eye. A towering and deep-bellied wave, toppling, encloses in its volute a quantity of air, and a few seconds after the spill this prisoned and compressed vapour bursts up through the boiling rush in feathery, foamy jets and geyser plumes. I have seen fountains here, on a September day, twenty and twenty-five and even thirty feet high. Sometimes a curious thing happens. Instead of escaping vertically, the rolled-up air escapes horizontally, and the breaker suddenly blows, as from a dragon's mouth, a great lateral puff of steamy spray. On sunny days, the toppling crest is often mirrored in the glassy volute as the wave is breaking. One lovely autumn afternoon, I saw a beautiful white gull sailing along the volute of a breaker accompanied by his reflection in the wave. (54)

Images of power and action abound in this description. Superlatives like "fine," "splendid," "lovely," and "beautiful" combine with such verb phrases as "taking pleasure" and "delight" to create an overwhelmingly rhapsodic representation of the Cape Cod surf. In this and other paragraphs, Beston provides substantial detail about the size and shape of the waves, and if he is trying to "persuade" his readers of anything here, it must be the potential of the sea to produce a benign and appealing effect on the human mind.

Occasionally in *The Outermost House* there are explicitly hortatory passages, but these are few and far between. The embedded persuasive rhetoric in Beston's work is virtually a force of nature—it flashes forth, reaches a pinnacle of eloquence, and then disappears into the general epistemological atmosphere of the text. For instance, in the early chapter called "Autumn, Ocean, and Birds," the author remarks that "No aspect of nature on this beach is more mysterious to [him] than the flights of . . . shorebird constellations" (23). He proceeds to describe and speculate at length about the flight of ocean birds, and then suddenly he springs into one of the few explicitly didactic comments of the entire book:

We need another and a wiser and perhaps a more mystical concept of animals. Remote from universal nature, and living by complicated artifice, man in civilization surveys the creature through the glass of his knowledge and sees therefore a feather magnified and the whole image in distortion. We patronize them for their incompleteness, for their tragic fate of having taken a form so far below ourselves. And therein we err, and greatly err. For the animal shall not be measured by man. In a world older and more complete than ours they move finished and complete, gifted with extensions of the senses we have lost or never attained, living by voices we shall never hear. They are not brethren, they are not underlings; they are other nations, caught with ourselves in the net of life and time, fellow prisoners of the splendour and travail of the earth. (25)

Then the next sentence returns the rhetoric to the epistemological, descriptive mode: "The afternoon sun sinks red as fire; the tide climbs the beach, its foam a strange crimson; miles out, a freighter goes north, emerging from the shoals" (25). The effect of Beston's intermittent exhortations, embedded as they are within extended narrative and descriptive passages that display an appreciative attitude toward nature without voicing an explicit ideology, is to crystallize and affirm the worldview that the text has gently, gradually, almost subconsciously communicated to the reader. And then, before the reader has a chance to feel repelled by the aggressive statement of ideology, Beston climbs down from his soapbox and becomes, once again, the passionate, attentive observer of the world.

The great Texas nature writer John Graves (best known for his 1959 book *Goodbye to a River*) published an article in the December 1963 issue of *College Composition and Communication* called "On the Desirable Reluctance of Trumpets," in which he asserts that the clearheaded, careful presentation of facts (e.g., natural historical information) is really more persuasive than what he calls "whole-hog exhortation" (210). In his own nature essays, Graves typically avoids explicit polemics, instead simply applying layer upon layer of narrative and discursive information. More recently, Ann Zwinger, one of the less overtly political contemporary nature writers, has expressed similar ideas in her public dialogue with Gary Nabhan (published in Edward Lueders's 1989 book, *Writing Nature History: Dialogues with Authors*). As Zwinger puts it,

I think we *are* out to save the world—in a very quiet, minor way. Nature writers, I think, are saying, "Look at this best of all possible worlds." My theory is that we should try to get the reader to really *look* at the natural world. If you once look at something, really *see* it, ask a question about it, get an answer, learn something about it, it becomes yours. And once it becomes yours, you'll never destroy it. I think that's one thing that nature writers do. Maybe that's hopelessly idealistic, because I certainly have long since given up the thought that anybody's going to change the world—least of all me. But there is a sense in nature writing of writing for nature, and there's a great comfort in that and a sense of home. . . .

Maybe that's what nature writers do: they write about home—and supposedly you don't mess up your home. And maybe we're saying we can acclimate to this world that seems so alien to so many, the natural world that we've built walls against. I have a friend whose idea of roughing it is when the color television is out at the Marriott—and *that's* my audience. If I can say to somebody like that, "There is something real and vital and exciting out there," catch their attention, pique their interest, nudge their curiosity, that's the audience I want to reach. Bless you for

being here and for reading what we write, but we're already on the same side. I
want to reach somebody who isn't, who's never been there, who's never stumbled
across an evening primrose, never held its bud in his hand one summer evening and
felt it open. I want to find somebody who can look at a Devil's Hole pupfish and
think, what a miracle that it's still there. I want to find somebody who is angry
about "these damned environmentalists." I want to find somebody who's not a
believer. (Lueders 72–73)

Unlike Henry Beston, though, Zwinger uses only sparse affective commentary in her own nature writing, preferring a more impersonal expository
style. Still, as she suggests above, even the unadorned presentation of natural information has the potential to inspire new awareness of and concern
for nature among readers. Nature writers like Beston, Graves, and
Zwinger, whose dominant rhetorical mode is epistemological exploration
and description, make only sporadic and subtle use of overtly persuasive
statements—and such statements have particular power because they ac-
cent the attitudes demonstrated elsewhere in the texts without alienating
readers with excessive stridency.

The idea of persuasion through epistemological exploration certainly
applies to Loren Eiseley as well. Like Beston, he used only intermittent,
"embedded" political statements (jeremiadic critiques of society) as a
means of subtly affecting his readers' values and attitudes without losing
sight of his primary epistemological goals. Eiseley is famous for steadfastly
avoiding politically volatile issues in his work. In his 1975 autobiography,
All the Strange Hours, Eiseley makes a point of placing his own literary and
scholarly interests in opposition to the highly politicized atmosphere of
American university campuses in the 1960s. When telling the story of a
lecture tour during which he spoke at various universities on the subject of
"Ice, Time, and Human Destiny," Eiseley commented:

I have never understood why my recondite subject matter drew the audiences that it
did, unless the campuses were so hot that . . . even students wanted a breath of cool
air off the ice sheet. I cannot think otherwise in one instance because shortly after I
departed a building was blown up and a death resulted. (132)

This comment could very well apply to the writer's dominant expressive
mode, that of apolitical, epistemological exploration—the effort to understand the nature of the self and the external universe (particularly the role
of the individual human being within the evolutionary process) without
trying to impart an explicit message to his society. A fine example of
Eiseley's epistemological mode appears in the opening paragraphs of his
essay "The Flow of the River" (from his 1957 collection of essays, *The
Immense Journey*):

If there is magic on this planet, it is contained in water. Its least stir even, as now in a rain pond on a flat roof opposite my office, is enough to bring me searching to the window. A wind ripple may be translating itself into life. I have a constant feeling that some time I may witness that momentous miracle on a city roof, see life veritably and suddenly boiling out of a heap of rusted pipes and old television aerials. I marvel at how suddenly a water beetle has come and is submarining there in a spatter of green algae. Thin vapors, rust, wet tar and sun are an alembic remarkably like the mind; they throw off odorous shadows that threaten to take real shape when no one is looking.

Once in a lifetime, perhaps, one escapes the actual confines of the flesh. Once in a lifetime, if one is lucky, one so merges with sunlight and air and running water that whole eons, the eons that mountains and deserts know, might pass in a single afternoon without discomfort. The mind has sunk away into its beginnings among old roots and the obscure tricklings and movings that stir inanimate things. Like the charmed fairy circle into which a man once stepped, and upon emergence learned that a whole century had passed in a single night, one can never quite define this secret; but it has something to do, I am sure, with common water. Its substance reaches everywhere; it touches the past and prepares the future; it moves under the poles and wanders thinly in the heights of air. It can assume forms of exquisite perfection in a snowflake, or strip the living to a single shining bone cast up by the sea. (15–16)

As in *The Outermost House,* there is a pervasive sense of wonder and awe in this passage (to use Barry Lopez's words), coupled with some extravagantly phrased speculation. Almost all of Eiseley's literary nonfiction—his nature writing—is in this rhetorical mode. If it enacts any persuasive effort, the goal is the very general Zwingeresque goal of inspiring curiosity about and interest in human nature and nonhuman nature alike, and consequently promoting the desire to protect the world. But Eiseley, like most writers, was not oblivious of his social and political context, and at the dawn of the modern environmental movement in the United States his voice made a strong contribution to the chorus of strident and eloquent new voices—those of Edward Abbey, Wendell Berry, Paul Brooks, David Brower, and Wallace Stegner, to name only a few.

The most forthright political statements that I have been able to find in Eiseley's work emerge intermittently in *The Invisible Pyramid,* an essay collection published in the propitious year 1970, contemporaneous with the first Earth Day. In the prologue to *The Invisible Pyramid,* Eiseley writes:

But I dream, and because I dream, I severally condemn, fear, and salute the future. It is the salute of a gladiator ringed by the indifference of the watching stars. Man himself is the solitary arbiter of his own defeats and victories. I have mused on the dead of all epochs from flint to steel. They fought blindly and well against the future, or cities and ourselves would not be here. Now all about us, unseen, the final desperate engagement continues.

If man goes down I do not believe that he will ever again have the resources or the strength to defend the sunflower forest and simultaneously to follow the beckoning road across the star fields. It is now or never for both, and the price is very high. It may be, as A. E. Housman said, that we breathe the air that kills both at home and afar. He did not speak of pollution; he spoke instead of the death that comes with memory. I have wondered how long the social memory of a great culture can be sustained without similarly growing lethal. This also our century may decide. (2)

At first glance this might seem like typical Eiseleyan gloom—or rather, as he liked to call it, "midnight optimism." But on further consideration, it becomes clear that Eiseley is here voicing an unusually humanistic concern, as opposed to his usual Jeffers-like inhumanism. Eiseley's concern in *The Invisible Pyramid* is with the need to salvage the earth for human habitation, and of course to achieve this end he must enlist the minds and muscles of his fellow humans. A more typical Eiseleyan epistemological comment would emphasize the transitory nature of organic existence, the probability that human beings, as they currently exist, will eventually die out or transmute, over the span of evolutionary time, into something different. So, he would imply, conservationist efforts are futile or unnecessary.

But this is not the message of *The Invisible Pyramid*—the final essay in the book, a moving piece called "The Last Magician," rails against the dangerous philosophical and emotional motivations of American space exploration. In what must have been a boldly unpopular statement at the time, Eiseley presents a scathing critique of modern science:

For centuries we have dreamed of intelligent beings throughout this solar system. We have been wrong; the earth we have taken for granted and treated so casually—the sunflower-shaded forest of man's infancy—is an incredibly precious planetary jewel. We are all of us—man, beast, and growing plant—aboard a space ship of limited dimensions whose journey began so long ago that we have abandoned one set of gods and are now in the process of substituting another in the shape of science. (152)

Eiseley goes on to recall that a "representative of the aerospace industry" recently told him "We have got to spend everything we have, if necessary, to get off this planet." Another space agency administrator stated in *Newsweek*: "Should man fall back from his destiny . . . the confines of this planet will destroy him." And in response to such assertions, the meditative essayist responds with the question, "Why?" Even in the process of voicing his own forceful counterargument, Eiseley presents his views in the form of an exploration rather than a direct truth statement:

It was a strange way to consider our planet, I thought, closing the magazine and brooding over this sudden distaste for life at home. Why was there this hidden anger, this inner flight syndrome, these threats for those who remained on earth? Some powerful, not totally scientific impulse seemed tugging at the heart of man. Was it fear of his own mounting numbers, the creeping fungus threads? But where, then, did these men intend to flee? The solar system stretched bleak and cold and crater-strewn before my mind. The nearest, probably planetless star was four light-years and several human generations away. I held up the magazine once more. Here and here alone, photographed so beautifully from space, was the blue jewel compounded of water and living green. Yet upon the page the words repeated themselves: "This planet will destroy him." (153)

Then, a page later, Eiseley boils down his own solution to the modern environmental crisis: "Today man's mounting numbers and his technological power to pollute his environment reveal a single demanding necessity: the necessity for him consciously to reenter and preserve, for his own safety, the old first world from which he originally emerged" (154). What interests me here is not just the fact that the epistemological writer here turns so explicitly political, but that Eiseley, who normally works in the sweet, gauzy language of rhapsody (as in the celebration of water discussed above), here communicates through fierce jeremiad. If we are to create a taxonomy of environmental rhetoric in twentieth-century American nature writing, though, we would still have to include Eiseley with Beston as a user of embedded persuasive rhetoric, for Eiseley's complaints and admonishments are placed within the larger context of his continued musings on the nature of existence. Both Beston and Eiseley display the hybrid language of the soapbox orator and the solitary journal writer, devoting most of their writing to exploring the relationship between the individual human being and the natural world, but occasionally pausing to address the implications of society's inattentiveness to this relationship.

Loren Eiseley's awareness of both environmental fragility and the jeremiadic mode of persuasive rhetoric, as demonstrated in *The Invisible Pyramid* did not come out of the blue. Two of the main antecedents for his approach to voicing environmental concerns in literary form are Aldo Leopold's *A Sand County Almanac* (1949) and Rachel Carson's *Silent Spring* (1962). However, unlike Eiseley and Beston, Leopold and Carson are examples of what I would call "discrete polemicists"—they work in the rhapsodic, epistemological mode at one time, and the jeremiadic, political mode at another. Seldom do they allow the two to merge. Like the embedded form of persuasive rhetoric demonstrated above, the discrete use of epistemological rhapsody and political jeremiad also has a long tradition in American literary nonfiction, as a few examples from Jonathan Edwards' writing will show.

Perhaps the most famous example of Edwards' rhapsodic mode is the sermon "A Divine and Supernatural Light," delivered in the year 1734. Without the slightest trace of warning and critique, this sermon aims to explain and celebrate the nuances of God's "spiritual and divine light." The following passage, glowing with benignity, exemplifies the tone of the entire sermon. "There is therefore in this spiritual light," states Edwards,

A true sense of the divine and superlative excellency of the things of religion; a real sense of the excellency of God and Jesus Christ, and of the work of redemption, and the ways and works of God revealed in the gospel. There is a divine and superlative glory in these things; an excellency that is of a vastly higher kind, and a more sublime nature than in other things; a glory greatly distinguishing them from all that is earthly and temporal. He that is spiritually enlightened truly apprehends and sees it, or has a sense of it. He does not merely rationally believe that God is glorious, but he has a sense of the gloriousness of God in his heart. There is not only a rational belief that God is holy, and that holiness is a good thing, but there is a sense of the loveliness of God's holiness. There is not only a speculatively judging that God is gracious, but a sense how amiable God is on account of the beauty of this divine attribute. (128)

Substitute "nature" for "God," and you end up with language eerily similar to the rhapsodic prose of nineteenth- and twentieth-century nature writing. But my purpose in presenting this example from Edwards' sermon is not, primarily, to suggest that modern environmental writers have inherited the spiritual tendencies of the earliest writers on the American continent. Rather, I am interested here in the pure delight of this passage and the 1734 sermon in its entirety, in the way Edwards relies exclusively on rhapsody to secure the sympathy and support of his audience during the early days of the religious movement known as "the Great Awakening." Several years later, Edwards explained in his "Personal Narrative" that his own religious conversion occurred years earlier in the condition of delight. Having spent considerable time reading the Bible and discussing his religious ideas with his father, Edwards one day went out for a walk in his father's pasture:

And as I was walking there, and looking upon the sky and clouds, there came into my mind so sweet a sense of the glorious *majesty* and *grace* of God, as I know not how to express.—I seemed to see them both in a sweet conjunction; majesty and meekness joined together: it was a sweet, and gentle, and holy majesty; and also a majestic meekness; an awful sweetness; a high, and great, and holy gentleness. (85)

In light of the joyousness of his own early religious experiences, it makes sense that Edwards should initially rely on rhapsody as a persuasive mode in his public sermons. The purely rhapsodic language of "A Divine and Supernatural Light" and the "Personal Narrative" is dramatically abandoned, though, in Edwards' most famous sermon—"Sinners in the Hands of an Angry God"—which was preached in Enfield, Connecticut, on 8 July 1741, at the peak of religious excitement during the Great Awakening.

The "amiable God" of 1734 is utterly absent from "Sinners." Instead, Edwards resorts to the jeremiadic trope of an "angry God" to command his listeners' attention in 1741. It is clear from the text of the sermon that the writer's primary concern is the inattentiveness of the congregation, their waning concern for religious ideas. Early in the sermon, Edwards takes a swipe at his listeners' complacency and disbelief in things invisible:

> It is no security to wicked men for one moment, that there are no visible means of death. It is no security to a natural man, that he is now in health, and that he does not see which way he should now immediately go out of the world by any accident, and there is no visible danger in any respect in his circumstances. The manifold and continual experience of the world in all ages, shows this is no evidence, that a man is not on the very brink of eternity, and that the next step will not be into another world. . . . Unconverted men walk over the pit of hell on a rotten covering, and there are innumerable places in this covering so weak that they will not bear their weight, and these places are not seen. . . . God has so many different unsearchable ways of taking wicked men out of the world and sending them to hell, that there is nothing to make it appear, that God had need to be at the expense of a miracle, or go out of the ordinary course of his providence, to destroy any wicked man, at any moment. (154–55)

The jeremiadic language of the sermon becomes ever more concrete and frightening. After first criticizing at length the foolish complacency of "wicked men," Edwards works his way toward the central image of the text, the image of a wrathful God holding the unfaithful over hell's flames and preparing to make a final judgment:

> So that, thus it is that natural men are held in the hand of God, over the pit of hell; they have deserved the fiery pit, and are already sentenced to it; and God is dreadfully provoked, his anger is as great towards them as to those that are actually suffering the executions of the fierceness of his wrath in hell, and they have done nothing in the least to appease or abate that anger, neither is God in the least bound by any promise to hold them up one moment; the devil is waiting for them, hell is gaping for them, the flames gather and flash about them, and would fain lay hold on them, and swallow them up; the fire bent up in their own hearts is struggling to break out; and they have no interest in any Mediator, there are no means within reach that can be any security to them. In short, they have no refuge, nothing to take hold of; all that preserves them every moment is the mere arbitrary will, and uncovenanted, unobliged forbearance of an incensed God. (156–57)

The physicality of this threat is then accented by its explicit application to the people in Edwards' church. "The use of this awful subject may be for awakening unconverted persons in this congregation," he explains: "This that you have heard is the case of every one of you that are out of Christ.—That world of misery, that lake of burning brimstone, is extended abroad under you" (157). Because Edwards' threat is directed at individual members of his congregation, not necessarily at the congregation as a whole, it differs from the jeremiads of twentieth-century essayists, which often contemplate—and sometimes predict—"the fate of the earth," as Jonathan Schell puts it in the title of his 1982 book. Nonetheless, in its unrelenting direness, this sermon from the year 1741 directly anticipates the discrete rhetoric of such twentieth-century writers as Aldo Leopold and Rachel Carson, including the rhetorical shift from rhapsody in early chapters or complete books to jeremiad in the end. Even when Edwards concludes "Sinners" with the offer of one last chance for salvation—"And now you have an extraordinary opportunity, a day wherein Christ has thrown the door of mercy wide open. . ." (165)—the offer is laced with continued threats. The final lines urge listeners to "fly out of Sodom . . . 'lest [they] be consumed' " (167).

Two centuries later, Aldo Leopold neatly divided *A Sand County Almanac* into epistemological and political sections. The book was published with a three-part structure, beginning with a group of seasonal essays set in Wisconsin and progressing through a series of more discursive pieces about different parts of the United States and concluding with a handful of lengthy polemical essays. But most of the material in the book clearly fits into either the epistemological category or the political category—this is especially true for the first and third parts, with the middle section functioning as a sort of transition. In his foreward to the book, Leopold writes: "There are some who can live without wild things, and some who cannot. These essays are the delights and dilemmas of one who cannot" (xvii). "Delights and dilemmas"—rhapsodic explorations of nature and the human experience of nature versus the sober analysis of how human behavior has come to jeopardize both the planet and humanity. The very language of *A Sand County Almanac* varies pronouncedly from that of the hundred-page "almanac" section at the beginning to that of the increasingly polemical essays throughout the remainder of the book. This split—the epistemological *here* and the political *there*—is what I mean by "discrete persuasive rhetoric." There is a pervasive sense of magic, humility, and excitement in the almanac narratives—even when Leopold is personifying nonhuman nature (as he does in the vignette called "Sky Dance" when comparing woodcock mating behavior to human dancers on a stage), he does so in the spirit of humility, noting that "It is fortunate, perhaps, that no matter how intently one studies the hunched little dramas of the woods, one can never learn all of the salient facts about any of them" (32–33). There is what we might call an "ecological sensibility" in this confession of ignorance, this acknowledgment of mystery—the human observer, far from being omniscient and omnipotent, occupies a limited niche within the same ecosystem as the animals under observation. Revisionary critics such as Harold Fromm have recently called into question Leopold's "purported biocentrism"—Fromm prefers to call the writer an "aesthetic anthropocentrist" rather than a "biocentrist" (45). Nonetheless, we can detect in both the epistemological and political sections of *A Sand County Almanac* Leopold's rethinking of modern civilization in light of the humbling discoveries of ecological science.

But after the introductory narratives of wonderment and celebration, the text gives way to the increasingly scathing social critiques of the book's later sections, including the famous chapters called "The Land Ethic" and "The Conservation Esthetic." "By and large," writes Leopold, "our present problem is one of attitudes and implements. We are remodeling the Alhambra with a steam-shovel, and we are proud of our yardage" (226). And in "Conservation Esthetic," he notes:

Scientists have an epigram: ontogeny repeats phylogeny. What they mean is that the development of each individual repeats the evolutionary history of the race. This is true of mental as well as physical things. The trophy-hunter is the caveman reborn. . . . The disquieting thing in the modern picture is the trophy-hunter who never grows up, in whom the capacity for isolation, perception, and husbandry is undeveloped, or perhaps lost. He is the motorized ant who swarms the continents before learning to see his own back yard, who consumes but never creates his outdoor satisfactions. For him the recreational engineer dilutes the wilderness and artificializes its trophies in the fond belief that he is rendering a public service. (175–76)

The task of "building receptivity into the still unlovely human mind" (177), as Leopold puts it in the final line of the chapter, is the overarching goal of the entire text, rhapsodic narrative and jeremiadic commentary alike. It's no accident, though that the author begins with rhapsody and then proceeds to jeremiad. The effect of the initial narrative material is to offer readers—especially nonbelievers like the ones Ann Zwinger writes for—a sympathetic glimpse of the natural world, a brief exposure to the appreciative perspective. In his book *The Sky's the Limit: A Defense of the Earth* (1990), John Nichols writes: "No way around it. To save the world, first we must love it" (80). Leopold's rhapsodies begin to inspire this love, and then the harsh jeremiads in the rest of the book provide sober notice of the discrepancy between the ideal condition of "receptivity" and our society's actual tendency to ignore and dominate nature. The virtue of the "ontogeny repeats phylogeny" formula is its intrinsic optimism—this is an optimism that includes Leopold's project as well.

For all the writers I have been discussing, there is a noticeable evolution or movement from the epistemological narrative of personal experience to the politicized analysis of environmental degradation. It's Ann Zwinger's paradigm all over again: experience leads to love, which in turn leads to responsibility, to the desire to protect one's "home." My final paradigmatic example of this movement from epistemological nature writing to political nature writing is the career of Rachel Carson. Carson initially earned her reputation as a writer with a series of best-selling popularizations of oceanography and marine biology, including *Under the Sea Wind* (1941), *The Sea around Us* (1951), and *The Edge of the Sea* (1955). Many contemporary readers are still familiar with her beautiful account of the natural history of tide pools and what it's like for the human observer to visit such places—the opening chapter of *The Edge of the Sea* called "The Marginal World"—which is frequently anthologized. Here is a typical passage from the "Marginal World:"

Whenever I go down into this magical zone of the low water of the spring tides, I look for the most delicately beautiful of all the shore's inhabitants—flowers that are not plant but animal, blooming on the threshold of the deeper sea. In that fairy cave I was not disappointed. Hanging from its roof were the pendant flowers of the hydroid Tubularia, pale pink, fringed and delicate as the wind flower. Here were creatures so exquisitely fashioned that they seemed unreal, their beauty too fragile to exist in a world of crushing force. Yet every detail was functionally useful, every stalk and hydranth and petal-like tentacle fashioned for dealing with the realities of existence. I knew that they were merely waiting, in that moment of the tide's ebbing, for the return to the sea. Then in the rush of water, in the surge of surf and the pressure of the incoming tide, the delicate flower heads would stir to life. They would sway on their slender stalks, and their long tentacles would sweep the returning water, finding in it all that they needed for life. (3–4)

Carson's epistemological description of the tide pool, much like Beston's descriptions of water and wildlife at the edge of Cape Cod, highlights the aesthetic qualities of her subject matter, but emphasizes the "delicate" and "fragile" beauty of nature. The predominant effect of *The Edge of the Sea* (and Carson's other books about the sea) is to instill protective concern among the audience, à la Ann Zwinger, by helping readers to look more carefully, more knowledgeably at the world. But, under the guise of nostalgia, the polemicism of *Silent Spring* is foreshadowed in subtle remarks about natural phenomena observed by earlier naturalists but now lost:

They were horn shells, and when I saw them I had a nostalgic moment when I wished I might see what Audubon saw, a century and more ago. For such little horn shells were the food of the flamingo, once so numerous on this coast, and when I half closed my eyes I could almost imagine a flock of these magnificent flame birds feeding in that cove, filling it with their color. (*Edge* 7)

Although the ostensible emphasis here is still on the aesthetics of the sea-coast, the beauty that concerns the author in this passage is *lost* beauty, as opposed to the *present* beauty suggested in the earlier quotation. The subtle shift from presence to loss, which is neither belabored nor even made quite explicit in the opening chapter of *The Edge of the Sea,* nonetheless anticipates the political stridency of Carson's best-known book, *Silent Spring.*

In fact, the jeremiadic focus of *Silent Spring*—beginning with the book's title—is on precisely this phenomenon of loss. But whereas the political element in her earlier books is muted and extremely sporadic, the effort to achieve public awareness and concern—even outright fear—dominates *Silent Spring.* Whether or not people actually act in accordance with jeremiadic rhetoric, there is something about the negative formulation of an idea that captivates the human mind—Garrett Hardin, following Freud, has suggested that "the subconscious mind cannot deal with negatives" (215), and this difficulty leads us to focus our attention on negatives. *Silent Spring,* with its litany of dire topics—"Elixirs of Death," "And No Birds Sing," "Rivers of Death," "Indiscriminately from the Sky," "Beyond the Dreams of the Borgias," and "The Human Price," to name just a few—makes unmistakable use of this rhetorical strategy. But it is fascinating to see how closely the jeremiadic structure of Carson's book—which begins with "A Fable for Tomorrow" that projects a bleak future if present behavior continues and eventually concludes with the more optimistic alternative in "The Other Road"—resembles the structure of Jonathan Edwards' late sermon, "Sinners in the Hands of an Angry God." Each of these works pushes its argument to the nadir of hopelessness before pointing out the possible solution. And curiously, just as Edwards is best remembered in the popular imagination as the fire-and-brimstone preacher of the Great Awakening, Carson's reputation as a polemicist has long since eclipsed her reputation as an exploratory, rhapsodic nature writer.

But Carson's major shift from the rhetoric of epistemology to the rhetoric of politics did not come easily or casually—and in noticing this, we begin to understand the dilemma that preoccupies many nature writers today. In 1957, Carson's friend Olga Huckins wrote an angry letter to the *Boston Herald,* complaining that the state of Massachusetts had sent spray planes over the marshes near her home in Duxbury, outside of Boston, to control the local mosquito population, but in the process had destroyed many birds in the area. Carson later attributed the writing of *Silent Spring* to Huckins's letter. "You deserve the credit (or blame, according to the point of view) for having brought my attention back to this problem," Carson wrote to Huckins:

I think that even you have forgotten, however, that it was not just the copy of your letter to the newspaper but your personal letter to me that started it all. In it you told what had happened and your feelings about the prospect of a new and bigger spraying and begged me to find someone in Washington who could help. It was in the task of finding that "someone" that I realized I must write the book. (Graham 310)

As Frank Graham, Jr., lucidly explains in *Since Silent Spring* (**1970**), Carson's decision to shift from epistemological nature writing to political nature writing came about as a kind of existential crisis. Although for many nature writers, as I have showed above, there is either an intermittent need to express political perspectives or an evolutionary movement from ingenuous exploration to strident polemic, Carson was a writer unusually committed to her identity as a scientist—her natural state of mind was that of wonderment, not argumentation. In 1956, just a year before she saw Huckins' letter about pesticide spraying, Carson published an article called "Help Your Child to Wonder" in *Woman's Home Companion,* and she hoped to expand this into a larger work. Graham quotes the following passage from Carson's personal papers as evidence of her struggle, in 1958, to decide between epistemological and political modes of expression:

I have been mentally blocked for a long time, first because I didn't know just what I wanted to say about life, and also for reasons more difficult to explain. Of course everyone knows by this time that the whole world of science has been revolutionized by events of the past decade or so. I suppose my thinking began to be affected soon after atomic science was firmly established. Some of the thoughts that came were so unattractive to me that I rejected them completely, for the old ideas die hard, especially when they are emotionally as well as intellectually dear to one. It was pleasant to believe, for example, that much of Nature was forever beyond the tampering reach of man: he might level the forests and dam the streams, but the clouds and the rain and the wind were God's. It was comforting to suppose that the stream of life would flow on through time in whatever course that God had appointed for it—without interference by one of the drops of that stream, Man. And to suppose that, however the physical environment might mold Life, that Life could never assume the power to change drastically—or even destroy—the physical world.

These beliefs have been part of me for as long as I have thought about such things. To have them even vaguely threatened was so shocking that I shut my mind—refused to acknowledge what I couldn't help seeing. But that does no good, and I have now opened my eyes and my mind. I may not like what I see, but it does no good to ignore it, and it's worse than useless to go repeating the old "eternal verities" that are no more eternal than the hills of the poets. So it seems time someone wrote of life in the light of the truth as it now appears to us. And I think that may be the book I am to write—at least suggesting new ideas, not treating them exhaustively. Probably no one could; certainly I couldn't.

I still feel there is a case to be made for my old belief that as man approaches the "new heaven and the new earth"—or the space-age universe, if you will, he must do so with humility rather than with arrogance. And along with humility, I think there is still a place for wonder. (28–29)

Although many contemporary rhetorical theorists and literary critics now believe that there is no such thing as apolitical, epistemological writing, nature writers frequently assume that their own work can be either artistic or political (in the case of Leopold and Carson, for instance), or that it must vacillate tenuously between the two extremes (as we have seen with Beston and Eiseley). But even as Carson prepared to write the major political statement of her literary career, she seemed to cling to her "old belief" that there might still be a "place for wonder," a need for literature that continued to explore humanity's primal niche in the natural world. Indeed, as the response to *Silent Spring* indicates, there is still an important role for epistemological nature writing to play. In *Seeking Awareness in American Nature Writing* (1992), I have explained that Carson's famous jeremiad, despite being perhaps the single most influential stimulus of public environmental awareness in American literary history, has had only a limited effect in its chief area of concern, pesticide use. *Silent Spring* struck American society in the face like a splash of cold water—it had the power of urgent alarm. But it has taken a new generation of writers, ranging from Wendell Berry to Richard Nelson, to guide the fearful or indifferent public, to begin the gradual process of inculcating a more appreciative—or "receptive," to use Leopold's term—attitude toward nature. Occasionally these writers will voice rather shrill political messages, as in Abbey's "Industrial Tourism and the National Parks: A Polemic" chapter in *Desert Solitaire* (1968) or more recently in Rick Bass's book *The Ninemile Wolves* (1992), but most of these messages have been presented in the subtle, "embedded" rhetorical mode.

Carson hints at the rationale for the embedded approach to polemicizing in her own comment about responding to threatening information by shutting her mind. In his book *Social Psychology: Attitudes, Cognition, and Social Behavior* (1986), J. Richard Eiser uses the "assimilation-contrast model," an idea proposed in 1961 by M. Sherif and C. I. Hovland, as a way of explaining this type of response. This model for the psychology of persuasion suggests, according to Eiser, "that people, exposed to a communication advocating a position somewhat discrepant from their own, may change their viewpoint in the direction of that advocated, i.e. they will be persuaded by the communication to a greater or lesser extent. On the other hand, if the advocated position is extremely discrepant from their own, an opposite 'boomerang' effect may sometimes occur" (152). In other words, the strident presentation of ideology or environmental information in the form of an overt and sustained jeremiad is likely not only to drive nonenvironmentalists further away from an environmentally concerned attitude, but to produce a response of denial even among an environmentally attuned audience. How many readers, even people who regularly read and think about the environment, routinely pick up and browse through books like *Silent Spring*? Is one reading enough? Or is the jeremiad an inherently limited form of communication because it causes readers to flinch, to pull back and say, "Wait a minute—things can't be that bad"? The great advantage of the jeremiad—in both the environmental context and other political contexts—is in the shock effect, which leads to immediate, albeit short-lived, awakening. But the more significant, long-term transformation of values is the work of writers who emphasize fundamental epistemological discoveries and whose political concerns, if any, are blurred with or deeply embedded in the epistemological.

D. W. Rajecki, in his 1982 book *Attitudes: Themes and Advances,* describes R. B. Zajonc's 1968 "mere exposure hypothesis" as an alternative to the "assimilation-contrast model "proposed by Sherif and Hovland. Zajonc's theory of persuasion holds that *"The repeated mere exposure of a stimulus is a sufficient condition to enhance an observer's attitude toward that stimulus"* (Rajecki 97). As Rajecki points out, this is a fundamental idea in the field of advertising, where frequent exposure is used to stimulate viewers' awareness of certain products. This psychological theory of persuasion through "mere exposure" corresponds closely with the intuitive rhetorical theories of John Graves and Ann Zwinger, and suggests the advantage of epistemological nature writing as means of changing public attitudes over the long-run, while the overtly political mode of nature writing (typically, the jeremiad) is particularly effective as an approach to grabbing immediate public attention.

I would like to conclude by referring to two of the most interesting literary efforts at environmental persuasion that I have encountered in recent years. The first is John Nichols' *The Sky's the Limit: A Defense of the Earth* (1990), which pairs sixty-six celebratory color photographs of the land and sky in northern New Mexico with jeremiadic statements (often disturbing statistics or quotations from such far-flung sources as Loren Eiseley, Anne and Paul Ehrlich, and Fyodor Dostoyevsky). Nichols explains that

At first, it may seem that there is little connection between the following text and photographs. Readers may ask: Why this exercise in antonyms? Yet . . . I cannot look at a lovely scene without being aware of the bulldozers just out of frame, waiting to plunder. There is no such thing, anymore, as an apolitical photograph. All environment is threatened; all air is poisoned. (xi)

Rather than relying exclusively on the techniques of either jeremiad or rhapsody, Nichols uses the two approaches in tandem as a way of expressing his own awareness and fear, a way of communicating these feelings to his readers/viewers. Many times Nichols' prose becomes aggressive, even shrill, such as when he states that "Orangutangs, Biafrans, giant sequoias, and impoverished Brazilians are interchangeably sacrificed so that the rich may dine on caviar or so that the middle class may watch Monday Night Football in an air-conditioned rec room" (60). But on the facing page we encounter the placid winter landscape of the Taos region: scattered brush, patches of snow with a few noticeable animal tracks, a layer of clouds pushing down on the mountains poking up over the horizon. Nichols thus achieves an intriguing form of provocation, neither chasing us away with unremitting apocalyptic rumblings nor allowing us the numbing luxury of "apolitical" aesthetic experience. Our repeated exposure to this conjunction of the dire and the beautiful leaves us more intensely aware of both the problems in the world today and our own attachment to the world. "No way around it," writes Nichols; "To save the world, first we must love it" (80)—but also, his juxtapositional strategy implies, to save the world, we must not ignore its jeopardy.

Richard Nelson uses a less confrontational approach in *The Island Within,* his 1989 book about Alaska. Rather than striking out at his readers or at certain nebulous agents of modern destruction, Nelson emphasizes his own private responses to the natural world; his various means of achieving respectful contact range from surfing in the frigid Arctic sea to hiking or running through dense forests, to hunting for deer. Repeatedly, Nelson experiences profound "congruence" between himself and the world, as Barry Lopez would put it; when surfing he "feel[s] like a particle hitching a ride on a meteor" (44), and when drinking stream water, eating huckleberries, and breathing cool forest air he realizes, "There is nothing in me that is not of earth, no split instant of separateness, no particle that disunites me from my surroundings. I am no less than the earth itself. . . . The life of the earth is my own life" (249). Though Nelson never explicitly asserts that his readers ought to live and think as he does, we find ourselves—through what the psychologist Zajonc would call "repeated mere exposure" and what Ann Zwinger would refer to as "really looking at the natural world"—attracted to the intensity of the author's experience, to the sense of meaning he derives from his relationship to the world.

Nelson actually goes out of his way not to antagonize readers who might think differently, to drive them away with his own extremism. In an excerpt from the book published initially in *Harper's* magazine under the title "Coming into Clearcut," he considers the difficulty of standing apart from his society's destructive treatment of the world, passing judgment on others. "I hold few convictions so deeply as my belief that a profound transgression was committed here, by devastating an entire forest rather than taking from it selectively and in moderation," he writes.

> Yet whatever judgment I might make against those who cut it down I must also make against myself. I belong to the same nation, speak the same language, vote in the same elections, share many of the same values, avail myself of the same technology, and owe much of my existence to the same vast system of global exchange. There is no refuge in blaming only the loggers or their industry or the government that consigned this forest to them. The entire society—one in which I take active membership—holds responsibility for laying this valley bare. (56–57)

The point of this statement is not merely to wallow in collective guilt or to distress readers by implying their similar participation in this "vast system of global exchange." Nor is it Nelson's goal to exonerate the government or the loggers by dispersing responsibility for decisions and actions. His point, rather, is to demonstrate the idea of universal responsibility for problems and for solutions. "The most I can do," writes Nelson,

> is strive toward a different kind of conscience, listen to an older and more tested wisdom, participate minimally in a system that debases its own sustaining environment, work toward a different future, and hope that someday all will be pardoned. (57)

As writers, scholars, and teachers, many of us share Nelson's sense of the need to use language to "strive toward a different kind of conscience." In times of straitened environmental conditions (and historians are now arguing that there has never been a time even prehistorically, when humans have failed to exert some stress on the environment), every human utterance about the relationship between human beings and nature bears a potentially political implication, even if the writer's conscious goal is simply to provide information about natural history or to offer the reader an aesthetic experience.

Richard M. Weaver has argued that all rhetoric, indeed all language, "is sermonic," that the ultimate goal of human expression is to persuade an audience to accept or reject particular attitudes toward the world, particular "values." "Rhetoric," claims Weaver,

> must be viewed formally as operating at that point where literature and politics meet, or where literary values and political urgencies can be brought together. The rhetorician makes use of the moving power of literary expression to induce in his hearers an attitude or decision which is political in the very broadest sense. . . . But there is nothing illegitimate about what he undertakes to do, any more than it

would be illegitimate to make use of the timeless principles of aesthetics in the constructing of a public building. . . . [W]e must never lose sight of the order of values as the ultimate sanction of rhetoric. . . . As rhetoric confronts us with choices involving values, the rhetorician is a preacher to us, noble if he tries to direct our passion toward noble ends and base if he uses our passions to confuse and degrade us. (225)

Viewed in the light of this notion of language, both of the epigraphs to this essay—Rick Bass's uneasiness about mixing art and politics and Garrett Hardin's fear that the glittery language of nature writing will block readers' rational thinking powers—must be called into question. If all literature, all language, is values-oriented and, by extension, political, then we as readers must simply be alert to this dimension of whatever text we're examining, whether its outward style is "poetic" or "prosaic." Rick Bass is not alone among nature writers in his idea that some writing leans toward art and epistemology, while other writing is mainly and overtly persuasive—writers ranging from Edward Abbey to Terry Tempest Williams have struggled to disentangle these overlapping goals. The point of my preliminary taxonomy of nature writing rhetoric in this essay is to suggest that, while all language may have political implications, we can view this particular literary genre as a spectrum with epistemological rhapsody at one extreme and political jeremiad at the other. Some writers, such as Aldo Leopold and Rachel Carson, tend to work discretely near each of the extremes at different times; other writers, and Henry Beston and Loren Eiseley are my examples of this, tend to embed their politics in their poetry, as Hardin would put it. By using the empirically based theories of the psychologist Sherif, Hovland, and Zajonc, we can begin to predict the potential efficacy of these various literary styles as determinants of our society's attitudes toward nature.

WORKS CITED

Beston, Henry. *The Outermost House*. New York: Penguin, 1928.

Buell, Lawrence. "American Pastoral Ideology Reappraised." In *Walden and Resistance to Civil Government,* ed. William Rossi. New York: Norton, 1992.

Buell, Lawrence. *The Environmental Imagination: Thoreau, Nature Writing, and the Formation of American Culture*. Cambridge: Harvard UP, 1995.

Carson, Rachel. *Silent Spring*. Boston: Houghton Mifflin, 1962.

Carson, Rachel. *The Edge of the Sea*. Boston: Houghton Mifflin, 1955.

Edwards, Jonathan. "A Divine and Supernatural Light" (1734), "Personal Narrative" (c. 1740), and "Sinners in the Hands of an Angry God" (1741). *Jonathan Edwards: Basic Writings,* ed Ola Elizabeth Winslow. New York: NAL, 1966.

Eiseley, Loren. *All the Strange Hours: The Excavation of a Life*. New York: Scribner's, 1975.

Eiseley, Loren. *The Immense Journey*. New York: Random House, 1957.

Eiseley, Loren. *The Invisible Pyramid*. New York: Scribner's, 1970.

Eiser, J. Richard. *Social Psychology: Attitudes, Cognition, and Social Behaviour*. 1980. Cambridge: Cambridge UP, 1986.

Fritzell, Peter A. *Nature Writing and America: Essays upon a Cultural Type*. Ames: Iowa State UP, 1990.

Fromm, Harold. "Aldo Leopold: Aesthetic 'Anthropocentrist.' " *ISLE* 1 (Spring 1993): 43–49.

Graham, Frank, Jr. *Since Silent Spring*. Greenwich, CT: Fawcett, 1970.

Graves, John. "On the Desirable Reluctance of Trumpets." *College Composition and Communication* 14 (December 1963): 210–14.

Hardin, Garrett. *Filters against Folly: How to Survive Despite Economists, Ecologists, and the Merely Eloquent*. New York: Penguin, 1985.

Johannesen, Richard L.; Rennard Strickland; and Ralph T. Eubanks, eds. *Language Is Sermonic: Richard M. Weaver on the Nature of Rhetoric*. Baton Rouge: Louisiana State UP, 1970.

Killingsworth, M. Jimmie, and Jacqueline S. Palmer. *Ecospeak: Rhetoric and Environmental Politics in America*. Carbondale: Southern Illinois UP, 1992.

Landow, George P. *Images of Crisis: Literary Iconology, 1750 to the Present*. Boston, London, and Henley: Routledge & Kegan Paul, 1982.

Leopold, Aldo. *A Sand County Almanac*. New York: Oxford UP, 1949.

Lopez, Barry. "Barry Lopez." *Antaeus*, ed. Daniel Halpern (1986):295–97.

Lopez, Barry. *The Rediscovery of North America*. Lexington: UP of Kentucky, 1991.

Lueders, Edward. "Field Notes and the Literary Process: Gary Paul Nabhan and Ann Zwinger." *Writing Natural History: Dialogues with Authors*. Salt Lake City: U of Utah P, 1989.

Mather, Cotton. *Days of Humiliation: Times of Affliction and Disaster. Nine Sermons for Restoring Favor with an Angry God (1696–1727)*. Ed George Harrison Orians. Gainesville, FL: Scholars' Facsimiles & Reprints, 1970.

Miller, Perry, ed. *The American Puritans: Their Prose and Poetry*. Garden City, NY: Doubleday, 1956.

Nelson, Richard. "Coming into Clearcut." *Harper's*, December, 1989, 28, 30–31.

Nelson, Richard. *The Island Within*. 1989. New York: Random House, 1991.

Nichols, John. *The Sky's the Limit: A Defense of the Earth*. New York: Norton, 1990.

O'Connell, Nicholas. "Barry Lopez." *At the Field's End: Interviews with Twenty Pacific Northwest Writers*. Seattle: Madrona, 1987.

O'Grady, John P. *Pilgrims to the Wild: Everett Ruess, Henry David Thoreau, John Muir, Clarence King, Mary Austin*. Salt Lake City: U of Utah P, 1993.

Rajecki, D. W. *Attitudes: Themes and Advances*. Sunderland, MA: Sinauer Associates, 1982.

Schell, Jonathan. *The Fate of the Earth*. New York: Avon, 1982.

Sewall, Samuel. "Phenomena." *The American Puritans: Their Prose and Poetry,* ed. Perry Miller. Garden City, NY: Doubleday, 1956.

Sherif, M. and C. I. Hovland. *Social Judgment: Assimilation and Contrast Effects in Communication and Attitude Change.* New Haven: Yale UP, 1961.

Slovic, Scott. "A Paint Brush in One Hand and Bucket of Water in the Other: An Interview with Rick Bass." *Weber Studies: An Interdisciplinary Humanities Journal* (Fall 1994): 11–29.

Slovic, Scott. "Ecocriticism: The Assumed Power of Awareness." Paper presented at the Western Literature Association Conference, Estes Park, CO. October 1991.

Slovic, Scott. *Seeking Awareness in American Nature Writing: Henry Thoreau, Annie Dillard, Edward Abbey, Wendell Berry, Barry Lopez.* Salt Lake City: U of Utah P, 1992.

Stewart, Frank. *A Natural History of Nature Writing.* Washington, DC: Island, 1995.

Weaver, Richard M. "Language Is Sermonic." In *Language Is Sermonic: Richard M. Weaver on the Nature of Rhetoric,* ed. Richard L. Johannesen, Rennard Strickland and Ralph T. Eubanks. Baton Rouge: Louisiana State UP, 1970. 201–25.

Wilson, E. O. *Biophilia.* Cambridge: Harvard UP, 1984.

Zajonc, R. B. "Attitudinal Effects of Mere Exposure." *Journal of Personality and Social Psychology Monograph Supplement* 9.2, part 2 (1968): 1–27.

CHAPTER 4

The Low-Level Radioactive Waste Siting Controversy in North Carolina

Toward a Rhetorical Model of Risk Communication

STEVEN B. KATZ and CAROLYN R. MILLER

Where Should We Put the Radioactive Waste?

The decision process was "a farce, a damn farce," said Vernon Malone, the chairman of the Wake County Board of Commissioners, upon learning that Wake County had been recommended as the preferred location for the Southeast's new low-level radioactive waste facility.[1] From the beginning, this feeling was shared by local antinuclear activists, environmental groups, and many citizens in the county and across the state as they followed the decision-making process and activities of the North Carolina Low-Level Radioactive Waste Management Authority. And the battle is not over yet. As Malone claimed, "We are dissatisfied with the site and the [Authority's] work . . . and we will make that dissatisfaction known through any channel we can find" (*N&O* 12/9/93, p. 20A).

Low-level nuclear waste, produced by power stations, universities, and medical research, amounted to 1,636,321 cubic feet in 1992 (*Radioactive Exchange* 2/8/93). Until 1980, the federal government accepted responsibility for storing this waste, along with high-level waste from nuclear power plants and weapons development. But in response to pressure from the three states with disposal sites (Nevada, South Carolina, and Washington), Congress passed the federal Low-Level Radioactive Waste Policy Act

111

of 1980 to give all states the responsibility for disposing of non-defense-related radioactive waste and to encourage regional cooperation in such disposal (94 U.S. Stat. 3347). The legislation was amended in 1985 to create regional "compacts" for cooperative waste disposal (Edgar Miller; 99 U.S. Stat. 1842).

Eight southeastern states joined in the Southeastern Compact, under which each state agreed to take twenty-year turns hosting a low-level radioactive waste storage unit for the entire region (99 U.S. Stat. 1981; North Carolina General Statutes Sec. 104F-1). According to the agreement, North Carolina was to develop and implement plans for the first regional facility by January 1993, replacing South Carolina's Barnwell facility, a longtime U.S. Department of Energy disposal site. To manage the process of siting, building, operating, monitoring, and closing such a facility, the North Carolina General Assembly in 1987 created the Low-Level Radioactive Waste Management Authority. The legislation established a detailed schedule for the process, which was to culminate by 31 December 1992 with a complete operational facility (N.C. General Statutes Sec. 104G-4). It also authorized the hiring of consultants to assist the Authority and stipulated some of the selection criteria to be used in choosing a county to host the site and the forms of decision making to be used. The Authority organized itself into four committees (Technical, External Relations, Legal and Finance, and Executive) and began its work in late 1987.

The early work of the Authority was characterized by idealism and optimism. On the basis of its first meeting, for example, the Technical Committee believed that some county would volunteer to host such a facility. According to its report to the full Authority, "it appeared that the law, the wishes of the people, and the intent of the Authority could come together in a harmonious way. Maybe by working closely with some 500 or 600 people around the state, we could avoid being confronted by 15,000 people!" (Technical Committee report attached to 11/2/87 Authority minutes). At a later meeting, the full Authority told itself that "The most important feature of what we are doing is to establish credibility and understanding that this is an open and fair process every step of the way" (Authority minutes, 6/29/89, p. 3).

But the process did not go as the legislature or the Authority intended. Delays, missed deadlines, and cost overruns plagued the Authority from the beginning. The final site decision, announced in December 1993, was supposed to have been made by 1 August 1989 (N.C. General Statutes Sec. 104G-9). When it became clear that the schedule could not be met, South Carolina threatened to close the Barnwell site and to levy stiff fines on North Carolina (*N&O* 12/12/91, p. B9). Lawsuits were filed against the Authority by counties representing the two sites selected for final characterization, alleging that the Authority had failed to follow legislated procedures, that the Authority had delegated too much responsibility to the primary contractor, and that political factors had entered into the technical decision-making process. Both suits also raised the possibility of conflict of interest on the part of one Authority member (N.C. Superior Court 90 CVS 524 and 90 CVS 186). An additional lawsuit was filed against the Authority by the North Carolina Press Association and four newspapers in 1991 to obtain all documents created by or for the Authority or its consultants. As late as June 1989 the Authority maintained that it could and would still meet all legislated deadlines and goals (*N&O* 10/26/88, p. 6D; 11/26/88, p. C2; Authority minutes, 6/29/89, pp. 2, 3). The Authority also continuously resisted requests for technical data, claiming that the data were not "public record" and had to be "verified" and undergo "quality assurance reviews" before being released to the public (MacMillan Informative #36, 1/24/92, p. 1).

Information that was released did not boost public confidence in the Authority. A 1991 court order forced the release of some data, which scandalized the public by showing that political assessments may have been used to characterize some potential sites.[2] A confidential 1989 memo, revealed in the discovery process for one of the lawsuits (*N&O* 9/25/91, p. B1), indicated that the Wake County site, near a nuclear power station, had first been eliminated because of unsuitable geology and then, under pressure from the Joint Utilities Commission, been put back on the list as a potential site (this is the site that was eventually selected). Despite assurances from the Authority that its decisions were based only on technical criteria, the public perceived the decision as a political one (*Independent*, 5–11 Aug. 1992). As the date approached for the Authority to make its decision, the state legislature called for an independent review of the entire siting process (*N&O* 3/18/93). And in the final months of the siting process, the chairman of the Authority requested not to be reappointed, and had to be replaced (*N&O* 7/3/93, p. B1).

The Authority's relations with the public were strained from the beginning. Citizens crowded into public meetings, organized protest groups, wrote letters to newspapers. The intensity of public disaffection is indicated by several incidents. In 1990, a live, televised meeting of the Authority was disrupted by an overflow studio audience before the minutes from the previous meeting could be approved, and the studio had to be cleared of visitors (Authority minutes, 2/21/90, p. 1). In 1991, the governor asked the highway patrol to provide security for members of the Authority and its contractors, and later, as an Authority document shows, protesters at one site were "verbally harassing" surveyors, as well as damaging portable latrines and survey markers (MacMillan Informative #25, 7/2/91). Later that year, the Authority approved the expenditure of $1.5 million by its main contractor, Chem-Nuclear, on security for personnel working at the potential sites (Authority minutes, 10/30/91, p. 4). The state highway patrol was accused in February 1992 of "intimidating" protestors (Richmond County) (*N&O* 2/7/92, p. A1; 2/8/92, p. B6). In March, death threats were received by the chairman of the Authority and a Chem-Nuclear official (*N&O* 7/3/93, p. B1). In marked contrast to its earlier optimism, the Authority's minutes for 30 October 1992 reflect a humbler, sadder perspective: "The effort required to site low-level radioactive waste facilities is now recognized to be much greater than first believed."

As we revise in the spring of 1995, the Wake County site is undergoing an extensive state licensing process, in which a virtual warehouse of technical data is being reviewed—a review that could find the site unsuitable (*N&O* 12/12/93, p. 2C). If that happens, Richmond County (the "runner-up") would probably be selected (*N&O* 12/9/93, p. 20A); if not, the entire selection process would have to begin again, or be abandoned. Originally supposed to take fifteen months and scheduled for completion in March 1995 (*N&O* 12/9/93, p. 20A), this licensing process will now take an additional fifteen months and won't be completed until 1997; state regulators pointed to Chem-Nuclear's inadequate information concerning geology, type of radiation to be stored, and the design of the facility itself as the cause of the delay (*N&O* 8/2/94, p. 1A), and an independent consultant has been called in by the Authority to evaluate the Wake site. "We are engaged here in an open-ended process to compile data to answer a question we don't understand," said the new chair of the Authority at a public meeting; "We don't want you to confuse our frustration with despair" (*N&O* 10/27/94).

Nevertheless, as a result of this delay, the licensing process in North Carolina has come under increasing political pressure. Waste generators point out and complain about the future problems of cost (and safety) of storing radioactive waste on their own sites (*N&O* 10/15/94, p. 3A; 10/25/94, p. 1A). In January 1995, North Carolina requested an additional $13 million from the financially strapped, somewhat dubious, and sometimes highly critical Southeast Compact Commission to fund further studies of the Wake site (*N&O* 1/13/95, p. 1B); the commission decided to give the Authority only $5.4 million, just enough for it to complete the first round of tests (*N&O* 1/14/95, p. 1B). The director of the Authority accused state regulators of dragging their feet and, much to the chagrin of citizens opposed to the site, urged the state to speed up the process (*N&O* 8/14/94, p. 22A). The governor of North Carolina joined the battle by saying he wasn't going to be pressured into sacrificing safety by South Carolina's schedule for closing Barnwell (*N&O* 8/12/94, p. 1A), but that pressure increased in April 1995, when South Carolina's governor decided to re-open the Barnwell facility—for every state in the nation *except* North Carolina (*N&O* 4/14/95, p. 1B)!

In fact, the licensing process and even the compact system itself are coming under attack from without as well as from within. In a move seen as an attempt to override safety rules in order to speed up the licensing process in North Carolina and other states, the Nuclear Regulatory Commission is considering policy changes that would allow it to overrule state standards that are higher than the federal government's, or to have sites privately owned rather than state-owned as is the current law; critics in North Carolina also fear that the Southeast Compact or the waste generators could use these new rules to challenge a siting decision not to their liking (*N&O* 12/13/94, p. 3A). A Supreme Court ruling in 1992 (*New York v. the United States*) also relieves the states of the legal obligation to accept the wastes of utility companies and thus of the necessity to remain in compacts, and some citizens continue to hope that this siting process will be abandoned on that basis. The affected counties in North Carolina will almost certainly renew their lawsuits, earlier ruled by the courts to be premature because the Authority's siting decision had not been made (*N&O* 12/9/93, p. 20A). And the public and the press continue to be skeptical of the legitimacy and fairness of the whole process.

"Not in My Back Yard"

This is not an unusual story. The siting of a low-level radioactive waste facility in North Carolina is a classic example of what has become a common occurrence: intense, focused, negative public reaction either prevents a decision about the location of a locally unwelcome facility or makes the process so acrimonious that the eventual decision has little legitimacy. The apparent inevitability of these failures has been called "environmental gridlock" by a New Jersey state official (Chess and Hance 12). More generally it is seen as part of a "crisis of confidence" in American political institutions (Fiorino, "Citizen Participation" 228), a threat to the "social contract through which citizens consent to be governed" (Laird 544).

This phenomenon has acquired a name, NIMBY, or "not in my back yard." As environmental law scholar Dennis Brion notes, "NIMBY has become a major theme in our political discourse" (xii). To understand better the nature and cause of the political impasse that NIMBY responses represent, in this essay we will examine the debates and decision mechanisms as communication processes. Using the North Carolina Low-Level Radioactive Waste decision as a case in point, we will bring to bear a rhetorical perspective that has as its central concern the ways in which communication structures the relationship between communities. Here we are particularly interested in the assumptions about communication that are revealed in the actions and discussions of decision makers, in this case the Authority. The duration, expense, visibility, and representativeness of the North Carolina case can make it a useful one for examining the contribution that a rhetorical perspective can make.

The NIMBY problem has elicited countermeasures on the part of decision makers to minimize the chance for gridlocked decisions, and these provide a focus for our inquiry. These measures are mostly procedural, since, as Chess and Hance note, communities "may object as strongly to the decisionmaking process as to the risk itself" (14). Such measures generally seek to enhance and encourage public participation in the decision process. Hence, we will focus on the rule-making process of the Authority and on the specific provisions it developed for involving the public, as two key places where the decision process is defined and worked out and where assumptions about the nature of communication and the role of the public come to the surface. Our material comes from minutes of Authority meetings, memos and reports to and from the Authority, memos to Authority members from the executive director ("Informatives"), and firsthand observations of several public meetings. These materials reveal the attitudes and assumptions of the Authority and its committees as captured in the style and content of its discourse.[3]

The broader context within which we will examine the processes of public participation in decision making is what has come to be known as "risk communication." Risk communication is an enterprise that includes not only communication about hazards within the context of decision making, but also community right-to-know programs about toxics used and stored by local industry,[4] and health and natural hazards safety campaigns.[5] In all of these situations, communication takes place between parties who have different (usually much different) knowledge about the risk and different degrees of access to power; the parties are often characterized as "experts" on the one hand and citizens, laypeople, or the general public on the other. In decision-making contexts, risk communication developed as an attempt to overcome these differences by "correcting" the public's "risk perceptions" so that they would better match the "risk analyses" made by the experts. The public's perceptions of risk are generally understood to be subjective, mistaken, emotional, and even irrational, whereas expert assessments are based on facts, knowledge, probabilities, and calculations. In this conception, then, experts engage in risk communication to inform and educate the public, to improve and correct their perceptions, and to persuade them to change their behavior.[6]

The difficulties that risk communication is designed to combat have appeared in other regional compacts created by the federal Low-Level Radio-active Waste Policy Act, as well as in North Carolina. According to a 1992 General Accounting Office report, most of the nine regional compacts are encountering "public opposition, legal challenges and uncertainty over is-sues such as liability protection." In Nebraska, for example, the host state for the Central Compact, a referendum in the community chosen for the site rejected it by a vote of 90 percent; in California, host state for a four-state compact, lawsuits and environmental concerns have delayed site selec-tion, and the waste contractor has sued the state over the delays; in Illinois a volunteer community was chosen to host a facility but an independent commission rejected the site because of groundwater and political con-cerns. In the past, the difficulties have led to retaliatory measures between the compacts, such as when the Southeastern Compact sought to prevent Nebraska from using the Barnwell facility (*N&O* 2/25/93, p. B7). And the failure of other compacts to site their facilities has added to the fears of some North Carolinians that their facility will become a national reposi-tory for radioactive fuel through emergency dumping authority of the Nu-clear Regulatory Commission (*N&O* 12/19/92, p. 12A).

NIMBY responses are not restricted to low-level radioactive waste, of course. They have become common for a wide variety of "locally un-wanted land uses," or LULUs; these include not only waste disposal facili-ties but also other high-tech facilities (manufacturing plants, transporta-tion centers, and the like), as well as social-service facilities collectively known as "halfway houses" (group homes for the mentally or physically disabled, AIDS residences and hospices, prerelease facilities for prisoners, etc.). Waste disposal facilities, however, present particularly difficult siting problems, since the dangers being imposed on a community or a neighbor-hood derive from *waste,* which by definition is what nobody wants; such facilities make neighbors think they are being treated like waste as well.

Brion's account of the NIMBY phenomenon helps put the North Caro-lina low-level radioactive waste case in perspective by indicating the depth and tenacity of the impasse that it represents. He takes the position that the LULU facilities are socially necessary (often, if not always) but also that the opposition to them is a justified response to inequities in the decision pro-cess; he suggests that the intransigence, anger, and shrillness that develop in NIMBY groups are a clue that more is at work than ignorance and selfishness. One inequity is that the political dimension of the process is "captured" by interest groups with economic and political influence (waste facilities are never proposed near country clubs), with the result that the government role in siting decisions almost always is to favor the devel-oper (although this phenomenon has been called "ecoracism," it might better be thought of as a form of "classism"). Another inequity is the asym-

metrical distribution of goods and harms: disposing of radioactive waste
(for example) is a general social good for all those who have benefited from
the use of radioactive material (through medical procedures, power production, scientific research, and the like, as well as those employed in producing and processing it); however, disposing of such waste is a localized
harm, disturbing only a small set of what Brion calls "Neighbors." As
Brion puts it, the Neighbors "provide a direct though hidden economic
subsidy to the LULU operation" (164).

Measures that have been used to counter or prevent NIMBY responses
have had limited success. These measures include opportunities for public
participation in the decision process, as noted earlier, as well as careful
attention to siting criteria, equitable selection of decision makers on
boards and commissions, and a general emphasis on procedural accountability. Specific measures for encouraging and enhancing public participation, such as public hearings, referendum initiatives, surveys, negotiated
rule making, and citizen review panels, have had some success in some
instances (Fiorino, "Citizen Participation").[7] However, public hearings,
which are perhaps the most common form of public participation, may be
the most ineffective and alienating (Kasperson 280); they are often dominated by organized economic interests and give little voice to neighbors
and risk bearers (Fiorino, "Citizen Participation"). We will suggest that
new forms of public participation need to be based on a rhetorical understanding of the communicative processes at work.

The Public Participation Plan in North Carolina

Public participation is nowhere required in the federal Low-Level Radioactive Waste Policy Act,[8] but the state legislation, the North Carolina Low-
Level Radioactive Waste Management Authority Act of 1987, does address this issue in several ways (N.C. General Statutes Sec. 104G, amended
1989). It establishes a policy "of negotiation and arbitration between the
Authority . . . and a committee representing the affected local govern-
ment(s) to assure that . . . the legitimate concerns of nearby residents and
affected municipalities can be expressed in a public forum, negotiated and,
if need be, arbitrated with the Authority in a fair manner and reduced to a
written document that is legally binding" (Sec. 104G-4). Any arbitration
was to be conducted by the Governor's Waste Management Board (Sec.
104G-21), established in 1981 to ensure a uniform system for managing
hazardous waste and low-level radioactive waste (Sec. 143B-285.10).[9]
One of the major duties of the board was "to promote public education
and public involvement in the decision making process for the siting and
permitting of proposed waste management facilities" (Sec. 143B-285.13).

The North Carolina legislation also requires the Authority to develop procedures and criteria for selecting a site, procedures that are to be "developed with, and provide for, public participation" (Sec. 104G-9).[10] Forms of participation that are specified include public information meetings in all areas that meet minimum site qualifications (Sec. 104G-9), "site designation review committees" (SDRCs) established by county commissioners in each county in which there is a site selected for detailed characterization (Sec. 104G-19), and a "preferred site local advisory committee" established in the county in which the final site is located (Sec. 104G-20); among the duties of this committee is "promoting public education, information, and participation in the licensing process." By the time the site was selected, the Authority had held over 350 public meetings. In addition, as a government body, the Authority was required to conduct all its official business in open meetings.

To begin to fulfill its legal mandate to inform and include the public in the decision-making process, the External Relations Committee of the Authority in January 1988 took the unusual step of organizing a private forum consisting of 35 members representing business groups, citizens, and the Authority. This group, known as the Public Participation Planning Group (PPPG), was to hold five sessions by 1 May with a consulting mediator, the Dispute Settlement Center. Their charge was to develop and approve unanimously a public participation plan (PPP) that could be passed on to the External Relations Committee, and then to the full Authority for final approval.

But the process of formulating a plan for public participation was beset by rancorous disagreement stemming from conflicts of interest. While members representing citizens favored substantial public involvement in the decision-making process of the Authority, members representing nuclear power, the N.C. Department of Administration, and the N.C. Citizens for Business and Industry saw parts of the plan as giving away to the public some of the legal responsibilities of the Authority (*N&O* 5/17/88, p. 3C). In the final meeting of the PPPG on 25 April 1988, the eight members representing the latter groups voted against those parts of the plan they objected to, scuttling any chance for consensus and effectively killing the draft proposal. On 5 May, the Dispute Settlement Center evaluated and submitted a plan to the External Relations Committee for resolving the conflict, and offered its services toward that end (report of Dispute Settlement Center, 5 May 1988). But the time allotted to the PPPG to make its decision had elapsed. With the planning group unable to reach a consensus, the External Relations Committee voted to "go ahead with a draft plan without receiving formal recommendations" from the PPPG (*N&O* 5/17/88, p. 3C), relying on the report by the Dispute Settlement Center and information on public participation plans in other states trying to site similar facilities (External Relations Committee minutes, 5/16/88, p. 2).

While the Authority was struggling to develop its PPP, technical and procedural decisions were being made at a rapid pace, dictated by legislative deadlines and the Authority's own schedule. Citizens continued to express their dismay that they weren't being notified of important decisions and requested greater involvement in the process (Technical Committee minutes, 4/14–15/88). In the meeting of the full Authority on 16 May 1988, members discussed the concerns of various environmental groups, concerns "that the work completed under the public participation planning process will not be incorporated by the Authority . . . that opportunities for public participation are missed every day that the Authority delays implementing a public participation plan" (Authority minutes, 5/16/88, p. 1). By July of 1988, with a draft plan for public participation only then being considered by the Authority, some environmental groups publicly decided to "drop out" of any formal decision-making process established by the Authority, despite assurances by the chair of the Authority that their views were represented in the draft (N&O 7/11/88, p. 16C).

To respond to the public's demand for more involvement in the Authority's deliberations and assure them that their views would be represented, the External Relations Committee on 11 July also approved a recommendation to seat three additional citizen members from the public, environmental, or other interest groups on three of the standing committees (excluding the Executive Committee), raising the total from five to eight members each. But this proposal was actually a pared-down version of an earlier one recommending the addition of four members from the public; apparently, some on the Authority feared "diluting" the decision-making ability of the five appointed members. There was also a question whether the additional members would have the right to vote, as well as questions concerning who would sit on the committees and how they would be selected (N&O 7/19/88, p. 3C). Although the proposal was initially hailed by some environmental groups as a breakthrough (N&O 7/13/88, p. B4), the expanded committees were to operate on a six-month trial basis only. And although the new members were granted the right to vote, nominations were to be approved by the full Authority based on information concerning "qualifications, interests, and availability" (Authority minutes, 8/9/88, p. 2).

The Authority knew from a 1988 report by the Southeast Compact Commission that "an effort to find a site for a waste dump would fail without a major public relations effort" (N&O 7/11/91, p. B1). On 1 June 1988, it hired a director of public information and rule coordinator, Chrystal Stowe. On 18 July, she presented to the full Authority the final draft of a public participation plan, as well as a plan for a proposal evaluation committee that would select the main contractor for the facility. This committee was to contain "two representatives of public interest groups, one each designated by the League of Women Voters and the Radioactive Waste Roundtable; two representatives of the business groups designated by the North Carolina Citizens for Business and Industry, including one generator of low-level radioactive waste; and one representative of local government," plus one member from each of the Authority's standing committees (Authority minutes, 7/18/88, p. 2). The Authority approved both the PPP and the Proposal Evaluation Committee. But again, there was concern about the members to be selected, as expressed at the August meeting of the Technical Committee: "it was suggested that the Authority carefully consider the qualifications of public participants as 'experts' " (Technical Committee minutes, 8/15/88, p. 2). After Chem-Nuclear was selected as the primary contractor, that company developed and spent one third of its initial research budget on a public information and involvement program (Authority minutes, 11/8/89, p. 3), which Stowe coordinated with that of the Authority.

The elaborate process we have described through which the Authority developed, approved, and implemented the PPP, as well as the additional measures taken by the Authority and Chem-Nuclear to involve the public, did not allay public concerns, as evidenced by newspaper reports and minutes of both the Authority and the county site designation review committees; opponents and citizens continued to decry the lack of information, notification, and public involvement in the decision-making process (Authority minutes, 11/15/88; Chatham County SDRC minutes, 12/12/90, 8/15/91).[11] Yet Raymond Murray, chairman of the Authority, continually expressed satisfaction with the public information efforts; in 1989, for example, he reported at an Authority meeting that "he was pleased with the community forums and responses he was receiving concerning these public meetings" (Authority minutes, 2/20/89, p. 2). To understand these conflicting assessments better, we will now examine the Authority's Public Participation Program in some detail.

The most recent report on the Authority's Public Participation Program includes the following description:

Since its inception in 1987, the North Carolina Low-Level Waste Management Authority has emphasized and encouraged public participation in all of its activities. A program to inform, educate, and solicit input and involvement from citizens has been actively under way. The objectives of the program include:

- Providing complete and accurate information about low-level radioactive waste, the site selection process and all related issues.
- Creating opportunities for the public to ask questions, provide comments and otherwise participate in all stages of the Authority's process.

• Using information and input provided by the public to contribute to the decision making process. ("North Carolina Low-Level Radioactive Waste Management Authority Public Participation Program," 1/6/93, p. 1)

Public participation is justified, according to this report, "for both philosophic and pragmatic reasons. A central philosophic reason is that the public's views ought to be sought before important government decisions are made. A central pragmatic reason is that, with public participation, the decisions in many instance will be both technically better and publicly more acceptable." The report claims that these considerations led the Authority to support public participation "beyond requirements mandated by law" (p. 5).

In addition to the public representation on committees and mandated public hearings, other efforts in the PPP were organized into four areas of effort, as follows:

Community outreach. Mass mailings, a mobile information resource center (a van outfitted for communication with the general public), traveling exhibits, a speakers bureau, open Authority and committee meetings, open houses in various counties, an "information campaign targeting school children" of educational packets on radioactivity for grades 4 through high school (External Relations Committee minutes, 4/17/89, p. 2).

Public response. Involvement in the Wake, Chatham, and Richmond SDRCs, written summaries of public comments and responses, a toll-free information line, answers to every written correspondence, the distribution of reports, impact statements, etc., and other documents free of charge.[12]

Media relations. Public transcripts of meetings; news releases in newspapers and on radio, public service announcements, briefings for state and local officials and others, including "background articles, media information kits, talk show interviews, and photo opportunities" (*PPP*, 1/6/93, p. 13).

Informational materials. An "Authority pocket folder with six fact sheets," a regularly issued newsletter, "brochures, slide presentations, viewgraphs, videotapes, and technical reports" in libraries across the state (p. 14).

By 1991, the *News and Observer* reported that the public relations effort of the Authority and its primary contractor, Chem-Nuclear, had already cost $2 million in state money (7/7/91, p. C1). By September 1993, at the height of the Authority's decision-making process, the total spent by the Authority through Chem-Nuclear and its subcontractors on public information alone since 1989 was $3,504,525 (table 2, *October 1993 Quarterly Review for July, August, and September 1993,* Chem Nuclear, Inc.).[13]

But despite the best intentions of the Authority, the massive amount of material generated, and the enormous sums of money spent, this huge effort was judged by those to whom it was addressed as a failure. These attempts at communication were obviously ineffective in creating the informed consensus the Authority had hoped for. In examining the PPP itself, public commentary about it, and relevant Authority minutes, we find four themes that summarize the Authority's official approach to communication with the public, themes that are characteristic of risk communication. These themes are, first, the Authority's complete control of the process, agenda, and rules; second, its faith in the power of information and education; third, its restricted understanding of communication; and, fourth, the seeming contempt for the public that results from all of the above. We illustrate these themes in detail below, in the belief that they can help account for the communication and decision-making failures in siting the North Carolina facility.

Control

The Authority's control took two forms: statutory control granted to the Authority as a government agency, and ideological control of language and values vested in the siting process by the belief in the efficacy of science and technology to solve all problems. As a government unit, the Authority is both constrained by and empowered by the processes encoded in the administrative procedures that govern the activities of all state bodies in North Carolina. One of these processes is the making of rules. Through its rule making, the Authority established criteria and procedures not only for site selection but for all of its functions.[14] The rule-making process, designed to regularize and formalize official power and ensure its accountability, also has the effect of enhancing official control. In addition, the administrative procedures governing business meetings and public hearings of all state government bodies grant similar power.

Several points to be noted here may underlie the public's belief that it lacked real political involvement, even when it was represented on committees. The first, and most general, was that the rule-making process is controlled by the appointed regulatory officials. The officials, in this case those of the Authority, set the agenda to which the public had to respond. They also decided when the public spoke, and when they just listened. And it was officials who evaluated the success of the communication process; for example, the External Relations Committee was instructed (somewhat tautologically) to "evaluate the Public Participation Program to determine how well the program is meeting the objectives of the Public Participation Plan" (Authority minutes 1/9/89, p. 2).

We also note the fact that the Authority, based on statutory procedure, allowed the public only a few "input points" in its decision process, and that the effect of that input was limited by other factors, such as the delayed release of technical reports and the explanatory documents that were legally to accompany these reports.[15] Public comment was in a sense excluded, a point not lost on citizens, who questioned "how meaningful public comment would be after the fact" (Chatham County SDRC minutes, 2/27/91, p. 2).

In fact, agendas for Authority subcommittee meetings show that public comment was almost invariably asked for at the end of meetings, after the "official business" was concluded; the implicit message to the public was that their comments were not part of the official business of the Authority. As one citizen later noted in a letter to the editor regarding a "public" meeting she had attended, "What a farce! After sitting through three hours of Chem-Nuclear's plans and promises, the Authority voted unanimously to approve all of the requests with very few questions. Only then, after all the voting was complete, did they take public comment" (N&O 12/27/94, p. 8A). In addition, public comments concerning rule changes or decisions were summarized (i.e., reconstructed) in response documents for the Authority by the staff. Although the practice of summarizing was started in response to a citizen's complaint that "her comments were not included in the revised proposal" (Authority minutes, 6/20–21/88, p. 2), the procedure had the unfortunate but inevitable effect of homogenizing and sanitizing public response by representing it in the language of the officials (see *Summary of Comments from March 21–23 Public Hearings and Recommended Response*, 1988). Finally, we observe that the public's concerns were often dismissed either by relegating them to nonlegally binding explanatory documents, or by citing relevant legislation under which those concerns were already covered.

Given the Authority's nearly complete control over the rule-making process, the central issue for the public became both the quantity and the quality of influence they could have in the decision-making process—not only *how much* input they were allowed in the process, but *how well* their comments were reflected and used by the Authority. While we don't have the space here to analyze this aspect of the process in detail, we wish to note that the quality of input is complicated and controlled by the highly scientific and technical nature of the issues, and by the degree of uncertainty surrounding technologies such as low-level radioactive waste management. The problem of the quality of public contribution was exacerbated early on, for example, when in a discussion of comments that had been received on "siting procedures and criteria," one member of the Authority strongly suggested that "future challenges . . . should be based on the technical language of a specific promulgated regulation and not on the interpretive layman's language which it includes"; this motion was supported by Chairman Murray (12/7/87, p. 2). The motion in effect invalidated the language of the explanatory documents intended expressly for public consumption and required the public to use technical language. The effect of the motion was to codify and "rank" language according to the official classification of documents and to put the public in a classic double bind. The import of such motions was not lost on the public. In a joint meeting of the Technical and External Relations Committees discussion touched on the public's awareness of and concern for how clear siting rules and procedures were, for what was included and excluded by classifications and language, and for how public impact was limited by whether their own language was appropriate for "rules formatting" (Joint Technical and External Relations Committee minutes, 1/11/88, p. 2).

The Authority's control of the decision-making process, inscribed in the law enabling the Authority and extended on ideological grounds by strict adherence to technical criteria and its own rules, was carried forward in all the Authority's attitudes and actions. For example, when the Technical Committee discussed the participation process for the original request for proposals from contractors, "It was agreed that since the Authority, not the public, will select the site operator, the public needed to feel confident in the selection process and needed to feel they had input into it" (Technical Committee minutes, 3/30/88, p. 1). In this view, the public does not participate but merely accepts. For another example, in an early meeting of the External Relations Committee, "Discussion focused on the concept of 'oversight' by the public over the Authority and a sharing of the decision making functions. It was noted by several members that the legislation governing the Authority does not allow for these concepts and therefore should not be incorporated into the public participation plan" (Authority minutes, 4/15/88, p. 1); the Authority's control, in other words, should not be ceded to the public. And in a letter dated 25 September 1992 to the Richmond SDRC, John MacMillan, executive director of the Authority, said: "If the SDRC is interested in presentations, workshops, seminars or discussion of current activities of the Authority and its contractors, we will consider written requests identifying the topics of interest. . . . We would expect such meetings to be conducted in an orderly and professional manner, with law enforcement officers present to maintain order, if necessary" (attachment to Informative #47, 10/1/92). The latter reveals not only an emphasis on order, but the ultimate extent of the power of a government body to enforce its mandate. The issue of control and the degree of public input was of course also a factor in the battle over the release of technical data. While trying to ensure quality control, the Authority maintained control over more than the quality of the data. The Authority essentially restricted the amount and kind of information the public had access to based on a set of assumptions about the nature of the issue being deliberated, the qualifications of the public, and the communication that was necessary to guarantee success.

Information and Education

The theme of control is very much related to the belief in the power of information and education to "correct" public opinion and thus resolve the siting controversy. From the start, the Authority believed that its program of information and education, the stated goal of the PPP, would be entirely adequate to dealing with the public. The sheer volume of informational materials produced and media employed in the PPP catalogued above is a sad testimony to the persistence of this faith in information and education.

The terms "information" and "education" seemed to be foundational ones for the Authority. They appeared in the report on the Public Participation Program submitted by the Dispute Settlement Center, which predated and informed that of the Authority. They were contained in the first objective of Chem-Nuclear's Public Information and Involvement Plan (Project Work Plan, 7/15/91). And they were central to the Authority's understanding of the goals of public participation: "to inform and educate the public on issues to be decided and the options for addressing them and to seek information from the public on resolving the issues" (PPP, 1/6/93, p. 9). Thus, in discussing the connection between the public forums and the choice of a couple of sites, the chair of the External Relations Committee "concluded that there are three things the committee needs to do: *explain* the process, *explain* the siting criteria and *explain* when the next announcement will be made" (External Relations Committee minutes, 4/17/89, p. 2; emphasis ours).

The Authority's optimistic belief that scientific data understood rationally will correct misperception was reflected in many of its documents and statements. In the conclusion of the PPP, for example, Stowe said, "It is vitally important that the Authority reach the larger, less vocal segment of the community with complete, accurate information. . . . An ongoing program of public participation is critical for educating the public if fears are to be minimized and acceptance is to be gained" (1/6/93, p. 20). Faith in the role of information also led the Authority to view any refusal to accept its version of the facts as unreasonable and improper. For example, the public's view was often characterized as a "misconception" (Authority minutes, 4/17/89, p. 3; Technical Committee minutes 3/13/91, p. 2), opposition to "educational materials" from Chem-Nuclear was dismissively characterized as "initial negative public reaction" (Informative #19, 3/14/91, p. 2), statements by the Chatham SDRC were "at least partially inaccurate and . . . wholly misleading" (Murray to chairman of Chatham County Board of Commissioners, 1/4/91, p. 3, attached to Mac-Millan Informative #16, 1/8/91). Thus, citizen opposition was regarded as "outside interferences" (Authority minutes 4/17/89, p. 3), lawsuits were a "distraction" (Authority minutes, 4/24/91, p. 1) and resulted in "management distractions" (MacMillan to Senator Richard Conder, 1/23/92, p. 3, attached to Authority minutes, 1/24/92), and other contingencies were characterized as "unexpected," "interruptions," "surprises" (Informative #8, 9/19/90, p. 2). For the Authority, disagreement on an issue "should not preclude the orderly exchange of information which provides a factual basis for . . . deliberations" (MacMillan to Richmond County SDRC, 9/25/92, attached to Informative #47, 10/1/92).

In the Authority's belief in "information," we see an example of the general assumption of scientific culture that facts are objective and autonomous and that social problems can be solved by acquiring more facts (rather than by agreeing on values).[16] In its belief in "education," we see the patronizing assumption, implicit in much risk communication, that NIMBY responses result from the public's ignorance of facts. It thus becomes the task of decision makers to provide the facts and to correct the "misperceptions" of the public. When understood under these assumptions, "public participation" is reduced to passive reception on the part of the public and can easily become a public relations campaign on the part of authorities.

Assumptions about Communication

Given the Authority's understanding of public participation as a highly controlled process of information exchange, it is worth focusing more closely on the assumptions about communication that are built into its processes and activities. In many places the importance of "two-way" communication was emphasized. For example, Stowe's 1993 report claimed that "The Authority sees public participation as a two-way process: to inform and educate the public on issues to be decided and the options for addressing them and to seek information from the public on resolving the issues" (9). We find a similar claim in a report from Chem-Nuclear's director of communications and community relations: "From the outset, Chem-Nuclear has stressed that effective communication is a two-way process in which listening is important and where meaningful communications are fostered only in an open atmosphere among well-informed parties. . . . Throughout our communications efforts, we will continue to strive to build great public understanding about this project. We believe this is essential" ("Statement of Gail Rosenberg, Director, Communications and Community Relations, Chem-Nuclear Systems, before the Low-Level Radioactive Waste Management Authority External Relations Committee," 7/30/91, p. 1).

The Authority's interest in dialogue has an interesting twist, however, which is illustrated in the following incident. In a letter responding to a request by the Richmond County Site Designation Review Committee, MacMillan said, "In the public information and business activities of the Authority, we have found that large public meetings are not a very effective forum for answering questions or having a meaningful exchange of information. Our experience has shown us that it is more productive to meet in small group settings to ensure that questions are responded to individually, with opportunity for dialogue. Therefore, I would not recommend that the Authority accept your request for a question and answer meeting" (attachment to Informative #58, 5/15/93). In his account of this exchange to the Authority, MacMillan added: "While declining to participate in a mass meeting, I did want to offer a constructive alternate to those who have a genuine interest in obtaining further information. I did not offer any participation by Authority members, rather working to treat this as our extension of our public information program" (Informative #58). While MacMillan's objection to a large public meeting agrees with Kasperson's claim that they are not effective, we also see here a constrained understanding of two-way communication: the Authority is taking the SDRC's suggestion for a face-to-face dialogue and transforming it into a controlled situation. For the Authority, communication may be a two-way process, but it occurs on one-way streets.[17]

In forums and situations that it selects and controls, the Authority *receives* comments, and through its public information program it *disseminates* information; in essence, the Authority and the public did not participate in the same communication process.[18] As already noted, public comment at open meetings was reserved for the very end, after the Authority had conducted its business. Furthermore, it was not necessary for members of the Authority to be present at public hearings: in one Informative before a public hearing on a proposed rules change, MacMillan suggested that "It is not necessary for Authority members to attend, but you are certainly welcome" (Informative #52, 2/12/93, p. 2). That only a few members did attend sparked criticism by citizens there, who saw it as a sign that the Authority didn't really care what the public had to say.

The language used by the Authority to discuss communication is also telling. The conclusion to Stowe's status report (attached to Informative #9, 9/26/90) reads: "It is clear that a great deal of public information has been disseminated and a large number of opportunities have been provided

for public input and involvement, above and beyond the statutory requirements. . . . Fairness dictates that the entire community that may host the
facility be given a chance to hear both sides of the debate and to understand
the real risks. . . . An ongoing program of public participation is critical for
educating the public if fears are to be minimized and acceptance is to be
gained." Early in the process, the Authority asked the League of Women
Voters to "develop a program of public education about low-level radioactive waste disposal issues and relay public comment back to the Authority
on a continuing and timely basis" (Authority minutes, 11/2/87, p. 3). In
these examples, especially in terms like "disseminate," "relay," even "hear
both sides," we again see a reliance on a common understanding of communication as a passive process of information transfer.

This understanding of communication, which we will call an "engineering" model, is based on Shannon and Weaver's model of information transfer developed at Bell Labs in 1948. It consists of a sender, a receiver, a
channel, a message, noise, and a feedback loop. This model has become
canonical in the fields of mass communication and communication psychology. From there it has been adopted widely by those studying and
practicing risk communication (Conn and Feimer; Covello et al.; Keeney
and von Winterfeldt; Renn; U.S. National Research Council).[19] All models, of course, are representations that serve certain ends and obscure others. The engineering model helps us to identify the parts of a communication situation and ask questions about or find alternatives for the various
components (who is the receiver? what channels are available—direct
mail, public hearings, news releases?). But in conceiving of communication
as a message that is transmitted in a channel to a receiver, it fails to explain
why the message sometimes isn't believed, even when it is clearly received.
In conceiving of messages as information, it fails to explain how different
versions of apparently identical information have different effects.[20] In conceiving of the audience's work as "receiving" information (adding it to a
database), it fails to explain effects on attitudes, emotions, and values,
which can only be "noise" in the system.[21]

Contempt for the Public

The engineering model of communication also fails to account for the role
of the public's emotions in North Carolina's attempt to site the low-level
radioactive waste facility and for that of the Authority's equally emotional
reactions. Although emotions are not obvious dimensions of bureaucratic
proceedings, one predominant tone in much of the Authority's interaction
with the public seems to have been contempt. The Authority communicated contempt by not showing up at rules hearings, by treating the PPP as
separate from the Authority's official business, by insisting on retaining

control, by refusing genuine dialogue. In fact, the engineering model of communication, as well as the elements of political control and the belief in information and education already discussed, can be understood to lead, almost inevitably, to contempt for the public.

Members of the Authority also occasionally communicated contempt in public statements. For example, Stowe responded to a letter in the *Chapel Hill Herald* by questioning the rationality of the opponents of the Authority: "The unreasonable fears of a few remain an obstacle to a rational understanding and awareness of effective, safe low-level waste solutions. That's the real scam" (attached to Informative #43, 6/19/92). Contempt was most clearly revealed in an offhand statement made by a member of the Authority at a public hearing in February 1993: "The more you give them, the more they misunderstand." This spontaneous statement is perhaps more indicative of the Authority's true attitudes about the public's ability to understand and engage in dialogue than are the cautious and diplomatic statements in the PPP. In these cases, the basis for contempt may be a belief that the Authority, by virtue of its scientific and political prowess, its technical criteria and legal rules, had the only solution to the problem necessary to consider.

Contempt for public participation was also communicated in repeated temptations to invoke temporary rules that would bypass the public comment period to meet deadlines, an entirely legal process, but one the public would suspect to be a loophole in law.[22] One Technical Committee report advised, "mechanisms are available to permit us to move ahead on the basis of temporary rules. We believe that if we do our homework properly and touch the necessary bases these procedures will not cause undue delay" (attached to Authority minutes, 11/2/87, p. 1). On 23 November 1987, the Technical Committee again thought "it may be necessary to utilize the Temporary Rules provision . . . to both meet the site rules deadline of May 1, 1988 and to allow adequate time for public meetings and evaluation of public inputs" (3). On 11 January 1988, the Authority encountered the problem of holding public hearings and also meeting a deadline for publication of rules, "leaving little time to review the comments and modify the rules. . . . While the comments received from the public hearings were important and should be considered, [the Chairman] expressed the hope that this could be accomplished within the existing time frame" (3). In these examples we see that the Authority was concerned about meeting its legal obligations regarding public participation, but we also see that schedules and other technical matters have priority.

We do not mean to suggest by our critique of the Authority's emotional reaction that all emotions are illegitimate in decision-making contexts, although this is the position that most discussions of risk communication take. Indeed, emotional reaction is sometimes a more appropriate and reasonable response than logic.[23] For example, in several quotations we have seen fear cast as irrational, something opposed and dispelled by the assurance of scientific facts and logical argument.[24] But the central problem with risky technology is that there is no scientific certainty, only probability. Fear is a psychologically natural and arguably justifiable response to risk that no amount of statistical data or probable argument can rationalize away. Fear is necessary for survival. When "Neighbors" are faced with the threat of risky technology and scientific uncertainty made all the more suspect by politics, fear may be a more reasonable response to the siting of a waste facility than scientific rationality.

Our critique supports the view that emotions, like values, are an integral part of decision making insofar as they inform human perception, understanding, and communication; emotions motivate and underlie all human knowledge and behavior, and thus any attempt to ignore, suppress, or exclude them in the decision-making process can result only in misunderstanding between parties to the decision. The engineering model of communication used by the Authority suppresses and excludes emotions and values, which are unmeasurable and to some extent unpredictable. Ironically, the result is the creation of contempt which, if not embodied in procedures, is communicated by them. Government and industry officials may need to recognize the legitimacy of the public's emotional reaction as an indicator of reasonable concern about and understanding of risk rather than regard it as an irrational reaction to a controlled situation. What we may need, then, is a model of communication that takes into account the role of emotions and values of all parties involved in decision-making processes.

Conclusion: Toward a Rhetorical Model of Risk Communication

The themes of control, information and education, one-way communication, and contempt that characterize the public participation in the North Carolina siting controversy also characterize most conceptions of risk communication broadly understood. We believe, therefore, that it is the underlying philosophy of communication, including assumptions about the relationship between language and knowledge embedded in it, that must finally be examined. Further research should examine the assumptions that underlie the arguments and strategies of NIMBY groups themselves, particularly whether they rely on the same or different philosophies of communication.

Most conceptions of risk communication embed a distinction between *informing* and *influencing,* a distinction implicit within the Authority's faith in information and education and explicit in the authoritative treatment by the National Research Council's Committee on Risk Perception and Communication. This distinction makes *informing* the basic communication function, which helps recipients understand and act "appropriately," and *influencing* a function that goes "beyond pure information," possibly into deception (U.S. National Research Council 82). The discussion by the NRC reveals a good deal of nervousness about the role of influence, admitting to some confusion about when and for whom influence is an acceptable goal and concluding that "no explicit guidelines can be drawn defining which techniques are appropriate or inappropriate in particular situations or for particular message sources" (87). The NRC lists the following "influence techniques" that do not necessarily "do violence to the truth" (and also can be used for informing): highlighting facts, framing information and decisions, persuasive use of facts, appeals to authority, and appeals to emotion (82–85). And the NRC did decide that "informing is always an appropriate goal . . . and that deception is never appropriate" (88).

The NRC's discussion of *influencing* suggests that an entirely different philosophy of communication would be helpful for understanding what risk communication should be doing. Appeals to authority and emotion and persuasive use and shaping of facts are canonical parts of the rhetorical tradition, but to our knowledge the risk communication literature has never made this connection.[25] The rhetorical model is not a linear schematic diagram of communication components, like the engineering model, but a conceptual approach that examines the suasory dimensions of language and its use in particular situations.[26] It cannot produce predictive rules, but rather evolves heuristic guidelines; it attends to the concrete details of situated practice as much as (or more than) to abstract theory. It sees influencing as the fundamental communicative relationship, not informing, because information is never pure but always comes shaped, selected, and intended in some way. It thus recognizes the important role that values and affect play in all aspects of a decision, and at its best attempts to use these in helpful and legitimate ways to achieve consensus and cooperation to further both immediate ends and those of society at large.

The rhetorical approach also assumes that the relationships among rhetor, audience, language, situation, history, and intentions are complex, themselves situated and historical, rather than discrete, objective, and measurable. It assumes that what is unsaid and what is implied are just as important as the overt "messages" in information transfer and can serve as indications to the values, relationships, attitudes, and historical trajectories of the parties to communication. Therefore, its preferred methodology is "criticism"—the detailed analysis of texts or events in order to learn what worked and why—rather than surveys, interviews, or experiments of the type that the engineering model leads to.

One issue of some concern to risk communication specialists illustrates the differences between these two approaches to communication. That issue is trust—or the lack of trust in institutions and officials by the public that leads inexorably to the NIMBY response; and it is the inverse of trust, "official contempt" for the public, that causes the public, in turn, to mistrust officials and institutions. Given that most risk communication researchers agree that trust is important in the reception of a message, they are left with a dilemma, because, as Keeney and von Winterfeldt point out, "while we have a fairly good idea about how to increase the chances of losing trust and credibility, our tools for restoring them are feeble" (423); the only tools they can suggest are honesty and openness. Similarly, the NRC includes a rather detailed list of how credibility is lost (having a reputation for deceit, for example, or contradicting past statements, 119–24) but no advice about how to regain it.[27]

In the rhetorical tradition, this issue is represented in the concept of *ethos,* the contribution that the character of the communicator makes to persuasion. In fact, Aristotle notes that ethos may be the "controlling factor in persuasion" (Aristotle, *On Rhetoric* 1.2.5). He suggests that there are three aspects of character that make a speaker persuasive: wisdom, virtue, and goodwill; for, he says, through wisdom we trust speakers to form opinions rightly, through virtue we trust them to be honest about those opinions, and through goodwill we trust them to give us the best advice based on their opinions; therefore, he concludes, "a person seeming to have all these qualities is necessarily persuasive to the hearers" (2.1.5). Now this is no formula for successful risk communication, but it does bring into play an entirely different perspective on the "sender" or "message source" and the way that authority can be effectively deployed. It suggests that risk communicators will (and should) fail to gain the trust of their audience if through lack of goodwill they do not have the best interests of that audience in mind—and that those best interests can be judged (and will be judged) only by the audience itself.

The rhetorical approach to risk communication that we advocate is compatible with the alternative proposed by Daniel Fiorino as a "democratic" model, based on recent issues in democratic theory. He compares the two versions of risk communication with two versions of democracy, elitist and participatory. Elite democracy places more emphasis on representation than on participation, with experts acting for citizens, maintaining stability, and applying specialized knowledge. Participatory democracy emphasizes process more than results, with participating citizens gaining not only results but satisfaction and investment from their engagement in decision making. Elitist democracy produces technical approaches to risk analysis and one-way models of risk communication. But, arguing that "the lay public are not fools," Fiorino sketches a model of risk communication that "accepts the legitimacy of lay judgments and the social and political values they reflect" ("Technical and Democratic Values" 294). That such an approach is not merely a figment of democratic idealism is suggested by the fact that three successful siting cases discussed in the risk communication literature did have extensive and innovative forms of public participation and enacted a truly dialogic and interactive sort of consensus building (see Harris; Lynn).

These two philosophies of communication—the engineering approach and the rhetorical—as well as the two approaches to democracy, are rooted in two different traditions of thought. Each one encourages us to ask different questions about communication, to understand our roles in it differently, to set different goals. They persuade us to understand communication itself differently. For this reason, we can say that each one has a different rhetoric—the closed rhetoric of authority, control, precision, associated with the power of science and technology and the cultural belief that these are the only valid methods of knowing and doing, versus the open-ended rhetoric of participation, engagement, ambiguity, associated with the ideals of democracy and the cultural belief that a plurality of perspectives and methods is probably necessary to arrive at the best decision. This essay thus presupposes a certain flexibility in the concept of rhetoric, such that it can constitute a specific philosophy of communication, as well as apply to the underlying assumptions and implications about which any theory of philosophy tends to persuade us while obscuring or ignoring others.[28] Such flexibility, or productive ambiguity, in rhetoric is one of the most important differences between the engineering approach to communication and the rhetorical one.

In the case we have examined, the Authority operates very consciously and conscientiously within a set of assumptions about decision making, participation, and communication, assumptions that are based on a one-way, asymmetric, elitist communication process, that is, the engineering model. It also operates within a set of related unconscious assumptions about the nature of science, knowledge, and rationality, assumptions that are deeply embedded in Western culture itself. We conclude that these assumptions, encoded in the legislation and procedures of the Authority, may in fact guarantee the Authority's failure. What is missing from public participation programs and from risk communication in general is an underlying conception of decision making as egalitarian, interactive, and truly dialogic, and of communication and consensus making as rhetorical processes, that is, as historically situated, persuasive, and open-ended. The philosophy of communication we advocate, based on equal participation, partnership, and mutual respect, is as much an ideal as the engineering model. We are under no illusion that trust can be manufactured on demand or that equal participation will prevent controversy. But we think this philosophy holds more promise than the ones currently dominating public decision making.

NOTES

We wish to thank our research assistant, Shawn P. Walsh, who many times went beyond the call of normal duty in tracking down the pieces of the story we tell. We are also indebted to Sara Voorhees, Information Officer of the North Carolina Low-Level Radioactive Waste Management Authority, for her cooperation in supplying us with reams of primary documents and in spending time explaining them to us, and to the Wake, Chatham, and Richmond Site Designation Review Committees for their minutes. Finally, we are grateful for support provided by North Carolina State University's College of Humanities and Social Sciences Organized Research Program, which helped make the research possible.

1.   Quoted in the Raleigh *News and Observer*, 12/9/93, p. 20A. Much of the background information in this essay was originally reported in this newspaper, the major daily paper in eastern North Carolina. Subsequent references will be given parenthetically as *N&O* with the date and page.

2.   This was in a report, known as the Epley Report, prepared in 1989 for Chem-Nuclear (the major contractor for the Authority) by a public relations consultant at a cost of over $21,000. It assessed political opposition from local and county officials, delegations to the state legislature, and environmental groups, as well as news organizations (*N&O* 7/7/91; *North Carolina Independent* 8/5/92).

3.   Although the minutes represent a reconstruction of discussions, they do capture some of the spontaneous interaction of events that were not staged for the public; they were written by information officers hired by the Authority, and thus, we believe, accurately represent the views and attitudes of the Authority as a political institution.

4.   Title III of the Superfund Amendments and Reauthorization Act (SARA) of 1986 requires industries to provide information on hazardous substances to local planning and emergency bodies, which then are responsible for communicating to the public. The requirements, inspired in large part by the Bhopal accident, have not worked well (Hadden; Rich et al.).

5.   There are several versions of the functions of risk communication. On the basis of an extensive literature review, Covello et al. list "information and education, behavior change and protective action, disaster warnings and emergency information, and joint problem solving and conflict resolution." Keeney and von

Winterfeldt give a similar list but also include improving the understanding (by government regulators) of public values and concerns (421). Fisher's overview of risk communication work within the Society for Risk Analysis adds some more politically realistic goals, including "damage control," overcoming opposition to decisions, and citizen empowerment (174).

6.   The versions of risk communication we describe here are similar to what Craig Waddell calls the "technocratic" and "one-way Jeffersonian" models of risk communication (this volume). As will become apparent in our analysis, Waddell is much more confident than we are that these models have been supplanted by more democratic understandings of what risk communication should be.

7.   In a study of the national siting process for high-level radioactive waste, Kraft notes that the failure of the federal government to site even the first of two repositories was at least partly due to "unclear guidelines" Congress gave to the Department of Energy on public participation and the ineffectiveness of the participation mechanisms that were used: "the public hearing procedure . . . led to the classic NIMBY response" (268). Kraft believes that we need to invent new forms of democratic participation to "reinvigorate the polity and citizens' involvement with it" (277).

8.   The Code of Federal Regulations provides only that state or tribal governments may participate in the licensing process of a "near-surface disposal facility" that affects their interests and that proposals for such participation must include a description of "plans to facilitate local government and citizen participation" (10 CFR 61.72). The Southeast Interstate Compact Agreement itself (Sec. 223 of USC 2021d), which establishes the Southeast Compact Commission, defines its powers, duties, and funding, and provides for the selection of a "host state," makes no specific provisions regarding the siting process.

9.   The Governor's Waste Management Board was disbanded in 1993.

10.   This wording is exactly the same as that in the companion legislation for hazardous waste management in North Carolina (General Statutes Sec. 130B), passed in 1989. Interestingly, the original version of the hazardous waste bill read: "The procedures and criteria shall be developed through public participation." We think this difference is significant; it seems to exclude the public from direct involvement in the decision-making process.

11.   The Authority itself criticized Chem-Nuclear's Public Involvement Plan, saying it "should focus more effort on their educational outreach program," and urged Chem-Nuclear to develop a more detailed plan for the next quarter (Authority minutes, 1/30/91).

12.   The Authority eventually implemented a copying charge policy to defray expenses, which the SDRCs claimed as a hardship and fought (Chatham County SDRC minutes, 1/23/91, 7/18/91).

13.   This figure did not include some of the Authority's separate expenditures, such as for the many community forums held around the state before and after Chem-Nuclear was hired, public meetings on rule changes and site selection, or the salaries and travel expenses, etc., of its staff, which fall under general operating budget. Sara Voorhees, information officer for the Authority, estimated that the $3

million plus figure above represents perhaps 80 percent of the money total spent on public relations by the Authority. An accurate total is not available.

14. The Authority first drafted its rules in 1988 and amended them once, in 1993. The process was based on the administrative procedures but also went beyond these requirements. Public input was sought in public meetings, a first draft was published in the *NC Register,* and there was a thirty-day public comment period during which public hearings were held to receive comments. After the comment period, the Authority held its official hearing (open to the public but not to public comment) in which the rules were discussed and adopted. Finally, the rules were forwarded to the state Rules Review Commission for approval and publication in the Administrative Code (N.C. Administrative Procedures Act, G.S. Sec. 150B-21.2).

15. Any time a rule is proposed or changed it must be explained in a "justification document" (Authority rule .0201). The difference between the "rule format" and the justification document is that the former is in technical language and is legally binding, while the latter is an explanation for lawmakers and the public. The justification is made available to the public after the rule is adopted. Early on, the chair of the External Relations Committee "wanted clarification as to why the rules did not resemble the justification document. Dr. Murray [Authority chair] explained that the rules format did not allow for the inclusion of some of the discussion that was contained in the draft justification document which made the justification document even more important in the process" (Authority minutes, 1/21/88, p. 2). Another concern was when the justification document becomes available. One member expressed concern that "the justification document . . . be available when the rules become effective. His concern was that the draft document be available at the time the rules are published in the State Register and that the public be made aware of this" (1/21/88, p. 4). They never were.

16. A particularly nice example of this occurs in a letter to the Chatham County Board of Commissioners from MacMillan, disputing reports that the board had received about the Wake-Chatham site. MacMillan says that the report "contains some conclusions that are simply not well grounded in the facts or consistent with local rigor. . . . Our attitude toward these reports is that they ought to be confirmed or refuted empirically, and we are anxious to do so. . . . Once we have done that, the regulators may assess the effect, if any, on site licensability. But, simply put, facts are needed to determine licensability" (1/4/91, attached to Informative #16, 1/8/91, p. 3). We do not mean to imply that empirical data are not necessary in cases like these, but we want to highlight MacMillan's total avoidance of the social values involved in licensing decisions.

17. The Authority's notion of dialogue is not unlike Plato's notion of dialectic, where one party (the teacher) has the truth, to which he leads the other party (cf. Rowland and Womack 16–17; Katz 46–47).

18. Interestingly, the Authority was frustrated by having to merely receive public opinion without commenting on it, according to Sara Voorhees, so in the preferred site selection meeting, the Authority set aside time to ask questions of each speaker. This procedure still did not allow for real dialogue. In fact, real dialogue is

probably not practical in the kind of large public hearings that the Authority found itself conducting.

19. Michael Reddy has noted that the language we use to talk about language and communication embeds this model, which he calls the "conduit metaphor."

20. For example, from the U.S. National Research Council: "Saying that cigarette smoking causes emphysema conveys the same information with or without an accompanying film of an end-stage emphysema patient, but with the film the message will have a different effect" (85).

21. This model underlies the first three of Waddell's risk communication models (this volume). Kasperson and Stallen provide a critique of the engineering model that is compatible with ours but offer no alternative, as we do below.

22. The North Carolina Administrative Procedures Act, General Statutes Sec. 150B-21.1. The temporary rules provision specifies the use of temporary rules only under extraordinary conditions; it doesn't totally eliminate the public comment period on a rule but delays it and allows the agency to act. Before the rule becomes permanent the normal rule-making processes must be followed.

23. Roland and Womack emphasize that Aristotle's analysis of the emotions in the *Rhetoric* makes them rational, or potentially rational, since they have a cognitive dimension and are capable of being influenced by reason. Waddell has also argued that rhetorical *pathos* should be recognized as playing a legitimate role in technological decision making.

24. In fact, the dichotomy between rationality and irrationality itself may be a false one insofar as notions of rationality and irrationality are political, historical, and social constructions. As the French philosopher Michel Foucault suggests, notions of "reason and folly," of "truth or falsehood," constitute rules of inclusion and exclusion that are institutionalized by political, legal, cultural, and aesthetic criteria which then determine the categories within which human thought and speech can or cannot operate; these prohibitions establish and limit the categories (such as rationality and irrationality) which are then used by those in power to arrive at, evaluate, and promulgate decisions. This is no less the case with the low-level radioactive waste siting in North Carolina (see Katz 58–59).

25. In their hope for a "science" of risk communication, which is a wistful undercurrent throughout the NRC volume and a refrain in other places, risk researchers have drawn on social-scientific approaches to communication (mass communication and communication psychology, as indicated above) and ignored the possible contributions of the humanities. In our view, risk researchers have committed an error Aristotle warned against, in his observation that "it is the mark of the trained mind never to expect more precision in the treatment of any subject than the nature of that subject permits" (*Nicomachean Ethics*). Communication scholars have begun to bridge the gap from their end; Waddell's "social constructionist model," for example, is similar to what we call the rhetorical approach to risk communication; Rowan also asserts the value of a rhetorical approach, but she draws primarily upon contemporary social science research in communication.

26. Our outline here is indebted only in part to Aristotle, representing, we think, a synthesis of contemporary thinking in the "epistemic" tradition. Epistemic

rhetoric assumes that language does not so much reflect thought and social reality as shape them. For a discussion of the relation between Aristotelian and epistemic rhetoric and a critique of both in regard to this low-level radioactive waste siting controversy, see Katz.

27. See also Renn and Levine, who review the "relevant psychological and sociological research on trust and credibility in communication" but conclude that it cannot provide solutions to the problems, in the sense of "recipes or fool-proof guidelines for dealing with the public." "The major finding of all the experiments and surveys conducted so far is that individuals as well as social units make use of a complex variety of internal and external cues to process messages and that the variation of one or two factors may only lead to marginal changes in the outcome. . . . [It is] difficult to create a communicative environment that guarantees the desired persuasive effect" (212).

28. One of us (Miller) has made this point in connection with another case study, of decision science, which resembles this one in some respects.

WORKS CITED

Aristotle. *Nicomachean Ethics.* Trans. J. A. K. Thompson. New York: Penguin, 1955.

Aristotle. *On Rhetoric: A Theory of Civic Discourse.* Trans. George A. Kennedy. New York: Oxford UP, 1991.

Brion, Dennis J. *Essential Industry and the NIMBY Phenomenon.* New York: Quorum, 1991.

Chess, Caron, and Billie Jo Hance. "Opening Doors: Making Risk Communication Agency Reality." *Environment* 31.5 (1989): 11–15, 38–39.

Conn, W. David, and Nickolaus R. Feimer. "Communicating with the Public on Environmental Risk: Integrating Research and Policy." *Environmental Professional* 7 (1985): 39–47.

Covello, Vincent T.; Detlof von Winterfeldt; and Paul Slovic. "Risk Communication: A Review of the Literature." *Risk Abstracts* 3 (1986): 171–82.

Fiorino, Daniel J. "Citizen Participation and Environmental Risk: A Survey of Institutional Mechanisms." *Science, Technology, and Human Values* 15.2 (1990): 226–43.

Fiorino, Daniel J. "Technical and Democratic Values in Risk Analysis." *Risk Analysis* 9.3 (1989): 293–99.

Fisher, Ann. "Risk Communication Challenges." *Risk Analysis* 11.2 (1991): 173–79.

Foucault, Michel. "The Discourse on Language." *The Archaeology of Knowledge.* Trans. A. M. Sheridan Smith. New York: Pantheon, 1972. 215–37.

Hadden, Susan G. "Institutional Barriers to Risk Communication." *Risk Analysis* 9.3 (1989): 301–8.

Harris, W. E. "Siting a Hazardous Waste Facility: A Success Story in Retrospect." *Risk Analysis* 13.1 (1993): 3–4.

Kasperson, Roger E. "Six Propositions for Public Participation and Their Relevance for Risk Communication." *Risk Analysis* 6 (1986): 275–81.

Kasperson, Roger E., and Pieter Jan M. Stallen. "Risk Communication: The Evolution of Attempts." In *Communicating Risks to the Public,* ed. Roger E. Kasperson and Pieter Jan M. Stallen. Dordrecht: Kluwer, 1991. 1–12.

Katz, Steven B. "Aristotle's Rhetoric, Hitler's Program, and the Ideological Problem of Praxis, Power, and Professional Discourse." *Journal of Business and Technical Communication* 7 (1993): 37–62.

Keeney, Ralph L., and Detlof von Winterfeldt. "Improving Risk Communication." *Risk Analysis* 6.4 (1986): 417–24.

Kraft, Michael E. "Evaluating Technology through Public Participation: The Nuclear Waste Disposal Controversy." In *Technology and Politics,* ed. Michael E. Kraft and Norman J. Vig. Durham, NC: Duke UP, 1988. 253–77.

Laird, Frank N. "The Decline of Deference: The Political Context of Risk Communication." *Risk Analysis* 9.4 (1989): 543–50.

Lynn, Frances M. "Citizen Involvement in Hazardous Waste Sites: Two North Carolina Success Stories." *Environmental Impact Assessment Review* 7 (1987): 347–61.

Miller, Carolyn R. "The Rhetoric of Decision Science." In *The Rhetorical Turn: Invention and Persuasion in the Conduct of Inquiry,* ed. Herbert W. Simons. Chicago: U of Chicago P, 1990. 162–84.

Miller, Edgar M. "Too Hot to Handle: Where to Put Radioactive Waste." *Environmental Politics: Lessons from the Grassroots.* Ed. Bob Hall. Durham, NC: Institute for Southern Studies, 1988. 48–55.

Reddy, Michael J. "The Conduit Metaphor: A Case of Frame Conflict in Our Language about Language." In *Metaphor and Thought,* ed. Andrew Ortony. Cambridge: Cambridge UP, 1979. 284–324.

Renn, Ortwin. "Risk Communication: Toward a Rational Discourse with the Public." *Journal of Hazardous Materials* 29 (1992): 465–519.

Renn, Ortwin, and Debra Levine. "Credibility and Trust in Risk Communication." In *Communicating Risks to the Public,* ed. Roger E. Kasperson and Pieter Jan M. Stallen. Dordrecht: Kluwer, 1991. 175–218.

Rich, Richard C.; W. David Conn; and William L. Owens. "Strategies for Effective Risk Communication under SARA Title III: Perspectives from Research and Practice." *Environmental Professional* 14 (1992): 220–27.

Rowan, Katherine E. "The Technical and Democratic Approaches to Risk Situations: Their Appeal, Limitations, and Rhetorical Alternative." *Argumentation* 11 (1994): 391–409.

Rowland, Robert C., and Deanna F. Womack. "Aristotle's View of Ethical Rhetoric." *Rhetoric Society Quarterly* 15 (1985): 13–31.

U.S. National Research Council. *Improving Risk Communication.* Washington, DC: National Academy P, 1989.

Waddell, Craig. "The Role of *Pathos* in the Decision-Making Process: A Study in the Rhetoric of Science Policy." *Quarterly Journal of Speech* 76 (1990): 381–400.

CHAPTER 5

Saving the Great Lakes

Public Participation in Environmental Policy

CRAIG WADDELL

A central concern in discussions about science policy in general and environmental policy in particular has been the role of the public in communicating risks and adjudicating environmental and science policy disputes (see, for example, Barke; Goggin; Goldhaber; Killingsworth and Palmer; Morone and Woodhouse; U.S. National Research Council; and Petersen). According to Petersen, "Citizen participation is nearly synonymous with democracy" (3); and Goldhaber suggests that "How to construct new forms of democracy that would allow us some influence over all the decisions that affect us is one of the daunting challenges of our time" (126). Although numerous models of public participation are possible, four are especially pertinent to the current discussion.

1. *The technocratic model.* Under this model, technical decisions are left to "experts" in science, engineering, industry, and government, and no appropriate role is defined for public participation or oversight. This model generally assumes that experts, deliberating among themselves, have reached or will reach consensus. We need only look to Eastern Europe and the former Soviet Union to see the potentially devastating consequences of this centralized approach. At the end of the Communist era, 65 percent of Poland's river water was so polluted that it could not be used even for industrial purposes, and one in seventeen deaths in Hungary was attributable to air pollution (French 5, 23).[1]

As Robert Oppenheimer said in the 1954 security clearance hearing that was brought on by his opposition to the development of the hydrogen bomb, some of our decisions both involve complicated technical information and have important moral and human consequences. There is danger, Oppenheimer went on to say, in making such decisions in secret "not because the people who took the decisions were not wise, but because the very need, the very absence of criticism and discussion tended to corrode the decision making process" (U.S. AEC 229–30).

2. *The one-way Jeffersonian model.* In an 1820 letter to William Charles Jarvis, Thomas Jefferson wrote, "I know of no safe depository of the ultimate powers of the society but the people themselves; and if we think them not enlightened enough to exercise their control with a wholesome discretion, the remedy is not to take it from them, but to inform their discretion by education" (278). One implication of this Jeffersonian vision of democracy for risk communication and environmental and science policy formation is that the public has a right to participate in decisions that affect its well-being and/or that of the larger ecosystem, but that it should be empowered to do so, simply and unproblematically, through a one-way transfer of expert knowledge. As Lin Chary said, speaking at the public discussion session of the International Joint Commission's Sixth Biennial Meeting on Great Lakes Water Quality, "I have heard more than once during these meetings the suggestion from government and industry officials that if they could just educate us, we'd understand" (IJC Transcript 211).

3. *The interactive Jeffersonian model.* In its 1989 report *Improving Risk Communication,* the National Research Council rejects the one-way Jeffersonian model in favor of a two-way, interactive model of risk communication, a model that might be considered a more charitable interpretation of the Jeffersonian vision of democracy. Under this model, technical experts communicate their expertise to the public, and the public communicates its values, beliefs, and emotions to technical experts. Thus, while the public adjusts to expert knowledge, experts adjust to public sentiments.

4. *The social constructionist model.* This model expands upon the interactive Jeffersonian model by acknowledging that the values, beliefs, and emotions of experts in science, engineering, industry, and government also play a significant part in risk communication and environmental policy formation. Furthermore, technical information also flows in both directions; thus, the distinction between "expert" and "public" begins to blur, as does the distinction between audience and rhetor. Under this model, risk communication is not a process whereby values, beliefs, and emotions are communicated only from the public and technical information is communicated only from technical experts. Instead, it is an interactive exchange of information during which *all participants* also communicate, appeal to, and engage values, beliefs, and emotions. Through this process, public policy decisions are socially constructed.

One example of this fourth model—at least in terms of the two-way transfer of technical information—can be found in the 1992 United Nations Conference on Environment and Development (UNCED) in Rio de

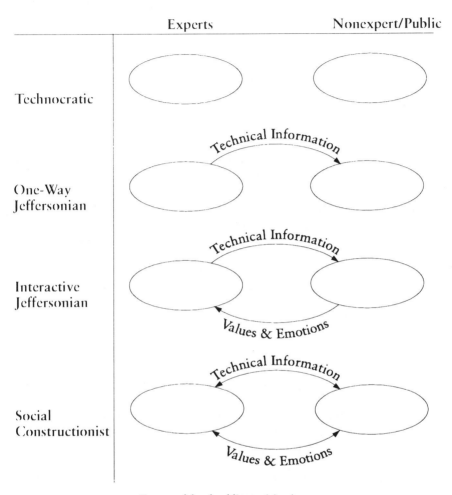

Four models of public participation

Janeiro. Here for the first time in a major U.N. conference, nongovernmental organizations (NGOs) played a major role as *generators* of information, rather than simply as disseminators of information that had been developed by others (Carpeling-Alakijah). Another example is *Toxic Wastes and Race in the United States,* a 1987 report by the United Church of Christ's Commission for Racial Justice. In his preface to this report, Benjamin Chavis, the commission's executive director, notes that "involvement in this type of research is a departure from our traditional protest methodology. However, if we are to advance our struggle in the future, it will depend largely on the availability of timely and reliable information" (Chavis x).

The interactive Jeffersonian model, as promoted by the National Research Council, is the current progressive paradigm for risk communication. That is, this model is offered as a progressive alternative to the one-way Jeffersonian model. However, the interactive Jeffersonian model is flawed at the outset by its implicit paternalism: the values, beliefs, and emotions of the public cannot truly be considered legitimate until those of technical experts are also acknowledged. Hence, the interactive Jeffersonian model is already being displaced by the social constructionist model in that (1) the public is developing greater technical expertise, and this expertise is being asserted and recognized;[2] (2) there is growing recognition and acknowledgment of the roles the values, beliefs, and emotions of technical experts play in shaping science and environmental policy; and (3) members of the public are increasingly asserting an appropriate role for their own values, beliefs, and emotions. To some extent, our increased recognition of the subjective side of science—in part, a contribution of history, philosophy, sociology, and rhetoric of science—has legitimized the subjective aspects of public participation in environmental and science policy disputes.

Public Participation in the International Joint Commission's Great Lakes Water Quality Hearings

This study examines what effect, if any, public testimony at the International Joint Commission's Sixth Biennial Meeting on Great Lakes Water Quality (1991) had on the commission's *Sixth Biennial Report* to the Canadian and American governments. My study of this case was motivated by three interrelated questions: (1) Did provisions for public participation in the IJC's Sixth Biennial Meeting provide only for catharsis, or did they provide a genuine opportunity for the public to influence the IJC's policy recommendations?[3] (2) What roles did emotion and technical expertise play in shaping the IJC's policy recommendations? and (3) What roles did egocentric, homocentric, and ecocentric appeals play? My analysis focuses on a four-and-a-half-hour public discussion session, held near the end of the Sixth Biennial Meeting; on analysis of videotapes and a transcript of the public discussion session; on informal interviews with twelve of the forty-nine people who testified at the public discussion session; on formal interviews with five of the six commissioners (conducted six days after the release of their report);[4] and on a rhetorical analysis of the commission's *Sixth Biennial Report on Great Lakes Water Quality.*

The International Joint Commission (IJC) is a Canadian and American organization, established by the Boundary Waters Treaty of 1909. The three Canadian and three American commissioners are appointed by their respective heads of government. At the time of the 1991 Biennial Meeting on Great Lakes Water Quality, the Canadian commissioners were Davie Fulton (co-chair), Robert Welch, and Claude Lanthier; and the U.S. commissioners were Gordon Durnil (co-chair), Hilary Cleveland, and Robert Goodwin. The commission investigates and monitors boundary water disputes—especially those concerning water quantity and water quality—and advises the two governments of its nonbinding recommendations. Over the past eight decades, the IJC has become a model for the resolution of international disputes, as is evidenced, for example, by a contingent of Russian observers who attended the Sixth Biennial Meeting in Traverse City, Michigan.

With a human population of over 40 million people, the Great Lakes basin, the world's second-largest reservoir of fresh surface water,[5] is subjected to immense environmental stress. This stress is perhaps most graphically illustrated by Detroit's Rouge River and Cleveland's Cuyahoga River, both of which dump directly or indirectly into Lake Erie, the shallowest and most degraded of the Great Lakes. Colborn et al. describe the condition of Lake Erie in the mid-1960s:

By the mid-1960s, Lake Erie was characterized widely as dead or dying, overloaded by wastes from human activities that were only slightly less damaging in the other lakes. The spectacle of a burning river in 1969 symbolized the degradation, when oil and debris in Cleveland's Cuyahoga River caught fire. Commercial fisheries in Lake Erie and Lake St. Clair were closed because of high mercury content in fish tissues. Eggshell thinning and adult mortality in bird populations indicated that DDT . . . and other pesticides were having unexpected and severe effects on wildlife. (2–3)

Canada and the United States responded to this degradation with the Great Lakes Water Quality Agreement of 1972, through which the two countries affirmed their commitment to restore and maintain the integrity of the Great Lakes basin ecosystem. Perhaps the most significant feature of the original agreement was its schedule for reducing the amount of phosphorus discharged into the Great Lakes in order to minimize eutrophication problems.[6] Having met with considerable success in reducing phosphorus inputs, the agreement, as revised in 1978 and amended in 1987, now obliges Canada and the United States "to virtually eliminate the input of persistent toxic substances" into the Great Lakes and commits the two countries to the strategy of zero discharge of such substances as a principal means of achieving this goal (70).[7] For over two decades now, the Great Lakes Water Quality Agreement has been a major focus of the IJC's activities.

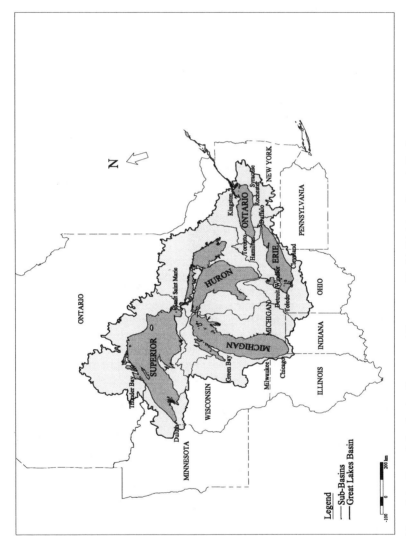

Map of the Great Lakes basin. Courtesy of Ecosystem Health Division, Ontario Region, Environment Canada.

The Boundary Waters Treaty, which established the IJC, requires that the IJC provide all interested parties with a "convenient opportunity to be heard" on matters under consideration (article 12). In including this provision in the treaty, the governments explicitly rejected the technocratic model of policy formation. However, which of the other three models the IJC does and *should* represent is open to interpretation.

In order to provide interested parties with a convenient opportunity to be heard, the IJC has, among other things, made its biennial meetings on Great Lakes water quality open to the public and has provided an opportunity for public testimony at these meetings. However, only since the Fifth Biennial Meeting in Hamilton, Ontario (1989), has there been significant public participation (Durnil 7). During the public discussion session at the Sixth Biennial Meeting, Lin Chary of Gary, Indiana, noted the limited opportunity for public participation during the Fourth Biennial Meeting in Toledo, Ohio (1987): "in order to ask a question, you had to write it down on a card and give it to somebody, and then they decided whether or not they would read your question" (248).[8] And Carol Sweinhart of Brighton, Michigan, who described herself as "a fairly long-time observer of the International Joint Commission and its processes," recalled when the biennial meetings were "a completely closed-door affair" (182). Since the 1989 meeting in Hamilton, however, public participation has increased, and Ms. Sweinhart was the first in a long series of speakers during the 1991 public discussion session to praise the commission for its respect for democratic processes and its efforts to protect the environment.

The Public Discussion Session

Environmental historian Samuel Hays has pointed out that "In our own day environmental affairs have evolved so that the expert thinks of the political context as one of 'us' and 'them,' of the knowledgeable and rational experts and the uninformed and emotional public" (9). The IJC's Sixth Biennial Meeting—which lasted from 29 September through 2 October 1991—provides a good example of such a conflict.[9] Early along in the meeting, a running commentary began on the distinction between the technical expertise of scientists and the emotions of the public. At a Zero Discharge Alliance demonstration immediately prior to the IJC's opening plenary session, a Greenpeace speaker, Jack Weinberg, said, "They [governments and industry] are out to get rid of this movement by saying that they're for science and we're for emotions. We're here to say that's not going to work." Commentary on the role of emotion was brought to a head during the 7–11:30 P.M. public discussion session on Tuesday, 1 October. During this session, the commissioners heard forty-nine speakers express their concerns about the Great Lakes basin ecosystem. I will summarize the comments of eight speakers who highlight the controversy about emotional appeals and who demonstrate that such appeals are used not only by the public, but also by technical experts.

Public testimony at the Sixth Biennial Meeting and my subsequent interviews with the commissioners suggest that at least some of the IJC's recommendations emerge from an interactive process that includes the five following stages: (1) folk epidemiology—possibly in conjunction with some preliminary scientific findings—alarms the public about a potential problem;[10] (2) public testimony on this problem is offered before the IJC; (3) the commissioners refer compelling issues to their various scientific advisory boards for investigation; (4) the scientific advisory boards confirm some of the public's concerns, leading the commissioners to be convinced (prepared to accept an idea intellectually), but not necessarily persuaded (committed to act on the basis of that idea); (5) on hearing further emotional appeals from the public on this issue, the commissioners become persuaded, but contend that public testimony only confirms what they already believe based on scientific evidence.

The first speaker in the public discussion session was Ira Markwood, a representative of the Illinois Section of the American Water Works Association. In 1986, the IJC's Water Quality Board had developed a working list of 362 chemical pollutants found in the water, sediment, and/or biota of the Great Lakes basin ecosystem; approximately half of these pollutants were synthetic chlorinated organic substances (*Sixth Biennial Report* 28–29). Fearing that growing public opposition to chlorine and chlorine-containing compounds might jeopardize efforts to disinfect drinking water and sewage, Mr. Markwood offered the following warning:

> If chlorine is no longer available for water treatment, we can expect major waterborne epidemics such as now are occurring in Peru, where out of a population of approximately 21,900,000, there have already been over 180,000 cases of cholera and more than 5,000 deaths. This epidemic is moving north. . . . Lack of chlorination of drinking water will result in a major reduction in population and in life expectancies in the area where chlorine and its disinfectant compounds are not available. . . . imagine the panic occurring from an epidemic such as cholera when death can result only hours after symptoms appear. (181–82)

The third speaker was Pamela Ortner-Mukavetz, a nurse who represented two grassroots environmental organizations from the suburban Detroit area (Clean Air Please and People United Against Incineration). Ms. Ortner-Mukavetz described the human health effects of toxic pollution and then read a letter to the commission from a woman whose eight-year-old son had been diagnosed with leukemia, a disease his mother believed was caused by environmental pollution. As Ms. Ortner-Mukavetz finished her statement, Chairman Durnil said, "as some of you attempt to tug at our emotions, there are others, including me, who have children similar to that situation you're talking about" (186). This statement triggered a running commentary on the role of emotion in the IJC's deliberations.[11]

Shortly after Ms. Ortner-Mukavetz's testimony, Robert Smerko, president of the Chlorine Institute, expressed his support for the goal of zero discharge of chlorine, but cautioned that "none of us can afford to be swayed by emotion from *any* angle" (195–96). After one intervening speaker, Mr. Smerko was followed by Ron Hohenstein, superintendent of environmental engineering for the Board of Water and Light in Lansing, Michigan. Mr. Hohenstein testified that "With the advent of chlorination of water supplies, such scourges as cholera, typhoid, diphtheria, bubonic plague, hepatitis, dysentery, or you name it, have been controlled, resulting in the saving of millions of lives" (199). He went on to implore the commissioners not to recommend banning the use of chlorine in water supply systems because "naturally evolved microbial life forms exist waiting to devastate vast numbers of human beings, now and into the future" (199). I do not want to diminish the concerns of the chlorine and waterworks representatives; however, I *do* want to point out that, despite Mr. Smerko's caution, emotional appeals were and are used not only by the public, but also by technical experts.[12]

As the hearing proceeded, speakers continued to employ emotional appeals and to comment on the appropriateness of such appeals. Bob Mondy, who identified himself as a Vietnam veteran, said:

all we really want to do is tug at your heart. As you said earlier, we're attempting to tug at your heart. Well, you better believe we are, because you're one of the best voices we have to tug at other hearts. If I don't get to your heart tonight, I hope somebody else in this room does, because we're not talking about fun and games. . . . We're tugging at your hearts because the facts don't seem to work. . . . I don't know what it takes to reach your hearts. I know I look at my seventeen nephews and nieces, and they get my heart real fast. I appreciate that you've got children, but I'm going to tug at your heart anyway, because I want to know that we've got your heart. I want to know that you're going to take a message from this group of people here forward for us that's strong enough that it implements serious action. (201)

Another speaker, Rob Taylor, a student from Toronto, said, "I know this is tugging at heart strings, but I think that's what we have to do, because going through brains doesn't work" (221).

Mr. Taylor was followed by Phyllis Gorski, a pharmacist from suburban Detroit and president of Parents Against Cancer Plus, an environmental health organization. After introducing herself, Ms. Gorski said, "Dr. Way-land Swain [vice president of Eco Logic, an environmental consulting firm] once said . . . that environmental problems are emotional, technological, and political, so we don't want to omit the emotional. . . . This is my emotional part" (221–22). She then proceeded to tell the story of her son David, who at age five was diagnosed with cancer, a disease Ms. Gorski believes was caused by environmental contaminants. She described eighteen months of painful chemotherapy, spinal taps, and bone marrow taps and how representatives of the local cemetery visited her home to ask if she wanted to buy a cemetery plot (221–22). She concluded by urging the IJC to involve more health professionals in the deliberative process (224).

Shortly after Ms. Gorski came testimony by Ann Hunt, from central Michigan, director of Citizens for Alternatives to Chemical Contamination, a regional grassroots group. Ms. Hunt said that those who attended the Workshop on Human Health Issues earlier that day "found out that as mothers of our children, we gave our daughters and our sons [voice breaking], excuse me, a tremendous load of toxic chemicals while we carried them in our wombs. We then compounded that when we breast fed them" (230, participant observation, and videotape). It is noteworthy that while Ms. Gorski felt obliged to justify her emotion and Ms. Hunt felt compelled to apologize for hers, the emotional appeals of technical experts passed without comment. At least three other speakers referred back to the issue of tugging at emotions or pulling at heartstrings (226, 228, 245); and Lin Chary of Great Lakes United complained that "we've been called emotional by industry, like that's an insult or something" (248).

General Influence of Public Testimony on the IJC's Recommendations

Early in the public discussion session, Carol Sweinhart, representing the League of Women Voters of Michigan, commended the IJC for its efforts to encourage public participation in the policy process and recommended that the commissioners take this process one step further by establishing a citizen advisory board. Chairman Durnil responded to this recommendation by saying that "you have no reason to presume that the advice we received from the [IJC's various scientific and technical advisory] Boards is any more likely to be taken than the advice we receive from you here tonight" (183). And Chairman Fulton closed the session by saying, "our next biennial report, I assure you, will also make clear what are the views that we have heard expressed tonight with such unanimity, such clarity, and such relevance; and they will be tied in with our recommendations that are made in that biennial report. I assure you they will be reflected"

(259). My interviews with the commissioners, however, suggest that the relationship between public testimony and the IJC's recommendations was somewhat complex: there was an acknowledged influence of public testimony on some recommendations, a displaced or delayed influence on other recommendations, and an unacknowledged influence on still other recommendations.

In my interviews with them, the commissioners reported that public testimony at the 1991 meeting *did* influence at least two of the thirteen recommendations in their *Sixth Biennial Report:* the weight-of-evidence and chlorine recommendations. Welch noted that "people were getting maybe a little impatient with further study. . . . and . . . we were attracted to the weight-of-evidence approach. That's fairly significant. And I think if you wanted a causal link [between public testimony at the Sixth Biennial Meeting and recommendations in the *Sixth Biennial Report*], you could find [it in] the seeming impatience with the endless debates" (Welch 13). Given that in some cases, "unequivocal evidence of injury to humans by persistent toxic substances may be difficult or impossible to obtain," the commissioners suggest in their *Sixth Biennial Report* that "At some point, the emerging mass of data and information must be accepted as sufficient to prompt or . . . ratify action against environmental contaminants" (21–22). Hence, they recommend that the governments "adopt and apply a weight-of-evidence approach to the identification and virtual elimination of persistent toxic substances" from the Great Lakes basin ecosystem (22). The commissioners also recommend that "the Parties [i.e., the Canadian and U.S. governments], in consultation with industry and other affected interests, develop timetables to sunset the use of chlorine and chlorine-containing compounds as industrial feedstocks and that the means of reducing or eliminating other uses be examined" (30).[13] Durnil indicated that "the chlorine [recommendation] was affected directly by what we heard from the public" (Durnil 16).

Cleveland pointed out that public testimony influenced not only what the commissioners recommended, but also what they *did not* recommend: "integrated monitoring *might* have been a recommendation in our *Sixth Biennial Report* . . . but nobody ever talked about it from the public. . . . So I guess we have to look at Traverse City from two ways: things that led to some of our recommendations, but *also* things that we decided *not* to recommend" (Cleveland 13).

The commissioners also commented on the influence of expert testimony from the public; for example, on Great Lakes United's report, "Broken Agreement: The Failure of the United States and Canada to Implement the Great Lakes Water Quality Agreement." Cleveland indicated that reading this report demonstrated to her that "a lot of the points of the [Great

Lakes Water Quality] Agreement have not been carried out" (Cleveland 19). Cleveland also indicated that her thinking had been influenced by reading *Great Lakes, Great Legacy?* (Colborn et al.), the report on a two-year study of the Great Lakes basin conducted by the Conservation Foundation and the Institute for Research on Public Policy (Cleveland 20).

Despite the acknowledged influence of public testimony, in their *Sixth Biennial Report* the commissioners say that the reports of their various scientific and technical advisory boards "provided the foundation for [their] conclusions and recommendations" (1).[14] And in my interviews with them, the commissioners indicated that prior to their 1991 Biennial Meeting, they had already anticipated much of what they would include in their report. Durnil, for example, said that "our planning for the meeting was geared to the things we thought we were moving toward putting in our report" (Durnil 9), and Cleveland said that prior to the Traverse City meeting, the commissioners "were already working on some of the recommendations that [they] made" in their *Sixth Biennial Report* (Cleveland 5).

In interviews, the commissioners suggested that public testimony primarily confirmed their prior conclusions. For example, Durnil said that public testimony "tends to be more reconfirming than it does give you original thoughts, because if you deal with it all year long, it's hard to hear something new, other than what the scientists are bringing you" (Durnil 11); and Welch said that "there was a lot of public *reinforcement* of the advice we were getting [from the IJC advisory boards]" (Welch 19). The commissioners also suggested that public testimony added political weight to their recommendations when they presented their report to their respective governments. Durnil noted that public reinforcement of the IJC's conclusions is "*important* because from a policy standpoint, from a realistic political standpoint, it gives more credibility to the report when it goes to a congressman or a senator, or whoever it goes to. . . . It's based on scientific input from a variety of sources . . . but also [on] the testimony of the public (Durnil 9).

Some of the commissioners' comments, however, suggest that public testimony may have helped to *shape*, rather than simply to *confirm*, more than the two recommendations I mentioned above. The commissions pointed out, for example, that (1) the structure of their 1991 meeting was strongly influenced by the public testimony that was given at the previous Biennial Meeting on Great Lakes Water Quality (Fulton 4); (2) their priorities and their instructions to their various advisory boards over the two intervening years had been influenced by this previous testimony (Fulton 2–4); and (3) public testimony given during the 1991 meeting would shape the priorities for and structure of their next biennial meeting, including, for example, the involvement of more health professionals (Durnil 38–41).

In describing the public discussion session in their *Sixth Biennial Report,* the commissioners say that "Many comments reiterated criticisms or suggestions made previously, while *many others provided fresh perspectives*" (51; my emphasis). Fulton said that during the 1989 Biennial Meeting in Hamilton, the public was unanimous in urging that the principles of the Great Lakes Water Quality Agreement be translated into effective and enforceable legislation (Fulton 4). According to Fulton, this was "something which we came to agree with, as a result of our own work, and as a result of the input from the public. So I would say . . . it had a considerable influence in shaping our work over the past two years and what went into our Biennial Report" (Fulton 4). Welch emphasized that one must "Keep in mind, too, that we're human and like to be seen as credible. . . . that's got to be seen as a very important matter, and that's why I think the Science Advisory Board and the Council of Great Lakes Research Managers are *tremendously* important to our operation" (Welch 19–20). Taken together, these comments suggest that in at least some cases, the commissioners pursued an issue on the basis of public testimony, sought the support of their scientific advisory boards before committing themselves, and then, having received such support, genuinely perceived subsequent comments on this issue from the public as simply confirming their scientifically based beliefs. Thus, although the commissioners have found it politically expedient to cite public support when presenting their recommendations to legislators, they have found it politically inexpedient to suggest that their recommendations *derive* from public (as opposed to scientific) testimony. As Killingsworth and Palmer have suggested, at times it may appear that the public has considerable influence on policy recommendations when, in fact, it has little (163–91); this study suggests that at other times it may appear that the public has little influence on policy recommendations when, in fact, its influence is considerable.

Influence of Emotional and Homocentric Appeals

Despite concerns about the role of emotion, public testimony was particularly effective when appropriate emotional appeals moved the commissioners from being convinced to being persuaded; that is, from intellectual acceptance of an idea to a commitment to act on the basis of that idea (cf. Perelman and Olbrechts-Tyteca 27).[15] For example, Fulton said that "where an emotional appeal tends to confirm the suffering . . . and the adverse effects of what's going on, it lends weight to the proposition that you must take action" (Fulton 8); Durnil characterized Phyllis Gorski's testimony about possible linkages between environmental contaminants and children's health as "very convincing" (Durnil 36); and Cleveland said that such testimony "struck me and made it seem very *necessary* to ban, or just sunset, some of these persistent toxics" (Cleveland 8). Cleveland went on to say that "a lot of [the public testimony] was information that I had . . . heard and read about before. But to see the people directly, in front of you, that were directly affected, there was an *emotional* impact. . . . that had a *tremendous* impact on me" (Cleveland 9). Public testimony was also important when it provided the commissioners with arguments that they could use to justify their recommendations. As Durnil pointed out, "it doesn't make sense to recommend things to governments that governments can't do, so you want to have realistic or actionable recommendations" (Durnil 31). He went on to say that the commissioners asked themselves, "What can we recommend to governments . . . that would be hard for them not to accept?" (Durnill 31).

In both of these respects, homocentric appeals (such as appeals to concerns about human health) were far more effective than ecocentric appeals (such as appeals for the protection of biodiversity as an end in itself) in providing an alternative to egocentric appeals (appeals to the vested interests of particular individuals, companies, or industries). As Carolyn Merchant points out, "A homocentric ethic underlies the social interest model of politics and the approach of environmental regulatory agencies that protect human health" (52). This seems to be the ethic the commissioners found most appropriate to their task. For example, Durnil indicated that "human health [was] a major priority" (Durnil 23); and Welch said that "we were apparently attaching even *more* importance to *human* health, and I put it that way because I'm sure human health considerations are always *important*" (Welch 13). Cleveland made the following observations:

the Human Health [Workshop] must have had three hundred people, and it was the biggest one. . . . I was very impressed by [arguments about human health], and that's why I think that our recommendations seem to stress the human health factors so much. . . . [Human health issues] seemed to be overriding. . . . It was largely human health that they talked about at that public meeting. Of course, they mentioned things like visibility and air pollution, but what it all came down to, really, was human health. I don't remember *another topic* other than the *bad* effects of pollution, one way or another, on human health. (Cleveland 16–17)

In fact, a number of speakers at the public discussion session expressed their concern about other species or about various ecosystems (islands, coastal areas, wetlands, etc.), but they generally did so without making specific, moving appeals. For example, David Stead, executive director of the Michigan Environmental Council, talked about preserving wetlands and maintaining biodiversity, but he offered no compelling reasons why we should do this; nor did he offer any examples of the suffering and destruction environmental contaminants were causing (206–7). As the commissioners say in their *Sixth Biennial Report,* studies of human health effects provide "rationale, incentive, and direction for public policy decisions" (7). The ecocentric appeals presented during the public discussion session often suggested direction for public policy decisions without providing an explicit rationale or incentive; they would have been more compelling had they done so. In my interview with him, Chairman Durnil said that "people *will* change their values if they know *why,* if they know the reason why they're doing it" (Durnil 39). He went on to offer the following critique of several recent television programs on the environment: "they went through this whole litany of things that people should be doing that would make the environment better. . . . But they never, ever, told them why. The *why* is what gets controversial, obviously" (Durnil 40).

Because of the prominence of human health concerns, Lanthier indicated that he had "strong reservations" about the wording of the following passage from page 18 of the *Sixth Biennial Report,* which is reproduced on the cover of the report: "Are humans and our environment in danger from persistent toxic substances now? Are future generations in danger? Based on a review of scientific studies and other recent information, we believe the answer to both questions is yes." Lanthier said, "I would have liked it better if [it had read] 'Are humans in danger,' and I wonder why *environment* was there. . . . if humans are not in danger, I don't care about the environment" (Lanthier 16–17; the context of the interview suggests that Lanthier may here be using *I* to mean people in general). He went on to say, "Let's not dilute with *environment. Environment* is a dilution [of] the danger" (Lanthier 18). Hence, he proposed the following alternative wording: "Are humans in danger from persistent toxic substances now? Are future generations in danger? Yes" (Lanthier 18); to which he added, "people will understand that. It's rendering the thing a little bit vulgar, maybe, but people understand more vulgarity than purity" (Lanthier 19). (Lanthier had earlier explained that he was using the word *vulgar* in its original sense to mean "obtainable by everyone," Lanthier 14.)

These observations about the effectiveness of emotional and homocentric appeals are subject to at least two qualifications. First, for both ethical and practical reasons, acknowledging an appropriate role for *some* emotional appeals should not be taken as licensing *any* emotional appeal. As Quintilian argued in his *Institutio oratoria:*

Too much insistence cannot be laid upon the point that no one can be said to speak appropriately who has not considered not merely what it is expedient, but also what it is becoming to say. . . . these two considerations generally go hand in hand.

For whatever is becoming is, as a rule, useful and there is nothing that does more to conciliate the good-will of the judge than the observance or to alienate it than the disregard of these considerations. Sometimes, however, the two are at variance. Now, whenever this occurs, expedience must yield to the demands of what is becoming. . . . the end which the orator must keep in view is not persuasion, but speaking well, since there are occasions when to persuade would be a blot upon his honour. (11.1.8–11)[16]

Perceived sincerity was one feature that the commissioners found persuasive. Welch, for example, said that those who spoke during the public discussion session were "very committed to this cause. There's . . . almost a missionary zeal. They really believe, and I think they do society a great service" (Welch 17); Fulton explicitly thanked one speaker "for the sincerity of [his] presentation" (Fulton 233); and Lanthier noted that the volunteers "are not animated . . . by any money or interest other than [our] better life; it *does* impress me" (Lanthier 10). Contrived emotional displays would have done more to discredit than to enhance the testimony of these speakers. However, acknowledging an appropriate role for emotional appeals in environmental policy disputes might sanction genuine expression of some emotions, particularly those emotions that evoke an empathic response.[17] In the absence of a social bias against such appeals, Ms. Gorski would not have felt compelled to justify her emotion, and Ms. Hunt would not have felt compelled to apologize for hers. Instead, they would have been free to feel their emotions without embarrassment and to express their emotions without commentary.

The second qualification to these observations about the effectiveness of emotional and homocentric appeals is that although homocentric appeals seem to have been more persuasive than ecocentric appeals, those who are concerned with the larger ecosystem may still find it prudent to couple or orchestrate ecocentric and homocentric appeals. Coupling homocentric and ecocentric appeals helps to bridge the gap between such appeals and, thus, makes ecocentric concerns more accessible to a larger audience.[18] Also, although in some cases an audience may be moved to address ecocentric concerns for homocentric reasons (e.g., to preserve a rain forest because it might harbor a cure for cancer), in other cases, homocentric appeals alone may be unable to move an audience to act in the interest of the larger ecosystem (there may, for example, be no compelling argument to be made for the human benefit of preserving some species or ecosystems). In anticipation of such cases, those who are concerned with the larger ecosystem would do well to cultivate ecocentric concerns even in situations when homocentric appeals may adequately address the issues at hand.

Several of the speakers during the public discussion session orchestrated homocentric and ecocentric appeals. For example, Bob Jones of the Northern Michigan Environmental Action Council appealed for protection of "the biological, botanical, scenic, recreational, historical, and economic resources of Great Lakes islands" on behalf of "all current and future inhabitants—human and otherwise—of the Great Lakes basin" (194). And Harold Stokes argued that "we need not only to be concerned with the health of people, but also the necessity of maintaining ecosystems that will sustain healthy life" (255).

Despite Lanthier's reservations, the commissioners did, in fact, orchestrate homocentric and ecocentric appeals. In the first paragraph of their *Sixth Biennial Report,* the commissioners argue that "urgent and continuing attention is needed by all sectors of society if it is to protect the environmental integrity of the ecosystem, which includes the humans who live within and depend upon it" (1). They go on to say that "Unless there is an increase in the extent to which environmental considerations are built into the process of values formation, and human behavior thus reflects those values, environmental progress will continue to be reactive in nature" (3).

Conclusions

The details of this case suggest that the IJC's deliberative process at least begins to approximate the social constructionist model of risk communication and environmental policy formation. This model is implicit in the IJC's *Sixth Biennial Report:* "we have undertaken a number of actions over the past two years to enhance two-way communication between the Commission and a variety of Great Lakes interests. . . . It is our aim not only to make information on Agreement progress and problems available to the public, but also to receive input to our deliberations" (54). Technical experts from the Chlorine Institute, the waterworks industry, and the IJC's various scientific advisory boards presented technical information to the IJC and to the public, but to some extent the public also presented technical information, both through public testimony and through documents such as *Great Lakes, Great Legacy?* (which the IJC's Water Quality Board and Great Lakes Science Advisory Board both refer to in their 1991 reports). In their *Sixth Biennial Report,* the commissioners note that over the twenty years since the Great Lakes Water Quality Agreement was signed, nongovernmental organizations working on Great Lakes issues

have grown considerably in their sophistication and ability to interact with other Great Lakes institutions, including governments and industry. Public consultation programs and reports produced over the past few years by these organizations have contributed greatly to the general awareness and understanding of Great Lakes issues and of the need for action. . . . the quality of research and action taken, and the level of interaction between and among all sectors of the Great Lakes Community, have been enhanced by the participation of these organizations. (11)

Clearly, members of the public conveyed their values, beliefs, and emotions to the commissioners. It should also be clear, however, that technical experts from the chlorine and waterworks industries also engaged in emotional appeals. Finally, it should be clear from some of the comments I have quoted (e.g., those of Durnil, Fulton, and Cleveland) that the commissioners' values, beliefs, and emotions were also engaged. If they were not, the public's expression of values, beliefs, and emotions would have been to no avail. To be sure, there is room for the development of greater technical expertise by the public, for greater recognition of the role emotions and values play in expert testimony, and for greater acceptance of an appropriate role for emotions and values in public testimony. Nevertheless, this case presents, at least in incipient form, all the defining features of the social constructionist model.

If the social constructionist model takes root, it should have significant implications for the expansion of democratic governance and the decentralization of political power. Hence, I propose this model both as a description of emerging public practice and as a prescription for enhancing public participation in environmental and science policy disputes. Paradoxically, however, the emergence of this model reinforces rather than displaces the spirit of the Jeffersonian vision of democracy. As the commissioners note in their *Sixth Biennial Report:*

An important element in the strategy to deal with persistent toxic substances, and Agreement requirements and environmental values generally, is education. . . . Effective environmental education is central to any effort to create a sustainable environment for future generations. When we speak of environmental education, we mean a process not confined to reciting facts and transmitting information, but one that helps people develop critical thinking skills and motivates them to seek the best decisions and actions for themselves and society. (36)

The social constructionist model calls for a public that is "enlightened enough to exercise [its] control with a wholesome discretion." And the education that must inform that discretion is not only technical, but also rhetorical.

Epilogue

Even before the IJC's *Sixth Biennial Report* was published, the chlorine recommendation—one of the two recommendations that commissioners acknowledged had been influenced by public testimony—was the subject of intense controversy. In my interview with him, Commissioner Durnil indicated that prior to the release of the *Sixth Biennial Report* the commission received "extensive submissions from the Chlorine Institute" (Durnil 11). According to Frank Bevacqua, the IJC's public information officer, of all of the recommendations the IJC has ever made, "few seem to have reverberated as strongly in both countries" as the chlorine recommendation (1). Drawn primarily by this recommendation, industry representatives comprised 300 of the approximately 1,900 participants in the IJC's Seventh Biennial Meeting on Great Lakes Water Quality—held in October 1993 in Windsor, Ontario—nearly a tenfold increase over industry representation at the Sixth Biennial Meeting (Bevacqua 1).

Discussion of the chlorine recommendation dominated the Seventh Biennial Meeting. However, despite the strong opposition from industry, the IJC confirmed its support for this recommendation in its 1994 *Seventh Biennial Report on Great Lakes Water Quality:* "The Commission formally emphasizes and confirms the recommendations of its *Fifth* and *Sixth Biennial Reports on Great Lakes Water Quality*" (46). By 1994, only one of the commissioners (Lanthier) who drafted the *Sixth Biennial Report* remained on the commission; nevertheless, the IJC continues to support its chlorine recommendation. In an October 1994 address to the Water Environment Federation, Thomas Baldini, the new chair of the U.S. Section of the IJC, said that the chlorine recommendation "has drawn the most comment and attention. . . . [it] has been pilloried by industry, championed by environmentalists, and championed *and* pilloried by scientists" (11–12). Commissioner Baldini went on to provide a context for the IJC's position on chlorine and concluded by saying that "We have yet to see any information that would cause us to reconsider that position" (Baldini 13).

At this writing, as the IJC prepares for its Eighth Biennial Meeting on Great Lakes Water Quality (to be held in September 1995 in Duluth, Minnesota), the proposal for sunsetting chlorine as an industrial feedstock continues to be one of the IJC's most controversial recommendations.

NOTES

1. In one variation of the technocratic model, scientific experts provide "unbiased" information—but not advice—to political or industrial decision makers. See, for example, Hammond and Adelman's discussion of this variation.

In either of these variations, from the perspectives of government and industry, one problem with the technocratic model is that it can eventually result in public rejection of a project or industry in which a substantial public or private investment has been made. For example, in *The Demise of Nuclear Energy? Lessons for Demo-*

cratic Control of Technology, Joseph Morone and Edward Woodhouse point out that "by the time it became apparent that the Shoreham nuclear plant might prove politically unacceptable, more than $4 billion had already been invested" (127).

2.   Public expertise takes various forms: folk knowledge, such as the folk epidemiology I describe below; mastery of the scientific literature that has been generated by various sources; and, increasingly, public interest science, such as that exemplified by *Toxic Wastes and Race in the United States.* Given the expense of basic research, public interest science is often (but not always) "second-order science"; that is, science that involves synthesizing, interpreting, or reinterpreting data that have been generated by government or academic scientists. For further discussion of the policy implications of the expense of developing empirical data, see Colborn et al. 114–15.

3.   There is, of course, the further question of what influence the IJC's recommendations have on governmental policy. Views on this point vary. In its September 1991 report *Broken Agreement,* Great Lakes United cites several instances in which the governments have responded to IJC recommendations (12, 15), but for the most part argues that the governments have ignored these recommendations (9–16). And although the Chlorine Institute was alarmed at what the IJC might recommend, during the public discussion session at the Sixth Biennial Meeting one Greenpeace representative registered the following complaint: "I understand the IJC is not a regulatory body but an advisory one. I've seen your advice, and much of it is good, and I thank you for it. But after what I heard this morning from [U.S. EPA] Administrator [William] Reilly and [Environment Canada] Minister [Jean] Charest, I must conclude that the only reason the federal governments fund the IJC is as a means of bread and circuses for the public. Because the voices of the people that have been spoken here don't seem to have found the ears of Messrs. Reilly and Charest" (237).

In its official response to recommendations in the IJC's *Fifth Biennial Report,* the United States government takes a more optimistic view, outlining point by point what actions it has taken. The IJC itself falls somewhere in between these two positions, pointing out in its *Sixth Biennial Report* that "Progress has been achieved, but much remains to be done" (5). The commissioners go on to commend the governments "for developing and at least partially implementing several recent initiatives or programs [that] begin to focus on the specific concerns the Commission [has] expressed about the state of the Great Lakes Basin Ecosystem" (6). Among the examples the commissioners offer of such programs are the Great Lakes Critical Programs Act of 1990, the Great Lakes Water Quality Initiative, and the National Environmental Education Act. The 1991 Binational Program to Restore and Protect the Lake Superior Basin also responds directly to IJC recommendations, as does the U.S. EPA's 1995 Water Quality Guidance for the Great Lakes System.

4.   Commissioner Robert Goodwin did not respond to my requests for an interview.

5.   The combined volume of the five Great Lakes is approximately 5,473 cubic miles, slightly less than the volume of Russia's Lake Baikal (approximately 5,520 cubic miles).

6. Eutrophication occurs when nutrients, such as phosphorus from municipal sewage treatment facilities, dramatically increase the growth of green plants and algae in a body of water. When this organic matter decomposes, it decreases the level of dissolved oxygen in the water, leading to the demise of various fish and insect species.

7. Annex 12 of the Great Lakes Water Quality Agreement defines a persistent toxic substance as "any toxic substance with a half-life in water of greater than eight weeks"; Annex 12 defines half-life as "the time required for the concentration of a substance to diminish to one-half of its original value in a lake or water body" (70).

In its *Sixth Biennial Report on Great Lakes Water Quality,* the IJC recommends that the definition of a persistent toxic substance be expanded to encompass all toxic substances "with a half-life in any medium—water, air, sediment, soil or biota—of greater than eight weeks, as well as those toxic substances that bioaccumulate in the tissue of living organisms" (26). Bioaccumulation is the retention and accumulation in the tissue of an organism of substances the organism has consumed or absorbed.

8. Page numbers in references to the public discussion session are to the official IJC transcription of this session. Where I have been able to identify speakers whose names were omitted or misspelled in the transcript, I have made the appropriate corrections.

9. The IJC's Sixth Biennial Meeting on Great Lakes Water Quality was the centerpiece of five coordinated meetings, which collectively lasted from 27 September through 2 October. The other four meetings were the 1991 Binational Great Lakes/St. Lawrence River Pollution Prevention Symposium, co-sponsored by Environment Canada and the U.S. EPA; the 1991 IJC Remedial Action Plan Forum; the Cause-Effect Linkages Symposium II, sponsored by the Michigan Audubon Society; and the Zero Discharge Mobilization for the Great Lakes, sponsored by the Zero Discharge Alliance, a coalition formed by Greenpeace and other environmental groups.

10. Phyllis Gorski's testimony during the public discussion session provides one example of what I have called folk epidemiology: "This is an observation that I have made personally after hearing that toxics may cause other diseases besides cancer. I observed, started to think in my own family, and I had had two miscarriages. I thought that was just by chance; a lot of people have miscarriages. Then I realized that our dog had a tumor and died, and my husband had asthma. So I started to ask other parents in the waiting room, did they have multiple health problems? At first, they didn't understand and said no. But when I asked them further, I found something like this: a parent whose child has cancer, plus a sibling with a club foot . . . ; a mother who had a child with cancer and also had a child with a learning disability or a hyperactive sibling or she had a still birth . . ." (222). Ms. Gorski goes on to describe additional cases of multiple health problems in families that live near landfills, incinerators, and other potential sources of toxic pollutants.

Epidemiologist Dr. Kenneth Rothman claims that "lay reports of disease clusters yield an extremely high proportion of false alarms" in that frequently either the cluster or the presumed cause of the cluster cannot be confirmed by conventional epidemiological methods (S10). However, Dr. Alfred Evans, professor emeritus of epidemiology at Yale University, notes that in the case of Lyme disease, a group of citizens became alarmed by a cluster of arthritis-like cases among children, went to the state department of public health, and were referred to Dr. Allen Steere in the Rheumatology Section of Yale's School of Medicine; Dr. Marvin Legator, a toxicologist at the University of Texas, Medical Branch, argues that the statistical methods of conventional epidemiology are not sensitive enough to establish causal relationships amidst the high "noise level" of community settings; and Dr. Lorann Stallones, past secretary-treasurer of the Society for Epidemiological Research, suggests that concerns about credibility may make some epidemiologists reluctant to acknowledge that citizens are the initiating factor in some epidemiological investigations (personal interviews with the author).

Folk epidemiology might be considered a subset of or model for folk knowledge or folk epistemology more generally.

11.   During my interview with him, Chairman Durnil expressed his surprise at the general response to this comment, the point of which, he said, had been simply to indicate that he had *personal* experience with environmentally related human health effects similar to those Ms. Ortner-Mukavetz described (Durnil 12–15).

12.   A similar strategy was used by some in the chemical industry in response to Rachel Carson's *Silent Spring*. For example, in the 1963 *CBS Reports* "The Silent Spring of Rachel Carson," Dr. Robert White-Stevens, assistant to the director of research for American Cyanamid, argued that "The real threat, then, to the survival of man is not chemical but biological in the form of hoards of insects that can denude our forests, sweep over our croplands, and leave in their wake a train of destruction and hunger, conveying to an undernourished population the major diseases and scourges of mankind. If man were to faithfully follow the teachings of Miss Carson, we would return to the Dark Ages, and the insects and diseases and vermin would once again inherit the earth."

Likewise, in hearings on conducting recombinant DNA research in Cambridge, Massachusetts, in 1976, scientists supporting the research made impassioned appeals on behalf of children with genetic diseases and cancer who might benefit from the research (Waddell, "Role of *Pathos*").

13.   The commissioners define sunsetting as "a program of staged reductions, leading to the total and complete ban on manufacture, generation, use, transport, storage, discharge and disposal" (*Sixth Biennial Report* 27). They do not suggest specific timetables for this purpose.

14.   They do go on to say that "presentations and workshops at the 1991 Biennial Meeting in Traverse City, Michigan contributed additional information" (*Sixth Biennial Report* 2); however, many of these presentations and workshops were conducted by the IJC's various boards.

15.   Mary Hesse has argued that "Theories are logically constrained by facts, but are underdetermined by them: that is, while, to be acceptable, theories should be more or less plausibly coherent with facts, they can be neither conclusively re-

futed nor uniquely derived from statements of fact alone" (187). Following Hesse, we might say that the IJC's policy recommendations are underdetermined by technical information in that they are partly determined as well by values, beliefs, and emotions.

16.   On this last point, I would depart from Quintilian. As Frederick Antczak says, "While 'successful' rhetoric may well involve moral standards, by definition it involves persuading the audience too" (90). It is a peculiar ethic that would inspire a rhetor to forgo, for example, homocentric appeals, concentrate exclusively on more noble-sounding, ecocentric appeals, and, as a consequence, leave his or her audience unpersuaded. While this approach might leave some rhetors feeling righteous, it also leaves the ecosystem at risk.

17.   For an extended discussion of the social construction of the appropriateness of emotional appeals, see Waddell, "Role of *Pathos.*"

18.   For an extended discussion of this point, see Waddell, "Perils of a Modern Cassandra."

WORKS CITED

Antczak, Frederick J. *Thought and Character: The Rhetoric of Democratic Education.* Ames: Iowa State UP, 1985.

Baldini, Thomas. Remarks. Water Environment Federation, 67th Annual Meeting. Chicago, 16 October 1994.

Barke, Richard. *Science, Technology, and Public Policy.* Washington, DC: Congressional Quarterly Press, 1986.

Bevacqua, Frank. "Chlorine Sunsetting Discussion Gains Momentum at Biennial Meeting." *Focus* 18.3 (Nov./Dec. 1993): 1–3.

Carpeling-Alakijah, Sharon. "The United Nations Development Fund for Women (UNIFEM)." The Citizens Respond: The Earth Summit and Beyond. Michigan State University, 26 September 1992.

Cleveland, Hilary P. Transcript of an interview with Craig Waddell. Washington, DC, 21 April 1992.

Chavis, Benjamin F., Jr. Preface. *Toxic Wastes and Race in the United States.* United Church of Christ Commission on Racial Justice. New York: United Church of Christ, 1987.

Colborn, Theodora E., et al. *Great Lakes, Great Legacy?* Washington, DC: The Conservation Foundation and the Institute for Research on Public Policy, 1990.

Durnil, Gordon K. Transcript of an interview with Craig Waddell. Washington, DC, 21 April 1992.

Evans, Alfred. Telephone interview. 19 May 1993.

French, Hilary F. *Green Revolutions: Environmental Reconstruction in Eastern Europe and the Soviet Union.* Washington, DC: Worldwatch Institute, 1990.

Fulton, E. Davie. Transcript of an interview with Craig Waddell. Washington, DC, 21 April 1992.

Goggin, Malcolm L., ed. *Governing Science and Technology in a Democracy.* Knoxville: U of Tennessee P, 1986.

Goldhaber, Michael. *Reinventing Technology: Politics for Democratic Values.* New York: Routledge, 1986.

Great Lakes United. *Broken Agreement: The Failure of the United States and Canada to Implement the Great Lakes Water Quality Agreement.* Buffalo: Great Lakes United, 1991.

Hammond, Kenneth R., and Leonard Adelman. "Science, Values, and Human Judgment." *Science* 194 (22 Oct. 1976): 389–96.

Hays, Samuel P. *Beauty, Health, and Permanence: Environmental Politics in the United States, 1955–1985.* Cambridge: Cambridge UP, 1987.

Hesse, Mary. *Revolutions and Reconstructions in the Philosophy of Science.* Bloomington: Indiana UP, 1980.

International Joint Commission (IJC) Water Quality Board. *Cleaning Up Our Great Lakes: A Report on Toxic Substances in the Great Lakes Basin Ecosystem.* Windsor, Ontario: IJC, 1991.

International Joint Commission (IJC). *Fifth Biennial Report on Great Lakes Water Quality.* Windsor, Ontario: IJC, 1990.

International Joint Commission (IJC). *The International Joint Commission and the Boundary Waters Treaty.* Windsor, Ontario: IJC, 1990.

International Joint Commission (IJC). Transcript: "Public Discussion Session on the Future Priorities for the Great Lakes Water Quality Agreement." 1 October 1991. IJC Sixth Biennial Meeting on Great Lakes Water Quality, Traverse City, Michigan. Windsor, Ontario: IJC, 1991.

International Joint Commission (IJC). *Revised Great Lakes Water Quality Agreement of 1978.* Windsor, Ontario: IJC, 1989.

International Joint Commission (IJC). *Seventh Biennial Report on Great Lakes Water Quality.* Windsor, Ontario: IJC, 1994.

International Joint Commission (IJC). *Sixth Biennial Report on Great Lakes Water Quality.* Windsor, Ontario: IJC, 1992.

Jefferson, Thomas. Letter to William Charles Jarvis, 28 September 1820. *The Writings of Thomas Jefferson,* ed. Ellery Bergh. Vol. 19. Washington, DC: Thomas Jefferson Memorial Association, 1907. 276–79.

Killingsworth, M. Jimmie, and Jacqueline S. Palmer. *Ecospeak: Rhetoric and Environmental Politics in America.* Carbondale: Southern Illinois UP, 1992.

Lanthier, Claude. Transcript of an interview with Craig Waddell. Washington, DC, 21 April 1992.

Legator, Marvin. Telephone interview. 18 May 1993.

Merchant, Carolyn. "Environmental Ethics and Political Conflict: A View from California." *Environmental Ethics* 12 (1990): 45–68.

Morone, Joseph G., and Edward J. Woodhouse. *The Demise of Nuclear Energy? Lessons for Democratic Control of Technology.* New Haven: Yale UP, 1989.

U.S. National Research Council. *Improving Risk Communication.* Washington, DC: National Academy P, 1989.

Perelman, Chaim, and L. Olbrechts-Tyteca. *The New Rhetoric: A Treatise on Argumentation.* Notre Dame: U of Notre Dame P, 1969.

Petersen, James C., ed. *Citizen Participation in Science Policy.* Amherst: U of Massachusetts P, 1984.

Quintilian. *The Institutio oratoria.* Trans. H. E. Butler. Cambridge: Harvard UP, 1980.

Rothman, Kenneth J. "A Sobering Start for the Cluster Buster's Conference." *American Journal of Epidemiology* 132.2 Supplement (July 1990): S6–S13.

"The Silent Spring of Rachel Carson." Written and produced by Jay L. McMullen. Reported by Jay L. McMullen and Eric Sevareid. *CBS Reports.* 1963.

Stallones, Lorann. Telephone interview. 17 May 1993.

U.S. Atomic Energy Commission (AEC). *In the Matter of J. Robert Oppenheimer: Transcript of Hearing before Personnel Security Board and Texts of Principal Documents and Letters.* Cambridge: MIT P, 1970.

U.S. Department of State. "United States Response to Recommendations in the International Joint Commission's Fifth Biennial Report." Washington, DC: U.S. Department of State, September 1991.

Waddell, Craig. "Perils of a Modern Cassandra: Rhetorical Aspects of Public Indifference to the Population Explosion." *Social Epistemology* 8 (1994): 221–37.

Waddell, Craig. "The Role of *Pathos* in the Decision-Making Process: A Study in the Rhetoric of Science Policy." *Quarterly Journal of Speech* 76 (1990): 381–400.

Welch, Robert S. K. Transcript of an interview with Craig Waddell. Washington, DC, 21 April 1992.

CHAPTER 6

Gold, Yellowstone, and the Search for a Rhetorical Identity

JAMES G. CANTRILL

Environmental rhetoric is exceptionally diverse. To the extent the environment overshadows *all* communicative practices, it is not surprising that human discourse, in turn, affects each environmental problem or policy we face. However, those interested in examining the rhetoric that surrounds environmental matters have focused mostly on the public utterances of major environmental organizations and spokespersons. Among others, Robert Gottlieb ("Odd Assortment" 47; cf. Strodthoff et al. 136) suggests that an obsession with broad-based persuasive campaigns and social movements tends to ignore the often more important drama of environmentalism that occurs in communities facing local threats to their health and lifestyles. This rhetoric may originate with a neighborhood association highlighting the danger posed by nearby toxic waste incineration; commonly, it is found in the voices of small communities competing for scarce resources such as water; often the discourse exists in the frustrated cries of those who were too naive to protect their own backyards when they had the chance. These smaller venues for environmental rhetoric are more pervasive than the mass-mediated disputes that monopolize national agendas, and, arguably, they are more significant sites for mobilizing local activism that will ultimately shape a global consciousness.

As a counterpoint to studies of larger controversies, the following analysis centers on the discourse of the Beartooth Alliance, a reasonably small community-based organization opposed to a mining project on the threshold of Yellowstone National Park. Examining how this group makes sense out of and discusses its rhetorical challenge in the isolated hamlet of Cooke City, Montana, holds great promise for studies of environmental rhetoric. In this setting we find the genuine symbolic artifacts of what has been

166

called "conservation from below" (McNeely and Pitt 1). Notably, local traditions and practices reveal what is considered important in an environmental dispute; they also provide inventories for what Dell Hymes calls the "selective metalanguage" of a culture or the way a culture talks about the language it uses (79).

Identifying the way members of the Beartooth Alliance speak about themselves and the code they use to depict their predicament does more than simply open a window onto an environmental dispute in the Rocky Mountain West. It tells us something important about our culture at large since it is in the isolated margins of society that the cultural milieu is most dramatically revealed (Fiske, "For Cultural Interpretation" 463; Bahktin 2). Paul Ricoeur, another social critic, observes that in appreciating others' use of language in times of stress and alien terrain, we reach a better understanding of who we are as cultural beings (33). In turn, we become adept in meeting the environmental challenges of our times. Because our ability to preserve the environment depends on collective action, understanding the discourse that helps or hinders the Beartooth Alliance may serve as a lesson for us all.

In the following pages, I briefly describe how it is we can use everyday language to identify the cultural underpinnings of environmental rhetoric. Next, I describe the way Beartooth Alliance members symbolically portray their situation with special attention paid to the themes that unify or fragment them as an effective grassroots organization. Following this analysis, I explain why the organization's discourse is shaped as it is and how this structure affects the group's rhetorical efforts. The chapter concludes with a suggestion as to what the study can lend to our understanding of other contemporary environmental campaigns.

Environmental Discourse and the Cultural Milieu

Scholars of rhetoric have long recognized that when people make arguments, their language also speaks of the society in which they live. Our discourses, in drawing upon current events and well-known examples, provide implicit reaffirmations or critiques of the social fabric for our lives. Beyond mirroring our constructions of society, however, rhetoric can also reveal the deep-seated cultural bases for how people view themselves and the objects of their concern. In this vein, prominent rhetorical critics such as Kenneth Burke, Michael McGee, and Michael Osborne suggest that the way advocates depict their situation not only fosters collective meanings for the world; these rhetorical choices are also rooted in the tacit understandings that ground human conduct and distinguish one culture from another.

All too often when we think of culture, the picture is one of some monolithic structure that governs everyone's lives in a unitary fashion. We speak of culture as *a* force that, in unseen ways, affects all people equally. In fact, if culture is considered a system of symbolic meanings, if symbols are imbued with meaning only in the context of how they are used, and if different groups in society use the same symbols differently, then we must consider the possibility of having to reckon with the force of *multiple* cultures in any given society. We can speak of an encompassing dominant culture only insofar as its members share and exhibit essentially the same meanings and symbolic constructions. In this sense, culture (as with language itself) is "polysemic" (Carbaugh, *American Talking* 7; cf. Bakhtin 85; Garfinkel 23–24); it erects different meanings for different people in different circumstances. Significantly, while people may use the same terms and conventions in describing the world, these rhetorical turns may obscure the very real, symbolic differences between groups (Cohen 444; Fiske, "British Cultural Studies" 268).

In her analysis of the "public sphere," Nancy Fraser observes that the presence of multiple cultures, as embodied in distinct symbolic traditions, reflects the fractured nature of a social system. For Fraser, following theorists such as Jürgen Habermas, the public sphere exists as a grand forum in which different groups compete within and amongst themselves for rhetorical high ground. In discussing matters of common interest, individuals participate in the life of grassroots politics, which either reinforces the dominant worldview or distances that group from mainstream society (cf. Williams 83). Especially when dealing with environmental matters, some groups may have greater symbolic resources (e.g., technical information) as well as more power to perpetuate their vision of culture through education and control of information sources (Cantrill 87–88; cf. Luhmann 32–36). Consequently, groups representing deviations from the dominant culture become impoverished and tend to keep their interactions to themselves. This sequestering produces language subcommunities, whose identity results from their common rhetoric and symbolic conventions.

In environmental controversies, the most logical place to locate discourses that oppose the dominant social paradigm would be in the rhetoric of activist organizations. And, as noted earlier, small grassroots alliances may exhibit the greatest rhetorical alienation exactly because they often are marginalized by more dominant cultural groupings. In these situations, especially when events unfold quickly, the conventions of language that characterize the membership are most dynamic. As John Fiske suggests, analysis of rhetoric in these situations allows a critic to observe cultural conflict at a specific place in time ("For Cultural Interpretation" 463).

In order to evaluate the symbol system and culture of a grassroots environmental organization, a critic must gain the confidence of group members as well as collect and decipher their discourse. One could examine public speeches, documents, and the like; pick apart naturally occurring conversations; scrutinize in-depth interviews. In this study, I was able to encourage a candid manner in the conduct of several intensive interviews with members of the Beartooth Alliance because I have been a member of the organization since its inception. This intimate knowledge of the group provided unique entrée into their systems of meaning. I typically employed the same interview schedule when soliciting remarks from respondents and encouraged them to elaborate in detail about their backgrounds, where they lived, the social and environmental conditions they faced, and the nature of the Beartooth Alliance. The interviews were subsequently transcribed for analysis and compared to observe common depictions, themes, and phrases. I then cross-referenced those passages with the person's location in the organization (e.g., officer or member; local resident or occasional visitor). In this manner, I obtained one possible interpretation of how the group was unified or fragmented as represented by its rhetoric.

Cooke City, the New World Project, and the Beartooth Alliance

It is useful to understand something of the sociogeographical backdrop for Beartooth Alliance discourse. The Greater Yellowstone ecosystem is estimated to comprise roughly 14 million acres spread across Idaho, Montana, and Wyoming. In addition to state and local governance, it is managed by four federal agencies affecting several national forests, recreation and wildlife areas, and parks. As the Congressional Research Service reported in 1987, this fragmented management structure has resulted in "difficult decision making in an area replete with virtually all of the classic natural resource development conflicts in the West—and in a setting deemed very special by Americans" (2). Unfortunately, a recently completed policy analysis concludes that even though the region's economy has moved away from land use practices that too often threaten the overall health of the ecosystem (e.g., extractive industries such as mining and timber operations), governmental policies continue to stress commodity production (Rasker et al. i).

Cooke City sits on the eastern edge of 2.2-million-acre Yellowstone National Park and adjacent to the Absaroka-Beartooth Wilderness Area. At an elevation just shy of eight thousand feet, the town has a year-round population of sixty-five that swells to roughly three hundred with the arrival of summer residents. This is an area of sparse settlement, harsh winters, and exceptional beauty; Charles Kurault once described the road that bisects the town (i.e., Montana Highway 212) as having the most spectacular vistas in the United States (Glidden 126). And, since the collapse of the mining industry in the 1950s, Cooke City has depended on tourism and recreation for economic subsistence. Skiers and snowmobilers flock to the area in winter months; fishing, hunting, and hiking are enjoyed the rest of the year. Beyond serving as critical habitat for a variety of endangered flora and fauna (including significant concentrations of grizzly bear), the high country above the town is a watershed for two of our most pristine Wild and Scenic Rivers: the Yellowstone and the Clark's Fork of the Yellowstone.

In 1988, Crown Butte Mines Incorporated (the U.S. subsidiary of Canada's Noranda Incorporated) successfully petitioned the State of Montana and the United States Forest Service for the right to mine gold and silver in the New World Mining District above Cooke City. In particular, the New World Project involves constructing a 68-mile-long powerline from Cody, Wyoming, hollowing out a mountain less than three miles from the national park boundary, and settling more than 150 miners and their families in the immediate vicinity. By July of 1992, more than 850 test holes had been drilled throughout the region and the company had filed over seventy patented claims in accordance with the Amended Mining Act of 1872.

The reason for Crown Butte's sustained interest and considerable investment in the New World Project: possibly the greatest gold strike of the century. Ongoing exploration has revealed 4.2 million tons of exceptionally high-grade gold deposits. With a projected 2.5 million ounces of the precious mineral in reserve and an expected profit over the fifteen-year life of the mine to exceed $800 million, the New World Project surpasses the ton-for-ton value of even the largest mining operations in Nevada.

Obviously, a project this big will create immense social and ecological changes in the Cooke City region. The influx of new residents will pump an estimated $7 million into the recession-strapped local economy and provide employment for those who traditionally depend on seasonal tourist dollars. On the other hand, the Greater Yellowstone Coalition (7) argues that such prosperity would be short-lived, limited by low-paying service economy jobs, and largely mitigated by the accompanying environmental and social disruptions. For example, water runoff from what some government personnel have called "the mine from hell" could threaten downstream ecosystems. Also, the availability of affordable housing in the vicinity could continue to shrink as the area's valued pace of life is compromised. Perhaps more significantly, by late 1991, deep polarizing rifts had developed between citizens who favored the New World Project on economic grounds and those who had social and environmental objections; as one resident was to later remark, "Friends who have been friends, are no more."

In the wake of Noranda's initial licensing successes with federal and state agencies, a small group of concerned Cooke City residents met in the winter of 1989–90 to assess the impact of the mine on their community. In a short time, and with the aid of the Northern Plains Resource Council, this group evolved into the Beartooth Alliance, bringing together more than two hundred ranchers, businesspeople, and occasional visitors to attempt to mitigate the changes and threats accompanying the New World Project. It quickly became obvious that the grassroots group could not compete with a major corporation supported by development-minded administrations; Crown Butte had the finances, government connections, and media savvy to stymie Alliance members at almost every juncture. Federal agencies and the State of Montana provided little opportunity to participate in decision-making meetings; notices of environmental impact assessment hearings were postponed to prevent effective counterresearch; the company reneged on promises of working with the townspeople to limit adverse changes in the community. In short, the kinds of forces that promote subversive environmental discourse converged in Cooke City.

Given the perceived indifference of corporate and governmental agents, those legitimately concerned with issues such as water quality and economic displacement felt themselves increasingly excluded from the policy-making loop and facing the very real risk of having their environment substantially degraded. In an effort to bolster their position, the Beartooth Alliance formally adopted the mantle of an "environmentalist" organization condemning the entire New World Project; in the case of the Alliance, this environmentalist stance was more closely allied with the preservation of land above Cooke City for recreation and aesthetics than with the conservation of natural resources, despite the fact that many in the group were opposed to an expansion of "wilderness" per se. Although this rhetorical move prompted 25 percent of the organization to resign, rejecting the mine resulted in increased media attention from outlets such as the *Christian Science Monitor* and the Canadian Broadcasting Company. In turn, Crown Butte changed the project to reduce its exposure, eliminating open-pit mining and cyanide-leeching processes from its plans.

In midsummer of 1992, there were 124 registered members in the Beartooth Alliance, 25 of whom served as my respondents. This was largely a self-selected sample of convenience (i.e., the interviews with members indicating a willingness to participate were conducted in and around Cooke City over a three-week period) that, nonetheless, captured roughly 20 percent of the active membership. These individuals ranged in age from twenty-three to seventy-nine, with most members being over fifty-three years of age. Seventy-three percent possessed at least a college degree, and a substantial number had gone on for advanced study. Informants were evenly split between those living in Cooke City, those from other areas in Montana, and residents of other regions of the United States; in fact, more than 75 percent of the Beartooth Alliance membership lives outside the vicinity of Cooke City.

Most of those interviewed considered themselves well-informed on current events and generally reported no more than a modest level of political participation or activity in organizations other than the Beartooth Alliance. Obviously, some were homeowners and other members only visited the area on occasion. More striking was the prevalent depiction of the Alliance as composed of either "winter" or "summer" people and this split between those who "lived with the mine year round" as opposed to those who only summered in the area generally matched that between the *core* leaders of the group and *peripheral* members as identified by my informants. This sense of implicit self-identity provides definitional benchmarks for analysis, with the core representing grassroots zealots in the Beartooth Alliance and the periphery composed of those not as fervent in their devotion to the cause. In particular, the remarks of these two broad subgroups in the Beartooth Alliance often demonstrate clear differences in perception. For example, local members considered their organization to be something more than a single-issue group opposed only to the New World Project; others defined the Alliance in light of the mine. Alternatively, although the Cooke City contingent clearly articulated the history and aims of the organization, when I asked those residing elsewhere if the aims of the Beartooth Alliance were being met, an alarming number of dues-paying members said, "Well, what *are* the aims?" or something very similar.

Apparent differences between Alliance members invite a more probing analysis. I examined more than fifty hours of transcribed interviews and meetings along with numerous private and public documents, searching for consistencies in the way different informants used various themes and symbols. What emerged is a more detailed picture of themes that unify or fragment the rhetoric and culture of the Beartooth Alliance. Specifically, talk that focused on *location, distrust, history,* and *hardship* draws Alliance members together as a marginalized group, while references to *community, commitment, outlook,* and *division* distance them from one another. After a deep analysis of these rhetorics of union and divorce, I shall argue that these themes conspire to limit the effectiveness of the grassroots group in shaping public policy.

Unifying Rhetorics of the Beartooth Alliance

One of the more informative ways of assessing the rhetorical unity of a grassroots environmental group is to inspect the extent to which they share meanings for significant symbols in their vocabulary. In the case of the Beartooth Alliance, four such symbolic convergences seem especially prominent and help define the collective identity of the group.

This May Not Be the Last Best Place, But You Can See It from Here

If there is one symbol whose meaning Beartooth Alliance members agree upon, it would be the location called Cooke City. Members of the group consistently echoed the letter and spirit of Kittredge and Smith's best-selling anthology *The Last Best Place* in depicting the area and responding to questions about the region. Comments such as "this is one of the few areas left," "one of the few relatively untouched places," and "To me, this is one of the last remaining places. Sort of pristine, fundamental, natural . . . unspoiled" typify Alliance impressions and signify their collective belief that the area remains an unblemished remnant of the American frontier.

Not only do group members describe current conditions as largely unsullied by civilization; several also locate Cooke City within an ongoing, almost sacred context of sanctified land. As one informant put it: "Well, of course, they saw it and it was wonderful. They told people about it and they kept coming back. Thank goodness President Grant, he should be a saint or something . . . what's the word, 'canonized'? . . . because of putting the park, making a national park. . . . thank goodness they preserved Yellowstone and that is a wonderful thing." This sense of being in a special place extends into the future as various informants position the area's potential against the backdrop of human choice: "If people would keep the area the way it is . . . the amount of tourists that pass through here and people who eat dinner and just want to sit at their cabin and watch the mountains because they feel like they are in paradise. I mean, that could last forever if people would let it last forever. And we could have an economy that would keep going because there aren't that many places left anymore."

It would be tempting to ascribe the outpouring of love for Cooke City to the normal tendency to elevate the status of one's home. Clearly, those who call the region "home" often employ hyperbole in discussing the region. "This community we're living in is very unique and it's hard to compare with almost any other place in Montana let alone any other place in the United States." "Some people have no dreams and all they do is work. Well, living in Cooke City is my dream." However, even those who do not own even seasonal accommodations uniformly praise the virtues of "life on the edge of Yellowstone." One resident of a distant metropolitan area captures the essence of this point in stating, "Even though I don't live here, that I only visit from time to time, it feels like home. No, that's not it, 'cause home was never this peaceful." Another visitor is more succinct in identifying what Cooke City is like: "the rest of the world could just drop off the map and it wouldn't matter."

Given the intensity of Beartooth Alliance members' feelings for the region, the fervor with which they rhetorically defend their "home" against the New World Project is understandable. Most of those interviewed juxtapose the existing beauty and "pristine wilderness" with the threats of a seemingly hostile government and foreign corporation. They consistently point to flaws in the 1872 Mining Law and the current bureaucracy in noting that "Companies coming in and staking up an area is antipublic development which is not what the 1872 mining law was all about." "The continued supremacy of mining in public lands planning must not be allowed to intrude on special places. . . ." Or "It's kinda like being a little David taking on a Goliath of a government and industry that wants to rape and plunder everything you hold dear." And, in discussing the impact of the mine, these individuals typically contrast the uniqueness of the region to the debasing nature of hardrock mining, stressing, for example, that the project "would be located at the apex of three of the most precious rivers in the Yellowstone system."

A very interesting element in Alliance descriptions of their location is the resemblance to the "outside world." For many, this small mountain town is a microcosm reflecting what is generally wrong with U.S. society. Several interviews contain references that cast the encroachment of renewed mining as a symbolic "analogue for" or "continuation of the way our country is going." These pointedly negative characterizations (e.g., "Progress is a nasty word") are directed solely at the New World Project rather than at other changes such as increases in tourism, more stringent Forest Service regulations, or economic downturns. "The New World Mining District is very similar to what's happening other places. You know, it's like everybody wants to screw up what's good and clean all for the sake of making a buck." Just as the governmental and corporate system has corrupted the rest of the world, so too is that system seen as coming to town in the guise of the New World Project.

And You'd Better Not Blink

In a number of ways, members of the Beartooth Alliance portray themselves as "hostages" to Crown Butte, with the mine, as weapon, "held to [their] collective heads." They are often careful in their choice of words to characterize the company and are typically distrustful of it and of those who support its aims.

Alliance distrust is heard in the manner in which they construct the company's relationship with the town. Historically, the management of Crown

Butte has been "less than candid with the town and [does not] really seem that committed to being good neighbors." Time and again, when they are asked to characterize their opponents, Beartooth Alliance members implicitly or explicitly compare their sense of decency (e.g., "We've played a fair game and that's important") with the perceived duplicity of the company. In making reference to the New World Project's chief geologist, one resident noted, "He seemed like a person you could trust yet I'm afraid to trust him. I'm afraid [to] trust because so often, you know, you trust somebody and then if you haven't read the fine print or if somebody who's pro-mine, you know, receives the permit, they could switch or change something because they don't think anyone will notice." Eventually, each of the respondents reported grave skepticism of the company's true designs for the project, declaring that "nothing short of the complete industrialization of the area will turn a profit for [the company]. . . . Crown Butte sells this as a small development but suddenly it's Pittsburgh."

Although Alliance voices occasionally single out specific company officers or, as is the case with many core members, personalize the company with general descriptors such as "bastards," they mostly speak of the New World Project in nonpersonal terms. The mine becomes "something else coming in from the outside that isn't just, you know, your neighbor next door, it's this whole big thing." The mine is a faceless entity that cannot be directly confronted, and its physical location *above the town* adds to the perceived alien nature of the threat. Reminiscent of what Donal Carbaugh discovered in a different situation (" 'The Mountain' " 365–68), group members characterize the threat as being "up there," "looming over us," and "The longer it goes on, the more destructive it becomes. It's like the nature of the disease. . . . people are tired of this hanging over their heads."

The combination of distrust and impersonal dread fosters another pair of related beliefs. First, residents and visitors often refer to "an alienated environment" that challenges their *freedom of choice.* One Montana resident comments that the mine will promote a lifestyle that is "alien to the existing chosen lifestyle. I think the word 'chosen' is really important here. People are there because of choice and they are about to be inundated by something that is not of their choice." Second, since the company employees represent the oppressive force, they are to be resisted, shunned, and denigrated. The only option becomes one of entrenchment: "You can't back off at all. Anytime you back off and make any concession to the mining company, it's seen as a major victory for them and they're eroding our base."

It is one thing to be wary of strangers: it becomes something far more serious when a group begins to distrust neighbors. The ill will toward the New World Project is often extended as well toward those in Cooke City who support the mine. Sometimes, the distrust is subverted in an effort to maintain harmony; a number of resident group members indicate they "just don't talk about it" with those who favor Crown Butte's plans because they "wouldn't want to ruin the relationship." Others are more forthright in their apprehension: "Another thing we've seen is a tremendous polarization of our community and it's gotten to the point that there is nobody sitting on the fence. . . . you're labeled so and it affects every aspect of your life. And you'd better not blink 'cause sure enough there's someone there to push you off and ruin your business." "We summer people are like fair game for the locals because this community has no way to generate income on its own. The place is culturally deprived . . . we often get left out." And yet, in the end, few in the group hold the citizens of Cooke City wholly accountable for the "rift" in town. "There are a number of townspeople who are unwilling to confront the choices presented by the Beartooth Alliance. But the Beartooth Alliance is not responsible for tearing the community apart, it's the mine's fault."

We've Become What We Were

The overwhelming sense of oppression in the discourse of the Beartooth Alliance may come from the way they construct history. Perhaps without recognizing the implications, group members generally frame the past and future in terms of hardrock mining. Consequently, the New World Project represents more than an environmental and social threat to Cooke City; it is the incarnation of an industrial devil that, ironically, they cannot avoid if they choose to live in the mountains of Montana.

Despite the fact that paleolithic Americans frequented the Cooke City region as long ago as 6,000 B.C. (Glidden 43), most respondents begin their historical narratives with the advent of mining. Even those who refer to native inhabitants do so only as a footnote to the search for precious minerals (e.g., "The area was based on mining though the Indians were here first"). Yet, by ignoring the original stewards of the Greater Yellowstone ecosystem, Beartooth Alliance members may be unwittingly endorsing a point of view that equates the area's values with only tangible wealth. One summertime resident best reveals this perceptual constraint in recounting the origins of Cooke City:

The only reason you and I are here today is gold and other assorted metals that people value. It's not Yellowstone National Park or the great hunting or fishing around here or the fact that you can wander for miles up on the [Beartooth] plateau without seeing anyone [or] any of the other stuff folks seem to like about this place. Hell, they probably wouldn't have blasted in, you know, the Beartooth Highway if Cooke City wasn't here and it's here only because of the mining up on Lulu and Daisy Pass. This country *is* mining; has been since the country was first discovered.

So, you see, it's downright stupid to talk about how mining isn't "natural" in this place since it brought the money that built the roads that carry the tourists that puts services in the area for people like us who don't live here. I guess I wish it were different, that there wasn't a nickle's worth of ore up there, but that's how it goes.

Another individual uses fewer words in summarizing, "We've become what we were. Folks groveling after chunks of yellow rock instead of sunshine."

As members' chronology of Cooke City begins with the search for gold, so too does the future depend on what happens with the New World Project. Although a variety of alternative forces such as the expanding tourism economy and recreational property market could figure prominently in their predictions, Beartooth Alliance members consistently foreground their belief that "the future depends on the mine." Mining thus becomes a significant symbolic anchor for thinking about what will happen in the region, since it could, potentially, rhetorically focus the group's energies on a single threat. Certainly, numerous voices reinforce the perception that the New World Project threatens future happiness and prosperity (e.g., "Nobody will want to visit a tailings impoundment"), and the fact that everyone believes that the mine controls their destiny means that advocacy often takes on fatalistic overtones. One Alliance leader notes that telling others about the mine requires "an interpretive exercise [highlighting] the ongoing and somewhat inevitable incremental deterioration" of the region's aesthetic and recreational resources.

Positioning themselves between a past that starts with mining and a future that depends on the same, the Beartooth Alliance seems collectively bound to a history defined by what they oppose. As a result, the group itself depends on hardrock mining, and any efforts to move the group beyond a strict focus on the New World Project are likely to meet resistance. In this sense, the comment that "the mine will eat the identity of Cooke City alive" takes on new meaning; the threatened "identity" is only that possessed by a people at odds with what they take to be the basis for their being in the area.

Citizens for a Poodle-Free Montana!

Many Rocky Mountain residents reject citified lifestyles, and this is certainly true of those living in the shadow of the New World Project. Members of the Alliance must embrace the hardships of living in the mountains if they reside, or even *want* to reside, in Cooke City. Even with modern transportation, "It's still isolated, that's how it's always been." And group members' discourse constantly reflects an admiration for the life of the "rugged individuals" who call Cooke City home. "They're tough and they,

they, you have to be . . . you have to be a special kind of person to put up with this [remoteness]." And more than one transient asserted, "I'd love to live here," or "there's something special about being able to get buried in a July snowstorm."

Beneath this discourse of admiration, however, exists a series of more disparaging characterizations. Not only do Alliance members appreciate the geographic remoteness and climatic severity of the area, but they also perceive a great deal of inbred *social* isolation in Cooke City. Members speak of being in a "culturally deprived area" fomenting "a different life" among "rugged individual*ists*" who "go their own way" and want little to do with others. "This is the weirdest community because everyone says, 'Oh, you live in such a small town you must know everyone, it must be really tight knit,' and it isn't at all. Everybody sticks to themselves." Other members offer similar characterizations: "I think people live here because they don't want to be bothered by other people. They live here because it's the kind of place where you can do what you kinda want to do without having . . . you know, we don't have a lot of regulations up here. . . . people are real into themselves. You see people and you wave and you know each other but you don't, you don't have any connection together."

Given the sense of social and physical isolation, the real value of an organization such as the Beartooth Alliance is immeasurably increased. In addition to disliking the prospect of the mine, members identify with each other as disenfranchised persons. "Being involved with [the] Beartooth Alliance, we often feel isolated, not just geographically, but from other individuals, experts, and groups." Alternatively, these respondents seem unified in their assessment of what it means to symbolically separate themselves from others. "Being in the Alliance means you don't feel all alone, you've got help."

Symbolic Distances in Alliance Discourse

Despite the few only-to-be-expected contradictions in Beartooth Alliance discourse (e.g., the group opposes the New World Project yet frames history in terms of mining), the fact that there is a good deal of unified symbolizing among its members should suggest that it could effectively muster collective energies to resist renewed mining in the area. Insofar as the group intensely values the Cooke City region and the spirit the land engenders, distrusts Crown Butte for what it represents and bodes for their livelihoods, and recognizes that hardrock mining *is* the issue of the hour, one might reasonably anticipate that Alliance rhetoric would exhibit a strong unity of purpose and design. However, a number of oppositional symbolic constructions serve to limit the effectiveness of the Beartooth Alliance in presenting a united chorus against the New World Project.

The Only Thing We Have in Common Is We Hate This Mine

Although Beartooth Alliance members seem unified in portraying the physical challenges faced by *individual* Cooke City residents, they are split in the way they portray the *community;* this division may significantly hamper their ability to stop the New World Project. On the one hand, core elements of the group characterize the fight against the mine as one of preserving the environment for the sake of the people that live in and visit the valley; their view of "community" is decidedly social. On the other hand, those who do not live in and around Cooke City focus on far more tangible aspects of the region. These peripheral Alliance members, who constitute the bulk of the group and who provide the financial backing for the campaign, do not typically think of a collection of people when describing the town. Rather, the "community" is a collection of buildings situated in a physical and economic space with little reference to social factors.

Asked to characterize their impressions of the Cooke City area, most of those who either visit or summer in the region focus on fairly obvious, tangible features. For example, they recall that "there were so few . . . there were *no* cabins between Cooke City and Silvergate [a nearby, smaller town]. It was just all wooded area," or that it was a "typical, small national park entrance community that was thriving on summer business." The noticeable absence of people from these depictions continues in describing the present; "We've had to adjust to an influx of cabins," "There still aren't very many side streets," and ". . . the [1988] fire opened up the view on the hillside." Other nonresident Beartooth Alliance members seem consciously to avoid references to the social dimension; "You know, you can't really talk about this being a community in the normal sense. I mean, the people really aren't that important. What *is* important is that Cooke City sits in such a beautiful location that isn't screwed over by a sprawling town. The geography hems in the town and limits the number of buildings and streets. I think I see this as the reason we ought to stop the mine, because if we don't at least try, there's going to be a waterslide here before you know it." In short, those who live in the area are not as important as the environment around them, and they serve subsidiary roles in the drama of the New World Project dispute.

Unlike nonresident members, the Beartooth Alliance members who live in Cooke City and who constitute the core of the group turn to interpersonal and socially driven perceptions of what makes up their community. There is a distinctly humanized tone to these depictions: "This is my home. I have always appreciated the lack of crime in my community, the unhurried pace of life for many months each year, the sense of community small towns engender. . . ." "I value small towns, communities, things I grew up with, trust in people, not having to lock your doors at night." Some even go so far as to discount the emergent differences in Cooke City. "Since the mine's come up, it's gotten to be a polarized community a lot more which is too bad 'cause everybody has their space and has a right to their space. And yet, if there's any problem, the community bands together to help each other and that's a good characteristic of a community and that's evident here." One charter member of the Beartooth Alliance provides a well-articulated summary of how most of the group's core feels:

I cannot imagine a better community to live in. Sure, it's a great thing, a very rare thing, to be able to have a bull moose in your backyard for breakfast or to take your bike and ride over to the park for some of the best fishing in the world or to walk home from the bars at night with no fear of getting run over or mugged. You can't deny that Cooke City is an incredible chunk of real estate! But, you know, if you could somehow, you know, somehow uproot the people who live in this town and, and move 'em somewhere else, leave behind the mountains and the clean air and somehow keep the community intact, I would still choose to stay with my neighbors. We may be a bunch of loners, but I'd trust these folks with my life. During the fires we did exactly that. . . . See, the thing that makes this place worth saving from those bastards [with Crown Butte] is that they want to split us up, to take the life away from some of the finest people I've ever known. I just couldn't live with it.

Yet another way the perceptions of community held by peripheral and core elements of the membership differ, and one that may be more significant, is that for summer residents and occasional visitors, the Alliance and the community are two separate entities. By contrast, core members repeatedly stressed the symbiosis between their group and the existence of the community. Core members see the group as existing for the society of citizens (e.g., "address what we felt was the more emotional side and the environmental side of what was going to happen to our community") and as having an impact on them (e.g., "We've empowered the people of the community to do something for themselves about things that are being done to them"). Some even go so far as to claim, "The organization and the community are essentially the same thing. There wasn't really a 'community' here until the Beartooth Alliance came along." Or, as one member summed up: "It's the old, 'As the BA goes, so goes the town.' "

The manner in which Beartooth Alliance members rhetorically present their community and group affiliation represents a very important division in the membership. If the majority of the Beartooth Alliance are focused on the physical aspects of the community, it seems likely that they would feel most threatened by the tangible dangers of renewed mining. Not only does this distance the Alliance leadership from the majority regarding motivations for contributing to the campaign, but it also provides Crown Butte with an opportunity to diffuse oppositional discourse by stressing how much it is mitigating the physical threat. Consequently, the company's slick packaging of high-altitude reclamation efforts, projected controls on acid mine drainage, and the removal of cyanide-base open-pit mining from the Yellowstone National Park watershed is sure to limit the dogmatism of most dues-paying members. Unfortunately, only a single informant explicitly recognizes this perceptual chasm: "Most of our members simply don't appreciate how this mine is destroying the sense of community we have here. They only think about the environmental damage from a break in the tailings pond, for example. That's important but it's not enough. The only thing we have in common is we hate this mine. But we've gotta hate it for the same reasons."

Only Some Give It All They Got

Arguably, the one thing that best sustains any culture is the willingness of a people to actively support the social structures that give it substance. People must participate in the life of a society in meaningful ways if that culture is not to become highly fractionated, with only a few carrying the load of maintaining the principles and values of the group. The same can be said of movements seeking change; protest groups live and die by the commitments of their members to work to perpetuate the oppositional views. In the case of the Beartooth Alliance, however, the way in which individuals speak of what it means to belong to the organization reveals a second significant symbolic rift. Whereas core members grudgingly accept the need for wholehearted commitment to the campaign against the New World Project, they also recognize that "only some give it all they got." This lack of unified ownership in the cause, while all too normal in a variety of group endeavors, further weakens collective identification with what the Beartooth Alliance is trying to accomplish.

For those beyond the ongoing center of the Beartooth Alliance, being a group member generally signifies one thing, financial support. When asked what role they serve in the Alliance, the most common response from non-residents is "I don't do much more than [provide money]." And most seem satisfied with this role, reporting that for their dues (ranging upward of fifty dollars a year), they are content with receiving timely news about the New World Project (e.g., "Being in the Beartooth Alliance requires me to keep abreast of what's up with the mine and I get a lot of good information from *The Alliance* [the group's newsletter]"). Those that offer more than monetary assistance generally seem unwilling to do more than is asked of them. "To me it means I'm supporting some other people's effort. In other words, I'm on the sidelines, kind of like a cheerleader. 'Yeah, you guys go ahead and I'll give some money, I'll give some time if you need some time, I'll write some things if you want me to write some things, but I won't be able to take a major role.' "

The reluctance to provide the organization more than a measure of financial equity may be a product more of uncertainty than of disregard for the work that needs to be done. One longtime summer visitor commented:

I don't know what they [the core] do, I assume they have jobs that keep them busy. You know, at least eight hours a day, and how much time they have to devote to meetings? The members like me who thus far have only contributed money and prayers to the effort. I mean, I don't know. There hasn't been a situation where I've had the opportunity or made it my business to [get involved]. . . . And I don't know whether that's in their thinking or not. Whether they think it's important for, to reach out and to, or whether they have the time, even if they want to do it whether they have the time to do that, to involve other people or make it known what kinds of things are necessary. I guess if I'd been up here more I would have known that, on least on some of the menial things like addressing letters and that kind of thing.

In contrast to the peripheral members, most of the leadership convey a sense of unified struggle in stating such generalities as "We've come a long way [beyond] the small core who live here in winter. [The situation] draws people together for a common cause . . . you have to put yourself on the line," or "We all share the responsibility." Nonetheless, these individuals describe the nature of being in the Beartooth Alliance in more strident terms. Belonging to the group is seen as mandating the loss of "free time" and necessitating "commitment, interpersonal trust [among group members], and distrust of everything Noranda says." An even more specific sacrifice inherent in being a part of the Beartooth Alliance is provided by a tenured resident who argues that "to belong to this group means that you have to give up a lot of things more than time and money. You don't see friends 'cause of always having to keep ahead of the company and you get a real headache trying to sort through all the documents they barrage you with. If you don't feel kind of burnt out from all this, and I think most members feel the stress, then you really can't relate to what we're up against."

Only a couple of core members' discourse reflects the sensed difference between themselves and the vast majority of their fellow Alliance members. They also seem to understand what that distancing means in terms of added burdens and implications. "We do have a good core group, and monetary support from a wide range of people, that it really comes down to a handful of people who are really dedicated. . . . [It] means giving up things, giving up your time and freedoms to go after the cause just because you feel strongly about it. There's no pay, there's no, I mean there may not even be, what do I want to say, the word, like a payback. You can never see it in your lifetime really. . . . but I think that's dedication."

It seems clear that despite their belief in the egalitarian sharing of burdens within the Alliance, the core of the group is symbolically constructing what it means to be a member in a more dedicated vein than most others. This may mean that the residents will be less vigilant in trying to mobilize seasonal visitors and property owners, assuming that these members *will* actively seek out tasks and information for themselves. Even more significant may be the unseen strain that is placed on those who expect others to assist them without provocation; as one resident confided, "Sometimes I wonder why the work never seems to end when there are so many of us trying so hard. It's times like those that I simply want to give up and move away but I don't because we're all counting on one another."

Don't Stop Thinking About Tomorrow

A third significant difference in the way Beartooth Alliance members define their situation is embedded in their outlook on the future. Generally, the core and periphery anticipate very different outcomes in the fight against the New World Project. In turn, their resignation or resolve is directly associated with the extent to which individuals believe that the group will or will not continue on into the future.

If we assume that the comments of transient members truly reflect their expectations, it is reasonable to conclude that most of this cadre is resigned to the eventual licensing of the mine and believe that it is "a lead-pipe cinch." More than half of the seasonal membership I interviewed identifies a financial warrant for the mine: "they're going to get in and work to do it, just to have a job. But I just see, I see the economics hurt people. How are they going to pay the utility bill next month? You know, what am I going to do? People have to live and they have to have food. You know, that's your necessity and they're going to say 'Environment, gosh I'm sorry, I love it, but how's [the] family going to eat?' How are they going to make it?" Notably, only the mine is seen as providing economic salvation.

As most peripheral Alliance members point to the difficulty of "educating folks as to the horrors of this mine," so too do they reveal their reasonably dismal outlook as to the future of the Beartooth Alliance. Many claim that "the mine fight is psychologically discouraging since it's inevitable that the mine will go in" or that "fighting them doesn't solve anything." An important part of this discouragement is tied to how the organization will, indeed, "collapse" or "just disappear" when the actual mining begins. Several respondents speak of a "bleak" future for the Beartooth Alliance, wherein "all the work they have accomplished will have been wasted because they'll not be able to keep members up." One especially disheartened interviewee stressed, "[It is] really kinda ironic that most of the other members I run into are all in favor of Clinton with his, you know, theme [song] 'Don't Stop Thinking about Tomorrow' when most of these guys can't see anything other than the mine and what it stands for. I mean, it's probably going to happen despite all we do to stop it. What then? I mean, what's the Beartooth Alliance going to do when it loses the fight? I bet, and it's sad but probably true, that everyone will shrug their shoulders and go back to doing what they did before."

Although representatives for the majority of the Beartooth Alliance present a rather discouraging prospectus for the organization, their core counterparts are much more upbeat in thinking about the future. If there is one term that could consistently characterize the Cooke City resident's expectations, it would be "hope." It is this sense of optimism, which is so distant from the perspective noted above, that compels a very different symbolic construction. "The future depends on what happens with the mine and the unity of the core members. We can beat this thing. We can pester the company to death or at least stall 'em till the price of gold goes down and it ceases to pay 'em a profit." And even when accepting the frustrations associated with trying to inform citizens and legislators about the social and ecological threats posed by the New World Project, the pervasive buoyancy of core expectations is readily apparent; as at least one group leader puts it:

I'm not going to say it's been easy or that we've got the mine on the run or that everyone is going to rush out and riot in order to prevent it. We still have a long way to go and I'm sure that they think they've pretty well got the EIS all sewed up. But, you know, it's amazing how far we've come in such a short time. Sure it's been hard, real hard to get folks to, to understand the problems we have here and more than once I've wanted to simply grab someone and give 'em a good shake. But slowly, most people are getting educated. . . . I think we really do stand a chance of convincing the government that, in this time and place, this mine really is a terrible idea.

Unlike the summer residents and visitors, core Beartooth Alliance members seem genuinely convinced that their organization will continue even if the New World Project is permitted to operate. Several in this group indicate that since the Alliance could serve a "watchdog" function to monitor and force mitigation of mining degradation, they "don't think that people are going to give up" or that the group will fold. Again, "hope" becomes a significant construct: when asked to predict if the group would survive the coming of the mine, they typically say such things as "I really have to hope that, you know, what we started a few years ago on a whim and a prayer would, you know, remain so . . ." or, more simply, "Well, I hope so." One member clearly articulates the perceived reality of group solidarity when noting, "we're changing from the organizing stage—just getting our shit together—to a group that will not just be something on the mine, will be a viable community group that will deal with other things." In other words, though the Alliance may stop the mine, the mine cannot stop the Alliance.

In summary, the two factions within the Beartooth Alliance represent very different outlooks on the future, especially as it involves the continuation of the group. In this, the core and periphery are consistent with their other beliefs. Because the nonresident members consider Cooke City little more than a physical place and the Beartooth Alliance an organization that they do not really own, the real progress Crown Butte makes in securing an operating permit signifies an inescapable loss of physical space and a concurrent decrease in the viability of the group. Alternatively, the resident core knows that people will continue to inhabit this place, that the Alliance invites commitment since it unifies the community, and that the mine cannot vanquish the spirit of a community that resists in spite of the forces aligned against it.

Sometimes, I Don't Think I Know Who the Beartooth Alliance Is

It might be possible to realign the perspectives of core and peripheral members in the Beartooth Alliance if, indeed, the group held the vision of a shared identity. If this were the case, they could educate themselves through open discussion in order to reconstruct what they take their community, task, and future to be all about. Unfortunately, the discourse reveals a final, far more fundamental division between group members couched in the all too familiar rhetoric of "we—they."

Although the leadership of the Beartooth Alliance has made a number of obvious overtures to incorporate nonresident members into the life of the organization (e.g., house meetings, newsletters), there is an underlying sense of exclusiveness in the core. The most significant way in which residents symbolically exclude most of the membership from the life of the group appears in their depictions of who is in the Alliance and what sorts of exigences *those* individuals confront. For example, it is not unusual for year-round residents to index their local status in their portraits of the *typical* Beartooth Alliance member (e.g., "The typical Beartooth Alliance member moved here for a reason"). Not only is the union of locality and group inclusion present in the rhetoric, but core members also distinguish between themselves as the vanguard of the organization (e.g., "We do all the work while they pay for it") and the "summer people" who are "only here for a short period of time and unless you live with this day in and day out you don't feel the constant stress and pressure that goes with the involvement in a project like this."

One of the more provocative twists in the core membership's symbolic distancing of themselves from the rest of the Beartooth Alliance is found in the fact that the leaders of the group publicly proclaim the need for unity. Writing in *The Plains Truth* and *The Alliance* (i.e., the membership media of the Northern Plains Resource Council and its affiliate, the Beartooth Alliance), the newly elected chair of the organization comments, "Often in grassroots organizations a few individuals take over. This causes some members to feel left out, others become apathetic, assuming someone else will do the work. Organizations need to realize that the membership is the organization . . . that without members, there is no organization"— nonetheless, the deeper layer of Alliance discourse, embedded in their less reflective comments, suggests that most of the core believe that they *are* the organization while others appear as mere necessities in the business of fighting the New World Project.

It is in their use of pronouns to describe the Beartooth Alliance that the greatest difference between core and peripheral members is observed. Whereas the year-round residents habitually employ a "we" convention in discussing the life of the group (e.g., "We are trying to save one of the last places"), those outside the core of the group characterize their own organization in terms of "they." These sentiments are echoed in references such as "I value their participation . . ." or "they've spent time to get information out to people like me" or "they're protecting our environment, they're protecting the community, and providing a service to the community" when describing who the Beartooth Alliance is. Alternatively, another member notes that he "joined the Beartooth Alliance 'cause I thought, '. . . here's some people who care about this area. I care about it. We have an interest in common.' I don't know exactly what they're going to do, but I certainly want to support them in that effort. At least financially." Here, again, economic contributions are foregrounded while the actual activity of the organization remains obscure to noncore members.

The symbolic distinctions being made by those who represent most of the Beartooth Alliance membership may play a significant role in the extent to which they accept a collective ownership and identification with the aims of the organization. Typical comments such as "what are the aims?" and "Sometimes, I don't think I know who the Beartooth Alliance is" may suggest something more than ignorance resulting from lack of organizational knowledge. Indeed, the combination of different pronoun usage and organizational uncertainty seems more closely allied with an explicit dislike for stratification in the Alliance. Sometimes, this negativity is seen in pointed objections to the way the organization is being run (e.g., "They don't make much of an effort to inform people of meetings. You can't just think that everybody will know these things"). More often, it is the core leadership that gets chastised, as in "the people who are involved in it really don't have the time, don't have the resources, to dedicate to it. I mean, they're on the margin anyway, almost all of them are." Or, more pointedly, "They go on welfare in winter and need us in summer to supply them with jobs."

The periphery is like the core insofar as both factions symbolically distance themselves from one another while accepting that the future of the social and physical community depends on what members can do collectively to stop the New World Project. The underlying schism is only exacerbated by the somewhat overly optimistic assessment the core has of membership abilities and motivations for joining the fracas. As a consequence, discourse aimed at rallying collective action is buffeted by currents of discontent that are rarely articulated and even less apparent, even to those whose rhetoric clearly indicates a sense of estrangement from the Beartooth Alliance.

Implications for Rhetorical Effectiveness

The previous analysis suggests a number of explanations for the specific rhetoric of the Beartooth Alliance. Of course, alternative interpretations are possible, but the argument presented here helps us to better understand the nature of this grassroots group as well as learning something about the symbolic promise and shortcomings of other environmentalist campaigns throughout the country. To develop this explanation, I consider two questions: Why do members of the Beartooth Alliance use *these* discursive conventions in describing themselves and the world around them? And, what implications do these choices hold for the effectiveness and long-term viability of the organization?

To the extent that there are systematic similarities and differences across Beartooth Alliance members' discourse, there may be any number of reasons why Alliance members use these particular symbolic patterns. One explanation suggests that because all Alliance members recognize the threat posed by the New World Project (in whatever way that threat may be mentally represented), they are compelled not only to generate agitative rhetoric but also to create a general system for symbolizing the situation. Dwight Conquergood could easily have been thinking of the Beartooth Alliance when he argued, "Betwixt and between worlds, suspended between a shattered past, *refugees and other displaced people* must create [a symbolic system] for recollecting, recontextualizing, and refashioning their identities" (185, emphasis added). If we consider Beartooth Alliance members as being, indeed, "refugees" from an outside world or "displaced" given the resource pressures ushered in with the mine, we would naturally expect them to forge new identities supported by rhetorical conventions.

The specific though varied symbol system used by the Beartooth Alliance largely depends upon the sociological foundation the members have for most of the year. Those who have recreational property or visit the region only for brief periods draw upon a different set of socio-economic conditions than are generally available to core residents. These basic differences are implicit throughout the discourse. The association between background and rhetoric seems to bear out Miles's Law: "Where you stand depends on where you sit" (Miles 399–400). That is, the position one takes on an issue or in reference to others depends on the dominant culture one generally represents. Visitors and seasonal residents represent the wealthier patrons of the organization and, for the most part, seem well enfranchised in the economy of the United States. Thus, despite their motivation to participate in the symbolic life of the group, they are more oriented toward fatalistic accommodation of powerful interests and tend to use their financial clout to mitigate potential problems linked to their possession of tangible goods (cf. Fiske, "For Cultural Interpretation" 459). They would naturally distinguish themselves from those less economically empowered, such as the core of the Alliance, by focusing on the material conditions in the Cooke City area. Conversely, year-round residents do not speak from a financially secure position and are more likely to reject in toto anything that might jeopardize the well-being of the one thing they possess that the seasonal members do not, their social community.

A key element of symbol systems based on different socio-economic orientations is the presence of particular terms and phrases that signify as much about the perspective of the rhetor as they do about the subject. For example, in characterizing the Cooke City region as "one of the last places" to find refuge, the group implicitly discounts the fact that past and future history depends on mining. What matters are the *present* values as embodied in the individualists and environmental conditions being threatened by a faceless company. However, what makes this a "best place" depends on who is speaking; the difference in members' constructs for "community" are quite significant. The speaker's social foundation determines his or her sense of commitment, hope, and joint participation; people cannot "commit" themselves to a physical layout that will always be "other" than a set of personal relations and inherently at risk from greater, tangible forces such as money and political clout. Here, the unity of one part of the Alliance symbol system is undercut by deeper divisions reflected in the rhetorical identity of the group.

There are at least two ways in which the unifying elements of Alliance rhetoric may result in an inefficient campaign to stop the New World Project. On the one hand, the shared belief that the region is populated by "rugged individuals" who can "go it alone" and tend "to isolate themselves from each other" can cripple the organizational efforts of the group. If members assume that the leaders of the organization are like the rest of the local population, they may be more accepting of a lack of structure, forethought, and planned strategy in Alliance activities. Living in the area may instill in core members less appreciation for organizational skills. On the other hand, by framing history in terms of mining, spokespersons may be obligating themselves to address only the physical effects of mining since that is all that is evident in the current epoch. As Michel de Certeau (122) cautions, depictions of history not only place current controversies in context, they also define how people should act as the future becomes the present. If hardrock mining results in environmental destruction, Alliance rhetoric should focus on that degradation rather than less historically tractable disruptions to social structures. Consequently, the Alliance leadership may unknowingly emphasize physical aspects over social effects in "educating" seasonal visitors about the New World Project despite the greater relative value the core places on the interpersonal community in thinking about impending threats.

The extent to which Beartooth Alliance members' symbolic constructions of the situation are fragmented is a more significant obstacle to effective collective action. For instance, there can be little argument that the Beartooth Alliance is focused on a local controversy and not a matter of principle; the members are opposed to mining in *their* region and not in general. Thus, their rhetoric can generally be categorized as being akin to many other "not in my backyard" (NIMBY) disputes (Mazmanian and Morell 233). Unfortunately, NIMBY rhetoric constrains effective participation in the public sphere because it is based upon the values of self-interest and not the public good. Although the Alliance asserts that hardrock mining is incompatible with the long-term viability of the Greater Yellowstone ecosystem, members' less posturing-prone discourse of everyday depictions suggests that these people are more concerned with their own needs than with those of a society they seek to escape. And this self-interest is compounded by being predicated upon the opposing core and peripheral assumptions of what constitutes the "community" at risk (cf. deHaven-Smith 194).

The potentially crippling effects of a NIMBY orientation can be extracted from various facets of Alliance rhetoric. For example, to the extent Crown Butte can act to lessen the distrust of nonresident Alliance members through public relations efforts and donations of tangible services to Cooke City (e.g., subsidizing emergency medical care equipment), and to the extent the company can show that the physical environment will not be significantly altered as far as the visitor or property owner is concerned, the major benefactors and constituency of the Beartooth Alliance will be less willing to contribute to the cause. As a result, the primary self-interest of the core, the social community, will be orphaned, and the ability of the group to act in concert against the mine will be severely hampered.

In arguing that the rhetorical identity of the Beartooth Alliance may have been imperfect in 1992, I do not wish to imply that the group is necessarily headed for utter failure. Indeed, with the introduction of "house meetings" in the summer of 1992, the election of new officers, and continued pressure for regulatory oversight in the national media, hard-rock mining has not resumed adjacent to Yellowstone National Park as of mid-1995. Significantly, legal opposition to efforts by Crown Butte to exempt the project from antidegradation water quality standards, combined with an objective environmental impact statement, resulted in lengthy delays. However, with the coming of the 104th Congress and the rise of a very powerful "Wise Use" movement in the West, the climate began to change to the extent that regulatory relief was not as assured as it may have seemed at the beginning of the Clinton presidency. Consequently, I want to underscore that the Beartooth Alliance's task of thwarting the New World Project has been made more difficult by the manner in which they have grown to see themselves in the early stages of the dispute. And, in some small way, the same may be true of the country as a whole as we survey the expanse of different environmentalisms in the United States today.

Alliance Discourse and the Context of American Environmentalism

In this final section, I want to briefly explore what the foregoing snapshot of discourse can tell us about the broader landscape of contemporary environmental communications. The Beartooth Alliance may face a unique configuration of exigencies and opportunities in rising to the challenge of stopping the New World Project, but the group is by no means an aberration. In general, environmentalists in our country (ranging from the radical fringe groups chained to trees in ancient forests to the conservative national organizations rooted within the Washington, D.C., beltway) face the same sorts of internal contradictions and deep-seated value conflicts apparent in the rhetoric of the Beartooth Alliance (deHaven Smith 177; Gottlieb, *Forcing the Spring* 318–19). Thus, an ethnography of the group can reflect at least a portion of the way in which significant symbols are entrenched in modern environmental thought.

Each of the themes that unify the rhetoric of the Beartooth Alliance has a complementary strain in the broad discourse of American environmentalism. Excepting those who have been pushed to the less desirable edges of society, most people highly value the places they live in or seek to visit. We also distrust faceless bureaucrats or those corporations that would limit our freedoms within or despoil the character of our cherished environs. We sanctify the right of individuals to stand up against long odds in the fight against pollution and admire those who have been able to "go it alone" in waging lonely environmental battles. And, as Sherry and Charles Cable observe (106–7), it is remarkable that most modern environmentalists at the grassroots define their "movement" as originating with as well as de-pending upon the ecological destruction of the earth. In this sense, the rhetoric of the Beartooth Alliance represents a microcosm of mainstream consciousness.

Beyond the tropes and schemes that unite environmental movements and that are heard in Alliance discourse, it is the sense of rhetorical distance that may be most problematic. Just as the core and periphery of the Beartooth Alliance are fragmented in the construction of a few significant symbolic markers, so too do other activists confront the same sorts of sepa-rateness. Most important would be the mental construction of "commu-nity." As Donohue, Olien, and Tichenor observed twenty years ago in the mining communities of Minnesota, the bulk of environmental rhetoric in the marketplace is focused on the physical threats posed by industry and development; many environmentalists approach their task as one of "edu-cating" others of the "facts" of the matter (Cantrill 83), and it is "facts" that are most obvious when we assess a decaying environment. Unfortu-nately, the widespread obsession with the environmental health of a *place* (be it a chunk of forest or an entire planet) tends to ignore the distinctly social causes and ramifications of ecological destruction. As a conse-quence, and quite like the Beartooth Alliance, most people ignore distant causes of decay such as overpopulation or economic stratification in think-ing about environmental problems, while searching for technical solu-tions. Social justice issues are obscured by campaigns promoting techno-logical fixes (Hofrichter 89).

There are a number of other thematic comparisons between Beartooth Alliance members' descriptions of their organization and what often oc-curs in alternative environmental arenas. Many lament the fact that there are so few "eco-warriors" who are willing to commit more than simply money to the cause of protecting precious resources; most seem content to pay their dues to gain tidbits of information or do not know what else they can do (Gottlieb, *Forcing the Spring* 198; cf. Wiebe 430). Furthermore, a great many environmentalists despair at the cabal of socio-economic forces that have rallied against efficient environmental policy making since Earth Day 1970. It seems as if only the movement leadership expresses hope of being able to forge a national consensus, let alone ratify international agreements. Just as the less empowered sectors of society are seen as having less valued cultural lifestyles and are marginalized in the public sphere by dominant groups (Fraser 68), many of the most ardent activists are castigated by their colleagues as being "tree spikers" and no better than those who would destroy the environment for short-term gain. As Bruce Piasecki and Peter Asmus (13) lament, few voices are heard that speak of inclusion, of moving beyond blame, and of finding solutions that will benefit everyone.

A popular way of phrasing the link between situated practices and ecological consciousness has been "Think globally, act locally." However, such well-intentioned recommendations may not take account of the possibility that individuals act at the local level precisely because of the way in which they mentally represent the world at large. Thus, it may well be that the symbolic character of Beartooth Alliance discourse is due more to who we are as a people beholden to the larger culture and less to the specific circumstances that promulgate them as a grassroots organization. If so, we have yet another warrant for changing the nature of our culture before trying to tackle the serious problems festering in various beloved corners of the world.

ACKNOWLEDGMENTS

Research for this chapter was supported by a Faculty Research Grant from Northern Michigan University. Grateful appreciation is extended to Perin Fenske and the Office of Research Development for their assistance in completing the project.

WORKS CITED

Bakhtin, Mikhail Mikhailovich. *Speech Genres and Other Late Essays*. Trans. Marvin Holquist. Austin: U of Texas P, 1986.
Burke, Kenneth. *A Grammar of Motives*. Berkeley: U of California P, 1969.
Cable, Sherry, and Charles Cable. *Environmental Problems, Grassroots Solutions: The Politics of Grassroots Environmental Conflict*. New York: St. Martin's, 1995.
Cantrill, James G. "Communication and Our Environment: Categorizing Research in Environmental Advocacy." *Journal of Applied Communication Research* 21 (1993): 66–95.
Carbaugh, Donal. *American Talking*. Norwood, NJ: Ablex, 1988.
Carbaugh, Donal. " 'The Mountain' and 'The Project': Dueling Depictions of a

Natural Environment." In *The Conference on the Discourse of Environmental Advocacy,* ed. Christine L. Oravec and James G. Cantrill. Salt Lake City: U of Utah Humanities Center, 1992. 360–77.

Cohen, Jodi R. "The 'Relevance' of Cultural Identity in Audiences' Interpretations of Mass Media." *Critical Studies in Mass Communication* 8 (1991): 442–54.

Congressional Research Service, Library of Congress. *Greater Yellowstone Ecosystem: An Analysis of Data Submitted by Federal and State Agencies.* Washington, DC: GPO, 1987.

Conquergood, Dwight. "Rethinking Ethnography: Towards a Critical Cultural Politics." *Communication Monographs* 58 (1991): 179–94.

De Certeau, Michel. *The Practice of Everyday Life.* Berkeley: U of California P, 1984.

DeHaven-Smith, Lance. "Environmental Belief Systems: Public Opinion on Land Use Regulation in Florida." *Environment and Behavior* 20 (1988): 176–99.

Donohue, Gordon; Charles Olien; and Paul Tichenor. "Communities, Pollution, and the Fight for Survival." *Journal of Environmental Education* 6 (1974): 29–37.

Fiske, John. "British Cultural Studies and Television." In *Channels of Discourse,* ed. Robert C. Allen. Chapel Hill: U of North Carolina P, 1987. 254–98.

Fiske, John. "For Cultural Interpretation: A Study of the Culture of Homelessness." *Critical Studies in Mass Communication* 8 (1991): 445–74.

Fraser, Nancy. "Rethinking the Public Sphere: A Contribution to the Critique of Actually Existing Democracy." *Social Text* 25/26 (1990): 56–80.

Garfinkel, Harold. *Studies in Ethnomethodology.* Engelwood Cliffs, NJ: Prentice, 1967.

Glidden, Ralph. *Exploring the Yellowstone High Country: A History of the Cooke City Area.* 2d ed. Cooke City, MT: The Cooke City Store, 1982.

Gottlieb, Robert. "An Odd Assortment of Allies: American Environmentalism in the 1990s." In *Media and the Environment,* ed. Craig L. LaMay and Everette E. Dennis. Washington, DC: Island P, 1991. 43–54.

Gottlieb, Robert. *Forcing the Spring: The Transformation of the American Environmental Movement.* Washington, DC: Island P, 1993.

Greater Yellowstone Coalition. "Gold Mine Threatens Yellowstone." *Inside Greater Yellowstone* (Summer 1993): 7.

Habermas, Jürgen. *The Structural Transformation of the Public Sphere: An Inquiry into a Category of Bourgeois Society.* Trans. Thomas Berger and Frederick Lawrence. Cambridge: MIT P, 1989.

Hofrichter, Richard. "Cultural Activism and Environmental Justice. In *Toxic Struggles: The Theory and Practice of Environmental Justice,* ed. Richard Hofrichter. Philadelphia: New Society P, 1993. 85–97.

Hymes, Dell. "Sociolinguistics and the Ethnography of Speaking." In *Social Anthropology and Language,* ed. Edwin Ardener. London: Tavistock, 1971. 47–94.

Kittredge, William, and Annick Smith. *The Last Best Place: A Montana Anthology.* Helena: Montana Historical Society, 1990.

Luhmann, Niklas. *Ecological Communication.* Trans. John Bednarz, Jr. Chicago: U of Chicago P, 1989.

Mazmanian, Daniel A., and David Morell. "The 'NIMBY' Syndrome: Facility Siting and the Failure of Democratic Discourse." In *Environmental Policy in the 1990s,* 2d ed., ed. Norman Vig and Michael E. Kraft. Washington, DC: CQ P, 1994. 233–50.

McGee, Michael C. "Text, Context, and the Fragmentation of Contemporary Culture." *Western Journal of Speech Communication* 54 (1990): 274–90.

McNeely, Jeffrey A., and David Pitt. "Culture: A Missing Element in Conservation and Development." In *Culture and Conservation: The Human Dimension in Environmental Planning,* ed. Jeffrey A. McNeely and David Pitt. Dover, NH: Croom Helm, 1985. 1–10.

Miles, Rufus E, Jr. "The Origin and Meaning of Miles' Law." *Public Administration Review* 38 (1978): 399–403.

Osborn, Michael. "In Defence of Broad Mythic Criticism: A Reply to Rowland." *Communication Studies* 41 (1990): 121–27.

Piasecki, Bruce, and Peter Asmus. *In Search of Environmental Excellence: Moving beyond Blame.* New York: Simon & Schuster, 1987.

Rasker, Ray. *The Wealth of Nature: New Economic Realities in the Yellowstone Region.* Bozeman, MT: Color World Printers, 1992.

Ricoeur, Paul. "The Model of the Text: Meaningful Action Considered as Text." In *Understanding and Social Inquiry,* ed. Fred R. Dallmeyer and Thomas A. McCarthy. Notre Dame: U of Notre Dame P, 1977. 27–48.

Strodthoff, Glenn G.; Robert P. Hawkins; and A. Clay Schoenfeld. "Media Roles in a Social Movement: A Model of Ideology Diffusion." *Journal of Communication* 35 (1985): 135–53.

Wiebe, George. "Mass Media and Man's Relationship to His Environment." *Journalism Quarterly* 50 (1973): 426–32.

White, Leslie A. *The Evolution of Culture.* New York: McGraw, 1959.

Williams, Raymond. *Problems of Materialism and Culture.* London: Verso, 1980.

CHAPTER 7

Landscape, Drama, and Dissensus
The Rhetorical Education of
Red Lodge, Montana

ZITA INGHAM

Some Better Way to Live

On the night of Friday, 19 June 1992, more than 120 people milled around in the main hall of the Roberts Senior Citizens Center in Red Lodge, Montana. An old Western drama was about to be enacted, with all the usual players: ranchers, townspeople, miners. The central player in the Western drama has always been the land—the land as water, timber, ore, grazing rights, creatures—and the subject of this drama is, as always, land use. Who has, and who will have, the right to do what with the land in and around Red Lodge? The conflict persists, down through the decades— "who runs this town?"—although more sophisticated ways of asking that question have evolved. If indeed the town will build an airport, what part of the landscape would become the runway, the parking area, the flyway? Who owns Rock Creek, the stream that runs through town? Who has the right to walk along it? Who controls—who determines and who benefits from—the zoning and taxing of the supremely developable ranch land surrounding the town? Who decides what constitutes "ownership" and "control" of the land and its resources?

The boundaries between the western dramas of novels and films, and the historical dramas of the West—range wars, Indian wars, all the larger and smaller conflicts over land use—have long been blurred; the qualities of each illuminate the other. In writing about the Western drama, as seen in movies such as *Shane* and *High Noon,* Jane Tompkins and, earlier, Peter Homans investigate this "moral dynamic." For Tompkins, as she argues in *West of Everything: The Inner Life of Westerns,* this dynamic culminates in

195

a "moment of moral ecstasy. The hero is *so right* (that is, so wronged) that he can kill with impunity. . . . The feeling of supreme righteousness in this instant is delicious and hardly to be distinguished from murderousness" (229). She argues that what's most important about this moment—the shoot-out as the moment of righteous violence on which the mythic stories of the West turn—is our ability to reflect on it. This "moment of righteous ecstasy, . . . the moment of murderousness. . . . [is] a moment when there's still time to stop, there's still time to reflect, there's still time to recall what happened in *High Noon,* there's still time to say, 'I don't care who's right or who's wrong. There has to be some better way for people to live' " (233). For Homans, "the key to the Western" is "[t]his process whereby desire is at once indulged and veiled. . . . What is required is that temptation be indulged while providing the appearance of having been resisted" (89). As the transparency of this dynamic of Western films and novels becomes more popularly evident, some communities in the West have begun attempts at living some better way.

This better way, at least for the community of Red Lodge, begins as a traditional Western, as what Homans describes as a "puritan morality tale in which the savior-hero redeems the community from the temptations of the devil" (89). In Red Lodge a group of concerned residents formed the Beartooth Front Community Forum and invited Luther Propst to conduct a series of community dialogue workshops. Propst is executive director of the Sonoran Institute, a nonprofit conservation organization based in Tucson, Arizona, that promotes the Successful Communities Dialogue program as a way to help resolve community disputes. The stage was set: a limited and unstable economic base made land use a charged issue, tensions arose from increasing population and impending development, and polarized factions in the community verbally fought each other. Enter the redemptive stranger, come to put things right and then vanish, leaving behind a more peaceful and productive, not to mention grateful, community.

But this is not the old West. Discussion, argument, legal actions, and decrees replace shoot-outs. Finding a better way to live and to manage environmental issues such as land use rests on language, on the use of language to discover, initiate, persuade, understand, anger, conciliate: on rhetoric. In June 1992, citizens in Red Lodge met to begin a process that has changed the economic, environmental, and sociocultural identity of the town and will continue to do so. Crucial to those changes has been the rhetorical education of many of its residents. Through public forums, workshops, committee meetings, committee reports to the communities, and news stories, residents of Red Lodge began to discuss and argue in public. Where once, for instance, townspeople grumbled about what the owners of large ranches might do when the financial rewards of development exceeded those of ranching, they now meet to develop plans. There is broad-based citizen participation in zoning and environmental impact studies and in grant writing to foster local economic development.

Because these situations—all rhetorical, all dependent on how people are persuaded by the use of language—now exist, residents are learning to articulate what they believe about the community, its past, present, and future, and their actions depend on what they articulate. The Beartooth Front forum meeting on that Friday night and the next day in June 1992 initiated a rhetorical education of active citizens—training and practice in how and what to argue with each other. This essay describes some features of the initial steps of this rhetorical education.

The Rhetoric of Community

Whether we adopt Aristotle's definition of rhetoric as the discovery of "the available means of persuasion" (24), or J. Frederick Crews's notion of rhetoric as "the placement of ideas" (6), or the definition of rhetoric as the possibilities of language to deform as well as formulate the truth of events, places, people, ideas, rhetoric is situated and can be analyzed only in the context of literal and figurative location. A speaker or writer—a rhetor— always occupies a particular ideological, cultural, geographical place from which to speak or write. The rhetor's rhetorical stance, as delineated by Wayne Booth, depends on the contexts of "the available arguments about the subject itself, the interests and peculiarities of the audience, and the voice, the implied character of the speaker" (141). Members of audiences, in turn, listen, read, and respond from their own places. As the messages fly back and forth in communities like Red Lodge, or even as they hang in the air without visible, immediate responses, communication changes the speakers and listeners, the writers and readers themselves, and this exchange can transform both the community and its environment. As M. Jimmie Killingsworth notes, "In addition to changing language and changing minds, the enterprise of rhetoric suggests that speakers and writers have the power to transform the site of discourse, the community itself" (110). In the case of Red Lodge, as in many other locations of environmental disputes, the rhetorical enterprise alters not only the rhetorical landscape, but the physical landscape as well.

The Scene

Red Lodge, Montana (population 2,000), lies at the foot of the Beartooth mountain range, northeast of Yellowstone National Park, and like other Montana towns in the Yellowstone area, Red Lodge is changing rapidly.

The area encompassed by the Greater Yellowstone ecosystem—which includes parts of Montana, Idaho, and Wyoming and all of the communities in and around Yellowstone and Grand Teton National Parks and the surrounding national forests—faces particular pressure to resolve issues associated with rapid population growth. The 1990 census shows that if the twenty adjacent counties in this area were considered as one state, it would be the fastest-growing state in the country. Between 1991 and 1992, subdivision activity in Carbon County, where Red Lodge is located, increased 44 percent, most occurring along the Beartooth Front. This figure does not include parcels twenty acres or larger, which are currently exempt from evaluation. Carbon County ranks first in Montana Greater Yellowstone ecosystem counties in land development on a per capita basis ("Successful Communities" 5).

Because of economic and demographic pressures, Red Lodge and towns like it are forced to resolve issues (even if by ignoring them) that will determine qualities of the population and of the environment in the future. To do that, and to insure that the resolutions consider the well-being of as many residents as possible, the citizens of Red Lodge need to learn how to argue better, how to speak and write to each other and to others about these issues. The first requirement for the "rhetorical health" of a community is that opportunities exist for all voices to be heard. Seeking consensus, in the context of a community beginning to grapple with issues of growth, is not perhaps as useful as the thorough exploration of "dissensus." Rhetorical theorist John Trimbur suggests that the goal of consensus in a community may not be as useful as was once thought. Depending on its political context, dissensus can replace consensus as "a powerful instrument . . . to generate differences, . . . and to transform the relations of power that determine who may speak and what counts as a meaningful statement" ("Consensus and Difference" 602). Before communities can approach the resolution of issues, Trimbur suggests,

> we will need to rehabilitate the notion of consensus by redefining it in relation to a rhetoric of dissensus. We will need, that is, to look at collaborative learning not merely as a process of consensus-making but, more importantly, as a process of identifying differences and locating these differences in relation to each other. (610)

Trimbur is speaking about the "community" of a writing classroom, but his insight into consensus and dissensus applies to other, larger communities; as we all know, consensus is notoriously difficult in environmental disputes. In order to resolve their disputes and protect their environment, communities like Red Lodge need to engage in the collaborative learning that characterizes Trimbur's rhetorical education. A community of residents who hold differing opinions about, for instance, whether or not to build an airport for their town must learn to articulate their differences and to explore their different values and how these would shape their environment.

The danger of beginning to talk to each other is always the same: the pressure for consensus, the ultimate requirement of consent, is always uncomfortable. If the nature of events or the community demands consensus, the situation can, paradoxically, dissolve, the rhetorical enterprise break down, and the various factions withdraw, taking with them the chance to resolve the issue. Everyone is aware of this risk; it often constitutes the basis of factional power. Everyone in Red Lodge knows, for example, that drawing larger businesses requires an airport, that airports destroy huge amounts of wildlife habitat, and that, eventually, some residents will have to concede something. That kind of anticipation of concessions inhibits the rhetorical process from the beginning. For Trimbur, as for the organizers of the Beartooth Front Community Forum, "The revised notion of consensus I am proposing here depends paradoxically on its deferral, not its realization" ("Consensus and Difference" 614). This essay describes the way this community and the Sonoran Institute use the strategy of deferred consensus.

The Script

The process of planning a future for Red Lodge was deliberate and initiated by local citizens but catalyzed by outsiders. The rhetorical education of Red Lodge began with the activism of an ad hoc group of citizens, but was guided by a Successful Communities Dialogue workshop developed by the Sonoran Institute. The Sonoran Institute, a nonprofit conservation organization based in Tucson, Arizona, was created in 1990 with technical and financial assistance from the World Wildlife Fund. The institute's mission is to work "nationwide to preserve the integrity of protected natural areas and adjacent communities by cooperatively resolving potential conflicts between conservation and meeting the needs and aspirations of adjacent communities and landowners. The Institute also works to insure that development occurring adjacent to protected areas adheres to the highest level of environmental compatibility and sensitivity" (*Annual Report 1991–1992* i). The institute first began with projects to protect Saguaro National Monument outside Tucson, but now has extended its work throughout the West and into Mexico. The institute is guided by a board of directors that includes conservation and business leaders, and "works with diverse groups (including natural resource managers, landowners, conservation leaders, and local officials) to create and implement tangible projects which link sustainable development and protection of natural resources" (*Annual Report 1991–1992* i). One such project, with the goal of initiating activities at the local level, is the Successful Communities Dialogue workshops. Such workshops (which began in 1988 as a pilot program of the Conservation Foundation, now incorporated in the World Wildlife Fund) have been held in various communities throughout the Greater Yellowstone area. These workshops use something like Killingsworth's idea of the enterprise of rhetoric to resolve environmental disputes and, ultimately, preserve natural resources. The emphasis on deferred consensus is key to the initial stages of community dialogue.

Propst and the Beartooth Front Community Forum organizers argue that community members must develop a consciousness of rhetorical stance, of how citizens stand in relation to each other, given their viewpoints. Community members must become more conscious and more deliberate in their uses of language so that they can know what they want to argue for in relation to Red Lodge and how to go about manifesting and settling those arguments. Increasingly, serious environmental disputes are resolved by outside mediators through a process that leaves existing community relations mostly untouched. In contrast, the rhetorical education promoted in Red Lodge helps communities develop and articulate working relationships themselves. Outside mediators help parties reach agreement relative to a specific conflict, with a process and outcome that may be voluntary or may be legally determined. But in the case of community dialogue, building and remaining a community is the goal, rather than more or less specific consensus. In the literature of environmental mediation, where building community is more likely to be seen as the "socialization of opponents" (Lake 62), leaving antagonisms and misunderstandings intact, less than ideal valuations of "community" are evident. In his investigation of the dynamics of mediation, Scott Mernitz uses social and psychological research into the nature of community conflict to argue for the positive social effects of mediation:

conflict tends to act in group-binding and group-preserving capacity. Conflict maintains, rather than disrupts, the well-balanced society by facilitating communication and defining relationships and group structures, so as to clarify for a participant his position and status relative to others. . . . conflict and the ensuing settlement establish and maintain the balance of power, so that a legitimate distribution of resources is achieved. Parties perceive themselves *in equilibrium*—a condition that is the desired end of most conflict situations. (51)

In this view, mediation—the search for a resolution of conflict that has escalated into litigation—seems successful when a balance of power is reached. In contrast, community dialogue has as its goal not equilibrium, but connection.

A crucial difference between the approach of community dialogue and that of mediation is in the timing of intervention in the community's history and in assumptions about the rhetorical effectiveness of community members and factions. The Sonoran Institute tries to intervene early in the process because it believes individuals can develop the rhetorical skills and set up the rhetorical situations that prevent litigious conflicts. Mediators, on the other hand, generally intervene only at the eleventh hour and use their knowledge of rhetorical skills and situations to facilitate agreements, not to facilitate the education of community members in ways to reach agreements on their own. Thus, the Sonoran Institute's idea of rhetorical dialogue about the environment ties the health of the environment to the rhetorical health of the community. If environmental health can be defined as the flourishing of diverse species, then rhetorical health denotes the flourishing of diverse voices.

The rhetorical education of Red Lodge began with this workshop in June 1992. The objectives of the two-day forum, conducted by Luther Propst, were "(1) to bring together diverse citizens, organizations, and government agencies to identify local values and assets, develop a vision for the future of the community and identify practical and tangible steps for realizing this vision; and (2) to provide a forum and process for informed communications and consensus-building that transcend the limits of single-value advocacy and special interest politics" ("Successful Communities" 3). These objectives are fundamentally rhetorical in nature: bringing members of the community into dialogue with each other, articulating a vision of the community's future and steps toward the manifestation of that vision (which only exists in language), and providing outlets and strategies for "informed communication." In essence, the workshop was a place, a situation, to display the value of skill in rhetoric, and to argue that changes in the community and its natural environment depend first on the kinds of rhetorical choices citizens make.

Advance Notice

The crucial step in this process of rhetorical education was to provide a forum for discussion. The rhetoric surrounding the invitation to discuss the town's future is an example of how rhetorical education begins with the demonstration and modeling of strategies, attitudes, rhetorical stances. In studying events at Red Lodge, Kenneth Burke's rhetorical concept of "identification" is useful, because the impetus for the entire process of planning the community's future depends on the reinforcement of Red Lodge *as* a community. The crucial strategy is an attitude of social cohesion: the adoption, by individuals, of a common identity from which to act together. In Burke's words,

"Identification" at its simplest is also a deliberative device, as when the politician seeks to identify himself with his audience. . . . But identification can also be an end, as when people earnestly yearn to identify themselves with some group or other. Here they are not necessarily being acted upon by a conscious external agent, but may be acting upon themselves to this end. ("Rhetoric—Old and New" 203)

The persuasive aim of the forum was to enable residents to envision themselves as a community—"acting upon themselves" by identifying with each other, by establishing stances in relationship to each other. In the context of the discussion at Red Lodge, the "external agent," the Sonoran Institute, uses the desire to facilitate identification between individuals within the community as a persuasive strategy—as a way of increasing its credibility in the community and as a way of demonstrating the power of such a strategy, such an attitude. All of the forum activities—the presentations by community members and by outside "experts," the recounting of regional and individual histories, the small and large group discussions— are strategies to increase group identification among community members.

Identification began with flyers posted around town in early June announcing that the Beartooth Front Community Forum (the group "dedicated to forging cooperative solutions to the challenges of tomorrow," as noted on the flyer) would be sponsoring a community dialogue, a Friday evening and all-day Saturday event to which "You're Invited! Share your thoughts about growth and economic development, preservation, and other important matters affecting you and your family." The sponsoring group, although anonymous, makes an appeal to its audience based on its credibility as constructed on the flyer: the group is "dedicated," earnest in recognizing and valiant in meeting the "challenges of tomorrow," and fair, not elitest but "cooperative." The flyer's authors also display the virtuous aim of including as many residents as possible in the invitation; the forum was advertised as "FREE," and "Lunch will be provided on Saturday. Babysitting is available if needed." Citizens were not only invited to lunch, but also to "Please lend a hand!" to participate in "forging cooperative solutions to the challenges of tomorrow." The initial anonymity of the group prevented its being dismissed because of objections to certain members, and no doubt such an appeal would draw the skeptical—those wondering who these people were and what they were planning—as well as those who wished to become proponents for change. Anonymity also prevented the forum from being perceived as a closed group. Cooperation and inclusion are further emphasized by the question posed in the largest type on the flyer, "WHAT KIND OF FUTURE WOULD YOU CHOOSE FOR RED LODGE AND THE BEARTOOTH FRONT?" The flyer invites identification with the community at large by suggesting that every community member can have a voice in planning. Over 120 residents attended the opening session of the workshop, more that 5 percent of the population of the town.

The Lights Dim: Opening Shots

The Friday evening session of the workshop began with an invocation by Kent Young, a Red Lodge attorney, to remember that these meetings were not about "what we *don't* want the community to be, but what we *want* the community to be." The question at the core of the long-standing Western dilemma—"who runs this town?"—is revised, cast positively, if a bit more vaguely: "What do you want Red Lodge to be?" The answer being formulated here assumes that individuals who make up the community will have the opportunity and ability to decide and to act on achieving those goals. For the moment—for as long as possible—the naiveté of these assumptions is suspended, as the organizers and other residents tacitly agree to participate.

The program begins with a visually rich, unabashedly emotional appeal to an idealistic sense of community in general, and an ideal sense of Red Lodge in particular. The audience watches a slide montage, by local photographer Merv Coleman, entitled "Red Lodge, A Place for All Seasons": fields of flowers, quaint downtown views, rodeo scenes, children playing in the snow, dancers at the town festival, all set to John Denver's sentimental and familiar "Season Suite" ("Oh, I love the life around me"). The audience oohs and aahs at the scenes, whispering to each other the names of particular places and people as they appear. Afterward, the moderator acknowledges the show as "meant to bring a tear to your eye." The strength of persuasion that rests on just such an arousal of the audience's emotions was articulated by Aristotle, who argued the importance of this appeal of *pathos:*

Particularly in political oratory . . . it adds much to an orator's influence that his own character should look right and that he should be thought to entertain the right feelings towards his hearers; and also that his hearers themselves should be in just the right frame of mind. . . . The Emotions are all those feelings that so change men as to affect their judgements. (91)

A sentimental view of Red Lodge appeals emotionally, but the program organizers cannot allow the audience to feel it is being manipulated, because that would undercut the program's *ethos,* its credibility. *Ethos* rests on the appeal of a speaker's character who "should be thought to entertain the right feelings towards his hearers." The argument for community connections rests on the perceptions that the program organizers have moral

authority, that they are committed to what's best for the community but
not domineering in their methods.

The *pathos,* the emotional appeal of the arguments, is established, as is
the *ethos*—the credibility, good will, and intelligence—of the program organizers. The work that remains is to get down to the subject at hand: Red
Lodge, as it exists now and as it is envisioned. The program completes the
triumvirate of Aristotle's modes of persuasion by moving on to *logos,* rational appeals. The appeals to logic—the most basic being the various reasons why Red Lodge, as an entire community, needs to plan for its future—
begin with a series of speakers, of whom Luther Propst will be the last. The
speakers are public figures and experts, specialists in the issues that affect
the community. The rhetorical intention of this part of the program is to
ground the discussions in evidence from authorities, to encourage participation, and to set the context—one of reasoned discussion—for tomorrow's workshop. The desired rhetorical effect is a commitment to action.

John Prinkki, a Carbon County commissioner, notes fundamental
changes in the area: growth in Red Lodge and the paradoxical decline in
the tax base. Because of the lack of oil revenue in recent years, the tax base
has dropped from $30 million to $17 million. He asserts the county's commitment to working with businesses, and reiterates what residents often
say: "We are looking for better than service industry jobs; we need a diverse business community." He ends by citing two instances of lack of city/
county planning that have created problems: the inability of the county to
maintain existing roads while building new, outlying roads, and a development, the Country Club Estates, that continues to draw heavily on tax
money because of a lack of controls on the developer. Prinkki aligns himself with his listeners by asserting that their concerns are his. He argues that
Red Lodge has severe economic problems, some of which could be averted
by better planning and by controls on development.

Other speakers include Barbara Campbell, head of a private community
development consulting firm and author of the 1989 Carbon County Economic Development Plan, who speaks on the three greatest needs of the
area: adequate infrastructure (roads, sewage), affordable housing, and
jobs. The most polemical, and also the most knowledgeable, of the speakers, she warns that "big developers *will* come, and they can easily take
away any chance you have for self-direction."

The participation of speakers such as Prinkki and Campbell, who are the
most knowledgeable about the economic issues of the county, insures that
the dialogue proceeds from a foundation of authority, of facts. Both authorities argue for planning, but implicit in these arguments is the notion
that the environment is at risk because of economic development. It is
assumed, by the speakers, the program organizers, and the audience, that

challenges to the environmental health of the community will result from the growth of its economy. Whether or not this assumption is valid, it underlies the entire workshop. Campbell's final remark, that developers are set to pounce on Red Lodge, is especially motivating, because anyone in the audience can reel off the names of small western communities that did not muster the resources and vision to remain "livable" as they grew. What these speakers most strongly argue for, based on the logic of their knowledge and experience, is immediate action.

The Hero: Where's the Shoot-out?

Luther Propst begins his presentation by establishing his own ethical appeal: as a former Washington lawyer, who worked there for the World Wildlife Fund, he tells a self-denigrating and actually funny lawyer joke, about the obsolescence of lab rats, who are being replaced by Washington lawyers because these occur in greater numbers and because "there are some things even rats won't do." In beginning his logical appeal, he cites demographic trends in particular counties in the Greater Yellowstone area, thereby assuring the audience that he's an expert, even though he's an outsider—perhaps an expert in ways only an outsider can be. He has a slide show of his own, displaying results of lack of planning for conservation from around the country. The scenes are familiar to anyone who has traveled even a little: conversion of farmland to suburbs, loss of regional architectural character and degradation of historical features because of commercial development, obliteration of landscape features, human conflict with wildlife. He contrasts these with views of instances of effective planning: clustered housing, retention of local architecture in commercial development, protection of views and wildlife habitat. He emphasizes the goal of these workshops: that residents of Red Lodge can set an agenda for action, whatever that agenda and action may be, but only if they act quickly and as a community. The urgency to act has been established by Prinkki and Campbell as well; Propst underscores it, and takes the further step of suggesting concrete possibilities.

Propst argues that the real power to effect conservation and preservation is always at the local level. He briefly delineates factors that "successful communities" have drawn on to best enact this power, including special physical aspects of the community, shared community vision, and proactive policies. Most important to successful communities is the willingness to look beyond ecological and economic factors to the quality of the lives of all community members and to work beyond laying down regulations, which, in Propst's words, "are too blunt a tool with which to fashion a livable community." Propst cites the need for "hometown heroes"—

local individuals who can channel energy into constructive rather than divisive agendas, who cultivate responsible, local developers, and who remain active to ensure plans are implemented and developments monitored.

In describing the factors of such communities, Propst constructs an ideal that Red Lodge can aspire to, while maintaining that this ideal has been successfully approximated in other places. To return to Burke's concept of identification, which "includes the realm of transcendence" ("Rhetoric—Old and New" 203), "The machinery of language is so made that things are necessarily placed in terms of a range broader than the terms for those things themselves" (*Language as Symbolic Action* 200). At the heart of the strategies used by Propst and the organizers of the forum are those that draw on transcending the view of Red Lodge as it is today, on Richard Weaver's ideal function of rhetoric, which, "at its truest seeks to perfect men by showing them better versions of themselves" (16). And better versions of their communities.

Propst ends with a series of rhetorical devices. He enhances his ethos, the credibility of his character, and disarms anticonservation arguments by citing research that shows that the economic vitality of a community is intimately connected to the quality of life of all inhabitants—that scenery does indeed provide jobs. He underscores his authority by elaborating on problems in nearby communities, such as those faced in relation to the proposed Targhee Ski Resort expansion in Driggs, Idaho, where, Propst suggests, residents have not yet identified common interests and goals. He casts the workshop experience itself positively, differentiating it from contentious public hearing processes, and suggests that nearby communities that face seemingly insurmountable problems have attempted too late the process the forum demonstrates, providing further motivation for the residents of Red Lodge to begin work now.

These presentations have moved from community members and to authoritative outsiders, from emotional appeals to appeals based on the credibility and authority of the speakers. The local presenters rely more on identification with the audience based on devotion to their hometown and its inhabitants, while the outside authorities use quantifiable information about the economic situation, or about cases of similar situations and outcomes in other communities. The combined rhetorical thrust, the major argument for action, rests on the premise that Red Lodge suffers from a variety of economic woes that will increase as environmental degradation increases, given present economic and demographic trends. The desired rhetorical outcome is the motivation of citizens to discuss and reach consensus on an agenda for action, although not yet to reach consensus on particular actions.

By forestalling consensus on particular decisions and actions the community should take, forum organizers hoped to solidify individual commitments to the community and to action on its behalf. Propst argues that the community can begin to create its agenda when it begins to identify where there is consensus, where there is not, and where there are degrees of consensus. To return to Trimbur's critique of "community" in the literature of rhetoric and social theory, "the ideal of community participates in . . . a metaphysics that denies difference" ("Ideal of the Community" 1). Although, as Trimbur believes, "the desire for mutual understanding and reciprocity underlying the ideal of community is similar to the desire for identification that underlies racial and ethnic chauvinism"—a community is defined by what it excludes—Propst aims for a wider definition of community in Red Lodge. Propst suggests that residence and action, not degree of conformation to viewpoints, determine membership in the community, and that the idea of community in Red Lodge admits differences, and in fact those differences are to be studied. The danger for the community is not lack of consensus on an issue, but divisiveness that prevents any possibility of action. While the Sonoran Institute is a proponent of environmental conservation and historical preservation, not interested in mediating neutral solutions, in this forum Propst's purposes are to increase awareness of options for resolving issues, not to push particular resolutions.

Audience as Actors

Saturday's forum begins with stories. Two residents speak; a local rancher in his sixties gives a brief history of ranching in Carbon County, and a young housewife and nurse recounts her personal history in Red Lodge. Both cover the changes in the area, recent and not so recent, and cite shared histories in support of the communal effort required today and in the future. Albert Ellis tells of one Montana pioneer who, when asked on his ninetieth birthday if he'd seen a lot of changes in his lifetime, answered, "You bet I have, sonny, and I voted against every one of them." In recounting the changes that have affected ranching, Ellis reminds us that, however stubborn Montanans are, change will come, and citizens need to direct it. Kim Shelley relies on a personal, emotional appeal to make her point: how her family were forced for economic reasons to move away for part of her childhood, and now she's grateful to be back. She reminds the audience of the biggest snowstorm last winter, and how cars parked in the streets were buried: "We all wondered, why do we live here? But that's why—because of nature." She shares her worries about having to leave again, forever, if the hospital, presently in a financially precarious position, should have to close, and reminds us that despite what she loves about living in a small town, a higher population would mean saving the hospital. She ends with a plea for concerted effort: "I know *I* just can't not try to give something back to this town." The audience, most of whom are at least acquainted with Ellis and Shelley, identify with the historical and personal narratives that range across time, gender, age, and profession and which constitute an acknowledgment of the foundation of the community (or an idealized view of that foundation): hard times, the identity of the region based on the difficulties encountered here, that identity in opposition to what lies beyond it, changes past, changes to come. Taken together, the two narratives set a rhetorical stage, a context in which discussion of community values will take place in a different light. Ellis and Shelley have modeled their stories, their rhetorical stances as community members, and now the other residents take up this same task in smaller groups.

All the other narratives come spilling out as audience members introduce themselves to each other in these smaller, randomly formed groups of nine or ten. For example, one group is facilitated by Keith Zimmer, owner of a T-shirt business on Red Lodge's main street, and includes a rancher's wife, housewives, a teacher, a city roads worker, the owner of a secretarial business, a ski resort worker. Their talk about positive aspects of living in Red Lodge provides common ground for the rest of the discussion. This common ground elicits Burkean identification and demonstrates the usefulness of story *as* argument, as Walter R. Fisher points out in *Human Communication as Narration:* "The world as we know it is a set of stories that must be chosen among in order for us to live life in a process of continual re-creation" (5). What these stories argue for, explicitly and implicitly, is action to preserve qualities of Red Lodge. In this group, Nancy Krekeler's story, for instance, is about how she left a lucrative job in Washington, D.C. years ago to join the working class of Red Lodge: "Tourists thought we all were twins, when they'd see us in the morning helping them onto the skilift and in the evening waiting on them at dinner. . . . Everyone gives up something to be here, whether you've always lived here or you're from somewhere else." Bob Holm, a city roads worker, recounts how he used to make his living working construction in other parts of the country, how his kids were really raised by his wife alone. These stories, and indeed all the stories and conversation that day, argue for particular visions of Red Lodge, past and future.

Even in the first round of discussion, the group is tempted to jump ahead to the town's problems, past defining "what we love about Red Lodge." Within five minutes, Bob Holm is wondering aloud if the town could ever pass a resort tax to pay for infrastructure development; Ruth Uebar says she thinks some development is good, that the golf course fits in with the atmosphere of the town, and then Mike Beye complains that the streets leading out of the golf course development look like "7-11 territory; is a strip mall next?" Zimmer calls them back to the task at hand, and the group devises a list of the town's positive attributes: its western flavor, natural environment, physical safety, political diversity, spirit of giving and openness, and its access to wilderness, health care, and skiing. People in the group state that what they like most is always meeting friends all over town, at the post office and stores, and "being able to hold a conversation with a 'wrong number' on the phone." Members of the group all agree that they don't want outside developers "to be able to do *anything*." After an hour, the small groups break up to form the large group (about ninety people in all), and the facilitators of each group report their group members' lists of attributes. The next two rounds of discussion proceed similarly.

In this way every participant at the meeting is guaranteed a voice, and at this point no hierarchy of problems or solutions is established, so all concerns can be expressed. In these discussions, individuals express concern over degradation of the environment as easily as concern over lack of economic opportunity, and these concerns are not seen as conflicting. Participants are tempted to voice their personal concerns and solutions, but because each group must report its results for the question being put to it, discussion irrelevant to the task is held in check.

In the third round of dialogue, the groups identify specific steps to meet threats and achieve goals. The group agrees on the needs to organize, to use the public forums—the newspaper, meetings like this, town government meetings—to insure better communication among the townspeople, to gather information about property restrictions and zoning, to establish committees to research and initiate action on particular issues. Imagining the individuals likely to be on these committees, the group begins to wonder, what's to stop committee members from acting out of special interests or not acting at all? Propst joins the group and points out that the first objective is to establish committees that will continue the dialogue, not solve problems or take positions on issues yet, and that diversity of committee membership is crucial to success. The priorities are community dialogue and recognition of dissensus. The rhetorical processes that may eventually facilitate consensus on particular issues—the processes, strategies, attitudes that individuals and committees use to persuade other people to align themselves with particular views and actions—depend on both the sense of community (the feeling that the people of the town are connected to each other in ways that benefit them) and the sense of diversity (that both individuals and the larger group will accommodate "other" viewpoints and actions).

Intermission: Implications

That a "rhetorical education" of Red Lodge began with this forum is seen by the continued dialogue in the public discourse of the town; the success of this education is seen in the activities and achievements of citizen groups originating at the June 1992 forum. In the months following the first forum, criticism of the workshop and meetings circulated, and response to rumors provided a forum for organizers and participants to further their work. In August 1992, these comments from the organizers appeared in a letter to the editor of the *Montana Free Press:*

We'd also like to take this opportunity to state again that the Beartooth Front Community Forum is a non-political community-based organization. We have no agenda and are not supported by any interest groups. While we hope to inspire people to express their opinions, the Forum as a body does not take stands. Our sole goal is to involve as many people as possible in discussions about planning for our community's future. (Beartooth Front Community Forum Steering Committee 3)

In November, the contradictory rumors that the Beartooth Front Community Forum is a front for developers and that its purpose is to halt all development were countered in another letter from the steering committee, appearing in the same newspaper, explaining that

The Community Forum is not an "it"—a political organization with positions or an agenda. The Community Forum is a process, a *vehicle*, through which any and all residents of the area can try to have a voice in the future of their home. ("Thanks From the Forum Front" 4).

In the March 1993 "Beartooth Front Community Forum Progress Report," the authors conclude with an emotional appeal that valorizes the sense of a community made up of individuals who hold different viewpoints:

Those involved in the Forum (as well as those on the sidelines) have been impressed with the scope and energy of their fellow volunteers. Many expected the community would not find such consensus; others expected that projects would not get off the ground so quickly; still others that enthusiasm would wane. Those expectations have been dashed magnificently. . . . the journey—the process—has been as exciting as its results. We have come together, in our disparate beliefs and needs and ambitions, to affirm our love for this area. We have come together to dream about its future, and share those dreams. We have seen how similar the dreams are, how within the realm of possibility. And in that process we have come together as that wondrous and often elusive entity, a community. (Beartooth Front Community Forum 7)

The forum participants tie the ideal of community to the ideal of every voice being heard, replacing, momentarily, the typical view of consensus, in which all community members agree to viewpoints and courses of action. They see consensus, as Trimbur does, as not necessarily "an acculturative practice that reproduces business as usual" but "as an oppositional one that challenges the prevailing conditions of production" ("Consensus and Difference" 614).

These kinds of sophisticated rhetorical moves continue: more letters to the editor, two more well-attended public forums with significant numbers of new participants, increased interest in local government as measured by attendance at town meetings. Committees formed at the end of the first forum, on 23 June 1992, have, by the persuasive strategies in their grant writing, received grants totaling over $300,000 to initiate a planning process for the town and its surrounding one-mile area, to establish water quality testing of the town's creek, to study the creation of a local development corporation, and to construct a site near the town for viewing local elk herds. The community of Red Lodge, through effective rhetorical work that realizes an agenda driven by both economic and environmental health, is forging some better way to live.

Red Lodge, 1995: The Sequel

Lest this movie seem saddled with an unrealistically happy ending, the results visible three years after the first Successful Communities Dialogue workshop continue to point to tangible successes. A specific, broad-based planning process has been established, led by the Beartooth Front Alliance, which enjoys the support of a wide range of citizens, including the chamber of commerce, a group of quilters who raise funds, and a group of ranchers. The Alliance is currently completing a planning initiative—funded by $20,000 from the city council—that has developed from several meetings, each attended by about a hundred people, over the last six months. Smaller but very important projects have developed as well: volunteer water quality monitors continue to gather data on the Rock Creek drainage, and the town now has a Boys and Girls Club that serves two hundred children, with an average of sixty children participating every weekday afternoon.

The Alliance has narrowed its focus to the town of Red Lodge for the present, although they continue to solicit rural participants especially, sometimes by inviting ranchers and cowboys to speak at the meetings. While the town has not implemented all the ideas that came out of the first meetings, successful planning efforts and other projects contribute to a heightened sense of shared community and viable opportunities in the town. These would not have developed without the community's deliberate and inclusive rhetorical activities, facilitated by the Beartooth Front Alliance and the Successful Communities workshops.

WORKS CITED

Aristotle. *The Rhetoric and the Poetics of Aristotle.* Trans. W. Rhys Roberts and Ingram Bywater. New York: Modern Library, 1984.

Beartooth Front Community Forum. "Progress Report." March 1992.

Beartooth Front Community Forum Steering Committee. Letter to the editor. *Montana Free Press,* August 1992, 3.

Beartooth Front Community Forum Steering Committee. "Thanks from the Forum Front." *Montana Free Press,* November 1992.

Booth, Wayne C. "The Rhetorical Stance." *College Composition and Communication* 14 (1963): 139–45.

Burke, Kenneth. *Language as Symbolic Action: Essays on Life, Literature, and Method.* Berkeley: U of California P, 1966.

Burke, Kenneth. "Rhetoric—Old and New." *Journal of General Education* 5 (April 1951): 203.

Crews, Frederick, and Ann Jesse Van Sant. *The Random House Handbook.* 4th ed. New York: Random House, 1984.

Ferguson, Gary. "Guest Opinion: Beartooth Front Forum Advocates Public Involvement in Planning Issues." *Montana Free Press,* November 1992, 6.

Fisher, Walter. *Human Communication as Narration: Toward a Philosophy of Reason, Value, and Action.* Columbia: U of South Carolina P, 1987.

Homans, Peter. "The Western: The Legend and the Cardboard Hero." *Look,* 13 March 1962, 82–89.

Killingsworth, M. Jimmie. "Discourse Communities—Local and Global." *Rhetoric Review* 11 (1992): 110–22.

Lake, Laura. "Characterizing Environmental Mediation." *Environmental Mediation: The Search for Consensus.* Boulder, CO: Westview P, 1980.

Mernitz, Scott. *Mediation of Environmental Disputes: A Sourcebook.* New York: Praeger, 1980.

Propst, Luther, and Trudy Halvorson. "Successful Communities in Greater Yellowstone: Revised Draft, May 13, 1993." Tucson: Sonoran Institute, 1993.

"Successful Communities Dialogue." Tucson: Sonoran Institute, 1992.

Tompkins, Jane. *West of Everything: The Inner Life of Westerns.* New York: Oxford UP, 1992.

Trimbur, John. "Consensus and Difference in Collaborative Learning." *College English* 51 (1989): 601–16.

Trimbur, John. "The Ideal of the Community and the Politics of Difference." *Social Theory and Practice* 12 (Spring 1986): 110–21.

Weaver, Richard. *Ethics of Rhetoric.* Chicago: Henry W. Regnery, 1953.

"The Sonoran Institute Annual Report, 1991–1992." Tucson: Sonoran Institute, 1992.

CHAPTER 8

Beyond the Realm of Reason

Understanding the Extreme Environmental Rhetoric of the John Birch Society

ROBERT L. BROWN and CARL G. HERNDL

The pickup that passed us had a scene in mylar on the window of the topper—three snow-capped mountains and a large bird flying in the foreground. The mountains were perfect Fujiyama cones, volcanic and prominent. The bird had the white head and tail fan of a bald eagle. "Nature," I say, "but not like any mountains in the real world. And that poor eagle has grown turkey vulture wings." Much laughter followed in the van, and much talk about who has and who hasn't climbed a mountain; about who can and who can't tell an eagle's pinions from a turkey vulture's; about who drives old pickups at 75 on icy roads.

Of course, we're right about how many glaciated cinder-cone mountains there are. And about the wings of eagles. And about art and representation. Later, in fact, we check the flight profiles of the eagle and the turkey vulture in Roger Tory Peterson's *A Field Guide to the Birds*. We like precision, the order of the field guide, the knowledge of the "flight profile" and that technical term. The name pinion feather. The money to travel to mountains and climb them, and the ingrained habits of bird-watching. They like the grand and the grandiloquent, the idealized. And on both sides, these "likes" are not isolated phenomena; they are deeply interested and political.

This is, of course, not a story flattering to us knowledgeable academics, however right we might have been about mountains, eagles, and art. And it is a story that involves a degree of generalization, a kind of stereotyping that is neither polite nor appropriate in careful scholarship. But it is representative; we weren't doing anything strange or rare. We were doing what all speakers and writers do—indeed, what all sign users do—when they

213

use words to describe the world. Knowledge is deployed in this story both then and now in the retelling. Our conversation and the knowledge we display locates us, the van full of academics, in relation to others whom we don't know. Using knowledge in this way conveys and cements a sort of symbolic power; using this language so easily locates us on a social and educational hierarchy. Our language has prestige; it is specialized; it distinguishes us as analytic and educated. Its power exists only when it is used in relation to others who don't, we assume, share that knowledge-power. It's the power of knowing, and knowing that we know, in the presence of others who don't: guys who buy pickups with toppers and put bad art on the tailgate window.

At first, this looks like a story of right and wrong, of getting it right and getting it wrong. Is this how the world of mountains and eagles really is? But that is too simple, and this is not really a story about truth. And why, we might ask, is it even important that art—in this case popular art—get it "right," scientifically? Our unexamined assumption that the discourse of science, of rationality, should dominate is telling. It tells us how thoroughly we believe that our way of seeing, our rhetoric is natural common sense. It tells us how important our ways of knowing can be to us. We think this story is really about the relationships of intellectual and social domination that shape all our social interaction.

Purchasing and displaying the window picture (and behind it, manufacturing and marketing the image), and our forming jokes at the expense of the pickup driver are cultural practices. When we engage in them, we consolidate and confirm our histories and our complex positions in the world, however flattering or unflattering, each against the other. Through our conversation in the van, we identify ourselves as people who study geology and nature. And our talk represents the driver of the pickup—correctly or not—as someone who reads the J. C. Whitney catalog and builds trucks as art. Rhetorically, we and the pickup drivers need each other. Our rhetorics, in a sense, are interdependent. Our knowledge, and theirs, become powerful only in relation to each other. When the two contrasting kinds of knowledge-power are deployed, they consolidate group identities and social positions, both the pickup driver's and ours. And this process of defining public selves operates everywhere knowledge is deployed, everywhere we present our views of the world to the world.[1]

Rhetoric as a Place to Be

Like other chapters in this collection, this essay assumes that the environment about which we speak and the rhetoric we use when we talk about it are inseparable. Certainly they are in practice. The job of many of us involved in environmental study and activism is to change minds so that actions toward the world may also change, and the business of rhetoric is to explain how words change minds. A number of rhetorical theorists have argued for some time now that our knowledge of things, the environment for example, is created through rhetorical activity. But we would push the connection between rhetoric and the environment one step further. We are interested in the ways that the words we use to talk about the environment establish and support us, the ones who talk about it. In our view, the rhetoric of the environment performs two different kinds of cultural work: one which produces knowledge about the physical world, and a second which produces the consciousness—indeed, the identities—of those who produce that knowledge. Environmental rhetoric, like all cultural work, sets relationships among its writers, readers, and the worlds of which they speak; it creates roles, formations, a place to be. Rhetoric represents the world and its history and locates its users in that world and in relations with other people. And when rhetoric does so, it provides its users a socially recognized identity and a position from which to speak and act coherently. Our story about the pickup is really about this second kind of cultural work; it reveals the way our language creates our identity and positions us in relation to the rest of the world.

In this essay, we examine the rhetoric the John Birch Society uses to write about the environment; we argue that this discourse which seems irrational and extremist to many environmentalists and academics can be understood as part of a contested cultural exchange, a contest not only about the nature of the world, but also about the identity and place of those involved in the debate. Certainly environmental rhetoric is powerful because it allows rhetors to manipulate the world to suit their interests. But environmental rhetoric is also powerful because it makes rhetors members of powerful social groups, and in doing so it helps create their social identity. We want to step back from our disagreement with the ultraconservative position of the John Birch Society—step back from our opposition to what seems to be bad policy, bad science, bad argument— and attempt to understand their rhetoric as a complex social exchange through which the members of the John Birch Society assert the power and prestige of their language, beliefs, and, as we argue, their social identity and position. Rather than engage in the debate about specific environmental issues, we describe the structure and nature of the contest itself. By doing this, we can understand the rhetoric of the John Birch Society as a strategic cultural and political move. Stepping back from the debate also helps us see that there is more at stake than any particular environmental policy or scientific position, and that this overabundance of stakes helps explain the vehemence with which groups like the John Birch Society assert their position. Certainly if recent history tells us anything, it tells us that merely offering more, and more careful, scientific arguments has little or no effect on the position and rhetoric of groups like the John Birch Society. We offer one explanation for why this is so.

The Sense in Talking Nonsense

This essay analyzes the environment as constructed by a group that seems alien to us: the John Birch Society, which we take as emblematic for much of the American political right. In June of 1992, the society brought out a special issue of their monthly magazine, the *New American,* focused on issues of the environment and subtitled "The Resilient Earth." These writings are fascinating in their own right, since to many of us they seem to be pure nonsense: They claim that there is no global warming. Either ozone depletion isn't happening, or if it is, it's not hazardous. The earth can support an almost unlimited population. The rainforests are unnecessary for ecological balance. Increased CO_2 concentration, and the resulting greenhouse effect, promise unimaginable improvements in agricultural production. Understanding a rhetoric which seems irrational and extreme to many of us is important to environmentalists, rhetoricians, and policy makers alike because the high visibility and resilience of this rhetoric indicate that it is deeply rooted in American culture. It won't disappear, and it is not readily understood.

It's remarkably easy to find flaws in both the arguments and the evidence supporting these claims: suspect sources, unmentioned political alliances and funding, lacunae, the whole suite of logical fallacies, shifts of focus and field. And it's satisfying to point them out. It's easy, in fact, to use the writings of the John Birch Society for the analytical equivalent of the game of making fun of guys who can't tell an eagle from a vulture and who advertise the fact on the back of their truck. We can easily use our knowledge-power to disenfranchise those other speakers. But it is precisely the act of being disenfranchised that lies at the very heart of their rhetorical and cultural behavior.

Why do we speak nonsense? According to the authors of "The Resilient Earth," most environmentalist rhetoric is pure, liberal nonsense. And to us the writings where they make this claim are pure, reactionary nonsense. We can't both be right—or can we? Certainly we're both right about our taste in rhetoric that positions us as writers and readers in relationships to each other and to the world—comfortable, whole, coherent, and secure. Certainly, we're both right about what we like to read and write, and about the effects this reading and writing have on us. It's this "common sense" based on socially distinctive systems of belief and complex relations of self and culture that we seek to explain. If we can understand what the John Birch Society is up to, rhetorically, in their writings on the environment, we may also understand what we are up to in the part of our own rhetoric that lies beyond the logical. Our argument does not deny the logical. Rather, it recognizes that our use of rational, scientific arguments always invokes their cultural power, and that these cultural relations create a social and extrarational context, what we will call an "economy" of self and culture, in which our arguments serve other, and multiple, purposes. We refer to an economy because our arguments have value and power, and we use them in the intellectual and cultural market. This terminology attests to the insight of the popular cliché used when someone makes a successful argument: "you can take that to the bank."

We preface our analysis with a necessary caveat on scientific truth dictated by recent rhetorical and cultural theory. All concepts and models in environmental science are in contention, as they are in all science. We can't claim privileged access to truth, or that we inhabit some neutral space, some ideology-free zone of pure, disinterested knowledge. Finally, we need to subject our own positions to reflexive analysis, recognizing that our most dearly held environmental beliefs—in the systemic nature of the physical world, in the unpredictability of technological innovation, in our skeptical view of modernist science in general—are always both interested and fallible (Herndl).

The Logic of "The Resilient Earth"

"The Resilient Earth" contains eighteen articles, each short and topical, in a newsmagazine format: color bar at the top with a descriptive headline ("Global Warming," for example), a figurative title ("Net Loss of Freedom"), one illustrative photo with caption, and two to five topical subheads. It looks like *Newsweek*. Authors are members of the "contributors" panel; no affiliations or biographies are given, and three of them write the majority of the articles.

It's important, we think, to examine one of these articles in order to gain a sense of the way arguments are constructed. One article will suffice, since the rhetoric of the entire edition is remarkably consistent. In "Fury of Mother Nature," written under the heading "Natural Pollutants," we hear that we need not fear the environmental consequences of greenhouse gas production (or the environmentalists who write about them). The piece treats three topics: volcanic effluent, Pacific Ocean currents and weather changes, and animal pollution. The controlling idea is the claim that human pollutants are insignificant when compared with other "natural" sources. The logical fallacies and bad data are everywhere obvious, even to the nonscientist. The irrelevant reason fallacy is so prominent that it becomes the organizing rhetorical motif, or trope, of the article. For example, the piece opens with an appeal to the authority of Dixie Lee Ray, who claims that "all of the air polluting materials produced by man since the beginning of the industrial revolution do not begin to equal the quantities of toxic materials, aerosols, and particulates spewed into the air from just three volcanoes: Krakatoa . . . Katmai . . . and Hekla" (quoted in Lee 5). From this, it's argued that man-made pollution is not a significant danger. Setting aside the category error in equating particulates and unspecified aerosols to greenhouse gases, the claim that more is okay because there's lots already is still prima facie absurd—and obvious. The same trope organizes a discussion of termite and ant activity that occupies over one-third of the piece. Assembling a long passage detailing the ability of gut bacteria in termites to reduce carboniferous material to CO_2 and methane, the writer claims—accurately but irrelevantly—that termites are an important source of methane and CO_2. The kinship of termites to ants allows a linking of global warming and acid rain. With ants, the issue is formic acid, said to be a major component of rainwater acidity in tropical wilderness areas. While true, this irrelevant claim elides the fact that such acidity is trivial and benign, and unrelated to industrial-based acid rain. With a grand rhetorical flourish detailing the number of ants in the acid-producing subfamily *formicinae,* the section ends with the claim that the 600,000 metric tons of ant-generated formic acid is "equal to the combined formic acid contributions of automobiles, refuse conbustion and vegetation" (Lee 5). The article fails to point out, however, that neither cars nor plants produce formic acid. But the accumulation of heavily qualified scientific data sounds persuasive and masks the fact that it is all logically irrelevant to the argumentative point.

The overall figure created by this article sees nature and man as opposing "despoilers," but membership in one or the other category is strikingly flexible. Spanish and Portuguese sheep, Indian cattle, and Dutch pigs are described, because they are animals, as "natural" forces of destruction rather than as agricultural technologies produced and controlled by man. Random forces of nature are invoked in the section on floods, droughts, and other weather disruptions through a detailed discussion of "Los Ninos," the tropical Pacific Ocean currents. Changes in these currents brought "both the US drought and the devastating floods that swamped Bangladesh" (quoted in Lee 5). Here the logical misstep is not irrelevance but the suppression of significant data: what caused the Bangladeshi floods? Certainly the rains did, but the deforestation and overgrazing from unhappy choices of agricultural and forestry practices were at least equally responsible. The nature vs. man opposition invoked by the article depends on a reductive isolation of the complex interconnections between phenomena.

And what caused the rains and the drought? According to "Fury of Mother Nature," it's chance. The possibility that climatic disruptions might result from changes in CO_2 levels and rising mean temperatures, for example, is excluded by a habit of mind everywhere evident in all of the articles in "The Resilient Earth": systematic/dynamic explanations are conspicuously absent. Explanation in these pieces is local, discrete, and built around a simplistic sort of Cartesian causality that's striking even on a casual reading. Typically the articles contradict themselves internally as they marshal opposing evidence to refute different points—here the flexible membership in the "nature" and "man" categories. The article's telling last words are another powerful example: "Clearly, man has a long way to go to match nature as a 'despoiler' of the environment" (Lee 5). Logically, this conclusion is untenable. Nature, of course, is the environment and cannot despoil itself. Nor can man logically be said to "match" nature as a despoiler; they are not in competition. Nature provides the background against which the effects of any human activity are measured, and it's the effect of technology on nature that environmental science attempts to model. But this sentence does make pragmatic sense if we read it as a defense against the claim that man is a despoiler—and indeed this defense of man and his activities is the overwhelming rhetorical goal of "The Resilient Earth."

There's an overriding sense that these articles are addressing a list of arguments external to them, propositions in the air, someone else's cultural knowledge. The essays, on first reading, appear to be standard, popular scientific essays, exercises in exposition. In style and format, they mirror popular news magazines. Yet they do not actually develop topics from any internal logic. Rather, they look outward, perhaps to a series of accusations, attacks which they address, each separately. As a result, the dominant rhetorical posture is defense, motivated by the political and economic argument that runs throughout the articles. Underlying all the John Birch Society publications we reviewed was a strident, virtually paranoid conspiracy theory. Government, international banking, the academy, business, and international socialism were consistently cast as parts of an unrecognized plot to attack individual autonomy and freedom. Readers are warned, for example, that the "inflammatory socialist rhetoric" of the Rio Earth Summit was not as important as the "dominance of the whole affair by internationalist banking/big business/media/ public policy elites of the Council on Foreign Relations (CFR) and Trilateral Commission (TC)" (Jaspers 35). Later in the same piece, readers are told that the "fictive covering of planetary 'democracy' " at the conference hid a conspiracy between "the socialist/communist Left and the corporate/banking capitalist elite" (Jaspers 36).

We can't, finally, read these pieces as autonomous texts. We cannot rest satisfied with refuting their arguments and data, no matter how gratifying the exercise. Perhaps here more than in most cases, we must treat these writings as parts of a cultural process that goes beyond the particular texts, as parts of a dialogue. The logical inconsistencies and the textual incoherence, so obvious to us as readers, are less strange when we begin to read this as a response of writers, and the community that identifies with that writer, who feel that they are under siege.

Understanding Nonsense

Three things trouble us about the John Birch Society writings on the environment and about our responses to them. And these troubling points are what make the rhetoric of the *New American* compelling to us as both concerned environmentalists and rhetorical theorists. First, they write nonsense and they must know it. These are educated writers; they simply can't not see the structural and scientific problems so obvious to us in their claims. Second, they look bad: extreme, combative, paranoid—at least to us. Finally, and paradoxically: our last observation can't be right—at least not in terms of the lived experience of many Americans. These writings are read, used, enjoyed by a substantial segment of the American people, and for every citizen who positions himself or herself around this extreme version of American political conservatism, there are many more delighting in the less extreme but strikingly similar performances of Rush Limbaugh or G. Gordon Liddy. So we propose a theoretical look at the cultural work being done both in the deployment of these arguments, positions, and identities, and in our response to them.

What rhetorical explanation would be adequate to explain these writings, our responses, and the cultural work that both are surely doing? The classical Aristotelian distinction of *logos, ethos,* and *pathos* goes some distance, and provides a useful way to define the architecture we have in mind. We focus less on the logical realm of facts and propositional relationships and more on the rhetor's credibility and presence, and the audience's fears, wishes, and dreams; less on *logos* than on *ethos* and *pathos*. But we're uncomfortable with classical rhetoric's easy confidence in these discrete categories. In our view, Aristotelian rhetoric (originally, and in its many classical and modern analogs) may be part of a way of thinking about rhetoric that makes it nearly impossible to understand the complex economy of self and culture that is invovled in this case. The classical notion of the writer or speaker always involves conscious, independent agency, the troubling assumption that rhetorical strategies are choices—as if the apparatus of ethical argument, for example, can be simply selected and used. A great deal of contemporary theoretical work, however, suggests that, to a considerable extent, existing cultural structures provide the categories and standards through which we perceive the world and guide the way we think. To exert this kind of influence, these cultural structures must necessarily remain largely hidden, even, or especially, from their willing participants.[2] Viewing rhetoric as cultural work asks us to examine how writing always participates in the social practices that maintain our social structure with its systems of power and that define who we are within these systems.

So what is "The Resilient Earth" doing, for the John Birch Society reader and for those of us who find it absurdly illogical? A useful way to begin is to examine the opponent created by the unremittingly adversarial writing in these articles. "The Resilient Earth" is coherent as a rhetorical action taken against an absent adversary who holds certain difficult beliefs: "the environmentalists," who in turn are the dupes and servants of international socialism. In the view from "The Resilient Earth," the opposition is characterized as either foolish or corrupt, consistently beneath contempt or consideration. A quotation pulled from a piece on global warming is prominently displayed in a block set in the center of the second page:

A "leading" climate model produced by the British Meteorological Office shows similar amounts of mid-summer rain falling in the middle of the Sahara Desert and in the notoriously wet Ireland and Scotland. (McManus 8)

According to the article, this comes from "several prestigious authorities" who earlier offered a "ridiculous 'ice age' scare." The bitter irony of this passage is characteristic of the article as a whole. Consistently, normal science, the environmental policy that draws on it, and the political systems that support such policy are held up to scorn: "unproven theories," "near-hysterical global warming non-science," "scary scenarios," "trendy theory," "global warming fanatics," "self-appointed experts," "Senators who pander to . . . environmental lobbies," all of them "riding the environmental wave." It's fairly unremarkable invective for the unremarkable end of casting the opposition as fools, or what seems worse in their particular rhetoric: as hysterical, emotional women or impressionable children.

But this rhetoric is more interesting when we treat it as a complex piece of cultural work, locating the writer and reader and those whom they oppose—and upon whom they depend for their carefully constructed identities. The worldview that informs "The Resilient Earth" (and all of the publications of the society one will receive after ordering any publication) is occult, suspicious, and radically individualistic. Environmental science and scientists are not the problem; they are puppets, blind to the implications of their work and publications, and ultimately controlled by a global conspiracy invisible to all but the initiated society member.

The longest article in "The Resilient Earth" occurs almost at the end and serves as a summary, and it offers a political reading that organizes the mass of isolated and miscellaneous claims of the rest of the issue. In a piece on the United Nations' "Earth Summit"—characterized as "environmental Woodstock," a "greater gathering of the greenies"—the society's official view of the coming "socialist new world order" is worked out in some detail. The piece is characterized by lists, typically of organizations or political leaders, blithely assigned to active roles in international socialism:

Who are "they" who are doing all this planning? Besides the hordes of UN bureaucrats, there is an army of ecology "experts" from Greenpeace, the Sierra Club, Friends of the Earth, Environmental Defense Fund, Natural Resources Defense Council, Nature Conservancy, Planned Parenthood, Zero Population Growth, National Wildlife Federation, Worldwatch Institute, National Organization of Women, World Council of Churches, Socialist International Women, and literally hundreds more of what the UN calls NGO's (non-governmental organizations). (Jasper 35)

In this piece that imposes easy coherence and order on remarkably dissimilar groups of organizations, we are told that "There is virtually no area of human activity or environmental concern that they have not arrogated as their own to plan, supervise, regulate and control" (Jasper 35). At the end of the piece we are warned that

The war is on and cannot be avoided. It is the US Constitution versus the UN Charter, inalienable God-given rights and freedom versus New World Order slavery, private property versus socialism, and pantheism versus biblical morality. (Jasper 38)

Anyone passingly familiar with the language of the American right has seen these lists used in this incantatory way, and the "war" figure used to position the sides of the debate. Probably most of us would resist the paranoid view that our lives are controlled by invisible cabals of Trilateralists, the Council on Foreign Relations, and the National Organization of Women. But it's critical to set our resistance to these arguments aside to see the order in this rhetoric. French language and culture theorist Pierre Bourdieu provides a powerful way to understand what is happening when writers marshal these masses of claims that appear so radically paranoid and extreme to readers like us. Bourdieu's theory allows us to see that this rhetorical strategy is multiply determined, and all the more intractable for the many things the rhetoric simultaneously accomplishes for its users.

The Linguistic *Habitus* and the Marketplace

Bourdieu offers three points which help explain the cultural work of "The Resilient Earth." First, all language comes to have meaning only in contrast to other socially constructed ways of using language.[3] Second, in a quite literal way, our words, our rhetorics are us; we "embody" them. Third, we must treat all rhetorical production as a complex system, understandable only through analysis of multiple, interconnected relationships. At the center of his analysis is the relationship between what he calls the *habitus* and the linguistic marketplace. The *habitus* is his general term for all of our dispositions to act in particular ways in particular settings. He defines a *habitus* as a set of "durable dispositions" that incline us to act in systematic ways without there being conscious rules; they are patterns of thought inculcated in us through a lifetime. These dispositions are durable in the sense that they tend to remain largely the same throughout our lives as we remain largely the same person. And the dispositions of social groups tend to be passed on to new members of the group; social structures and the behaviors characteristic of them tend to be consistent over time. In a sense, these dispositions are "habits" of linguistic/rhetorical behavior regular and definable, but operating beyond the regularities of simple linguistic rules. After a lifetime of inculcation from all aspects of our everyday lives, our habitus is us, in a manner of speaking, because in using it in our everyday lives, we present ourselves to the world, elicit reactions from the world, and in so doing, confirm and conform ourselves. For Bourdieu, the habitus is a mental entity not amenable to direct access or explanation, but revealed everywhere we act, especially when we act through language (Bourdieu 82–84). It might be thought of as a persistent style of thought, speech, and action.

In making his second point, Bourdieu argues that our language practices are literally embodied in us as the habitus. "All groups," he says, "entrust the body, treated like a kind of memory, with their most precious possessions," their cultural, institutional records (123). We walk, talk, dress, behave, and live in ways that mirror the complex processes that formed us, and we reproduce and represent these processes in all our social behavior. This seemingly radical idea need be no more surprising than the realization that we can tell a great deal about someone's life from the way he speaks, the way he dresses and acts in social settings, the kinds of relations he assumes in conversational encounters, from what we colloquially call "body language." A useful illustration from popular culture might be Eliza Doolittle in Alan Lerner and Frederick Loewe's *My Fair Lady,* an adaptation of George Bernard Shaw's *Pygmalion.* To change her language, deportment, and social sense, she has to change social class. Or rather, in changing her language, bearing, and behavior, she changes class, and thus her social identity. So for Bourdieu, rhetoric is very nearly somatic; the deployment, in a particular setting, of our habitus. His account focuses on the way all language use expresses, reproduces, and consolidates the relations of power underlying culture: our many institutional relationships—ties to hearth, home, community—everywhere present when we contact culture. They are literally carried in and on our bodies.

> More convincingly than the external signs which adorn the body (like decorations, uniforms, army stripes, insignia, etc.), the incorporated signs (such as manners, ways of speaking—accents—, ways of walking or standing—gait, posture, bearing—, table manners, etc. and taste) which underlie the production of practices aimed, intentionally or not, both at signifying self and at signifying social position through the interplay of distinctive differences, are destined to function as so many calls to order by virtue of which those who might have forgotten . . . are reminded of the position assigned to them by the institution. (123–24)

If Bourdieu's habitus looks inward, to the socially constructed self, his notion of the "marketplace" looks outward, to the places where we contend with words and the power that they represent and create. The model of a "marketplace" of cultural contact and exchange invokes exactly the sort of "economy" of selves and culture that we have been describing. In our view, and Bourdieu's, the presentation of self in words is literally an economy, a complex system of exchange and value creation. We may find that our views, our linguistic styles, our complexes of underlying beliefs find immediate "currency" when we speak them; they may be respected and successful. But we may also find that they have little "value" or that they are rejected as "counterfeit." In any case, self is a fragile construct, at stake in every exchange, and held intact only by the reception it finds when deployed in the marketplace. Our value, personally, and in the direct, literal sense, is a function of our reception in various marketplaces. In Bourdieu's theory, our rhetoric is always shaped by our habitus and our sense of the linguistic marketplace; the push and pull of each system against the other determines what we say and how we say it. In this two-sided, systemic view, rhetoric becomes a theory of the constant, social, economic, dialectical building and rebuilding of self in which we engage when we meet the world with words and other signs.

What rhetorical, political marketplace do the writers of "The Resilient Earth" intend? A commonsense, impulsive answer might be: "surely not one where they look like fools for bad science and a paranoid outlook." But the complexity of their rhetoric makes us take a harder look, and see some patterns we claim may locate rhetoric of the environment and its practitioners in general. Said briefly: the extremity of the John Birch Society's rhetoric marks their habitus as socially marginal, a reactionary and even desperate rhetorical action against a dominant, coherent, liberal discourse. If they feel defensive, they are probably right. The extremism and energy of their rhetoric, and of most environmentalist responses to them, are symptoms of the polarity and the degree of antipathy between positions. And the society's rhetoric also underscores both the institutional power of standard environmental science with its conventions for reporting data and making arguments, and the political formations that support standard science. In a way, their extremity should encourage partisans of environmentalism: they are telling us that the battle is over and that they have probably lost.[4] Unfortunately, this is not the only battle and theirs is not the only, and certainly not the most powerful, opposition to environmental action.

Read in this way, the John Birch Society's appropriation of scientific discourse, and of the forms and format of the consensus press newsmagazines, makes sense as a striking reversal of what Bourdieu calls the "strategy of condescension." For Bourdieu, linguistic condescension occurs when a powerful member of the dominant linguistic community temporarily adopts the language of a marginal or disenfranchised group. When this occurs, two things happen simultaneously. First, if he is successful, the speaker builds a social link to the disenfranchised because he recognizes and attributes value to their habitus. But in doing so, he paradoxically reinforces the power of his own privileged language. In the case of the John Birch Society writer, when he adopts the language and style of the mainstream press he recognizes the cultural power of the dominant press and simultaneously marks his own habitus as marginal.

When a member of a marginal group, speaking from a marginal habitus, appropriates the rhetoric of the dominant class, who is he fooling? Never, Bourdieu would say, will he fool the dominant classes. But probably "fool" is an inelegant expression for the cultural work such rhetorical appropriations seek to accomplish. What, after all, is the *New American*? A teaching tool? Or a recruiting tool? Scientific reporting? News reporting? Does it set out to change minds? Or is it epideictic rhetoric, seeking only to please and affirm the beliefs of a group already sure of its positions?

Probably it is many of these things, but it is almost certainly not a tool to teach us a new way of seeing the environment and our relationship to it. In the simplest sense, it is not written for us—and our reactions confirm this. So it makes sense to read "The Resilient Earth" as a tactical appropriation of the dominant rhetoric in a reversal of the strategy of condescension. In the local rhetorical marketplace of like-minded readers, this appropriation makes the writer and the readers he binds to him look like heroic rebels. He has taken the opposition's means of language production and used it for his own ends: he offers evidence of equivalent power. This is the rhetoric of group solidarity, not of deliberation or proof. From this perspective, the fact of flawed logical and scientific particulars matters little; this is an economic action, a significant rhetorical "taking" of linguistic, rhetorical power. That the writers and readers of the magazine do see themselves as a coherent but marginalized group is obvious from their language. Throughout the longest piece in the issue, William Jaspers describes the powerful "new enemy"—the UN and the startling collection of nongovernmental organizations we described earlier—as a group that combines everyone from the "socialist/communist Left" to "the corporate/banking capitalist elite" (Jaspers 36). Representatives of this environmentalist coalition are repeatedly, and scornfully, identified as "insiders," "insider experts," and "one-world Insiders," marking the writer and his readers as outsiders, excluded from this powerful, global coalition.

The John Birch Society's attempt to appropriate the language and style of scientific news reporting and to give their rhetoric symbolic value might succeed, except that, as Bourdieu points out, the dominant classes and their language can never finally be excluded from the larger marketplace. In fact, their control of the linguistic marketplace is a functional definition of cultural domination. So any rhetorical battle won in the local community constituted by readers of the *New American* is inevitably lost in the larger social context, as the larger linguistic marketplace assigns value to the entire rhetorical act. The power of normal scientific method with its systemic analyses and of consensus news reporting with its complexes of beliefs and value is validated and reinforced as the writers in the *New American* try to appropriate them for their cause. Their act of imitation and appropriation acknowledges that the dominant language is valuable, that it is legitimate and worth appropriating. And while they succeed in their local market, they fail utterly in the larger market. We read them as fools.

Significantly, we are not claiming here that they are fools, or even that the methodology and rhetoric of environmental science are finally "right"—even though we may believe it. What Bourdieu's view offers is a way to trace the operations of language and power in public rhetoric independently of the truth claims of that rhetoric.

Bourdieu offers a telling illustration of power at work in language in a reading of what American sociolinguists have named "hypercorrection." When a speaker tries to produce the speech forms of a dominant linguistic group, and fails, partly, we call this hypercorrection. The simplest examples are "malapropisms," but the more interesting ones occur in syntactic and sound structures. A speaker who hypercorrects has partial knowledge of the rules governing the forms he or she's trying to produce, but only partial knowledge. So if we say "credible" and mean what is meant by "creditable," for example, we've gotten close to the word—and told our knowledgeable hearers that we don't know the distinction. Similarly, speakers who use "whom" where "who" would be called for in the prestige dialect reveal several things: that they don't have the who/whom distinction in their linguistic habitus, and that this distinction, rightly made, confers the power of prestige in the larger linguistic marketplace. Linguist William Labov did the first and most extensive work on hypercorrection in his study of the language practices of inner city street gangs; the Jets and Thunderbirds he studied would occasionally produce forms that were not governed by either the rules of their own dialects, or by those of the prestige dialects. We read the rhetorical practices that inform the articles in "The Resilient Earth" in a parallel way: they are "rhetorical hypercorrections," texts approximating the forms and formations of the dominant groups, but missing significantly.

But Bourdieu acutely points out what Labov's formal account overlooks: the powerful do not hypercorrect. They don't need to; they have no economic motive to do so. So hypercorrection, like condescension, is an asymmetrical relationship, and its asymmetry marks the flow of power. When the writers of "The Resilient Earth" rhetorically hypercorrect, they are telling us about the way power is manifested in specific rhetorical and methodological practices. They may consolidate their fellow believers' sense of their own integrity, but they show themselves marginal—always—in the larger linguistic marketplace.

Do these writers "know" what they are doing? We think probably not. But a more interesting way to view their practices might begin with another simple concept from sociolinguistics. Linguists studying the practices of disenfranchised groups (like the gang members Labov studied) find a sort of cultural work in speakers' violating the rules, in being bad—linguistically and otherwise. Most obvious are practices that value taboo words, but equally compelling are research data confirming that certain groups—African American adolescent males, say—"violate" the rules of the standard dialect two to three times as often as do their female counterparts. Linguists call this "covert prestige," power gained in flouting the practices of the dominant culture. Rappers call it being "hard men," or, in the oldest street term of all, "being bad." In Bourdieu's terms, it's a value creation process, a process of creating power by refusing to bow to the rules and practices controlling the marketplace. Always, Bourdieu explains, this sort of practice confers a local and temporary advantage among a speaker's immediate group and a global, long-term penalty in the larger social context.[5] A speaker gains "covert prestige" at the cost of reinforcing the group's disenfranchised status.

What if we saw the positions and personae created by the writers in "The Resilient Earth" as forms of rhetorical covert prestige, as tactics to build power (and solidarity and coherence) by voicing the extreme, the overt, and (from our viewpoint) the bizarre?[6] What if these writers anticipate, in some sense, the scorn and derision of the environmental establishment, and figure them into their tactics? In this view, we, and the complex of beliefs we share with others in positions of linguistic and political power, are part of the marketplace in which these writings are offered. It is our "scorn"—a strategy operating much like Bourdieu's "condescension"— that assigns value to these covert floutings of the norms of science, reasoning, and writing. The more extreme our response, the more effective this covert tactic of resistance. So in a descriptive sense, the extremism of "The Resilient Earth" is a mark of the isolation of the political group that the John Birch Society represents. In an explanatory sense, the extremism gains local value from our hostile, often dismissive response. Both the Birchers and we are present in the environmental rhetorical marketplace; we each depend upon the other for coherence, for the means to mean.

Why It Matters So Much

What remains yet to be explained is why these issues matter so much to the members of the John Birch Society, why these writers and readers invest so much energy and cultural capital in this virulent rhetoric. We can offer two explanations: the first an application of a psychological theory of how we form our sense of self, the second an extension of the social theory we have offered throughout.

If we are to understand the writings of groups so alien in their reasoning and motivation as the John Birch Society are to most of us, we must finally arrive back at the self, the place where institutions inculcate the habitus, the body—and the psyche. Bourdieu's dynamic account of language as a system of value and power creation is elegant as a political explanation. But beliefs are held by the self—even a socially constructed one—and no political theory, finally, explains its internal dynamics. Much current theory rejects all talk of the self as an artifact of a humanist, inherently reactionary way of reading cultural and political relations. Talk of the self is often regarded as a holdover from nineteenth-century romantic individualism that excludes the power of the social and the political, and, indeed, much of it is. As a result, theories of political and social structure such as the one we have offered usually reject any theory of psychology, any talk of the internal dynamics of the psyche. But we see the self as part of the social, as the embodiment of cultural and political history. As we read through "The Resilient Earth," we are struck by the intensity and depth of the writers'—and presumably the readers'—resistance to and resentment of environmentalist rhetoric. And so we close with a brief account that might explain the irrational power of the need for coherence and community— even at the expense of reason—exemplified by the John Birch Society's rhetoric.

Our account is based on the theory of "object relations" and the central concept of "self objects" as articulated by Heinz Kohut, D. W. Winnicott, and Alice Miller.[7] These theorists hold that we form our initial sense of self, our internal sense of who we are, through our earliest relationships with things in our world. We develop a sense of self through the way things outside us act on and react to us; we come to know ourselves through these everyday relations with the objects in the world. At base, the fundamental objects through which we develop our self are the folks who raised us, who gave us our view of the world—not objects at all, but people. Fathers and mothers, of course, but beyond them, all the members of our community who tell us, discursively, who we are and how to be. Having formed our self through relations with these objects, these people, we tend to reproduce these self-constructing relationships everywhere in our symbolic and cultural creations. Individually and as a culture, we make things (physical things, discursive things) that repeat our earliest relationships because doing so reinforces the self created by those relationships. That is, we surround ourselves with stand-ins, substitutions for our familiar, primal objects. So it seems natural and human for us to seek those things and people that serve to mirror back and support our image of coherent selves.

Certainly people are the obvious candidates as self objects in later life, but rhetoric, too, can serve as a self object—and not just for members of the John Birch Society. In fact, rhetoric may be the most powerful of self objects. As we have argued, it always sets relationships among its participants: roles, formations, a place to be. Rhetoric invokes a world and a history and locates its users in that world. It does so in "The Resilient Earth," and it does so in our opening story about pickups, mountains, and eagles' wings.

In order to explain how we surround ourselves with familiar objects, reproducing our earliest self-constructing relationships, Heinz Kohut describes two basic principles that structure object relations: the mirroring and the idealizing relations. The mirroring relation provides a sense of security, support, coherence, trust. It's hard not to see the mother as the mirror and slip into a gendered reading that does some violence to the elegance of Kohut's conception; a person of either gender can fill this role. She/it reflects back to the young child a sense of being loved, accepted and valued. When we enter our favored environmental rhetoric as native speakers, we reenter a world mirroring wholeness—one we worked hard for, and one we're good at. As we hear familiar words, familiar references, familiar names, we're accepted. In a way, rhetoric can be the enfolding, supporting place where we feel safe, complete, at home.

The idealizing relationship, in Kohut's conception, is the site of power—and for our reading, the more important concept. Either parent may be a source of vicarious strength that we seek to recreate later in the relationships we set with the world and its inhabitants. So as we watch the people who represent our ideal self—our mentors, or in this case the John Birch Society writers and spokesmen—making hash out of our enemies while using their own tools to do it, we're filled with a sense of the rightness of our beliefs and choices, of our life—protected, defended, whole, coherent. We transfer onto these people our earliest relationship with the powerful figures who spoke for and protected us.

In object relations terms, "The Resilient Earth" is a celebration of affiliation with the ideal. The writers speak for us, and of us. And they speak (and speak against) a totalized, coherent other that embodies all that we are not. It's a seductive relationship, and one hardly isolated in this group or this rhetorical foray against environmentalism.

The psychological explanation of why many people are so attracted to powerful ideal objects helps extend our political analysis of the John Birch Society rhetoric. In his explanation of linguistic practices, Bourdieu argues that rhetoric is shaped by the relation between a speaker's or a group's habitus and the values of the linguistic market. When a person's linguistic habitus, and the social identity that goes along with it, are not compatible with a particular field or market, when they have little or no value, a speaker may be at a loss for words. In our increasingly bureaucratic world, where politics have become professionalized, individuals who feel marginalized by the powerful "insiders" mentioned so often in "The Resilient Earth" may also feel disenfranchised and silenced. As individuals, they have no power to speak effectively. But they can make themselves heard as members of a group constituted around a spokesperson vested with the right to speak on the group's behalf. Thus, by publicly articulating the habitus of society members, the spokespersons (in this case the spokesmen—women are notably absent from the whole issue) of the John Birch Society create a forum through which members can be heard and through which they can assert their social identity. Society members identify with the writers, granting them the authority to speak for them while getting in return the satisfaction of being enfranchised, valued, and heard. In object relation terms, the spokespersons become powerful ideal objects. For John Birch Society writers like Lee and Jaspers, their rhetoric is not simply an attempt to represent their particular vision of the social world, and thus of themselves. It is also the means through which they mobilize the support of the readers on whom their rhetorical power depends. Although their rhetoric may ultimately fail on the larger market, it gives these writers and their readers a powerful voice, if only locally, and a recognized and coherent social identity.

The position occupied by the John Birch Society reader and writer is everywhere demonstrated in its writing. Indeed, the ideological constructs are almost obsessively present. The clearest illustration, and one that provides an elegant close to our reading, is a single sentence printed on the cover of "The Resilient Earth":

Far from being fragile, our planet is a vast and versatile creation designed to flourish under man's innovative stewardship.

This is a strikingly "overdetermined" statement, with multiple layers of meaning all pointing to the same ideological position, the same construction of a self and its relationships to the world. The nominalization "creation" hides a verb—create—which in turn entails a creator. With this move, the writer sanctifies the universe by implying the existence of a creator, but by turning the relationship of creator to planet into a noun, "creation," and omitting any explicit mention of a creator, he masks the ideological claim for a divine creator. The hidden creator, and the planet created, are further specified through the passive-voice verb "designed." Its unrealized subject is ambiguous, but will be read as the creator/ designer already entailed. And the word "designed" requires a designer and a design. With the design theme comes a particular ontological construction: an ordered and teleologically coherent world. When the writer adds the predicate "versatile," he claims that the earth was created resilient and, by implication, that those who deny such resilience are apostate, unbelievers. By aligning the writer and reader with this ideological position, the text banishes relativism and the skeptical enterprises associated with it.

Putting the content of the claim aside, we see a clear opposition between an implied reader who agrees and others who resist, one a believer (in a very particular cosmology) and the others rebellious. This opposition is reinforced by the opening clause "far from being fragile"; those who believe that the earth is fragile reject the versatile creation and those who believe in it. This clause, and the use of "far" to introduce it, make rhetorical sense only if we read it as a refutation of an offstage claim: that the earth is fragile. That the position being formed here rests on particular and familiar religious beliefs is supported by the connotation of "stewardship" from the King James Bible and its associations with Renaissance British property law. With the addition of "innovative" to modify stewardship, the proposition is moved into the present by invoking entrepreneurship and its particular embodiment of individuality and autonomy, the "freedom" that the writers of "The Resilient Earth" assert so insistently throughout their essays.[8] Indeed, a full-page advertisement near the end of the magazine reproduces the U.S. Bill of Rights, our guarantee of freedom, above the statement: "We at DEAN SELLERS FORD believe freedom of mobility is as fundamental as our 'Bill of Rights.' " The advertisement encourages readers to "See Dean Sellers Ford for your new freedom machine."

Conclusion

Is the planet fragile? Certainly we think so. Certainly much environmentalist writing says so. Certainly the writer captioning "The Resilient Earth" knows that much environmentalist writing says so. But critical for our case is the way this text locates its writer and readers in relation to others in the culture, to certain ideological positions and to particular ways of using language to draw absolute boundaries between groups and to establish a coherent, political self. The cultural work being done here, like that done by the pickup driver's love of nature displayed on his window—and our love of knowledge displayed in our scorn for it—is beyond the realm of reason. It is performed in the complex marketplace of language and power, and finds its final location in the habitus that locates our fragile selves. Reading "The Resilient Earth," the intended reader finds a clearly defined self: believer, Christian, owner, steward, innovator, essentialist, individualist, agonist. What can we offer that compares with the seductive political and psychological identity provided by this rhetorical place/object?

The answer, as we have said earlier, to the John Birch Society rhetoric is not simply more and more careful rational argument. Our analysis suggests that their rhetoric emerges from the relationship between their habitus and the cultural market, a relationship between their identity and the dominant hierarchy of value and social power. This suggests that, as with complex environmental problems, solutions to this rhetorical problem are not local but systemic. Their rhetorical position is at least partly, we would claim mostly, the result of social and political marginalization and domination. If this is in fact the case, it suggests two kinds of response to extremist environmental rhetoric, neither one easy. When we are engaged in specific, local exchanges, we need to respond not only to substantive disagreements over "facts," but also to the social and psychological motives behind the Birchers' rhetoric. But to change the rhetoric itself, we need, collectively, to address the material and social conditions—economic, political, educational—that produce and maintain both their habitus and our own and their respective relations to the linguistic and cultural market.

NOTES

1.   In Pierre Bourdieu's view, everyday language-life is an encounter between our various *habits* and the cultural "fields," the sites or playing fields on which everyday life is "played." When we are accepted as players, we are confirmed—as a teacher might be every time she successfully conducts a class, or as a physician might be when she treats a patient. The product of many such confirming encounters is a coherent sense of our selves, and a coherent sense of the social fields on which we play.

2.   This model of action draws, of course, on Louis Althusser's disturbingly constricting notion of the "good subject" interpellated by her material conditions of existence into a consciousness she neither sees nor is able to criticize. A less deterministic and, for us, more convincing view can be found in Bourdieu's *habitus* or Giddens' theory of "structuration." In both models subjects are guided to act in particular ways, not necessarily with conscious awareness, but not blindly or hopelessly.

3.   Bourdieu's structural sociology of language is obviously inspired by Saussure. Bourdieu is at pains, however, to reject Saussure's formalism, arguing that Saussure's theory takes language as a "pre-constructed object, ignoring its *social laws of construction* and masking its social genesis" (44). The meaning-making contrast, in Bourdieu's view, comes from "sociologically pertinent" oppositions created by the political distribution of power within society. His social theory takes as its object "the relationship between the structured systems of sociologically pertinent linguistic differences and the equally structured systems of social differences" (54).

4.   We are indebted here to a conversation with Noam Chomsky on the rhetoric (and funding) of the organized American political right. In Chomsky's view, and ours, the rise of the right—however frightening—is a cause for some hope. Their program to restore "family values," a teleological view of reality, a fixed social order, and so on indicates the destruction, probably permanent, of that ideological complex after the 1960s.

5.   For an analysis of hypercorrection as a self-defining act in the absolutely hegemonic setting of corporate America, see Brown and Herndl (1986).

6.   This model of rhetorical action, and the terminology of "strategy" and subversive "tactic," is described by Michel de Certeau in *The Practice of Everyday Life*. De Certeau follows Bourdieu in looking at language practices as complex "economies" of self and power, but he is usefully more explicit in naming the devices of the underclass, the powerless, as "tactics," deployed against the official "strategies" of dominant groups. Both Bourdieu and de Certeau take their cues from Michel Foucault, particularly his study of the creation and power of "disciplinary" systems in *Discipline and Punish*.

7.   The central appeal of object relations theory is the elegance with which it allows us to read current behavior as a trope of childhood experience. While most of its proponents consider (or once considered) themselves psychoanalysts, they have all abandoned the rigidity of the classical drive-and-stage theory for a view much less essentializing and more amenable to crosscultural application. All, with

Lacan, would see the unconscious as structured like a language, but they would seek the structure of this language in the cultural matrix that supports us. This makes it possible to understand the individual psychodynamic as part of the social and political. Thus, while we recognize the difficulty of using psychoanalytic theory within political analysis, we think that this model of the self is essentially consistent with Bourdieu's idea of the habitus—in both, the self is constructed in relation to the surrounding cultural and material circumstances.

The best overview of object relations theory is Heinz Kohut's "The Disorders of the Self and Their Treatment: An Outline." Kohut's two major books, *The Analysis of the Self* and *The Restoration of the Self,* are complex but accessible. But most interesting for our work is Alice Miller's work tracing the consequences of German ideology through centuries of child-rearing (and abusing) practices. Her method is unremittingly hermeneutic, revealing the meanings of social and personal behaviors from their roots in early experience. Best known is her first book, *The Drama of the Gifted Child,* but more useful is *For Your Own Good,* where she shows how charity and understanding come from understanding the social and psychic sources of "dissonant" behavior.

8. Several sorts of linguistic analysis shape this analysis, primarily H. Paul Grice's account of the strategies of conversational cooperation. Like Bourdieu, Grice proposed a conversational competence best represented as a set of dispositions to act in predictable ways in particular situations. Formulating these as his "Cooperative Principle," Grice set out a loose calculus by means of which speakers form their semiotic contributions (linguistic and otherwise) to fit and make sense in the communicative events in which they find themselves. Grice's principle posits an "economy" of communication in which any speaker's "contribution" is guided by the speaker's sense of its relevance to the topic or activity, its sufficiency as a contribution, its truth value, and its linguistic form, broadly conceived. So any language use allows inferences beyond what is literally said. In this way, the "far from being fragile" line we examined fits the conversational economy only if we assume that it is a comment on someone's belief that the planet is *near* to being fragile—and that believer, by implication, becomes part of the whole rhetorical sense of the passage.

WORKS CITED

Althusser, Louis. "Ideology and Ideological State Apparatuses." *Lenin and Philosophy and Other Essays.* Trans. Ben Brewster. New York: Monthly Review P, 1971. 127–86.

Bourdieu, Pierre. *Language and Symbolic Power.* ed. John B. Thompson. Trans. Gino Raymond and Matthew Adamson. Cambridge: Harvard UP, 1991.

Brown, Robert L., Jr., and Carl Herndl. "An Ethnographic Study of Corporate Writing: Job Status as Reflected in Written Text." In *Functional Approaches to Writing: Research Perspectives,* ed. Barbara Couture. London: Frances Pinter, 1986. 11–28.

De Certeau, Michel. *The Practice of Everyday Life*. Trans. Steven Rendall. Berkeley: U of California P, 1984.

Foucault, Michel. *Discipline and Punish: The Birth of the Prison*. Trans. Alan Sheridan. New York: Vintage, 1979.

Giddens, Anthony. *Central Problems in Social Theory: Action, Structure, and Contradiction in Social Analysis*. Berkeley: U of California P, 1979.

Giddens, Anthony. *The Constitution of Society*. Berkeley: U of California P, 1984.

Grice, H. Paul. "Logic and Conversation." In *Syntax and Semantics 3: Speech Arts*, ed. Peter Cole and Jerry Morgan. New York: Academic P, 1975. 41–58.

Herndl, Carl. "Cultural Studies and Critical Science." In *Understanding Scientific Prose*, ed. Jack Selzer. Madison: U of Wisconsin P, 1993. 61–81.

Jasper, William F. "Rio and Beyond." *New American*, June 1992, 35–38.

John Birch Society. *New American*, June 1992.

Kohut, Heinz. *The Restoration of the Self*. New York: International UP, 1977.

Kohut, Heinz. *The Analysis of the Self*. New York: International UP, 1971.

Kohut, Heinz, and Ernest S. Wolf. "The Disorders of the Self and Their Treatment: An Outline." *International Journal of Psychoanalysis* 59 (1978): 413–25.

Labov, William. "Field Methods of the Project on Linguistic Change." In *Language in Use: Readings in Sociolinguistics*, ed. J. Baugh and J. Sherzer. Englewood Cliffs, NJ: Prentice-Hall, 1984.

Labov, William. *Language in the Inner City*. Philadelphia: U of Pennsylvania P, 1972.

Labov, William, and David Fanshel. *Therapeutic Discourse: Psychotherapy as Conversation*. New York: Academic P, 1977.

Lee, Robert W. "Fury of Mother Nature." *New American*, June 1992, 5.

McManus, John F. "Nothing More Than Hot Air." *New American*, June 1992, 7–8.

Miller, Alice. *For Your Own Good: Hidden Roots of Cruelty in Child-Rearing and the Roots of Violence*. New York: Farrar, Straus, & Giroux, 1983.

Miller, Alice. *The Drama of the Gifted Child*. New York Basic Books, 1981.

CHAPTER 9

Environmental Rhetoric in the Age of Hegemonic Politics
Earth First! and the Nature Conservancy

MARILYN M. COOPER

In the broadest sense, the question that drives the environmental move-ment is how to resolve the contradiction between the lifestyle of modern industrial society and the continued existence of life on earth, or, further, the existence of a diversity of life, something beyond humans, seagulls, and cockroaches, for example. As Jimmie Killingsworth and Jacqueline Palmer put it, "how can the standard of living attained through technological prog-ress in the developed nations be maintained (and extended to developing and undeveloped nations) if the ecological consequences of development are prohibitive?" (3). Although the question of the environment is most often represented in popular media as a stark choice between economic prosperity and an Edenic vision of nature (jobs versus owls, for example),[1] the question is really much more complex. How much and how fast do we have to change the way we live? How much biodiversity do we need in order to have a "healthy" environment? Is a healthy environment one that sustains human life, or must it also sustain as many other life forms as possible? Can economic prosperity for all and biodiversity be compatible, or do we have to sacrifice our living standard (and reduce our population dramatically) if we wish to avoid ecocatastrophe? Among environmental organizations, the fundamental question under debate is, how much change is necessary in our society to preserve the environment?

Not surprisingly, the diverse groups that make up the environmental movement have developed significantly different answers to this question, and they employ a variety of different rhetorical strategies in their joint effort to realign public opinion and policy on environmental issues—and to renovate, as well, the fabric of our everyday lives. In this chapter, I want to examine the complexities of how two national environmental groups position themselves and are positioned by others in the debate over the environment. Although my focus is on the rhetoric of the environmental movement, I find it useful to place my analysis within a broader framework of political theory, for the environmental movement is a political movement. In particular, I will be looking at the rhetorical strategies of these two groups through the lens of radical democratic theory, which emphasizes the role that rhetoric plays in changing or maintaining the structure of our society.

Radical democratic theory focuses on how the various groups in a society struggle to gain acceptance for their views in the arena of public discourse. This struggle is especially important in contemporary society because what is accepted common sense about what people value and how they live and behave strongly influences not only the practices of our everyday lives but also policy decisions in government and in industry at all levels. Accepted common sense, sometimes called a society's ideology or belief system, evolves in public discourse, and in radically democratic societies, where everyone is free to participate in public discourse, what is accepted as common sense evolves and changes rapidly in response to changing conditions and to the ebb and flow of the struggle between different points of view. When participation is more limited, accepted common sense may lag behind changing situations and impede a society's ability to adapt its practices to new situations. Radical democratic theory is especially interested in how adaptation does occur when participation is not completely free, which is the more usual situation in mass society.

Using radical democratic theory to look at the rhetorical strategies employed by Earth First! and The Nature Conservancy in the public debate about the environment enables me to describe the causes and the effects of these different strategies and to begin to assess how effective these strategies are, both separately and jointly, in bringing about changes in how our society thinks about the environment and in environmental policies and practices. Each group's strategies are linked to the particular history and experiences of the group and to their particular beliefs about how and how much the practices of modern industrial society must change if we are to preserve biodiversity in our environment. As a consequence of these different beliefs and strategies, each group plays a different role in the effort to reorient our society's relationship to the environment. Although it is difficult, in the midst of the ongoing debate, to accurately assess how effective each group is in this effort, I conclude that each makes important contributions and that the effect of their different strategies is synergistic, that is, that the success of the environmental movement will in large part depend on different groups employing different strategies and playing different roles in the debate.

Dave Foreman, founder of Earth First! recognizes the value of these differences: "We need many paths; we need to ask many questions. . . . there are countless tools suitable for tackling different aspects of each problem" (*Confessions* 172). As an example, he notes, "even though The Nature Conservancy and Earth First! have similar goals of saving native diversity, our techniques are . . . different, our styles . . . divergent" (173). The mission of The Nature Conservancy, as stated on the masthead of their magazine, is "to preserve plants, animals, and natural communities that represent the diversity of life on Earth by protecting the lands and waters they need to survive." Although Earth First! does not speak with nearly so unified a voice, the group is considered to be the action arm of the deep ecology movement,[2] a biocentric movement committed to the principles that "the well-being and flourishing of human and nonhuman Life on Earth have value in themselves," that "these values are independent of the usefulness of the nonhuman world for human purposes," and that "richness and diversity of life forms contribute to the realization of these values and are also values in themselves" (Devall and Sessions 70). The mission of the most recent offshoot project from Earth First!—the North American Wilderness Recovery, or "Wildlands" Project—is even more explicitly parallel with that of The Nature Conservancy. In announcing the project, Foreman and his colleagues write: "The mission of The Wildlands Project is to help protect and restore the ecological richness and native biodiversity of North America through the establishment of a connected system of reserves" (Foreman et al. 3).

Despite these similar goals, these two groups are radically divergent in structure, strategies, politics, and rhetoric. With a membership of 10,000 and an annual budget of $100,000, Earth First! looks every inch of its marginal status in contrast to the mainstream Nature Conservancy with its 588,000 members and annual budget of $100,500,000.[3] Earth First! prides itself on its "disorganization" (Kane 100): Foreman argues that "the nature of the Earth First! movement made it . . . important that . . . a centralized administration never be established" ("Foreword" 10). The Nature Conservancy, in contrast, is an efficiently managed corporate enterprise. *National Geographic* comments: "The business-like approach to environmental matters can strike an air of incongruity, as though one were watching Wall Street make preparations for the second Earth Day" (Grove 831–32). Earth First! is famed for its dramatic and sometimes violent defense of nature. Although officially the group disclaims responsibility for acts of ecological sabotage such as spiking trees marked for logging, as Foreman explains, the group specializes in "confrontational civil disobedience, monkeywrenching, and uncompromising advocacy" (*Confessions* 172). The Nature Conservancy, in contrast, concentrates on buying land of environmental value and in building alliances among individual landowners, environmental groups, governmental agencies such as the Bureau of Land Management and the National Forest Service, and corporations; its current president, John Sawhill, remarks that such activities "make the point that there are environmental groups such as ours that have chosen to work cooperatively, rather than confrontationally. . . . and . . . illustrate ways in which business and environmental groups can work together for the common good of society" ("How to Think" 576).

The Nature Conservancy was founded in 1951, when the scientists who formed the Ecologist's Union (which had split off from the Ecological Society of America in 1946) joined with Dick Pough, an engineer by training and an entrepreneur with a reputation as a manager who had "acquired a deep love and broad knowledge of the environment" (Grove 837).[4] Thus, the Conservancy was marked from the beginning as an alliance between scientists and business, and its first project demonstrates how the group would continue to use economic power to protect significant ecosystems: purchasing a "two and one-half mile stretch of [Hudson River] riverfront untouched since the arrival of the first white settlers in 1640, [which] was home to an old growth hemlock forest which was being threatened by construction of a new reservoir" (Lavine 24).

In response to the United States Forest Services decision to open over 90 percent of federally protected wilderness to development, Earth First! was founded in 1980 by Dave Foreman, a lobbyist for the Wilderness Society, and several of his friends who were also staff members of mainstream environmental organizations. Inspired by Edward Abbey's novel *The Monkey Wrench Gang* (1975), the strategies and projects of Earth First! are strongly marked by the personal vision of Foreman, its most articulate member.[5] One of the first actions of the new, radical group was to unroll a banner depicting a giant crack down the side of the Glen Canyon Dam, symbolically enacting the group's proposed solution to the ecological destructiveness of modern industrial society, but Foreman and co-founder Howie Wolke also compiled and published an exhaustive inventory of wilderness (*The Big Outside*, 1989), and the group has had from the beginning a close association with scientists developing the notion of deep ecology, an association that was strengthened in 1990 when Foreman left Earth First! to found Wild Earth.

In politics, Earth First! is one of what Michael McCloskey calls the new radical groups that emerged in the mid-1980s: "some of the new radicals were radical in their demands, and others were radical in the means they used. . . . The deep ecologists . . . wanted sweeping changes in society and living patterns but were largely apolitical. . . . groups such as Earth First! and the Sea Shepherd Society actually used radical means, resorting to sabotage and other illegal techniques, although their demands for changes in public policy were not always radical" (78–79). Believing that the current socio-economic system is incompatible with a healthy earth—as Christopher Manes puts it, "that our culture is lethal to the ecology that it depends on and has been so for a long time" (22)—and thus that this system must be overturned, the radicals are often criticized by more moderate environmentalists for polarizing the issues and for tainting the whole movement with the image of lawless hooliganism.

At the center of the political spectrum lie most of the large, mainstream environmental groups (e.g., the Sierra Club and the Audubon Society), which McCloskey calls the pragmatic reformers, those groups who believe "that progress toward environmental protection could be achieved best through government action" (78). Although The Nature Conservancy is one of the "Big Ten" environmental groups who often collaborate in endorsing or opposing governmental policies, the Conservancy differs from the pragmatic reformers in focus: its emphasis on buying land of ecological significance places it among the groups McCloskey calls accommodators, who believe that "a new era was beginning in which industry and environmentalists would work together harmoniously" and who "look less to the heavy-handed governmental regulation favored by the reformers and more to market-like mechanisms to achieve their ends" (79). The Nature Conservancy is often accused by radical environmentalists of being overly accommodating to industry and developers and of needlessly compromising important environmental principles. *Outside* magazine's guide to environmental groups notes, "The most salient criticism of the Conservancy's approach is that its cozy ways with big business (it cashes huge annual checks from Mobil, Weyerhaeuser, and other industrial patrons) buy its silence during regulatory squabbles" (Martel et al. 70).

Both Earth First! and The Nature Conservancy are explicitly aware of their strategies as distinct and not necessarily exclusively the best. Foreman says: "We did not form Earth First! with the thought that we had the only proper methods: confrontational civil disobedience, monkeywrenching, and uncompromising advocacy. We founded Earth First! because these particular tools were not otherwise being used in defense of native diversity" (*Confessions* 172). Pat Noonan, the president of The Nature Conservancy from 1973 to 1980, says, "Corporations and environmentalists were butting heads, but we knew the free-enterprise system was a fantastic motivator. So the Conservancy decided to reach out to corporate America. No other environmental group was doing it" (quoted in Grove 837). To demonstrate how these different strategies are embodied in the rhetoric of the two groups, and to demonstrate more clearly the differences between the strategies, I will in a moment look closely at a pair of articles that argue the positions of the two groups on land management in the western United States. But in order to characterize the rhetorical strategies I see at work in these articles, I need first to introduce some more specific concepts from radical democratic theory.

Formulated most articulately by Ernesto Laclau and Chantal Mouffe in their *Hegemony and Socialist Strategy,* radical democratic theory derives from the writings of the Italian communist Antonio Gramsci. Laclau and Mouffe argue that beginning with the French Revolution it has become increasingly difficult to see political struggle as based on a confrontation between predefined groups or classes, the lords versus the peasants, for example. Instead, they argue, political struggle is a matter of the construction of opposing positions wherein groups attempt to define a place for themselves in the political structure by linking together their positions (and those of their allies) into a coherent vision, or common sense. After the French Revolution, Laclau and Mouffe say, "there was no politics without hegemony" (151). For them, as for Gramsci, hegemony refers to this general process of building alliances among groups in order to gain a consensus that will enable a group to lead the society through intellectual and moral principles as well as rule it by force; it is the process I earlier referred to as the establishment of accepted common sense.[6]

In introducing his notion of political power, Gramsci distinguishes between "domination" and "leadership" (57). Domination is the naked exercise of power, the use of the law or armed forces to "liquidate" or "subjugate" opposing groups; leadership is the winning of power through building an intellectual and moral consensus, the establishment of hegemony. Both are necessary, he argues, for a group to gain and maintain power in a society. And while hegemony definitely sets up a hierarchical relationship between groups in which the dominant group attempts to subordinate the interests of other groups to its own interests, at the same time, "the fact of hegemony presupposes that account be taken of the interests and tendencies of the groups over which hegemony is to be exercised, and that a certain compromise equilibrium should be formed—in other words, that the leading group should [also] make sacrifices" (Gramsci 161). Furthermore, along with Marx, Gramsci asserts the possibility—and the necessity—of alternate or counterhegemonies, "new popular beliefs, that is to say a new common sense and with it a new culture and a new philosophy which will be rooted in the popular consciousness with the same solidity and imperative quality as traditional beliefs" (424). Although the possibility of revolution lies in the potential building of a counterhegemony, wherein the common interests of a new group are forged into a coherent philosophy, a principled intellectual and moral awareness, hegemonic politics recognizes the immense capacity of modern states to avert revolution through redefining the interests of potentially opposing groups in terms of its own interests and principles. Gramsci believed that military revolution was outmoded as a process of changing social structure and had been replaced by a rhetorical struggle for hegemony in which the nature and extent of change were a great deal more problematic.

I will return to a more detailed discussion of radical democratic theory and how it can explain the differences in strategies between Earth First! and The Nature Conservancy later. At this point, I will simply suggest that the rhetorical strategies operating in the article published by Earth First! might be thought of as an attempt to establish a counterhegemony, a new common sense, while the strategies operating in the article published by The Nature Conservancy might be seen as extending the power of the established hegemony.

"Livestock Grazing on the National Parks: A National Disgrace," by Dale Turner and Lynn Jacobs, appeared in the *Earth First! Journal* in December 1990. Turner and Jacobs detail the history and extent of livestock grazing in the national parks, monuments, and recreation areas in the West, and comment in caustic terms on the cost of this practice to taxpayers and on the damage it does to "fragile natural environments." The villains of the piece are greedy ranchers and western politicians (who are also often ranchers), and the National Park Service is depicted as complicitous in the process of degrading these public lands.

The piece begins with a characteristically blunt and unqualified statement of the problem:

America's National Parks are world-famous for their beauty and grandeur. Since the late 1800s Congress has been setting aside these lands as the most impressive examples of untrammeled Nature in this country. Today they comprise the most extraordinary system of natural preserves on Earth.

Naturally most Americans think their National Parks and Monuments are protected from commercial exploitation. And generally they are, outside certain heavily visited locations, where concessionaires are permitted to operate stores, gas stations, lodges, and other services deemed necessary for tourists. However, ranching is a glaring exception. (118)

Turner and Jacobs go on to explain that since most of the lands now included in the park system in the West were originally open to ranching, ranchers have had a strong influence in the fate of these lands, and, for the most part, the goal of the ranchers has been simply to make the most money they can out of the situation. In contrast to Congress's desire to preserve the "grandeur and beauty" of the western lands, ranchers are depicted as interested in preventing the establishment of parks, limiting the size of parks, insisting on retaining grazing rights in parks for as long as possible and at the lowest fees possible, selling grazing rights at high profits, threatening to despoil the scenic beauty of inholdings in park lands in order to extort high prices for scenic easements, and allowing or encouraging their cattle to trespass on park lands.

Language used in describing the ranchers is consistently negative: ranchers "refused to relinquish 'their' grazing permits" (118); they "forced the government into special agreements" (118); they "convinced the government to allow them to maintain ranching operations in new Park units under guise of 'preserving the historic Old West' " (119). Members of Congress from the West are characterized as completely supporting the ranchers in these activities, are called "politicos," and are accused of "political string pulling." The National Park Service receives little better treatment. In Grand Teton National Park, where grazing is permitted, "Park visitors are encouraged to view the overgrazing cattle, fences, and other range developments as part of the natural scenery" (121), and in Great Basin National Park, "a Park brochure assures tourists that 'cattle grazing [is] an integral part of the Great Basin scene' " (122). Turner and Jacobs comment, "It fails to say that visitors will see thousands of cattle en route to the Park and will hardly wish to see more, especially in the campgrounds, where they now graze" (122). Even the cattle are characterized negatively, as "huge bovines." The ecosystems of the parks are depicted as fragile and vulnerable to the effects of overgrazing and trespassing cattle, which also upset and disgust park visitors. In Zion, trespassing cattle are accused of "upsetting fragile riparian corridors and desert ecology" (122); in Big Bend, trespassing cattle "so heavily degrade the Rio Grande canyon that in many riparian areas cottonwood regeneration is virtually nonexistent" (122); in Lake Mead National Recreation Area, cattle "trample and erode the fragile desert soil, crush the cryptogams, and consume the scant greenery. They congregate around the area's few water sources and along 'Lake' Mead and Colorado River shorelines where they invade campgrounds and foul beaches" (124). The solution Turner and Jacobs propose to these problems is equally blunt: "Nearly every NPS unit where ranching has been banned shows significant recovery. . . . So the solution to the overgrazing problems on National Park Service lands is obvious: Remove all livestock and ranching developments from all Park Service lands" (125–26).

In this article the lines of opposition are clearly drawn: Congress (with the exception of western senators and representatives) and park visitors value pristine nature, untrammeled by cattle; cattle ranchers, supported by their congresspeople and by the National Park Service, value the land only in terms of profits. Ranchers, who are seen as being motivated only by economic considerations, and the National Park Service represent the established hegemony which considers the natural environment primarily as a resource to be managed for human economic prosperity. Turner and Jacobs attempt to promote instead their biocentric belief in the spiritual value of "untrammeled Nature" by linking it to a value already embedded within (yet at the same time potentially contradictory to) the established hegemony inasmuch as the beauty of wilderness areas was enacted in the setting aside of national park lands. They attempt to construct a new position, a counterhegemony that takes into account some of the values of the larger society yet is founded on a biocentric rather than on an economic principle. In order to shift the ground this radically, they must separate the valuing of the beauty of nature from the valuing of nature as a resource, and they do so by sharply distinguishing the actors in the drama of land management: Congress and park visitors versus ranchers and the National Park Service.

Consequently, we hear nothing of ranchers who also appreciate the beauty of nature, of park visitors who are undisturbed by the presence of a few cows, of park rangers who work to resist overgrazing practices; our attention is not drawn to how representatives from western states resolve the conflict between their support for ranching and serving in a Congress that has agreed to set aside national parks as preserves of natural beauty. The solution proposed by Turner and Jacobs grants no ground to the ranchers, and no credence to any suggestion that natural beauty and economic benefit could be reconciled: national parks are not to be used as a resource for ranchers. This rhetoric delineates clear alternatives in order to create a mandate for a significant redirection of policy; it deals in absolutes in order to emphasize the fundamental difference of the position being recommended from existing positions; it refuses to be coopted by the established hegemony.

In contrast, ranchers and other landowners are given more hospitable treatment in Hugh Zackheim's "The Blackfoot Valley and the River that Runs through It," from *The Montana Nature Conservancy Newsletter,* where they appear as knowledgeable managers of land opposed to the inroads of developers. The purpose of the newsletter is to report to members on the progress of Nature Conservancy projects and to increase support for them; thus this discourse is characteristically optimistic and rather self-congratulatory. At the same time, the intent of The Nature Conservancy to cast its net as broadly as possible, to include in their consensus as many perspectives as possible, is also clearly evident.

After a brief evocation of the beauty and biological diversity of the Blackfoot river valley, the article opens with a statement of The Nature Conservancy's commitment: "Protecting the natural environment of the Big Blackfoot has been a priority for the Montana Nature Conservancy for nearly two decades. And the Conservancy's projects have by design gone the extra mile to accommodate the land's traditional, economically compatible land uses, such as ranching, farming, small-scale logging, dude ranching, hunting, and river recreation" (1). In contrast to the depiction of the land by Earth First! as pristine, here the land is seen to have a history of uses. But, although practically every economic interest imaginable is included in their project (a highly significant and, from the perspective of more radical environmental groups, dangerously accommodating inclusion), there is, as in the Earth First! article, a villain who is threatening the land: developers.

Interestingly, however, these villains—and the ranchers who are briefly cast as villains later in the article—are never named and never appear as agents of any villainous actions. Zackheim laments "skyrocketing public use of the river [that] was virtually unmanaged," and "development pressures [that] jeopardized the continued existence of agricultural operations in the corridor" (1). He points out that the Conservancy's actions have prevented "the subdivisions and 20-acre ranchettes rapidly becoming the rule in many other Montana river valleys," and he notes that easements donated by landowners, including ranchers, ensure that "subdivision and other developments not compatible with agriculture and the natural values are forever prohibited" (1). He notes that the degradation that has occurred is the result of "present trends in land use," and he describes it in passive voice: "Sections of native prairie are being plowed; floodplain cultivation and locally unmanaged grazing are damaging the fragile riparian zone and adding silt to the river; and some potholes are being dewatered" (2). In short, he characterizes the actions as undesirable but avoids blaming the agents of the actions, and the only motive implied for these unnamed actors is a lack of forethought and planning, deficiences The Nature Conservancy stands willing to help rectify.

This is a rhetoric of inclusion aimed at winning consent; readers are not offered any position except as willing, wise, and wonderful collaborators with The Nature Conservancy's project "to promote land and river management that would conserve environmental values, protect private rights, ensure agricultural continuity, and provide compatible public recreational opportunities" (1). Everyone is assumed to be involved in or invited to participate in this endeavor, and all are characterized positively, praised for their "cooperation, creativity and . . . generosity" (1). Volunteers have been "tireless in efforts to restore the Blackfoot's fabled fishery" (1–2). "Private and governmental groups" are also lauded for "playing key roles" in the collaborative project (1). The Conservancy "strongly supports" the acquisition of land on the river by the Bureau of Land Management, which "has pledged to manage [it] for recreation and habitat protection" (2).

Management is the key term in this discourse, and it signals the difference in attitude toward the land that separates The Nature Conservancy from Earth First! and enables the Conservancy to align itself with the established hegemony. Alan Holt, director of stewardship and science for the Pacific region of The Nature Conservancy, notes, "In Hawaii and in many other areas of the world, if you just set aside a natural area without a commitment to active, long-term management, you may be sending it to its biological grave" (27). The Nature Conservancy's belief in the possible coexistence, through careful management, of "traditional, economically compatible land uses" and natural biodiversity contrasts with the belief of Earth First! in the spiritual value of untrammeled nature, and this concept of proper management of natural areas allows the Conservancy to argue that natural beauty and diversity can coexist with economic prosperity. The concept of management also allows Zackheim to avoid creating villains in his story: developers are not inherently evil and misguided; rather, they simply must learn to be better managers, to avoid unrestrained development or development that is inappropriate to particular areas.

In the conclusion to the article, Zackheim asserts the value of this strategy of inclusiveness and grounds it in the deep connection between Westerners and the land they live on: "Decades of strong, broad-based support for conservation efforts in the Blackfoot testify to the depth of Montanans' attachment to this river and its valley. Private and public partnerships have been key to the project's success, providing the nation with a Montana model of how to achieve on-the-land conservation" (2). Also notable is the way The Nature Conservancy, despite its status as a national organization, manages to adopt a grassroots stance on their projects: each of the state chapters includes the state name in the name of the group, and here the *Montana* Nature Conservancy is seen as providing a model to the nation.

As in the Earth First! article, however, much is being left out. We hear nothing of the inevitable conflicts between the interests which are being drawn into this coalition: nothing about how cattle trampling riverbanks cloud the water and disturb trout reproduction, nothing about the runoff of agricultural fertilizers and pesticides that deplete the biodiversity of the valley, nothing about how river rafters disturb nesting bald eagles and ospreys, nothing about how protections for endangered species restrict individual landowners' uses of their land. If recognized and examined, such conflicts potentially could result in the formulation of a counterhegemony (as does with Earth First! the conflict between the use of nature as a re-source and the valuing of the beauty of nature), but whenever such issues are mentioned in Nature Conservancy discussions, it is always in the context of successful solutions to these conflicts, win-win solutions in which all interests are satisfied within the established system.

These two rhetorical strategies could not be more different: while Earth First! polarizes the issues and provides a compelling critique of the effects of capitalism on the land, The Nature Conservancy constructs a broad area of common ground and argues, equally compellingly, for the benefits that can accrue to ecological values from the wise application of capital. This difference is compatible with, and partly motivated by, the difference in these two groups' fundamental beliefs—Earth First!'s adherence to bio-centrism and The Nature Conservancy's belief in management—beliefs that affect the groups' conceptions of how natural biodiversity can best be preserved or enhanced. For Earth First! putting human concerns first will always restrict biodiversity, and they doubt, with some reason, that human management, dependent upon very limited knowledge of the intricacies of ecosystem dynamics, can achieve the same results that unrestricted natural forces do. Thus, they call for a fundamental reorientation of priorities and the overthrow of the established hegemony. Foreman, speaking of the Wildlands Project, says, "Our goal is to create a new political reality based on the needs of other species" (quoted in Pennisi 168).

For The Nature Conservancy, in contrast, saving biodiversity does not require an overthrow of the current system: lands can be purchased and ecosystems can be restored by proper management. The Conservancy recognizes that ecosystems do not have any essential state they revert to if left alone but are always changing in response to the changing forces within them, which can and necessarily must include humans. Thus The Nature Conservancy works to integrate the value of biodiversity as completely as possible into the established hegemony. Greg Watson, director of the eastern regional office of The Nature Conservancy, argues, "In practical terms, we can no longer afford to consider humans as externalities. Indeed, the continued success of our efforts to preserve biodiversity in the face of mounting threats will depend on our ability to integrate socioeconomic factors into our conservation equations" (33).

From this perspective, these two groups might be seen as working against each other: to the extent that The Nature Conservancy succeeds in integrating the interest in saving biodiversity into the established hegemony, Earth First! will fail in bringing about any real change in priorities. Hegemonic politics is dialectical: because situations are always changing, the established hegemony must adjust or be vulnerable to revolution, but,

at the same time, to the extent that the establishment can redefine potentially disruptive interests in line with its own imperative, it can postpone
revolution indefinitely. Walter Adamson argues that Gramsci

saw what later Western Marxists would increasingly ignore, namely that the incumbent regime's increasing need for hegemony could also decisively increase its vulnerability. When a regime recognized this need and was generally successful in
meeting it, the proletariat was pushed to the defensive and forced to engage in a
protracted war of position in which the prospects for victory were indeed discouraging. When, however, the incumbent powers failed to forge their own hegemony or
to recognize fully the imperative for it, their vulnerability to an alternative hegemony was very great. (228)

   It is here that the question of how much change is necessary in our society to preserve the environment becomes relevant. It could be argued that
The Nature Conservancy (along with other mainstream groups) has successfully met the establishment's need for hegemony and thus strengthened
its resistance to an alternative hegemony and that this failure to reorient
our society's priorities will lead to the destruction of the environment.
Gramsci characterizes this situation as a "passive revolution" (59), a revolution that contains rather than liberates progressive forces. Adamson explains that a passive revolution does not necessarily prevent change, but it
does limit the extent of change. The Nature Conservancy has promoted
greater awareness of the environment and the value of biodiversity without
any radical demands for reorientation of the socio-economic system, or for
any very great changes in lifestyle. And, despite the optimistic tone of their
promotional materials, the Conservancy's rhetoric belies some some
awareness of the limited success of their efforts on behalf of the environment. The name of their recent initiative, "Last Great Places," which is
"aimed at preserving the planet's remaining intact ecosystems" (Watson
33), tacitly recognizes the rearguard actions the environmental movement
finds itself resorting to. In the opening chapter of their collection of essays
on the recent history of American environmentalism, Dunlap and Mertig
argue that the success of the movement has been ambiguous:

Many leading environmentalists, including McCloskey in this volume, have acknowledged that the movement has largely failed in its goal of protecting the quality of the environment. As Denis Hayes, key organizer for both the first and twentieth Earth Days, stated, "The world is in worse shape today than it was twenty years
ago." Of course, others are quick to point out that the situation would be far worse
had the movement not been around. Although the primary purpose of this volume
has been to examine environmentalism's success as a social movement, history will
judge it in terms of its success in halting environmental deterioration rather than in
simply avoiding its own demise. (8)

Furthermore, the relatively moderate stance of The Nature Conservancy also allows those who resist changes in our society's attitude toward the environment to call on the Conservancy to curb the more progressive force of the radical environmentalists. An article published by the Heritage Foundation demonstrates how the work done by groups like The Nature Conservancy can be used as the basis of an effort to discredit more progressive efforts. After detailing the "extreme" views of deep ecology and the monetary and physical damage done by Earth First! ecoterrorists, the article concludes:

Americans want to preserve a clean world—to conserve their environment. Americans too want an economy that offers them increasing economic opportunities. How to balance these two goals all too often splits Washington between myopic conservationists and equally myopic developers. Out of this split comes [*sic*] the ecoterrorists, who believe that anything short of complete victory for "the environment" is a moral as well as a practical disaster. . . . The environmental movement has a special responsibility. It must no longer tolerate, let alone encourage, the ecoteurs. In particular, environmental groups should publicize the fact that the ecoteurs' violence sabotages legitimate environmental groups. These mainstream groups thus should speak out forcefully to encourage their members to distance themselves from violent and destructive activities.

If Deep Ecology is not challenged at the philosophical level, the number of environmentalists committed to ecotage is likely to grow. And as more people put the "rights" of nature before those of humans, the more likely it is that innocent people are going to be killed. (Bandow 10)

Although the position staked out here is quite different from that of The Nature Conservancy,[7] the Heritage Foundation, which is actively working to contain and resist the interests of the radical environmentalists in shifting the basis of society from humanism to biocentrism, can align themselves superficially with the more moderate demands of groups like The Nature Conservancy and can then call on the Conservancy to reject the strategies and principles of the radical groups. For the most part, this strategy has not succeeded, for the diverse environmental groups generally avoid criticizing one another or commenting on differences in goals.[8] Furthermore, in this context, even the accommodationist strategies of The Nature Conservancy seem progressive,[9] for, although they insist that economic and environmental values can both be served through careful management, they do not see the environment solely as a human resource as does the Heritage Foundation. Current president of the Conservancy John Sawhill explains, "What does protecting biodiversity really mean? It doesn't mean any one thing—it means working with government, business, farmers, ranchers and people like you and me to protect all living things" ("Nature Conservancy" 9).

Radical democratic theory helps us see that assessing how much change is necessary for the success of a progressive cause is not simple. The environmental movement is not faced with an either/or choice between the Earth First! attempt to overthrow the current system and The Nature Conservancy's attempt to support and strengthen it. For Gramsci, the ideal successful counterhegemony was the Jacobin revolution, which brought about a radical reorientation of the society, while the prime example of passive revolution was the Risorgimento in Italy, which "involved the gradual but continuous absorption . . . of the active elements produced by allied groups—even of those which came from antagonistic groups and seemed irreconcilably hostile" (58–59). But Adamson argues that Gramsci also saw in the Risorgimento "certain new factors which had at least raised the possibility" of change, and Chantal Mouffe's interpretation of Gramsci's complex discussion of hegemony suggests that the success of a counterhegemony has less to do with the fact that it opposes and overthrows an established hegemony and more to do with how hegemony is attained:

if hegemony is defined as the ability of one class to articulate the interests of other social groups to its own, it is now possible to see that this can be done in two very different ways: the interests of these groups can either be articulated so as to neutralise them and hence to prevent the development of their own specific demands, or else they can be articulated in such a way as to promote their full development leading to the final resolution of the contradictions which they express. (182–83)

Thus, we might account for the difference in the positions of the Heritage Foundation and The Nature Conservancy by noting that the article published in the Heritage Foundation series attempts to neutralize the interests of Earth First! and the deep ecologists, while The Nature Conservancy's initiatives can be seen as attempting to include the Earth First! demand that the rights of nature also be taken into consideration in the established hegemony in such a way that the contradiction between modern industrial society and biodiversity will be resolved though careful management.

From this perspective, then, the efforts of Earth First! and of The Nature Conservancy can be seen as building on one another to create a new attitude toward the environment, rather than working against one another. Mouffe argues that

The objective of ideological struggle is not to reject the system and all its elements but to rearticulate it, to break it down to its basic elements and then to sift through past conceptions to see which ones, with some changes of content, can serve to express the new situation. Once this is done the chosen elements are finally rearticulated into another system. . . . Ideological struggle in fact consists of a process of *disarticulation-rearticulation* of given ideological elements in a struggle between two hegemonic principles to appropriate these elements: it does not consist of the confrontation of two already elaborated, closed world-views. Ideological ensembles existing at a given moment are, therefore, the result of the relations of forces between the rival hegemonic principles and they undergo a perpetual process of transformation. (192–94)

Revolution in the age of hegemonic politics is a matter of struggle over priorities, not of wholesale change. Any successful counterhegemony will contain transformed elements of the established hegemony. Radical groups like Earth First! struggle to disarticulate positions and principles from the established hegemony and transform them in line with their own priorities; thus, the "traditional" American love of wilderness is disarticulated from the notion of nature as an economic resource and transformed into a respect for the diversity of life (a spiritual value that was also present in the established belief system but suppressed in favor of the economic agenda) that will serve as a basis for a sustainable way of life for human beings and for the planet as a whole. The more ambiguous status of accommodationist groups like The Nature Conservancy results from the difficulty of ascertaining, in the midst of this process, whether their efforts to rearticulate positions prevent or bring about some significant change (if not as much change as radical groups demand); more particularly, whether in their efforts to articulate the principle of biodiversity to the principle of economic prosperity the Conservancy has simply been coopted by the position that nature is valuable primarily as an economic resource or whether they have created a new hegemony that resolves the contradictions between protecting all living things and achieving economic prosperity.[10]

While this question may be impossible to answer definitively, what seems more clear is that radical groups like Earth First! and accommodationists like The Nature Conservancy seem to have divided up between them the disarticulation-rearticulation process that Mouffe describes. Gramsci described a similar two-step process in the development of a new ruling class: "1. autonomy *vis-à-vis* the enemies they had to defeat, and 2. support from the groups which actively or passively assisted them" (53). Earth First! specializes in emphasizing the autonomy of their positions: Foreman argues, "I think the greatest strength and accomplishment of Earth First! has been our ability to redefine the parameters of the national environmental debate" (*Confessions* 30). Insisting single-mindedly on such notions that live redwood trees are not to be sacrificed to redwood decks, the group strives to break down the links that hold the established hegemony together. These links, or articulations, are strong, held in place not only by "tradition" but by the strength of the interests they serve (e.g., the timber industry), and, thus, because we often do not even perceive these links, they can be difficult to break. Herbert Marcuse describes how possibly disruptive contradictions within the established hegemony are systematically neutralized by "harmonizing" realizations; for example:

I take a walk in the country. Everything is as it should be: Nature at its best. Birds, sun, soft grass, a view through the trees of the mountains, nobody around, no radio, no smell of gasoline. Then the path turns and ends on the highway. I am back among the billboards, service stations, motels, and roadhouses. I was in a National Park, and I now know that this was not reality. It was a "reservation," something that is being preserved like a species dying out. If it were not for the government, the billboards, hot dog stands, and motels would long since have invaded that piece of Nature. I am grateful to the government; we have it much better than before. . . . (226)

Our gratitude to the government for protecting the park keeps us from seeing how "unnatural" a park is and how bad the environmental crisis is. The "realization" that government protection has solved the environmental problem harmonizes the contradiction between nature and industrial civilization and draws attention away from the question of how governmental protection allows and encourages environmental degradation to take place everywhere else and how setting aside a park makes the irruption of billboards, hot dog stands, and motels seem to be an unavoidable process. In short, governmental protection of national parks keeps us from facing the question of the extent to which decisions about land use are made democratically in our society. The Turner and Jacobs article I analyzed earlier works against such harmonization of contradiction by drawing attention to just this question through their attack on cattle grazing in national parks.

Scott Elliott refers to the theories of Robert Cathcart concerning the rhetoric of social movements to explain the contribution radical groups like Earth First! make to the success of the environmental movement: "The radical provides the audience with clear cut lines of decision. Does the audience accept or reject the position of the revolutionary? Cathcart notes that confrontation is an essential element of a movement's success. It is the confrontational form that produces 'dialectical enjoinment in the moral arena' " (7–8). But what Earth First! does not do much, or do well, is to seek support from other groups, especially those that might not agree with them on all concerns. As Killingsworth and Palmer observe, although "Foreman has occasionally appealed to other groups or social radicals. . . . This interest in hegemonic links . . . along with his pride over the ability of Earth First! to influence the public, has always been subordinated to his nonconformist, antinomian passion for the individually motivated and furtive righteousness of the radical acting alone or in small gangs of fellow seekers" (218).

Killingsworth and Palmer trace Foreman's attitude to the influence of Edward Abbey, author of the novel that introduced the notion of environmental monkeywrenching, and, further back, to the influence of neoromantic wilderness preservationists like Thoreau: "For Abbey, as for other existentialists and romantic individualists in the mold of Thoreau, Whitman, and the beat poets of the 1950s, radicalism arises most directly from personal experience, not from ideology. . . . Abbey's writing thus coincides with that of the deep ecologists, who suggest that their work is more a form of personal seeking than a systematic philosophy" (223). The stance of the romantic individual, however useful it may be in disarticulating radical positions from the established hegemony (and, I would argue, it is not a stance necessary to this effort), is not conducive to building a new hegemony, for it refuses to consider how the radical group may share interests with other groups and to educate people about these possible links. This failing is well illustrated by a confrontation between two smaller environmental groups in Montana. Louise Bruce, a representative of the moderate, consensus-building Montana Wilderness Association, takes issue with the radical and "exclusionary" strategies of the Alliance for the Wild Rockies (a group that is associated with the Wildlands Project). She quotes a statement by Steve Kelley, the president of the Alliance for the Wild Rockies, "When people get in the way, we ask them to move. When they don't move, you've got to go around them," and comments: "That's the language of exclusion and proscription, the antithesis of grass-roots activism. Wilderness will endure only with popular support; people won't change their environmental attitudes simply because someone who professes to know better has told them to do so. At MWA, when people get in the way and don't move, we strive to listen, to inform and— if we're good at our work—to build new support for preservation of the wild" (15).

This lack of interest on the part of Earth First! in reaching out to a broader range of people is particularly troublesome in light of the potential of the deep-ecology-inspired Wildlands Project to serve as the basis of a new hegemony. Killingsworth and Palmer note that the established hegemony has promoted attitudes toward nature that combine the attitude of traditional science (nature as object) with the attitude of business/ industry and agriculture (nature as resource), and they suggest that "we may now, however, be witnessing an attitudinal shift and a corresponding power shift that would cause the continuum to 'roll,' leaving a new alliance of deep ecology, science, and government—the environmentalist alliance" in the dominant position (15). This new alliance would need to develop a new attitude toward nature that somehow adjudicates between the deep ecologists' notion of nature as spirit and the scientific notion of nature as object—"for science to form a hegemonic link with deep ecology . . . it would have to be a transformed science, not the positivistic science that formed the model for scientific management and that provided the impetus for large-scale technological development" (15)—but Killingsworth and Palmer argue that "the connection between science and the environmental reform movements . . . has become the most problematical and the most important link in the evolution of environmental politics in America" (48).

In fact, the Wildlands Project, which proposes to set aside a system of wildlife reserves that would dwarf the largest national parks in extent, has attracted a surprising amount of support from scientists. As reported in *Science News,* "the plan drew strong applause from participants at the annual meeting of the Society for Conservation Biology in June [1993] when it was presented by Foreman, Soulé, and Noss" (Pennisi 169). Pennisi concludes: "At first glance, the Wildlands project seems too wild to warrant consideration by practical people, environmentalists included. But actually, research that is reshaping conservation science justifies some of Wildlands' underlying premises. Consequently, a growing group of scientists and activists, though critical of the details, find merit in this very radical plan. Already they have begun to focus on large-scale preservation" (168). The question for Earth First! is whether they should (or can) modify their oppositional stance and begin to work more actively on consensus building with other groups to broaden the base of their support. If they do so, they risk losing the advantage of representing a clear alternative; if they do not, they risk having their positions excluded from the newly developing hegemony.

The work of rearticulating positions into a broad-based hegemony, of seeking the support of a broad range of groups in society and combining their interests into a new common sense (whether genuinely new or merely a transformed consensus) is the specialty of The Nature Conservancy. As demonstrated by Zackheim's article about the Blackfoot River project, the Conservancy seeks to build broadly based support for projects to preserve local ecosystems that contain significant biodiversity. Because of its efforts to include everyone in its projects, it is difficult, as I mentioned earlier, to precisely characterize the Conservancy's attitude toward nature or where it would fall on the continuum described by Killingsworth and Palmer; instead, the notion of management allows the Conservancy to include the perspectives and the interests of all groups—scientists, government, business/industry, farmers, social ecologists, and deep ecologists—in its agenda. Characteristically, official statements from Conservancy personnel use the terms "preserve" and "conserve" interchangeably, terms that are precisely discriminated by other environmental groups (cf. Killingsworth and Palmer 23–48).

Notorious for their efforts to align the policies of corporate America with environmentally friendly principles, the Conservancy now also reaches out more formally to farmers, loggers, fishermen, and underemployed minorities under the rubric of sustainable development. This initiative, along with the increasing commitment of The Nature Conservancy to projects in all parts of the world, aligns the Conservancy with another group of environmentalists that Killingsworth and Palmer call the globals, who "argue for positive, sustainable development" while at the same time contributing to "the ecologically based critique of standard economics" (240). Greg Watson defines the Conservancy's vision of sustainable development "as the successful integration of compatible human activities into our biodiversity preservation strategies" (33). He notes that recent environmental conflicts have created "an impression that healthy economies and environmental quality are not compatible" and lists several Conservancy projects that attempt to refute this impression:

At Ohio's Big Darby Creek watershed, we are working with local farmers and other residents to reduce soil erosion and chemical runoff that threaten aquatic biodiversity. The project seeks to implement land-use practices that allow economic progress while protecting the creek's water quality. . . . Our flagship effort in sustainable development is the Virginia Coast Reserve. In 1991, the Conservancy joined with the local chapter of the National Association for the Advancement of Colored People (NAACP) and Citizens for a Better Eastern Shore to form the Northampton Economic Forum. The forum's mission is to create good jobs for local citizens and protect the area's natural resources. (33)

The Virginia Coast Reserve project, in addressing the needs of minorities, reaches out even further to include groups involved in the recent environmental justice movement. Benjamin Chavis, one of the leaders of a protest against the siting of a hazardous waste landfill in a black community in North Carolina, reports, "I said to The Nature Conservancy a little while ago: if you really want to conserve the earth, then join the environmental justice movement, because this is the movement that is going to constrain the destroyers of our neighborhoods and our communities" ("Place at the Table" 50).[11]

How The Nature Conservancy responds to such challenges will serve as a measure of their commitment to the creation of a truly progressive hegemony that serves the whole of society. Nevertheless, their achievements in obtaining big business support for environmental projects have been impressive. Douglas Hall, director of communications for the Conservancy, explains that as well as working with local farmers and residents on the project at Big Darby Creek, the Conservancy has also enlisted the aid of Honda of America: "Honda not only is making cash donations to our ecosystem preservation model on the Big Darby Creek in Ohio, but it is also independently mobilizing its workers to participate in tree planting along the Darby. And Honda management is continuing to talk with us about other long-term ways to aid the economy of the region in a manner that also benefits conservation of the watershed" (25). Hall echoes Foreman's assessment of how the strategies of radical and accommodationist groups can combine to produce changes in our society's attitudes and behaviors toward the environment:

> The Nature Conservancy thinks that change requires both protesters and accommodators; corporate support need not undermine the process. A number of recent efforts underscores the importance of environmental groups playing this dual role—good cop/bad cap, if you will.
> McDonald's may not have chosen to evaluate its practices without protest from grassroots environmentalists. But it was the Environmental Defense Fund that aided the fast food gaint in analyzing and planning dramatic reductions in packaging waste. Dow Chemical may continue to raise the ire of Greenpeace, yet Dow has begun working with Ducks Unlimited, the Conservancy, and others to protect significant wetlands throughout North America and has made great strides in voluntarily reducing pollutants from its facilities.
> . . . Just as we continue to need advocacy groups to push agendas of both industry and the environment, we increasingly need groups who can act strategically as catalysts for a truer greening of business. (25)

Whether The Nature Conservancy is contributing to a progressive hegemony remains an open question, as does the effectiveness of Earth First! and its associated projects in creating a counterhegemony. I would agree with McCloskey that the problem within the environmental movement lies not in the lack of agreement over how to pursue the goal of protecting biodiversity but rather "in the absence of healthy interaction between the more radical groups and the mainstream groups, or even between the pragmatic reformers and the accommodators. Increasingly, the radical groups embody the passion over the issues and articulate the visions of what the future should hold, whereas the mainstream organizations have far more resources and strong management. The dilemma is how to get these two ingredients into a productive relationship. Apart, the radical groups may expend their energy with little tangible results, whereas the mainstream groups may lose their way with no clear vision to pursue" (85). If such healthy interaction is to occur, it is important for environmental activists to recognize the importance and value of all the rhetorical strategies being employed by the different groups, and especially to recognize that in the struggle to develop a new accepted common sense about the the environment, positions must be clearly separated from traditional practices and redefined in line with the priorities of the new situation as well as being related in a new way with the concerns of a broad range of interests in our society.

NOTES

1. Killingsworth and Palmer see this reduction of the issue as a conservative strategy, and name this kind of discourse "ecospeak."

2. On the connection between Earth First! and deep ecology, see Elliott.

3. Membership and budget figures are from the *Encyclopedia of Associations 1994*.

4. Pough suggested modeling the new organization on the British government's Nature Conservancy, with the exception that the American group would remain private in its funding.

5. In fact, I am using the name Earth First! as a shorthand way of referring to the organizations associated with Dave Foreman, who in the early 1990s left Earth First! to form Wild Earth and the Wildlands Project.

6. Hegemony is more commonly used to refer to an established and oppressive regime, that which progressive forces are always striving to disrupt, and these negative connotations linger in Laclau and Mouffe's and Gramsci's use of the term. Nevertheless, as I will discuss further below, radical democratic theory sees the hegemonic process not only as that which impedes change but also as that which enables change in a society.

7. Bandow argues that environmentally committed Americans aim to strike a balance between commitment to the environment and commitment to the economy, and the commitment to the environment is cast in terms of a clean—that is, safe for humans—environment rather than of biodiversity. Drawing attention to the conflict between human rights and the "rights" of nature and implying that nature has no rights is also a move The Nature Conservancy would not make.

8. There are exceptions, and one instance of criticism cited by Killingsworth and Palmer illustrates how the strategies of radical groups enable mainstream groups (whom Killingsworth and Palmer call reform environmentalists) to position themselves more advantageously: "The argument that Earth First! muddies the face of environmentalism may be necessary, for reformers like Jay Hair [of the National Wildlife Federation] need to maintain their foothold in the Washington establishment; for them to condone violence—against either private property or people—would be the equivalent of negotiating with terrorists. But in many ways, ecotage helps the reform environmentalists both by stalling and frustrating developmentalist progress and by making liberals seem all the more moderate and appealing" (227).

9.   As Gramsci's analysis of fascism shows, a passive revolution can play "an historically progressive role": "like many, though not all, passive revolutions, fascism was progressive in a defensive fashion, since it was designed to curb a still more progressive political force. Its peculiar feat was to have promoted the development of industrialism without the radical cataclysm of a proletarian revolution" (Adamson 201).

10.   The conclusion to the *National Geographic*'s 1988 profile of The Nature Conservancy demonstrates the ambiguity of the Conservancy's attitude toward nature:

> Practicality is not the only reason for preventing extinctions, according to Larry Morse, who manages the Conservancy's national data center at the Virginia headquarters. "You can also argue that we have no right to wipe out species that have existed for millions of years or you could say that with every species lost in the chain of life, we humans are that much closer to extinction.
>
> "Practicality just happens to be the argument that most people can accept."
>
> Perhaps the point was best made by botanist Peter Lesica to a rancher in Montana on whose land grew a threatened prairie carnation. The Conservancy wanted to protect it with a conservation easement that would restrict some use of the flower's surroundings but allow the rancher a tax deduction.
>
> "This flower you want to save," asked the rancher testily, "is it good for anything?"
> "We don't know yet. But if you see a bolt on the ground, do you throw it away?"
> "Course not. I might need it some day."
> "We feel the same way," said the botanist, "about the prairie carnation." (844)

11.   The Nature Conservancy was also one of the eight groups accused in a letter from "several organizations of color . . . not only of lack of diversity in their staffs, but also of isolation from communities of color and of the poor, who are the chief victims of pollution" (Hahn-Baker 41).

WORKS CITED

Adamson, Walter L. *Hegemony and Revolution: A Study of Antonio Gramsci's Political and Cultural Theory.* Berkeley: U of California P, 1980.

Bandow, Doug. "Ecoterrorism: The Dangerous Fringe of the Environmental Movement." *Heritage Foundation Backgrounder* no. 764. 1990.

Bruce, Louise. "Wilderness Politics Are Anything but Simple." *High Country News,* 25 January 1993, 15.

Cathcart, Robert S. "New Approaches to the Study of Movements: Defining Movements Rhetorically." *Western Journal of Speech* 36(1972): 82–88.

Devall, Bill. "Deep Ecology and Radical Environmentalism." In *American Environmentalism: The U.S. Environmental Movement, 1970–1990,* ed. Riley E. Dunlap and Angela G. Mertig. New York: Taylor & Francis, 1992. 51–62.

Devall, Bill, and George Sessions. *Deep Ecology: Living As If Nature Mattered.* Salt Lake City: Peregrine Smith, 1985.

Dunlap, Riley E., and Angela G. Mertig. "The Evolution of the U. S. Environmental

Movement from 1970 to 1990: An Overview." In *American Environmentalism: The U.S. Environmental Movement, 1970–1990,* ed. Riley E. Dunlap and Angela G. Mertig. New York: Taylor & Francis, 1992. 1–10.

Elliott, Scott M. "Radicalism and Its Effects on the Environmental Movement." Paper presented at the Conference on Communication and Our Environment, Big Sky, MT, 1993.

Foreman, Dave. *Confessions of an Eco-Warrior.* New York: Harmony Books, 1991.

Foreman, Dave. "Foreword: Around the Campfire." In *The Earth First! Reader: Ten Years of Radical Environmentalism,* ed. John Davis. Salt Lake City: Gibbs-Smith, 1991. 7–10.

Foreman, Dave, et al. "The Wildlands Project Mission Statement." *Wild Earth* Special Issue (n.d.): 3–4.

Gramsci, Antonio. *Selections form the Prison Notebooks,* ed. and trans. Quintin Hoare and Geoffrey Nowell Smith. New York: International, 1971.

Grove, Noel. "Quietly Conserving Nature." *National Geographic* 174 (1988): 818–44.

Hahn-Baker, David. "Rocky Roads to Consensus: Traditional Environmentalism Meets Environmental Justice." *Amicus Journal* (Spring 1994): 41–43.

Hall, Douglas. "Building Green Corporate Partnerships: Cooperation between Companies and Environmental Groups." *Communication World* (April 1992): 25.

Holt, Alan. "Management and The Nature Conservancy." *Nature Conservancy* (Jan.–Feb. 1994): 27.

Kane, J. "Mother Nature's Army." *Esquire,* February 1987, 98–102.

Killingsworth, M. Jimmie, and Jacqueline S. Palmer. *Ecospeak: Rhetoric and Environmental Politics in America.* Carbondale: Southern Illinois U P, 1992.

Laclau, Ernesto, and Chantal Mouffe. *Hegemony and Socialist Strategy: Toward a Radical Democratic Politics.* London: Verso, 1985.

Lavine, Carolyn S. "The Nature Conservancy Turns 40." *Conservationist* (July–Aug. 1990): 24–28.

McCloskey, Michael. "Twenty Years of Change in the Environmental Movement: An Insider's View." In *American Environmentalism: The U.S. Environmental Movement, 1970–1990,* ed. Riley E. Dunlap and Angela G. Mertig. New York: Taylor & Francis, 1992. 77–88.

Manes, Christopher. *Green Rage: Radical Environmentalism and the Unmaking of Civilization.* Boston: Little, Brown, 1990.

Marcuse, Herbert. *One-Dimensional Man: Studies in the Ideology of Advanced Industrial Society.* Boston: Beacon P, 1964.

Martel, Ned, et al. "Inside the Environmental Groups, 1994." *Outside* (Mar. 1994): 65–73.

Mouffe, Chantal. "Hegemony and Ideology in Gramsci." In *Gramsci and Marxist Theory,* ed. Chantal Mouffe. London: Routledge, 1979. 168–204.

Pennisi, Elizabeth. "Conservation's Ecocentrics." *Science News* 144 (1993): 168–70.

"A Place at the Table: A Sierra Roundtable on Race, Justice, and the Environment." *Sierra* (May 1993): 50.

Sawhill, John C. "How to Think about the Environment: The Impact of New Behavior." *Vital Speeches of the Day* 56 (1990): 573–76.

Sawhill, John C. "The Nature Conservancy and Biodiversity: 1993 in Review." *Nature Conservancy* (Jan.–Feb. 1994): 5–9.

Turner, Dale, and Lynn Jacobs. "Livestock Grazing on the National Parks: A National Disgrace." In *The Earth First! Reader: Ten Years of Radical Environmentalism,* ed. John Davis. Salt Lake City: Gibbs-Smith, 1991. 117–26.

Watson, Greg. "Sustainable Development and The Nature Conservancy." *Nature Conservancy* (Jan.–Feb. 1994): 33.

Zackheim, Hugh. "The Blackfoot Valley and the River That Runs through It." *Montana Nature Conservancy, Big Sky Field Office Newsletter* (Fall 1991): 1–2.

CHAPTER 10

Thomas Cole's Vision of "Nature" and the Conquest Theme in American Culture

GREGORY CLARK, S. MICHAEL HALLORAN, and
ALLISON WOODFORD

Thomas Cole is the acknowledged founder of what art historian Matthew Baigell calls "the first coherent school of American art, the Hudson River School of landscape painters" (107). Like many American intellectuals of the antebellum period, Cole and the other Hudson River School painters celebrated "nature," in the sense of a landscape touched only lightly if at all by human works. Their canvases represented an America of rolling hills, pristine lakes, and dense forests, of occasional farms and villages surrounded by a vast, Edenic, and often intimidating wilderness. Another art historian, Barbara Novak, uses the term "rhetoric" in connection with their work, referring in a general way to its affective power and its connection with the nationalistic pride that motivated much literary and artistic work of the 1820s and 1830s (*Nature and Culture* 19 and passim). Their imagery is familiar to us today, not only through the widespread reproduction and conscious imitation of their work for popular consumption, but also through unconscious imitation by countless amateur painters and photographers. A recent effort to identify by survey what the American public prefers in art produced a general description of a Hudson River-style landscape (Melamid and Woodward). The Hudson River-style landscape surrounds us—in advertisements for everything from environmental activism to instant coffee, in the photo albums and slide shows in which we memorialize our vacations. It seems to have instantiated in the visual discourse of the developing national culture a rhetorical aesthetic that enabled citizens to articulate the indeterminate

261

wilderness they were working to inhabit in terms consistent with their aspirations.

Our purpose in this chapter is to explore the rhetorical dimensions of nineteenth-century American painting by focusing specifically on Thomas Cole's understanding and representation of the natural environment. One of us has argued that contemplation of scenery took on for nineteenth-century Americans some of the functions traditionally associated with epideictic rhetoric: the landscape came to be seen as an embodiment of cultural values and a locus of praise for the nation. Halloran has emphasized the work of writers who represented the landscape in picturesque terms, including Emerson, Thoreau, William Cullen Bryant, and particularly Nathaniel Hawthorne. Here we explore the rhetoric of landscape representation during this period through a focus on the visual artist who clearly inspired the poet and orator Bryant as well as a generation of painters.

We should also note here that most of the aspects of Cole's work we will be dealing with would more properly be categorized as "sublime," though the distinction between sublime and picturesque has little relevance to our argument. Both are aspects of what Barbara Warnick has called "the sixth canon," a range of aesthetic effects that achieved prominence in the rhetorical theories of such eighteenth-century Scottish belletrists as Adam Smith, George Campbell, and Hugh Blair. The intellectual context in which Cole worked was shaped in important ways by belletristic theory, which aestheticized oratory and rhetoricized the other arts, making of rhetoric a kind of architectonic for all modes of expression, including painting.

We will argue that in his painting and writing, Thomas Cole articulated attitudes toward the American landscape that were developing rapidly in the United States during the early nineteenth century and that continue to shape the relationship of this national culture to nature and the land. In making this argument, we will first characterize an iconology and ideology of "nature" that we find in Cole's paintings and writings in order to identify their rhetorical function in the community to which he addressed them. Then we will explain how that iconography and ideology, since perpetuated and to some degree transformed through the nineteenth and twentieth centuries, have shaped American attitudes toward nature that help define our cultural relationship with—and thus our national policies toward and actions upon—the landscape that is our environment.

The Rhetoric of Cole's Landscapes

Cole's influence in the art world dates from 1825, when three of his paintings depicting scenes in the Catskill Mountains came to the attention of established artists John Trumbull and Asher Durand, and artist-critic William Dunlap. The son of a shabby-genteel English immigrant who had failed more than once in business, Cole spent some time living hand-to-mouth as a minimally trained itinerant painter and painting instructor, though he was only twenty-four years old when he achieved "overnight success." The landscapes he produced in the 1820s, many of them depicting specific mountain scenes in the Catskills of New York and the White Mountains of New Hamsphire, no doubt both reinforced and benefited from the rapidly growing popularity of these locales as resorts for well-to-do American and European tourists. The Catskill Mountain House, for example, opened in 1824 as a small but comfortable resort hotel for well-heeled seekers after the picturesque and the sublime. Just one year later—in the year when Cole's paintings of scenes around the Mountain House first came to public notice—fifty more rooms were added, and by mid-century the Mountain House would accommodate several hundred guests and had become, according to Roland Van Zandt, virtually synonymous with "the Catskills" for fashionable tourists (43 and passim). As such, it became a characteristic feature of the Catskill landscape, appearing in countless paintings and prints including some by Thomas Cole. Cole's success in the twenties was such that by 1829 he was able to embark on a three-year tour of England and the continent, where he met and talked shop with such artists as John Constable, spent long days examining masterworks in the museums, and painted numerous studies of the European landscape to develop his artistic technique.

In addition to the more literally representative landscapes that first brought him success and helped maintain it throughout his career, Cole also painted didactic allegorical narratives—often in multicanvas cycles with titles such as *The Voyage of Life* and *The Course of Empire*—these set in landscapes that were both imagined and idealized. Novak makes a distinction between "the still small voice" and "grand opera" that, while perhaps somewhat overstated, aptly expresses the rhetorical flavor of these two strands of his work (*Nature and Culture* 18–33). In both genres, Cole exhibited an interest in capturing the particular look of natural phenomena. Other Hudson River School painters would share this interest, and some would surpass Cole in the ability to represent the natural world faithfully. Jasper Cropsey, for example, is said to have exhibited a handful of leaves next to one of his canvases to demonstrate to skeptical Londoners the accuracy of his depiction of the autumn colors of a Northeast American landscape (Novak, *Nineteenth-Century American Painting* 13). Cole was a genuine lover of the outdoors and an enthusiastic reader of the new empirical science, and he introduced what would quickly become the standard practice of sketching directly from nature in order to achieve a faithful representation of it. As a result, the depictions of natural phenomena such as clouds and the effects of light in the open air in works by Cole and other Hudson River School painters are accurate to a degree no previous artist had achieved with any consistency, perhaps because they were the first to whom "nature" in this romantic sense mattered so much. When Cole's most famous pupil, Frederick Church, exhibited his monumental painting *Heart of the Andes* in 1859, viewers were advised to bring opera glasses in order to appreciate more fully the rich detail of flora and fauna, and among those who testified enthusiastically to the vividness of the experience was Mark Twain (Avery 43).

This passion for direct and close observation of "nature" was grounded in an empiricist spirit that had been important in science, art, rhetoric, and philosophy since the time of Locke. But for Cole and his followers, it was powerfully inflected by romanticism's inclination to understand nature as excluding and even opposed to the human. The English painter William Hogarth, who flourished a century before Cole, had shared the empiricist preference for direct observation of "nature" over the imitation of established models, but to him observing and representing "nature" meant observing and representing the life of London's streets and coffeehouses and parlors. For Cole, "nature" was rural and wild, and humans were visitors who came to witness and appreciate, ideally leaving little trace of their presence.

As the canvases in his "grand opera" mode most clearly demonstrate, appreciation of the natural world was for Cole not simply a matter of detached scientific study or aesthetically pleasing representation. Like many artists and intellectuals of the 1820s through 1840s, Cole found the landscape rich in spiritual meaning. With contemporaries in Europe and America, Cole viewed the natural world as an embodiment of divine beauty and truth—essentially, as a mode of access to God. Further, the category of the aesthetic itself was, for Cole as it was for many readers of the developing English philosophy of the time, a mode of access to the divine in the human: it awakened and refined an innate moral sense that was understood to be the only common ground of human virtue in a culture that was remaking people as increasingly self-absorbed and atomized. For people living according to these cultural assumptions, the aesthetic provided the primary basis for virtuous community by enabling mortals to connect with the godly in each other as it enabled them to connect to God. (Clark describes this aesthetic in detail in his analysis of the rhetoric taught at Yale and practiced throughout New England at the turn of the nineteenth century by Timothy Dwight—an aesthetic rhetoric born of his union of the secular notion of taste and the sacred notion of grace.) By portraying the natural world in this moralized and religious context, Cole's landscapes, whether subtly in the picturesque mode or more overtly in the "operatic," attempted with lesser or greater intensity to do the ideological and rhetorical work of sermons.

In Cole's own terms, this work was the transmission of a kind of refining "delight" that, as his "Essay on American Scenery" explains, is accessible only to those who encounter the natural world with perceptions trained in this aesthetic. The function of this delight is specifically spiritual and moral in his description, and ideological and rhetorical in ours. Such delight, he wrote,

> is not merely sensual, or selfish, that passes with the occasion leaving no trade behind; but in gazing on the pure creations of the Almighty, he feels a calm religious tone steal through his mind, and when turned to mingle with his fellow men, the chords which have been struck in that sweet communion cease not to vibrate. (5)

And Novak notes that it is only where this experience is shared that Cole can locate the ground for reliable community. For him, and for many of his like-minded contemporaries, only the godly in nature can awaken the godly in men and women. And only that mortal godliness, awakened and enacted upon the ground of a shared contemplation of divine creation, can enable people to maintain a redeeming rather than a corrupting kind of collectivity (Novak, *Nature and Culture* 15). Indeed, Cole was impatient with those who viewed nature for purposes less lofty than that, declaring in his 1844 essay "Sicilian Scenery and Antiquities" that "he is unworthy of the privilege of traveling who gleans not from the fields he visits some moral lesson or religious truth" (49). More bluntly and personally, he recorded in his journal that

> my admiration for the beautiful is a source of irritability & uncharitableness towards those who do not seem to feel as I feel & see as I see, & instead of pitying them for their obtuseness & want of taste I speak of and to them as if they were vile and criminal. (138)

Clearly, at stake for Cole in the landscapes he painted was the presentation of truths that are moral and religious as well as aesthetic, truths upon which, for him, hopes for virtue and progress in the young American nation were founded.

Given these ideological assumptions inherent in his work, we can review Cole's career in a way that identifies both the intentions behind the iconography of nature he bequeathed to Americans and its rhetorical functions in their culture. In terms of the development of subjects and technique, his work can be divided somewhat arbitrarily into three phases. Works of the first phase, most prominent in the period from 1822 to 1829, are marked by relatively limited technical skills, an overwhelming attention to detail, and experimentation with elevated and often precarious viewpoints that violated accepted aesthetic standards and conveyed a sense of risk and hardship endured in the effort to see something. The often reproduced *Falls of the Kaaterskill* (1826), for example, places the viewer opposite a cliff down which the falls plunges; in the foreground is a twisted and dead tree clinging to a rocky crag in the lower-right-hand corner, placing the viewer high up on the side of what appears to be an extremely steep slope overlooking the precipice into which the falls empties. The vantage point is a consciously contrived one; there is at the actual site of the Kaaterskill Falls no opposing slope on which to stand. While this and other works of Cole's early period are in many ways immature, they capture something that seemed both artistically new and uniquely American, compounded of the rugged and wild landscape itself and the daring of the viewer, powerfully signified in the contrived vantage point, who proves equal to the challenge of the landscape. These early paintings won both popular and critical notice and firmly established Cole as a figure in the American art world.

Cole's second phase is characterized by a significant improvement of his technique and some initial important changes in his content. It begins with an 1829–32 trip to Europe—during which his deliberate study and practice improved his technique substantially—and extends through about 1842. During this phase Cole began to center more attention on lighting effects, and his composition became less complicated as he concentrated on larger forms and left out inessential details. Secular philosophical themes began to take on some importance in increasingly ambitious choices of subject matter, particularly in the two famous cycles *The Course of Empire* and *The Voyage of Life*. However, whether his paintings took this operatic or, as he called it, "fancy" form, or that of the well-known and more readily marketable realistic "views" that he continued to paint (Parry 176), the depiction of landscape still remained his primary concern. And in both forms he continued to experiment with the elevated and seemingly risky viewpoint that is a distinctive feature of many famous Hudson River School works.

The final phase of Cole's work emerges clearly in 1842, the year of his return from a second trip to Europe, and ends with his untimely death on 11 February 1848. In this phase religious and allegorical themes began to dominate his paintings, and landscape took on the character of a more generalized backdrop for the moralistic narratives that had become primary subject matter. Art historian Ellwood C. Parry III notes that as early as 1827 Cole had adopted as his own a strict hierarchy of genres in painting that placed his commercially successful landscapes at no higher than a fourth level, well below in both cultural significance and professional value the "historical landscapes," the "historical or poetic portraits," and the "epic, dramatic, and historical paintings" that held his clear aesthetic prior-

Falls of Kaaterskill (1826), by Thomas Cole. Photograph courtesy of The Warner Collection of Gulf States Paper Corporation, Tuscaloosa, Alabama.

ity. From this point in his career on, Parry argues, Cole attempted to move up that hierarchy in his work, an ambition that was continually undermined by his need to produce and sell those more marketable fourth-level landscapes that made him a living (52–53, 67). His letters and journals record on the one hand his persistent desire to produce the first-level epics that would instruct and inspire, that would provide "a means of lifting the mind of the plain laborer and mechanic above its dull common course"

(Cole 113) and "teach him that the beauty [Art] displays is a type of coming and enduring glory" (Cole 118–19), and on the other hand the constant frustration of that desire by the market demands that he had to meet to support himself and his family.

They also record that even as he aspired upward in the aesthetic hierarchy to which he subscribed, Cole remained deeply interested in portraying the American landscape. And like his friends William Cullen Bryant and James Fenimore Cooper, Cole recorded in his best-known paintings a distinctly American nature marked by qualities of purity and wildness that set the New World apart from the Old. Here they could see no ruins of ancient empires, no historic cathedrals, but instead lush forests, high mountains, and freshwater streams all largely unmarked by human works. Bryant remarked publicly on the importance of this emerging American aesthetic of wildness in Cole's early landscapes in an 1829 sonnet addressed "To Cole, the Painter, Going to Europe," urging him to relish the "different" and more tamed European landscape, but to "keep that earlier, wilder image [of the American landscape] bright." Cole expressed virtually the same sentiment in a letter addressed to his patron, Robert Gilmour, written very shortly before his departure on this first venture abroad: "I wish to take a last lingering look at our wild scenery. I shall endeavor to impress its features so strongly on my mind that, in the midst of the fine scenery of other countries, their grand and beautiful peculiarities shall not be erased" (Noble 72). Like the poem, Cole's letter is dated 1829, and he may have had Bryant's sonnet in mind as he wrote, or the two friends may have been drawing upon a common source, perhaps a conversation.

The striking similarity of their sentiments suggests the crucial importance of the theme of "wildness" in Cole's early work. In the early nineteenth century, the Puritan vision of America as a "howling wilderness" was still a commonplace, though others such as Washington Irving and DeWitt Clinton had commented more recently and more favorably on wildness as a distinctive quality of the American landscape. But for Cole wildness was much more. Upon returning from this first trip to Europe, he elevated it to a moral principle in the "Essay on American Scenery," which argued eloquently that Americans would be spiritually improved if they would learn to appreciate the uniquely wild beauties of their native landscape. And in eulogizing Cole nearly twenty years later, it was this aspect of Cole's work that Bryant would recall most fondly:

I well remember what an enthusiasm was awakened by those early works of his, inferior as I must deem them to his maturer productions,—the delight which was expressed at the opportunity of contemplating pictures which carried the eye over scenes of wild grandeur peculiar to our country, over our aerial mountain-tops with their mighty growth of forest never touched by the axe, along the banks of streams never deformed by culture, and into the depth of skies bright with the hues of our own climate; skies such as few but Cole could ever paint, and through the transparent abysses of which it seemed that you might send an arrow out of sight. ("Funeral Oration" 14)

Bryant's hyperbolic claims to the contrary, Cole's vision of virgin forests, pure streams, and bright skies was no longer unique by 1848. Indeed, Bryant himself would soon possess a particularly brilliant example of Cole's influence—Asher Durand's *Kindred Spirits,* a representation of Cole and Bryant standing on a rocky crag in a typically wild Catskill woods. One of the most famous canvases of the Hudson River School, *Kindred Spirits* was commissioned as a gift to Bryant on the occasion of his Cole eulogy, and as a memorial to the artist Durand had helped "discover" just twenty-three years before. In the brief ensuing period, a generation of artists including Jasper Cropsey, Frederick Church, and Durand himself, formerly an engraver and portraitist, had taken up landscape painting with an emphasis on the unspoiled northeastern woods and mountains that Bryant associated with Cole. Cole's vision of the landscape was not his alone, but a shared one, and in the decades to come Church and others would press south and westward in search of the wildness that was becoming increasingly rare as a fact though increasingly important as a value in the Northeast.

Kindred Spirits both depicts and adopts the precarious vantage point that was one of Cole's contributions to the tradition of American landscape painting. Durand places Cole and Bryant on a rocky crag overlooking a deep gorge, and views them from what appears to be another outcrop at the edge of a steep plunge into the same gorge. Like Cole, he represents nature as inviting and spiritually uplifting, but at the same time dangerous and difficult, a challenge to one's courage and determination. The refining delight of which Cole had written in the "Essay on American Scenery" was apparently accessible in its highest form only to the man—it would for Cole and Durand and their fellow artists have been a man specifically— with a certain disregard for his own physical comfort and safety, a wildness, perhaps, to parallel the wildness of the American landscape itself. And implicit in this juxtaposition of the wild in an idealized man and in an idealized landscape, we read at that moment of early national culture an invitation to conquest.

The central character in the quasi-mythical "discovery" of Cole was John Trumbull, who was later quoted as saying that "This youth has done at once, and without instruction, what I cannot do after 50 years practice" (Myers 41). Trumbull may actually have said something like this, and in

Kindred Spirits (1849), by Asher B. Durand. Photograph courtesy of The New York Public Library. Collection of The New York Public Library, Astor, Lenox, and Tilden Foundations.

any event he allowed the words to be put in his mouth. Alan Wallach records evidence of a more concrete and material contribution Trumbull made to Cole's early success: he introduced Cole to many of the wealthy patrons who sponsored his work and his travel during the 1820s and 1830s. What was the achievement that Trumbull, probably the most distinguished and highly regarded American painter in 1825, so admired in Cole's youthful landscapes? Trumbull was himself best known as a painter not of landscapes but of patriotic historical scenes, such as *The Battle of Bunker Hill* and *The Declaration of Independence,* and in view of what later commentators and Cole himself had to say, it seems possible that the political implications of his own work were precisely what Trumbull saw realized in Cole's somewhat different style of painting. Like so many other artists and intellectuals of his time, Trumbull had been striving not only to master a medium of expression, but to articulate in that medium an identity for a young nation self-conscious about its exceptionality. Trumbull had striven to fix that identity in images of heroic people and historical events, but Cole brought into visual focus a new possibility that had recently begun to emerge in the writings of Bryant and Cooper: the nation could be understood as neither more nor less than the land itself, a rugged land "never deformed by culture," challenging the courage and determination of its people to assert their own heroism.

This vision of a land unmarked by culture was nostalgic when Cole first came to prominence and grew increasingly so as his career progressed. Though less overtly political than Trumbull, Cole shared his Federalist sympathies, and in the context of Jacksonian politics and an increasingly industrial economy both tended to see the unfolding historical scenario as tragic. This is perhaps most apparent in Cole's *Course of Empire* series, in which five canvases show the evolution of a landscape from the wild state, through the pastoral, to the establishment of an apparently flourishing empire which is then wracked by civil disorder and finally collapses into picturesque ruins. Wallach offers a detailed and persuasive interpretation of the series as the allegorical expression of both a pessimistic philosophy of history, according to which all societies inevitably rise and fall, and a more specific "agrarian republican critique" of the optimistic tendency of Jacksonian democrats to hold the United States immune to the more general cyclical "laws" of history (90–98).

As a beginning painter Cole may or may not have attributed political meaning to his landscapes, and he was reticent throughout his life about political allegiances (Robinson 70). But Bryant's 1829 sonnet made explicit the idea that the "wilder image" represented on Cole's earliest canvases was not only an object of aesthetic pleasure and source of moral improvement, but a subject of national pride as well. And the "Lecture on American Scenery," delivered before a meeting of the American Lyceum in New York City after Cole's return from his first trip to Europe, clearly suggests a political as well as a moral and cultural significance for the wild landscape. To take delight in the landscape would be to participate in the lyceum ideal of forming a morally responsible and politically competent public, an ideal rooted, as Frederick Antczak shows, in both the current Jacksonian populism and the much older rhetorical tradition of civic discourse. Barabara Novak attributes a similar political significance to Durand's *Kindred Spirits,* noting that it represents a transcendentalist ideal of communion with and through nature, of "a potential community" of human beings (*Nature and Culture* 15). The Hudson River style of landscape painting was the iconographic expression of an ideology based on a tacit premise articulated by Myra Jehlen: "the decisive factor shaping the founding conceptions of 'America' and of 'the American' was material rather than conceptual; rather than a set of abstract ideas, the physical fact of the continent" (3). But as we will argue below, "the physical fact of the continent" was itself transformed by Cole and his artistic successors into something immaterial, to the peril of our physical environment.

Cole's Nature and the Rhetoric of the American Land

Killingsworth and Palmer's *Ecospeak* (1992) frames the various discourses of the environment in contemporary North America between two ethical poles: "One group will view nature as a warehouse of resources for human use, while an opposing group will view human beings as an untidy disturbance of natural history, a glitch in the earth's otherwise efficient ecosystem" (4). The polar positions and the various others arrayed between all assume a radical distinction between the human on the one hand and nature on the other. As human beings, we are either more or less prudent stewards of natural resources put here for our use, or more or less destructive intruders on a natural world that would be better off without us, but never ourselves an integral part of what we treat as "nature." (The movement known as "ecofeminism" represents an important exception. We do not consider it here, except to note that it underscores the masculine bias of both the exploitative ideology within which we place Hudson River School art and those ecological discourses examined by Killingsworth and Palmer.)

That politicized concept we now call "the environment" thus tends to exclude human works except as exploiters, and what might be called "mainline" environmentalism tends to disregard natural forces at work in the human world except in such extraordinary cases as the erosion of the Parthenon by polluted air. A somewhat paradoxical expression of this insistent distinction between humankind and nature is the often-heard slogan that we must "save the planet" through environmental activism. A moment's thought tells us that it is beyond our power to save or destroy the planet. It will survive whatever depredations we wreak upon it, and life too will undoubtedly adapt to changed atmospheric and climatological conditions. It is neither the planet nor the biosphere we need to save, but rather our own species. But to talk that way would be to acknowledge that we are a species, like the spotted owl or the snail darter, that we are an integral part of nature rather than either an alien visitor or a designated steward. We would like to suggest that this alienation and the attitude of domination that follows from it were strongly reinforced in the notion of "Nature" that was popularized by Cole and other nineteenth-century artists and writers. To the extent that later environmentalisms in the United States as well as North American culture more generally have inherited the iconography of the Hudson River School, this alienation is reinforced by tacit attitudes operating as an ideology that fundamentally separates humankind from the realm of nature, whether ascribed the role of spectator, steward, or exploiter.

Patricia Nelson Limerick, whose work examining the history of the American West explores the social function of this sort of ideology, can help us identify attitudes toward the American land that are perpetuated by this iconography, an iconography that was translated freely between American painting and writing during the nineteenth century and that seems to have saturated our popular culture in the twentieth. Arguing that "Western history has been an ongoing competition for legitimacy—for the right to claim for one's group the status of legitimate beneficiary of Western resources," Limerick articulates the foundational assumption that the land is material for our use, and she identifies the political function of perpetual competition for a free claim on this material as nothing less than conquest. This process of conquest, in her words,

basically involved the drawing of lines on a map, the definition and allocation of ownership . . . , and the evolution of land from matter to property. The process had two stages: the initial drawing of lines . . . , and the subsequent giving of meaning and power to those lines, which is still under way.

This definition of the process of conquest supports Limerick's argument that "Conquest forms the historical bedrock of the whole nation, and the American West is a preeminent case study in conquest and its consequences. Conquest was a literal, territorial form of economic growth" (27–28). Although the notion of conquest in American cultural history is more commonly used to describe the relations of peoples—specifically the domination by immigrant Europeans of the indigenous North American cultures—conquest is also a useful concept to apply to an examination of the attitudes of these European Americans toward the land that they came to dominate.

The inherent violence of the concept of conquest may seem at first inappropriate to our project of describing the rhetorical function of nineteenth-century landscape paintings, particularly those of an artist whose work exhibits a deep and demonstrably sincere reverence for the land. The American land was for Cole "the pure creation of the Almighty" (5). Our claim is that this attitude of reverence could and did function rhetorically to fuel a process of conquest. To understand how it did that, we must return to Limerick's observation that the process of conquest was enacted first in the graphic work of drawing maps, which she describes as "the definition and allocation of ownership," and then in the rhetorical work of interpreting them as guides for social policy and action. Making a map is, in effect, making a text, and texts are at once both selections and appropriations of reality, as careful readers from Plato to Derrida have observed. Simply put, the act of making a text—whether map, graphic representation, or verbal description—is essentially the act of taking control. Paul Carter observes that the conquest of the continent of Australia progressed as the Europeans treated the land "like their language," taking elements of it "out of context, like quotations, to symbolize their own historical presence" (344). The same metaphor can be applied not only to the conquest of the continent of North America in general, but more particularly to the textualizing of that continent that was the work of landscape painting. As Kenneth Burke observes, the making of a text entails the seeking of "faithful reflections of reality" that ironically turn out to be "selections of reality" and "deflection[s] of reality" (*Grammar* 59), that have the rhetorical function of inviting readers "to make [themselves] over in the image of the imagery" (*Philosophy* 281).

This is a description of the ideological function of rhetorical texts, a description that we assume applies to visual as well as to verbal representations. Given that assumption, we turn to Cole's writings to understand the rhetorical purpose that he had in mind for his painted imagery of the American land. Barbara Novak has observed about Cole the commonplace that other cultural historians have observed about many of his contemporaries—that they saw Nature as a divine handiwork, and thus believed that seeing the divine in Nature was analogous to seeing the face of God (*Nature and Culture* 5). We are arguing that Cole's aesthetic project, like those of many other American painters and writers of his time, involved a conscious attempt to present that divine handiwork to others in the form of what amounts to visual sacred texts that, like all sacred texts, function to explain and direct the relationship of humans to the divine. Cole's belief that this relationship was founded upon a clear distinction between the human and the natural is explicit in his writings throughout his career.

Not long before his death, Cole wrote to a friend that "An artist should be in the world, but not of it; its cares, its duties he must share with his contemporaries, but he must keep an eye steadfastly fixed upon his polar star, and steer by it whatever wind may blow" (quoted in Parry 343). Years earlier, in his "Essay on American Scenery," he had insisted that this land as rendered in painting and poetry should "sublime and purify thought, by grasping the past, the present, and the future" in ways that "[give] the mind a foretaste of its immortality and thus prepare it for performing an exalted part in the realities of life" (3–4). Later in the same essay he described this "exalted part" that Americans were to perform in terms that made the American land the setting for divinely approved actions of dominance by human culture over nature: "Where the wolf roams, the plough shall glisten; over the gray crag shall rise temple and tower—mighty deeds shall be done in the now pathless wilderness; and poets yet unborn shall sanctify the soil" (17).

But while in his public utterances Cole could celebrate the conquest of the American land, he had moments of profound pessimism as well. In a remarkable fragment of an essay called "Verdura, or a Tale of After Time—," unpublished and unfinished in his lifetime, he looked forward to our own time and envisioned the outcome of these "mighty deeds" in less celebratory terms:

The close of the twentieth century was a fearful season in the history of man—for the world was filled with outrage & wrong. This vast continent of America was peopled with its hundreds of millions. The plough had furrowed the last prairie & every green nook of the Rocky Mountains had its inhabitants. The desire of wise men of two centuries past was fulfilled & there was a great multitude spread over the land. The principles, as they called them of those sages were also wrought out— The Freedom of the individual man—and the dignity of human nature—favorite notions—were now developed & exhibited themselves in vice profligacy of irreligion & anarchy. As long as the lands were ample & large tracts unoccupied & every man had his road of ground the States which once held the proud title of the "United" bound in a loose band of interest & pride moved among nations as one nation. Though among themselves they jostled & quarrelled & blood had oft been shed, and love was not the Chain that encircled them. But when the population became dense & multitudes began to clamor for bread the filmy threads of vanity and worldly prudence were broken and the pride of man with its haggard offspring like a tempest broke up the great deep bosom of society and there was no more calm; but a fearful heaving hither & thither of passions of men. . . . (Robinson 82)

Some signs of the pessimistic vision are visible in his paintings, most obviously in the tragic narratives of *The Course of Empire* (1834–36) and two pairs of allegorical canvases called *The Departure* and *The Return* (1837) and *Past* and *Present* (1838), more subtly in the ugly rows of tree stumps in the foregrounds of such paintings as *A View of the Mountain Pass Called the Notch of the White Mountains* (1839) and *The Hunter's Return* (1845), and perhaps even in the lightning-blasted tree that stands as Cole's most recognizable signature in the foreground of most of his early "literal" landscapes.

Novak has described Cole's vision of the natural world as one that claims a place for the human in a "new Trinity of Nature, God, and Man" (*Nature and Culture* 17). In light of "Verdura" and the pessimistic notes of his visual landscape, perhaps the Devil should be seen lurking at the fringe of this Trinity. With or without a devil, such a relationship makes humans as much other to the natural world as they are to God. We see the theology implicit here as going beyond the simple opposition between humans and nature suggested by Novak's formula. Our claim is that Cole's vision of nature entails not just a separation of human culture from nature, but an insistent dominance over it. We base this claim on two aspects of Cole's work. First, he made statements throughout his career to the effect that the act of painting nature is an imitation of the creative act of God. Second, his frequent use of an elevated and precarious viewpoint signifies an act of dominance over nature, of risking and surmounting its challenges. Bryant's "Funeral Oration" gives metaphorical expression to the sense of dominance over nature conveyed by Cole in "pictures which carried the eye over scenes of wild grandeur . . . , over our aerial mountain-tops."

In describing Cole and other landscape painters as "priests of the naturalist church" (*Nature and Culture* 9), Novak enables us to consider Cole's project in terms of the project of the clergy, but also to rethink the political alignment inherent in the clergy's role, at least as Cole practiced it in his art. As interpreters of the divine, the clergy are situated somewhere between the divine and the human; are they aligned more closely with God or with their fellow mortals? Limerick's discussion of mapmaking as an act of conquest, and our discussion of painting nature as the making of a sacred text, lead us to conclude that in his role as priestly iconographer of the divine, Cole aligned himself more closely with the divine than with the human, reading his work as a reenactment of the act of divine creation. In "A Letter to Critics on the Art of Painting," Cole described the kind of painting he attempted as "the imitation of the creative power" that "forms, on the principles of eternal nature, a world of its own" (62). In "A Lecture on Art," he described art as "the Atmosphere which encircles the sphere of our humanity, kindles the dead soul, and raises it above the dullness of mere animal existence," and the act of making art as "man's imitation of the great Creative power" (103). Such a role not only separated Cole from the nature that it was the purpose of his art to recreate and interpret but also raised him, like the Creator, to a place somewhere above it. Further, the rhetorical function of his art was to separate its viewers from and elevate them above the nature that it represented to them as well. And in doing so it simultaneously transformed the natural world into something capable of domination by an essentially spiritual being—an ideal rather than a material landscape.

Terry Eagleton observes that in the high culture of England and the United States at this time, the notion of the aesthetic as a rhetorical address to an innate and refinable human capacity to recognize and reenact the divine became central to the operation of the "public sphere" (32), that place where decisions are made about collective policy and action. Cole's contribution to that public sphere in America at a time when the American landscape was undergoing unfettered and sustained destruction was to separate its beauty from its material reality. In doing so, it explicitly revered moral and religious form perceived in the land while accommodating, in an iconography and ideology that separated the human from the natural, the political and economic destruction of its content. Certainly this aesthetic is not the only source of the ethic of conquest and exploitation that has been central to the relation of Americans and their land since their culture's beginnings. But it has supported that ethic. The iconography of the American land developed by Cole and perpetuated by others has located the material reality of nature—the American land—within the realm and responsibility of human control and dominance, even while professing reverence and respect for the moral and spiritual lessons that land might teach.

Novak's argument in *Nature and Culture* about the ideological consequences of nineteenth-century landscape painting in the United States is summarized in this statement: "Each view of nature, then, carried with it not only an aesthetic view, but a powerful self-image, a moral and social energy that could be translated into action." This vision of nature, she argues, operated then and has operated since in the culture "as an imperial iconography" (7). For the purposes of our discussion, Novak's "imperialism" and Limerick's "conquest" both enact an attitude that seems pervasive throughout the history of this culture, an attitude that demands explicitly of Americans their separation from and, implicitly, their conquest of the land where they live. And in keeping with the history of imperial conquest, it is also an attitude that designates Native Americans as a part of that land which European Americans can and must control, a pattern that is also subtly apparent in Cole's work.

Plainly apparent in his paintings and writings is Cole's preference for the wildness of the American landscape, in contrast to the more domesticated landscapes of European art. The established European norms of scenic beauty insisted that a landscape appeals to our sense of beauty through its historical and cultural associations rather than any intrinsic qualities. To be beautiful, a landscape thus required some traces of history and culture—buildings, ruined temples, etc. The American landscape was by this standard dull, since its most notable distinguishing feature was the general absence of marks of cultivation. Cole's rhetorical legacy was to establish the new aesthetic standard we have described, a standard that found in the wild American landscape the divinely beautiful and true. He did so by painting sacred texts in which American nature is pure and wild, distinct from American culture and available for its conquest.

Cole developed this new landscape aesthetic at the very moment when our rivers and hillsides were being reformed and often deformed by culture. The year of his "discovery" by John Trumbull was the year in which the Erie Canal was completed. By the 1830s the Hudson River teemed with both wind- and steam-powered boat traffic. The Catskill Mountains were home to a thriving tanning industry that would collapse when the stands of hemlock that provides bark for the tanning process were exhausted in the latter part of the century. Most of this is hidden from sight in the work of Cole and the other Hudson River School painters. Perhaps that is because such was not for them the American landscape at all. That landscape was, rather, the one they themselves created—a landscape intended to be read as a text with spiritual, moral, and intellectual instruction for Americans. The trajectory of Cole's career suggests that the material land of America became less real to him than the ideal landscape he created and interpreted to his community.

ACKNOWLEDGMENTS

This project has been supported by the Educational Leadership Corps of the Hudson Mohawk Consortium of Colleges and the Undergraduate Research Program of Rensselaer Polytechnic Institute. The authors also acknowledge the help of Alan Wallach, whose thoughtful and careful reading of the essay prompted important final revisions.

WORKS CITED

Antczak, Frederick J. *Thought and Character: The Rhetoric of Democratic Education*. Ames: Iowa State UP, 1985.
Avery, Kevin J. *Church's Great Picture: The Heart of the Andes*. New York: Metropolitan Museum of Art, 1993.
Baigell, Matthew. *A History of American Painting*. New York: Praeger, 1971.

Bryant, William Cullen. "A Funeral Oration, Occasioned by the Death of Thomas Cole, Delivered before the National Academy of Design, New York, May 4, 1848." New York: D. Appleton, 1848.

Bryant, William Cullen. "To Cole, the Painter, Going to Europe" (1829). *Poems of William Cullen Bryant,* ed. Humphrey Milford. London: Oxford UP, 1914.

Burke, Kenneth. *A Grammar of Motives.* Berkeley: U of California P, 1969.

Burke, Kenneth. *The Philosophy of Literary Form.* 3d ed. Berkeley: U of California P, 1973.

Carter, Paul. *The Road to Botany Bay: An Essay in Spacial History.* London: Faber and Faber, 1987.

Clark, Gregory. "The Oratorical Poetic of Timothy Dwight." In *Oratorical Culture in Nineteenth-Century America: Essays on the Transformation of Rhetoric,* ed. Gregory Clark and S. Michael Halloran. Carbondale: Southern Illinois UP, 1993. 57–77.

Cole, Thomas. *The Collected Essays and Prose Sketches.* ed. Marshall Tymn. St Paul: John Colet Press, 1980.

Eagleton, Terry. *The Ideology of the Aesthetic.* London: Basil Blackwell, 1990.

Halloran, S. Michael. "The Rhetoric of Picturesque Scenery: A Nineteenth-Century Epideictic." In *Oratorical Culture in Nineteenth-Century America: Essays on the Transformation of Rhetoric,* ed. Gregory Clark and S. Michael Halloran. Carbondale: Southern Illinois UP, 1993. 226–50.

Jehlen, Myra. *American Incarnation: The Individual, the Nation, the Continent.* Cambridge: Harvard UP, 1986.

Killingsworth, M. Jimmie, and Jacqueline S. Palmer. *Ecospeak: Rhetoric and Environment al Politics in America.* Carbondale: Southern Illinois UP, 1992.

Limerick, Patricia Nelson. *The Legacy of Conquest: The Unbroken Past of the American West.* New York: Norton, 1987.

Melamid, Komar, and Richard B. Woodward. "The Perfect Painting." *New York Times Magazine,* 20 February 1994, 36–37.

Myers, Kenneth. *The Catskills: Painters, Writers, and Tourists in the Mountains, 1820–1895.* Yonkers, NY: Hudson River Museum of Westchester, 1987.

Noble, Louis L. *The Course of Empire, Voyage of Life, and Other Pictures of Thomas Cole, N.A., with Selections from His Letters and Miscellaneous Writings.* New York: Cornish, Lamport, 1853.

Novak, Barbara. *Nature and Culture: American Landscape and Painting, 1825–1875.* New York: Oxford UP, 1980.

Novak, Barbara. *Nineteenth-Century American Painting: The Thyssen-Bornemisza Collection.* New York: Abbeville Press (Artebras), 1986.

Parry, Ellwood C., III. *The Art of Thomas Cole: Ambition and Imagination.* Newark: U of Delaware P, 1988.

Robinson, Christine N. *Thomas Cole: Drawn to Nature.* Albany, NY: Albany Institute of History and Art, 1993.

Van Zandt, Roland. *The Catskill Mountain House.* Hensonville, NY: Black Dome P, 1991.

Wallach, Alan. "Thomas Cole: Landscape and the Course of American Empire." In

Thomas Cole: Landscape into History, ed. William H. Truettner and Alan Wallach. New Haven and Washington: Yale UP and the National Museum of American Art, 1994.

Warnick, Barbara. *The Sixth Canon: Belletristic Rhetorical Theory and Its French Antecedents.* Columbia: U of South Carolina P, 1993.

CHAPTER 11

"The Curious Peach"

Nature and the Language of Desire

CHARLES BERGMAN

> The body moves, though slowly, toward desire.
> We come to something without knowing why.
> —Theodore Roethke, "The Manifestation"

The common Darwinian wisdom has it that nature is a jungle. The common environmental wisdom has it that nature is, well, a national park. But I think nature is a labyrinth in which, when we walk, we are tracing the tracks of our own desire. When we walk in nature, we walk within ourselves.

A brief example will illustrate how human desire is written onto nature. I visited a prehistoric cave recently in the north of Spain, along the verdant coast of the Bay of Biscay. A remote cave, high in the jagged mountains of the Cantabrian Cordillera, *El Horno de la Peña*—"the oven of the mountain"—is not visited by tourists. I went with the provincial *encargado,* the man in charge of caves of the region, José Maria Ceballos. We stepped out of the damp gloom of a drizzly autumn day into a labyrinth of darkness. By the feeble light of our headlamps, Jose Maria traced for me the outlines of virtually dateless creatures, painted and carved onto the seeping stones of the cave. Some of the first humans created these images, working in the darkness, at various points between 25,000 and 14,000 years ago, and they filled me with an inarticulate awe: big-jawed horses with their manes waving in an ecstasy of implied motion; the exquisitely carved heads of female deer, scratched lovingly into the seeping rock; the round and ominous profiles of predatory cave bears.

But at the end of the twisting tunnel of this cave was hidden its true secret. I had to squeeze into a small corner, a *rincon,* to see it. In the darkest

281

recess of the cave was the profile of a standing human being, its rough crudity suggesting that it is, perhaps, one of the oldest images in the cave. He had the head of a bird, his nose sharp as a beak. His feet were vaguely reminiscent of bear paws, stepping forward. And his arms stretched before him, raised, palms up, in an attitude of supplication and yearning. As if, within the ardent Spanish earth, he were praying.

It is the human image, carved on the face of nature, the image of human desire and longing, that we continue to discover under all the other images of nature that we create.

The two bodies—the physical body of humans and the physical body of nature, the flesh and the planet—are written upon and through each other. The body of a man, scratched and engraved upon the rocks of the cave in Spain, combines human and animal shapes; and that body, supplicating with desire, is marked upon nature. Human desire emerges from the body, and it finds its expression in our lives in nature. We are drawn to nature, impelled by some desire, like body moving to body. And if, for Western culture now, in the late twentieth century, desire is experienced primarily as an absence, a sense of lack, even a wound, it must be that the longing for nature is more intense, more poignant, more cut with a sense of its own inevitable impossibilities, than ever before. For increasingly we are coming to know nature through what is no longer available to us—through lack and absence and loss. And through the wounds we have inflicted ourselves upon animals and land. Upon the body of nature.

The largest question that faces us, in trying to decipher the human relationship with the natural world, is precisely what it is that draws us to nature, what desire drives us to seek beautiful creatures in the forest, lovely vistas in the mountains, and strange forms painted and engraved in the recesses of caves. For though we may tend to believe that the preservation of species and the salvation of natural spaces is largely a scientific or a political question, involving us in the various discourses of ecology and bureaucracy, the discourses of "data" and "resources," I believe that the issues we face in nature are essentially issues about relationship, and in our relationships with nature the same issues apply as in our relationships with other people.

Desire moves, as the quotation from Theodore Roethke's poem says, through the body, takes concrete physical forms. We embody our desire, just as it seems to move through the body. It is not clear whether desire is actually located in the body, or whether we have deposited it there. Perhaps desire does move through the body, but the shapes we give it are constructed by us. Certainly, one of the ways desire is embodied is through language and images. In the Western tradition, in the language and imagery by which nature has been described and comprehended, nature itself is regarded as a kind of body, sometimes literally, but usually metaphorically. Our relationships to nature are similar to those which we have with our own bodies and others' bodies. And so nature can often be used in poetry, for example, as a kind of language of our own physical desire, the evocation of a specific image—a peach, for example—serving as a metonymic substitute for human body parts. Nature becomes a kind of language by which human desire is expressed, comprehended, and justified. By turning this old convention of using nature to express human desire around, or viewing it from slightly shifted positions, it's possible to see how desire itself draws us toward nature, entwines us in nature at the same time that it draws us into various relations with our own bodies. The various psychological theories of the body, and its relations to power and desire, can help us read our own relationships to nature. These theories can help us see how we construct the two bodies—human and natural—out of language and cultural norms and practices. These theories can help us understand more deeply what it is that has drawn us toward nature, following the movements of our own often confused desires, toward ends we may not often have fully understood. The traces of desire, left for us in metaphor and image, mark out a labyrinthine path over which we conduct a complicated traffic between nature and culture. The body of nature and the human body intersect in the wild and even dangerous terrain of human desire.

The human figure at the end of the dark cave in Spain suggests the double nature of this intersection of human desire and nature, humanity and earth. He is at once composed of various animal features, bird and bear. The man is constructed out of natural images. And the human is written, or engraved, upon the rocks deep in the earth. The image and its placing upon nature are a description of the process of representation of nature itself, looking two ways at once—inventing ourselves out of natural images, and simultaneously placing ourselves as human animals within nature. It is a process we negotiate with language and images. It is the process of rhetoric itself.

In other words, what are the forgotten animals that have been scrawled in the dark caves within us? Stepping back from those symbols of nature—both the linguistic and nonlinguistic forms of representation of nature that we create to make sense of nature for ourselves—we can study the symbols not for their truths, as it were, about our emotional investments in nature, but for the way in which those symbols reveal something about the person or culture that produced them. We make out of nature a text, a set of symbols, both linguistic and nonlinguistic, and out of those symbols we can learn about ourselves, our own desires in nature, and the meanings we write into nature. This is the first and most important step in the process of restructuring our relationship with nature. And inevitably, with ourselves as well, since what we are able to see and imagine in nature is so deeply dependent on who we are.

The languages and the images we use to interpret nature also make nature speak to us. These languages speak *of* us. They offer us a semiotics of our representations of nature. A valuable summary of semiotics is given by Terence Hawkes in *Structuralism and Semiotics*. Semiotics as a discipline is the "science of signs," he says. In both linguistic and nonlinguistic, verbal and nonverbal ways, humans generate language. Semiotics suggests that any social practice, from speaking a word to giving someone a bunch of roses, involves signifying, that is, it is articulated like a language. Talk is one language, for example. But we also, of course, make elaborate messages out of our gestures, posture, clothing, hairstyle, perfume, and much more—a kind of body language. And when we begin to analyze the ways in which these "signs" produce both explicit and implicit meaning, we begin to understand more about ourselves and the way we make meaning in our lives. As Hawkes says, this is the process of "signification," and with it "we have, of course, encountered an extremely powerful, because covert, producer of meaning at a level where an impression of 'god-given' or 'natural' reality prevails, largely because we are not normally able to perceive the processes by which it has been manufactured. [This] analysis of *semiosis* . . . begins to take us 'behind the scenes' as it were of our own constructions of the world" (123–36).

This semiotics of our representations of nature is a diagnosis of our desire. A culture writes its own values into nature, so that it can then, in discovering those values "in" nature, justify itself. As Hawkes explains, out of its images of nature, both linguistic and nonlinguistic representations, a culture creates myths that sustain and authenticate its sense of its own being. In these naturalized images, a culture locates its own values, at the same time grounding itself in what it imagines to be "natural."

The first task is in acknowledging the place of desire in structuring our language of and relations to nature—we have to clear out a space in which desire can be reinscribed, rewritten, reenvisioned. We don't have to go back to paleolithic caves to encounter the prominence of desire in the discourses about nature. In the Western tradition, desire animates nature and inspires the writing about nature. The great Roman poet Lucretius opened his quasi-philosophical treatise on nature, *De rerum natura* (The nature of things), written in the first century B.C., with a beautiful paean to Venus. "Since you," he writes,

> and you only, rule the world of nature,
> and nothing without you, comes forth to the coasts

of holy light, or makes for joy or love,
I pray you be with me as I write these verses
that I compose about the world of nature. . . .
(Book 1, lines 21–25)

Shakespeare's Falstaff is another example, a man of gross appetite and wild linguistic extravagances. That hugely corporeal and lustful figure calls himself one of the "squires of the night's body," one of "Diana's foresters, gentlemen of the shade, the minions of the moon"—a devotee of the goddess of the hunt and the mistress of the animals (*1 Henry IV,* 1.2.24–26). There is a kind of fury to desire that makes it subversive.

Yet in the tradition of American natural history writing, which focuses on the relationship between humans and nature, there is a marked tendency to eschew desire as a theme. Perhaps more accurately, this language prefers to bracket off desire, subjecting it to cultural constraints and ideals. The tidy, middle-class comfortableness that surrounds so much environmental discourse now, a discourse of lovely animals in family groups and idealized landscapes in softened light, can too easily be perturbed by the desire Falstaff invokes. In *The Merry Wives of Windsor,* he enters one midnight scene in the forest wearing the head of a buck over his own head. He's a beast: "For me," he says, "I am here a Windsor stag, and the fattest, I think, i' th' forest. Send me a cool rut-time, Jove" (4.5.12–14).

But American natural history writing eschews these subversive pleasures—the confusing vitalities and the rending tumults of passion. Thoreau himself defines one of the central features of natural history writing in dealing with desire: it is disembodied. Nature becomes the scene of pure and spiritual longings, rarefied into a "transcendent beauty." Standing on the frozen Walden Pond during winter, Thoreau looks down through the ice, as through a window, into the "quiet parlor of the fishes, pervaded by a softened light as through a window of ground glass, with its bright sanded floor the same in summer; there a perennial waveless serenity reigns as in the amber twilight sky, corresponding to the cool and even temperature of the inhabitants. Heaven is under our feet as well as over our heads" (314).

Nature is the heaven we learn to walk above, looking down. This urge to spiritualize the body of nature, to turn the solid body into water and light, grips contemporary nature writers. Barry Lopez, for example, writes of "Imagination and Desire in a Northern Landscape," in *Arctic Dreams.* In his passionate and beautiful prose, however, the subjectivity of desire is held in check, disciplined even, by the ethical schoolroom of nature. Human desire is tutored by the natural world. He writes at the end of *Arctic Dreams* of bowing, hands folded at his parka, to the great expanse of water in the Bering Sea, a spiritual gesture:

When I stood I thought I glimpsed my own desire. The landscape and the animals were like something found at the end of a dream. The edges of the real landscape became one with the edges of something I had dreamed. But what I had dreamed was only a pattern, some beautiful pattern of light. The continuous work of the imagination, I thought, to bring what is actual together with what is dreamed is an expression of human evolution. (371)

Thoreau and Lopez turn to water to see a purified, clarified, almost baptized desire. The desire of Narcissus, for example, bending over a pool of water to see his own image, is hinted at, but obscured by the gesture of a genuflection.

Terry Tempest Williams calls her most recent book *Refuge,* and puts her unease about desire most directly in a book review in a recent issue of *Orion* magazine. "What are the essential questions that drive natural history writing?" she asks:

In the end, they may be sexual. But I choose to believe our yearnings, our desires to learn about the land, to live among its creatures, are how we remember the spiritual ties that bind us to life, to those invisible strands that connect us to all that is dark and bright and mysterious (60–61)

I admire these writers deeply, their passion and their commitment to the natural world. But in generating a language of ethics and spirituality to describe our longing in nature, we have excluded and domesticated the wilder, unruly passions that nature itself seems so often to evoke in us. The spirituality we discover in nature is sublimated sexual desire.

Perhaps desire is a matter of choice, but I do not experience it that way. I have never yet eliminated a feeling by choosing not to feel it. I merely repress it, often by a process of idealization. One need not be a Freudian to recognize, in Terry Tempest Williams' lines, an almost classic sublimation. Desire is a deeply charged issue, politically as complicated now as it has ever been. So in nature writing we more or less avert our faces from desire, or at least that messy desire associated with the body and its passions that intrude upon the calm order of our solitary meditations. After John Hay, in *The Undiscovered Country,* witnesses a mass of tiny eels on the shore of the ocean, and an elver come among them, he meditates:

I am told that there is a Chinese instrument called the ch'in whose sounds are said to be "the sounds of emptiness," which pervade the universe and set the heart of the player in tune with mystery. So the sight of an elver put me in touch with reaches out of mind. (28)

We have constructed, through our language, a desexualized image of nature, and a desexualized human desire within nature. Of course, some current American writers deal, not so much with sexual impulses in nature, but with desire in nature. Edward Abbey can watch a billboard flame, from "plutonic pyromaniacs," in the desert its pine and paper wrapped in flames in a "mad lust," with the "rapt intensity, of lovers fecundating" (10). But his wild-eyed passion is an aggressive, masculine form of desire, attacked by some critics as the same kind of destructive desire that destroyed the landscape—"raped" it—in the first place.

Ours is largely, strangely, even sadly an eviscerated human presence in nature, our desire neutered, emptied into a kind of Buddhistic, desireless vacancy, summarized by Ralph Waldo Emerson's famous description in "Nature" of the self turning into a "transparent eyeball" (6).

The engraved, human-animal figure in the Spanish cave revealed perhaps something of why we now, at this precise time, are so reluctant to address desire directly in American natural history writing. It was a startling image in several respects beyond its open-handed vulnerability. It juxtaposed what appears as a spiritual longing with a blatant sexuality that always strikes us so powerfully when it appears in earlier times and other cultures. Desire is a labyrinth of strange associations, troubling impulses, sexual urges. The figure in the *rincon* was deformed, and not simply with animal features. His humanness was itself deformed through an exaggerated sexuality, an exuberant and even demonic eroticism. Projecting from under a slightly bulging stomach, he had an erect penis almost as large as his body itself.

The connection between humans and nature has been made through metaphorical parallels since humans have left records. Human desire, especially in its darker forms, is a deeply troubling mystery, connected at once with both the body and nature. In the cave in Spain, the erect phallus serves as a great symbol for desire, an image. The bird and bear man with the erect penis is a metaphor at once of animal desire within humans, and of the connection of human desire within the natural world.

We think of desire as literally located within the body, and the body locates us within nature. Yet, like the erect penis in the cave man, the body is a way of giving metaphorical expression to desire as well. The body provides the metaphors for desire. Metaphor is the language of desire. It is the language of relationship. It likes, or makes an equation between, two entities, A and B. It establishes a relationship between them: a man is like a bird or a bear; desire is like an erect penis. Metaphor goes to the heart of desire itself, since this equation is a kind of paradoxical copula, merging two images or ideas. Julia Kristeva, a French post-Freudian theorist, argues that metaphor is sexual in nature, the linguistic equivalent of the motions of desire. The term metaphor, she argues, should not "bring to mind the classical rhetorical trope (*figurative* vs. *plain*), but instead . . . the modern theories of metaphor that decipher within it an indefinite jamming of semantic features one into another, a meaning being acted out . . ." (30).

Equally as important, metaphor is the way in which human desire embodies itself, both in language and by its investment in particular body parts. The feeling of desire, a fantasy, a longing for what is absent, attaches itself to the specifics and concretes of the body, and these body parts are the living metaphors of that desire. Desire is a metaphorical phenomenon: the act of desiring another person or thing is, psychologically speaking, a metaphorical act. As Kristeva explains:

Metaphor should be understood as movement toward the discernible, a journey toward the visible. . . . The object of love is a metaphoric of the subject—its constitutive metaphor, its "unitary feature," which, by having it choose an adored part of the loved one, already locates it within the symbolic code of which this feature is a part. (37)

Specific body parts are themselves the metaphors of desire. And yet the focus on a particular part of the body, as metaphoric or metonymic object of desire, already makes this body part "symbolic." It takes on meaning apart from its physical being, within a "symbolic code" that will be at once personal and cultural, psychological and anthropological. That symbolic part helps constitute the person experiencing the desire, it is the feature that helps unify the person's psyche. It is through the psychological and linguistic operations of metaphor that desire is structured within the psyche, and it's through metaphor that a culture is able to give shape to and understand the meaning of relationship—to other people and to nature.

In the man in the cave, we are given the mysterious animal aspect of desire—he is transected by gestures of spirituality and sexuality, at once a bird and a bear and a man. And yet it is the large penis that becomes the overriding metaphor of desire, and that metaphor has persisted. It has been, in fact, the primary signifier of desire for us. And this, I suspect, is precisely the reason that desire is so increasingly suspect for us in our relationships with nature. The link between desire and particular body parts, especially the highly sexualized body parts like the penis, now makes the topic of desire uniquely volatile for us, leaves us with unique problems in dealing with desire and its inevitable associations with aggression, vulnerability, and danger. Desire now locates us in the shadow of the phallus, with all its associations of an erotics of power.

Kristeva, for example, argues that all Eros is, insofar as it is about relationship, phallic and "essentially manic": "Eros is essentially manic. Its infatuation with power, idealized as it might be, hence its joying in the Phallus, has its reverse side—depression, the destructive relish that takes pleasure in dissolving the Ego and even the living being itself" (79). She is arguing that the demonic in desire, its manic and wild lawlessness, is its central element. The power of the phallus is not, she claims, simply a feature of desire. We might try to idealize phallic power, give it joy and pleasure, but it is destructive as well. Desire is linked with wounds, with suffering, with craziness, with death.

It is this specter of erotic, male domination that enforces much of a current erasure of desire—and human agency—in nature. We live in a double habitat—our bodies and nature. And both are inscribed with boundaries and taboos. Increasingly, under the feminist analysis of the rhetoric of male relations with nature, the phallic prejudice has been exposed. The destructiveness of the phallus has come to stand for the rape of the land. Annette Kolodny, for example, has documented the role of sexual metaphors in American encounters with the land, with its connotations of exploitation, in her *Lay of the Land*. The metaphor of the land as female, encountered by male desire, served for early Americans as their *experience* of nature. "At the core," Kolodny writes,

lay a yearning to know and to respond to the landscape as feminine, a yearning that I have labeled as the uniquely American "pastoral impulse." Obviously, such an impulse must at some very basic level stem from desires and tensions that arise when patterns from within the mind confront an external reality of physical phenomenon. But the precise psychological and linguistic processes by which the mind imposes order or even meaning onto phenomenon—these have yet to be understood. (8)

But this gendering of the land, this overlay if you will of topography and anatomy, was not merely a literary language—"it became the vocabulary of everyday life" and guided male action. As Kolodny writes, the tradition of this "pastoral impulse" in American literature leads to the "multifaceted and growing awareness that, before the masculine, the feminine is always both vulnerable and victimized" (143).

This suspiciousness of desire in the discourses of nature is also linked with a deep prejudice against discovering human qualities in nature, the distrust of metaphor itself in describing nature. Since the seventeenth century, we have been deeply suspicious of locating subjectivity in nature. We look to nature as something distinct and external. Michel Foucault is the great French poststructuralist philosopher, noted for his examinations of the way in which power operates in all relationships, and the way sexuality has been constituted and experienced from classical Greece through nineteenth-century Europe. He argues that our subjectivities, our identities, are now most deeply linked precisely with our desire. We seek our identities in our desire. As Foucault said in an interview, we characterize individuals through their sexual behavior: "Tell me your desires, I'll tell you who you are" (11). Breaking subjectivity from nature has meant censoring desire, and the language of desire, from our relationships with nature. So a kind of rigorous incompatibility exists between our sense of nature and our sense of ourselves in nature. We are precisely now learning, through the language of metaphor and story, how to rewrite our place in nature—and coming straight up against that mysterious animal aspect in desire that still holds us in its fascinating grip.

The heat that desire evokes in our discourse is, I think, a sign of its importance, a marker of the vitality we place in it, in issues of both identity and relationship. It is in the contested meaning of desire—in the metaphors and myths, in the stories and images of humans in nature— that we will find how nature lives inside us. And it is in understanding human desire in nature more completely that we can begin to reinscribe humans more fully into the body of nature. This is a question as much about language and meaning as it is about the body itself. The question is, how is power articulated in desire? How is it distributed in relationships? We need to know the shape of our desires, the forms our passions take, and the mirrors that nature holds up to us. Choice is the rationalist's virtue, and the ethicist's; transformation is the hope of the emotional. It is not choice I believe in, finally, but transformation.

The best place to turn to see how nature and desire have been intimately associated is the pastoral genre of poetry. This genre shapes one of our main myths of nature, a central trope for the relationship between humans and nature—nature is a paradise, the idealized home the civilized, urbanized human spirit has lost and longs for. The poet Theocritus invented the pastoral poem, and with it the connections between love, erotic longing, and nature. Theocritus lived in Alexandria in the first half of the third century B.C., a city of great wealth. But he had grown up in Sicily, and he longed for the simpler joys of his childhood. So he created a poetry in which he could wander in the solace of cool breezes and chestnut trees. In his poems, shepherds sing and wrangle. Cows low. And a prominent feature of these lovely, dreamy idyls is the lament of the forsaken lover, his or her song an incantation under the silence of a silver moon. In one idyll, Theocritus stands upon the shore and sees a crystal stream leap down from the cliffs. The waves of the sea break around him, until he sees the breasts of nymphs shine in the whiteness of the foam and their hair spread wide in the weed, and the nymph Galatea, enticing and fickle, mocking the clumsy longing of the Cyclops. She tosses upward the bitter spray of the sea from her shining arms (see Greg 8–10).

What's merely pleasurable in Theocritus becomes something more in the Roman poet Virgil. Virgil's bucolic blisses have a political edge to them—

he writes satires from the country, in which the Roman farm becomes a kind of utopian country seat. There's a straight line of descent in pastoral from Theocritus to Thoreau, from Virgil to Grizzly Adams. The desire for nature in the pastoral genre, in its idyllic form, is largely regressive, the longing of the child for the mother.

Shakespeare uses the genre frequently in his drama, but to trouble the easy fantasy of escape. In Shakespeare, nature is the scene in which human desire is released. Beyond the walls of the city, lovers traverse the fields of desire that are not sanctioned by parents and princes—a strange world of excess and transgression. Shakespeare complicates the simple nostalgia of Theocritus and Virgil, while maintaining the opposition between city and nature. Hermia speaks to Helena, as she plans her flight from both father and Athenian law in *A Midsummer Night's Dream,* of the "new friends and stranger companies" she seeks in the woods:

> And in the wood, where often you and I
> Upon faint primrose beds were wont to lie,
> Emptying our bosoms of their counsel sweet,
> There my Lysander and myself shall meet:
> And thence from Athens turn away our eyes,
> To seek new friends and stranger companies.
> (1.1.214–19)

The escape into nature is a cultural trope, a great myth of Western literature. Nature in the pastoral becomes linked with "stranger" desires, and a deeper personal energy that is opposed to the city, with its emphasis on law and reason and authority. The lovers of the play enter the woods, fleeing the city and following their desires, and the woods become the symbol of a deeper experience of themselves. Driven through the woods by dream and desire, lust and love, the young lovers find in the release of their passions a strangely transformative experience, a clarifying renewal after a bout of nocturnal chaos.

As George Bataille writes, more modernly, more perversely, in *My Mother:*

I believe I have never loved anywhere except in the woods. I did not like the woods, but I loved immoderately. I have never loved anyone but you, but what I love in you, make no mistake about it, is not you. I believe I love only love, and even in love, only the anguish of loving, I have never felt it except in the woods. . . . (Quoted in Kristeva 366–67)

Yet one of the great writers of the pastoral, Andrew Marvell, suggests that nature is more than the scene of desire, more than provocateur of human sexuality. It is somehow more intimately connected, the source and

object of desire itself. In "The Garden," he also gets us closer to some of the
problematics of desire:

> Nor white nor red was ever seen
> So am'rous as this lovely green.
> Fond Lovers, cruel as their Flame,
> Cut in these Trees their Mistress name:
> Little, Alas, they know or heed
> How far these Beauties Hers exceed!
> Fair Trees, where s'eer your barkes I wound,
> No Name shall but your own be found.
>
> When we have run our Passions heat,
> Love hither makes his best retreat.
> The *Gods,* that mortal Beauty chase,
> Still in a Tree did end their race:
> *Apollo* hunted *Daphne* so,
> Only that She might Laurel grow;
> And *Pan* did after *Syrinx* speed,
> Not as a Nymph, but for a Reed.
>
> What wond'rous Life is this I lead!
> Ripe Apples drop about my head;
> The Luscious Clusters of the Vine
> Upon my Mouth do crush their Wine;
> The Nectaren and curious Peach
> Into my hands themselves do reach;
> Stumbling on Melons, as I pass,
> Insnar'd with Flowers, I fall on Grass.
>
> (51–53)

The white and the red in the first lines here quoted refer to human lovers,
to female beauty, white skin, red lips, lilies and cherries. Perhaps science is,
as that same stanza suggests, the sublimated passion of love, a passion
redirected from the sentimental carving of lovers' names into the trunks of
trees—a favorite pastime of forsaken lovers wandering hurt and alone in
the woods, singing their love complaints—to carving instead the names of
the trees themselves in the bark. The more powerful naming and knowing
of science itself is, like amorous desire, a kind of erotic wounding of the
body of nature. This is the controlling gesture of the zoo as well, in which
each species is identified and interpreted for spectators by an engraved
metal plate with its Latin name, and the range of the animal if it were free in
its natural habitat.

And yet the very words of natural objects, our naming of them, can
evoke a thrill of desire, a passion felt in the body. Take the third stanza
quoted: the words embody the fruits, and that embodiment can create in us

a physical sensation. The ripe apples, the melons and the flowers, all swirl in their own kind of linguistic seduction: "I fall on grass."

The "curious peach" seems a harmless joke, reaching out to the stumbling nature lover while he "falls" among the flowers. The fruit is a kind of body, evoking the appetite for the female flesh, though there is no inherent reason why the peach might not as easily suggest, say, a male ass as various parts of the female body. But what is most likely to disturb us now, in these stanzas, is the soft-core violence that has been swathed in the beautiful and seductive language. The wound has been installed at the heart of passion. Lovers are more than fond; they are cruel to trees and each other. It may seem an idyllic world, where even plants are as "amorous as this lovely green," but the trees bear the marks of our longings. Even the gods—especially the gods—join the conspiracies of desire: Apollo hunts Daphne, who flees and escapes only by becoming a tree herself; Pan the satyr gallops after the nymph Syrinx, follower of the goddess Diana, who becomes reeds in Pan's arms when he catches her. These are quasi-rape sequences—desire as pursuit, desire as capture. Desire here is the appropriation of the pursued, even in its transformation: Apollo takes the laurel for his victory wreath, and Pan makes his panpipes, the shepherd's pastoral instrument, out of the reeds.

These cultural myths follow us, precede us even, into the woods, and the darkness we dread will accompany us there. The nature we enter is always in some degree prewritten for us in the language and the myths we have inherited, and controls the way we are able to imagine ourselves in nature. Probably one of the great myths we hold is that the phallus is the signifier of power. Phallic aggressiveness seems to lurk at the heart of desire. Power is no doubt located there, but it is located in images like "the curious peach" as well—in images we associate more with the female. One need only think of caves, secrets, holes—and biting—to realize the distribution of power to the phallus is culturally conditioned. We locate desire in nature, and in specific body parts, not because that is where it really resides, any more than sexuality itself resides in a single act or body part, phallic or vaginal, titillating or orgasmic. This is a production of a certain politics of the body—the suturing of power to particular organs, the colonizing of the body by our own discourses of desire. These are our metaphors.

The moral response to the disturbing presence of desire in our relationships with nature is a kind of censoring, a repression of the disturbing impulse. As I have suggested, that has been the impulse in modern American nature writing: desire is largely silenced or domesticated. We can repress desire from our relations with nature. But the very urge to transgress that is so much a part of desire itself—that leads to the great loves being represented as adulterous, even impossible—will create a new movement of power in desire, the power of resistance. And the hope of censoring power from desire, in a kind of modern pastoral in which humans merge with nature as children into an idealized mother, will perhaps lead only to a countervailing emphasis on power itself, on an erotics of exploitation. Perhaps this is already happening, with the increasing call for an inclusion of human values, the values of utility and economics, for example, in the revision or reauthorization of the Endangered Species Act.

If desire is linked for us, in our cultural myths, to power and physical domination, of both our own bodies and the body of nature, we need to try to understand that relationship. Is power inevitable in love and desire, whether the relationship is with another person or with nature itself? Kristeva argues, in an essay on Romeo and Juliet from *Tales of Love*, that power is not simply masculine. The drive to dominate stems from the feeling of love itself, or more accurately, from the feeling of hate that is let loose from repression inside the feeling of love. She writes:

> More deeply, more passionately, we are dealing with the intrinsic presence of hatred in the amatory feeling itself. In the object relation, the relation with an other, hatred, as Freud said, is more ancient than love. As soon as an *other* appears different from myself, it becomes alien, repelled, repugnant, abject—hated. . . . But as soon as the strength of desire that is joined with love sets the integrity of the self ablaze; as soon as it breaks down its solidity through the drive-impelled torrent of passion, hatred—the primary bench-mark of object relation—emerges out of repression. Eroticized according to the variants of sadomasochism, or coldly dominant in more lasting relationships that have already exhausted the delights of infidelity, as delusive as it is seductive, hatred is the keynote of the couple's passionate melody. (222)

One need not agree with Kristeva here, or with Freud as he is invoked by her, that hatred is primary in relationships. But she raises a useful caveat, that power is not simply male, even if she uses the phallus as the signifier of Eros. Power may be deeply connected to Eros itself, manifested in the struggle to control, and resist, the person or thing that we love—and hate. The denial of this power in Eros, she writes in the same paragraph, is the attempt to idealize love, to create "the paradise of loving understanding between the child and its parents." This longing for, and escape into, maternal embrace precisely traces the psychological movement of the pastoral impulse—the harried, civilized self merges with an idealized, feminized nature. In the older vocabulary of the classics, wounded lovers sing their laments to the nymphs of woods and stream.

Michel Foucault argues that power is implicit in all relationships, but the forms that power may take are culturally produced. The power we seek as a culture, he argues, the domination over nature required by our economy, produces its effects not abstractly, but corporeally. It is exercised upon and through our bodies. The cult of the healthy body, of the slim body disciplined by fasting and exercise, by aerobics and muscle building, is the cult of mastery at work at the level of our own desire. In an interview published under the title "Body/Power," he says,

> Mastery and awareness of one's own body can be acquired only through the effect of an investment of power in the body: gymnastics, exercises, muscle-building, nudism, glorification of the body beautiful. All of this belongs to the pathway leading to the desire of one's own body, by way of the insistent, persistent, meticulous work of power on the bodies of children or soldiers, the healthy bodies. (56)

The power he speaks of is an unspecified social power, a cultural power working to create the kind of body the culture needs. He is thinking in economic, Marxist terms. Power works through us, through our own internalized desire to attain for ourselves "the body beautiful" that is the cultural ideal. And our glorification of this disciplined body is really the worship of our own longing to control. His point is that it is a mistake to imagine that we have merely repressed and negated the body, with power operating upon it from the outside. Rather, we have affixed power to desire, and it finds its expression in the shapes our body takes. We make metaphors of our bodies.

Our relationships with nature now are a mirror of this relationship with our own body. Our desire to dominate nature does not operate simply in a repressive way, upon nature, power imposed from without. Power is even now linked, as we try to save nature, with the kinds of desire we express toward the body of nature we at once long for and invent, place before us but keep nicely managed and sanitized. We are in love with the beautiful in nature. For most people, experiences in nature are largely visual—at least, this is how nature is marshaled before us now in nature photography and television documentaries. The contours of nature, the bodies of animals, are bathed in the glows of soft and gorgeous lighting. We are tourists of nature, watching it from our living rooms and cars. These ways of representing nature—visually more than linguistically—are the front line in the environmental battle with the economic forces of exploitation. The visual has largely displaced the verbal in our representations of nature, with its own luminous rhetoric of romantic twilights and intimate encounters with beasts, and created a kind of voyeur's desire.

The desire to be close to nature is allied to a new species of power and control. We will redeem nature, save it, but the bargain is: we get to be the stewards of nature. We are making ourselves, slowly, the new masters over the idealized body of nature that we ourselves are constructing. Yet stewardship, deriving as it does from deeply felt cultural traditions with their roots in the Christian myth of the Garden of Eden, does not simply confer preservation of and access to nature. It does more than validate human mastery and domination. It creates a new category of people who have power over, and control of access to, nature and wildlife. These are the wildlife managers—scientists and bureaucrats, largely. Nature is exclusive property, and opportunities for intimate experiences are increasingly restricted. Some people manage animals, for example, quite closely. But the mass of people are reduced to experiencing nature at a great distance, if at all, from places marked beside the road with a sign that makes the image of a camera.

Our love of nature is structured along a new kind of power—not economic exploitation, but a kind of cultural mastery nonetheless. We now design the nature we want. Nature is increasingly reduced to our national parks and wildlife refuges. What we once did in medieval, Renaissance, and eighteenth-century gardens, we now extend to nature itself, to all of our natural world. We have parceled out the body of nature, and in the preserved areas we manage the land and the animals to keep them clean and healthy. These parks are the metaphors of our desire, the parts of the body of nature that we have dumped our desire into—trimmed and brushed and made presentable to the Americans in the white Adidas and summer shorts. The boundaries of the parks are clear, the parking lots are kept clean, the forests penetrated by trails we are admonished to stick to, and the animals carefully monitored. The American family visits this nature, on the weekend or on summer vacation, and rarely strays far beyond the interpretive center, where the park has been carefully constructed in dioramas and displays—strange tableaus of *nature vivant*. We are told what it means, and we are controlled in our responses. Nothing is allowed to be unruly—in either the management of the animals or the management of the people who come to look at them.

We have made new divisions between the sacred and the profane in nature, between the parks and the exploited areas. The map of this new landscape is also the geography of our own fragmented and regimented bodies.

A new landscape of ethical duty has emerged in our relationship with nature, articulated originally by Aldo Leopold's concept of "the land ethic," and elaborated by a huge literature on environmental ethics, outlining the "rights" of nature and the restraints that need to be imposed upon human desire. Even as it is disappearing, nature is strangely becoming more powerful as a moral and legal entity. Nature must have a "right," for example, to be preserved or protected, to receive dollars, to have a kind of legal "standing." But surely this involves the redistribution of power between humans and nature, and it makes that power productive of both money and feelings. Paradoxically and inevitably, as nature takes on a new kind of social power, and as it exists marked off and apart from us, behind boundaries and at a distance, another kind of desire is also generated, a transgressive desire. This can be the kind of reactionary anger of loggers, say, who want to kill the spotted owl because they think it is costing them their livelihoods. But there are other impulses toward violation of the new ethic, and they are more complex. These are the violations that result from the desire to get closer to nature even as it is becoming set apart from us. And these violations occur among the very people who love nature. Take the common example of birdwatchers or photographers who, in their zeal to see the rare bird, trample its habitat and harass it from the nest. All this energy that we invest in nature, all this desire to see it and feel close to it, emerges from our sense of lack and want. From the self in its fire for the distant other. The idealized imagery and the utopian rhetoric applied to nature now are made possible by the great distance from nature at which we live, so that we can enter nature, as it were, only in brief affairs.

Yet we long now for a new and greater intimacy, for more complete and satisfying relationships, between the sexes and between humans and nature. This longing for intimacy exists even as power and desire are being redistributed through our bodies. And so, we might ask, where are we, realistically, in our relations to our own sexualized bodies and the eroticized body of nature? A great classical myth represents our situation very clearly. It is the story of Actaeon and Diana, a hunter and the goddess of the hunt, as told by Ovid. In the classical period, hunting was an activity that conducted humans to the frontier between human and nature. It was a symbolic activity, expressing at once the desire to enter nature and the desire to dominate or control nature. And hunting led as well to borderline experience, subjective and often disturbing. Hunters often found that their confrontations were not simply with animals, but with unsuspected parts of the self, with startling impulses. Ovid's tales of changes, *The Metamorphoses*, written between 2 and 8 A.D., betrays a culture for which identity and the anxiety over boundaries of the self were extremely important. Yet desire seems to inhabit just exactly those borders of selfhood and self-transformation. Actaeon's story describes one such "error," or wandering, in which he went too far (Ovid 61–64). A grandson of Cadmus, Actaeon loves to hunt with his companions on the mountain outside of Thebes. By noon one day, he and his men have taken many species of game. With their nets and spears dripping "with the blood of our successful hunting," Actaeon orders his men to rest for the day. "Tomorrow," he tells them, "we try again."

On his way down the mountain, he comes across a valley, highly feminized in its description. It is a "secret grotto," dark and shaded. A slender archway in the rock leads to shining water, a crystal pool with grassy banks all around it. In this pool, the "goddess of the woods," Diana, loves to bathe, her arrows and her spear laid aside. Diana's female companions pour water over the naked goddess from large urns. But this purely feminine moment, so richly suggestive, is interrupted by the unsuspecting Actaeon, wandering through this unfamiliar and pristine part of the woods, a man entering "the cool and dripping grotto":

> The nymphs saw him immediately:
> The nymphs, all naked, saw him, a man,
> And beat their breasts and screamed, and all together
> Gathered round their goddess, tried to hide her,
> With their own bodies, but she stood above them,
> Taller by head and shoulders.

Diana could not be hidden, and she "blushed at being seen." Unable to find her arrows, she scoops a handful of water into Actaeon's face.

The water transforms the man into a beast. He becomes a stag, a hunter turned into the hunted. On his forehead, where the water was splashed, he feels horns begin to sprout. His nose stretches long, his ears grow long and pointed, his skin turns to dappled fur. He becomes the body of the beast he has always coveted. In his muteness, he is unable to tell anyone who he is or what he has seen. It is this loss of language, the sign of his impotence, that marks his loss of human identity—he cannot put his experience into words. He has lost the ability to represent for himself what nature is, what his experience has been, and who he is. Human power over nature lies in language itself.

Actaeon's dumbness leads directly to his destruction. As he wonders where to go, he sees his own hounds come baying over the hill, full of the lust of blood. When they see him, a stag, he cannot tell them he is their master. He cannot utter his name. They see only a beast. They attack:

> Actaeon, once pursuer
> Over this very ground, is now pursued,
> Fleeing his old companions.

The dogs bring him to bay, biting and nipping and slashing. Actaeon fills the mountains with his moaning, uttering a groan neither human nor cervine, and drops to his knees like a man praying. He has no arms to plead with, but his eyes are full of mute appeal. The dogs dismember the body of their former master:

> They circle him, dash in, nip, and mangle
> And lacerate and tear their prey, not master,
> No master whom they know, only a deer.

And so he died, and Diana's anger
Was satisfied at last.

Which is the metaphor, and which the meaning—human relations with nature, or sexual relationships? Voyeurism and revenge—these themes describe a contest over engendered bodies in nature. The female body: chaste, hidden and protected, exposed and violated. The male body: guilty, wandering and intrusive, attacked and broken. What is powerful about this story is that the goddess, presiding over the secret grove and hunted animals, has laid her weapons aside, yet finds a new one. Water is her weapon, and her attack leaves the hunter the victim of his own hounds. The goddess, at once female and nature, triumphs over Actaeon, who is surprised by his own culpable desire, which betrays him like his own dogs. In the retaliation of female power, we have invented a new erotic moment, one in which the male body is left silent and dismembered.

Perhaps we are in a necessary historical stage, in which men feel at once silent and defensive, assertive and unsure of themselves. In which women have increasingly taken it upon themselves to identify with and speak for nature. In which culture continues its war upon nature, and nature (or the advocates of nature) finds ways to fight back. In which the boundaries between men and women, nature and culture, are contested and shifting. It is a time for new images of ourselves and nature to emerge. I long for some newer intimacies that concentrate on something other than the broken and guarded parts of the body we have inherited as the locus of desire. Perhaps Kristeva is right in locating desire in the body: "this body, the center of desire" (231). Perhaps desire is actually, physically located in our cells and hormones. But the way we experience that body, the way the desire moves through us, the places in the body where that desire is located—in short, the meaning of desire for us—these are generated by the work of culture and metaphor. We can begin to realize that nature is so endangered and exploited, not merely because a group of men are exploiters, but because we have written mastery into the structure of our desires. We have written power into desire. And our only alternative to the myth of power and domination, to desire in nature, seems to be a regressive pastoral fantasy, an idealized escape into maternal embraces or virginal purity. But if desire is written in language, inscribed upon the body, we can begin to imagine new possibilities, write new metaphors. Metaphors that have less to do with domination and escape, that think of desire as something other than lack and absence and wounds. Foucault says in an interview that he looks to a reversing of the trend of a great " 'sexography' which for centuries makes us try to decipher sex as the universal secret." It will not come out of an "anti-sex" reconstruction of our relationship to ourselves, he says:

it is a matter—I don't say of "rediscovering"—but rather of inventing other forms of pleasures, of relationships, coexistences, attachments, loves, intensities. (116)

I have come increasingly to venture into nature searching for these new intensities and new relationships. They derive from and lead to moments of self-discovery and self-transformation. I have felt such moments in nature, in which I have suddenly found that nature lifts me out of myself somehow, above the fragmented wilderness of my desire, into glimpses, not just of a new nature, but of a new self in nature, more complete than the anonymous bodies living in modern cities.

In the cave of Altamira, in Spain, I was lucky enough to see a series of prehistoric images, animal and human images, that were explicitly about borders and transformations, metaphor and relationship. These images focused on the body, on the relationship between bestiality and humanness. But the images were of a body part we usually ignore as body part, associating it with the "head." It is the face. In the cave of Altamira, outside the medieval village of Santillana del Mar, along the north coast of Spain, the famous images of the bison are dizzying in their beauty and their awe-inspiring significance. It is one of the most famous of prehistoric caves. Most people who visit Altamira see the great chamber with its beautiful reclining bison cows, standing pony, and the incomparable female deer walking away, head turned gracefully as if glancing over her back. But there is a small passageway with images that were to me even more startling. I saw them through the help of Dr. Leslie Freeman of the University of Chicago and the Rev. Joaquin Gonzalez Echegaray of the Institute for Prehistoric Investigations, two of the major figures in paleolithic art in Spain. They have conducted a recent reexamination of the entire cave of Altamira. Their most exciting finds were in this small and cramped passageway in the far rear of the great cave, a ragged corridor called in Spanish the *Cola de Caballo,* the Tail of the Horse. You have to scoot and scuttle through the passageway, almost crawl in places. It's long, but only two meters wide and waist high in some spots. Large sharp rocks jut from the walls, and rubble lies on the floor.

The entrance is marked with primitive forms, vaguely like finger-paint squiggles—indecipherable lines that researchers call "macaroni." Goats and deer are incised on the rock walls at various points, as are strange black marks, lines really, whose meanings have been fiercely but inconclusively debated. You can easily tell, entering this strange space, that you're moving into a different consciousness, a darkness filled with meanings, but meanings that are always somehow out of reach—a disturbingly beautiful, wonderfully disorienting sensation.

The defining images of the corridor of the Cola, however, are the bison.

Their faces are carved on large stones that poke out from the wall and ceiling. As so often and so beautifully in prehistoric art, the shapes of the rocks have been exploited. The natural shapes of these rocks were carved for slight alterations, and enhanced with bits of black pigmentation. The faces occur at dramatic points along the cramped passage. They are haunting, both because they are simply faces, or "masks" as Dr. Freeman calls them, and because they loom out at you, barely discernible at first, but unmistakable and unforgettable once you've traced them out on the stones. The faces seem to come to you out of the cave itself, like optical illusions.

The first bison image was barely ten meters from the entry, chunked out of a squarish block of stone, enigmatic eyes gouged roughly and painted black, a long vertical fissure in the rock forming the nose. At the bottom of the stone, the fissure bent from my right to left, had been scraped by some tool, and formed a line for a mouth. It was the image of a beast, but the face was eerily human. It seemed half beast, half human—a human-animal double.

There are nine "masks" altogether in the Cola, as you go deeper into the darkness of the tunnel. Just before the end of the passageway, the narrow tunnel widens slightly, into what Dr. Freeman calls the "Chamber of the Masks." In this small chamber, not so much a room as a darkness made replete with significance, the prehistoric people carved out five faces. Two are quite clearly animal faces, both bison, easily recognized because they are in profile. Two other bison, however, merge the bestial with the human. One of these is carved out of a long vertical rock hanging from the ceiling, an almost threatening projection. On either side of a sharp vertical ridge in the rock, which serves as a nasal shape, two dark circles have been painted in, black and ghostly eyes, like the kind scrawled on white sheets for Halloween ghosts. At the bottom, a curving gouge serves as a heavy, slightly gaping but silent mouth. The human-animal double is powerful for its crudeness, so at odds with the technical sophistication of the bison in the large, main chamber of the cave. I remember thinking, was the artist learning, in this carving, how to render the shape of the human face, the look of the human, the idea of humanness, out of the face of the animal?

These artists were clearly looking at inner realities, in animals and themselves. They were looking into the mirror of another's eyes. And in seeing these faces, I was looking into the mirrors of their eyes.

Just beyond this human-animal double is the startling culmination of these masks. I had to look hard to see it, turning around in the tunnel, having a companion light the proper stone from below while I squeezed up against the far wall for perspective. In the strange light, emerging out of a play of shadow and light and rock, the image begins to appear—an engraved human face. It is utterly recognizable. Heavy, pondering brows hang over deeply recessed, darkly peering eyes. One of the eyes is large, punched out of the stone. The other is tight and small, as if the face is squinting, even winking at you. The nose is much more subtle than those on the other masks, and the mouth has small human lips, vaguely like the rosebud mouths in Gothic paintings, tight-lipped and pursy. There is the trace of a scowl in them. It is a lonely, tense, brooding face.

In the presence of such images, I felt a raw sensation, a feeling of things stripped away in the underground darkness. The images before me were familiar, but finally unintelligible. Freeman believes that these masks demonstrate that, for these early *Homo sapiens*, symbolic capacity was fully developed, and played as prominent a role in early evolution as material culture. These people were capable of making a metaphoric connection between themselves and bison, human and animal, in this case probably deriving from the close connection they felt between themselves as predators to their prey. He argues that these masks constitute a whole composition, and bear a relationship each to the others as you enter and leave the Cola—a relationship of transformation.

I am struck by how these people, the Cro-Magnons, seemed to be learning how to think about who they were through the animals. They were groping through desire, in a literal darkness, to think themselves. Relationship itself, the value celebrated by the language of metaphor, was represented in a long series of images, a series that seems to portray not so much static concepts of animal and human as a process of difference and identity, distance and nearness. The human face, tucked into a special spot, visible unlike the others only by assuming a special posture and special lighting, emerges from the dark rock, flickers with a fragile tentativeness, as if even this image of self is likely to merge back into the cave, to sink back into the animal. The transformation of the beast into the human seems the explicit theme, but it is also a merger of human and animal. This desire to know ourselves through animals, through others, is recognizable in the haunting gazes of these masks that return to us, images of the stranger in ourselves, from across the vast ages. I left the Cola de Caballo filled with the beautiful, brooding darkness of faces.

WORKS CITED

Abbey, Edward. *The Monkey Wrench Gang.* New York: Avon, 1976.

Emerson, Ralph Waldo. *The Complete Essays and Other Writings of Ralph Waldo Emerson.* ed. B. Atkinson. New York: Modern Library, 1940.

Foucault, Michel. *Politics, Philosophy, Culture: Interviews and Other Writings, 1977–1984.* Lawrence D. Kritzman. New York and London: Routledge, 1988.

Greg, W. W. *Pastoral Poetry and Pastoral Drama: A Literary Inquiry, with Special Reference to the Pre-Restoration Stage in England.* New York: Russell and Russell, 1959.

Hawkes, Terence. *Structuralism and Semiotics.* Berkeley: U of California P, 1977.

Hay, John. *The Undiscovered Country.* New York: W. W. Norton, 1981.

Kristeva, Julia. *Tales of Love.* Trans. Leon S. Roudiez. New York: Columbia UP, 1987.

Kolodny, Annette. *The Lay of the Land: Metaphor as Experience and History in American Life and Letters.* Chapel Hill: U of North Carolina P, 1975.

Lopez, Barry. *Arctic Dreams: Desire and Imagination in a Northern Landscape.* New York: Charles Scribner's Sons, 1986.

Lucretius. *The Nature of Things.* Trans. Frank Copley. New York: W. W. Norton, 1977.

Marvell, Andrew. *The Poems of Andrew Marvell.* ed. Hugh MacDonald. Oxford: Clarendon P, 1952.

Ovid. *Metamorphoses.* Trans. Rolfe Humphries. Bloomington: Indiana UP, 1955.

Roethke, Theodore. *The Colleced Poems of Theodore Roethke.* Seattle: U of Washington P, 1982.

Shakespeare, William. *The Riverside Shakespeare.* ed. G. Blakemore Evans. Boston: Houghton Mifflin, 1972.

Thoreau, Henry David. *Thoreau: Walden and Other Writings.* ed. Joseph Wood Krutch. New York: Bantam Books, 1962.

Williams, Terry Tempest. *Refuge: An Unnatural History of Family and Place.* New York: Pantheon, 1991.

Williams, Terry Tempest. Review of *The Moon by Whale Light and Other Adventures among Bats, Penguins, Crocodilians, and Whales,* by Diane Ackerman. *Orion* 11 (Autumn 1992): 60–61.

Index

Index

307